M000168974

APPETIZERS

Socca

YIELD: 4 TO 6 SERVINGS / **ACTIVE TIME:** 30 MINUTES / **TOTAL TIME:** 1 HOUR

7 TABLESPOONS EXTRA-VIRGIN OLIVE OIL

3 SMALL ONIONS, CHOPPED

1½ CUPS CHICKPEA FLOUR

½ TEASPOON KOSHER SALT, PLUS MORE TO TASTE

1 TEASPOON TURMERIC

1½ CUPS WATER

BLACK PEPPER, TO TASTE

2 TABLESPOONS CHOPPED FRESH CHIVES

TZATZIKI (SEE PAGE 42), FOR SERVING

1. Place 1 tablespoon of the olive oil in a small cast-iron skillet and warm it over medium-high heat. Add the onions, reduce the heat to low, and cook, stirring occasionally, until the onions are caramelized, about 30 minutes. Transfer the onions to a bowl and let them cool.

2. Place the chickpea flour, salt, turmeric, and water in a mixing bowl and whisk to combine. While whisking, slowly drizzle in 2 tablespoons of the olive oil. When the mixture comes together as a smooth batter, season it with salt and pepper.

3. Warm the cast-iron pan over medium-high heat. Add 1 tablespoon of the olive oil and then add ⅓ cup of the batter, tilting the pan to make sure the batter is evenly distributed. Reduce the heat to medium and cook until the batter starts to firm up, about 2 minutes.

4. Sprinkle some of the caramelized onions over the socca and cook until the edges are golden brown, 2 to 4 minutes. Flip the socca over and cook until golden brown and cooked through, about 2 minutes.

5. Gently remove the socca from the pan and repeat Steps 3 and 4 until all of the batter and caramelized onions have been used.

6. When all of the socca have been made, sprinkle the chives over the top and sprinkle with Tzatziki.

Hummus

YIELD: 20 SERVINGS / **ACTIVE TIME:** 1 HOUR / **TOTAL TIME:** 12 HOURS

2 LBS. DRIED CHICKPEAS

1 TABLESPOON BAKING SODA

12 CUPS ROOM-TEMPERATURE WATER

12 CUPS VEGETABLE STOCK (SEE PAGE 484)

1 CUP TAHINI PASTE

2 TABLESPOONS ZA'ATAR (SEE PAGE 501)

2 TABLESPOONS SUMAC

2 TABLESPOONS CUMIN

2 TABLESPOONS KOSHER SALT

2 TABLESPOONS BLACK PEPPER

2 GARLIC CLOVES, GRATED

½ BUNCH OF FRESH CILANTRO, ROUGHLY CHOPPED

1 CUP EXTRA-VIRGIN OLIVE OIL

1 CUP SESAME OIL

1 CUP ICE WATER

½ CUP FRESH LEMON JUICE

1. Place the chickpeas, baking soda, and water in a large saucepan, stir, and cover the pan. Let the chickpeas soak overnight at room temperature.

2. Drain the chickpeas and rinse them. Place them in a large saucepan, add the stock, and bring to a steady simmer. Cook until the chickpeas are quite tender, about 1 hour.

3. In a blender or food processor, combine all of the remaining ingredients and puree until achieving a perfectly smooth, creamy sauce; the ice water is the key to getting the correct consistency.

4. Add the warm, drained chickpeas to the tahini mixture and blend until the hummus is perfectly smooth and not at all grainy, occasionally stopping to scrape down the sides of the bowl. This blending process may take 3 minutes; remain patient and keep going until the mixture is ultra-creamy and fluffy, adding a little water as necessary to make the hummus move.

5. Taste, adjust the seasoning as necessary, and enjoy.

Hummus
SEE PAGE 15

Grilled Cantaloupe

YIELD: 4 SERVINGS / **ACTIVE TIME:** 20 MINUTES / **TOTAL TIME:** 20 MINUTES

1 CANTALOUPE

1 TABLESPOON EXTRA-VIRGIN OLIVE OIL

4 OZ. FRESH MOZZARELLA CHEESE, TORN

1 TABLESPOON BALSAMIC GLAZE (SEE PAGE 508)

FRESH PARSLEY, CHOPPED, FOR GARNISH

1. Prepare a gas or charcoal grill for high heat (about 500°F). Remove the rind from the cantaloupe, halve it, remove the seeds, and then cut the cantaloupe into ½-inch-thick slices.

2. Place the cantaloupe in a mixing bowl, add the oil, and toss to coat.

3. Place the cantaloupe on the grill and cook until it is lightly charred on both sides and warmed through.

4. To serve, pile the warm cantaloupe on a platter, top with the mozzarella, and drizzle the Balsamic Glaze over the top. Garnish with parsley and enjoy.

Sicilian Bar Nuts

YIELD: 4 SERVINGS / **ACTIVE TIME:** 10 MINUTES / **TOTAL TIME:** 20 MINUTES

¾ CUP WALNUTS

¾ CUP CASHEWS

¾ CUP PECAN HALVES

2 TABLESPOONS UNSALTED BUTTER, MELTED

2 TABLESPOONS CHOPPED FRESH ROSEMARY

1 TEASPOON CAYENNE PEPPER

1 TABLESPOON BROWN SUGAR

1 TABLESPOON FLAKY SEA SALT

1. Preheat the oven to 350°F. Place the nuts on a baking sheet, place them in the oven, and toast until fragrant, about 12 minutes. Remove from the oven and transfer the nuts to a mixing bowl.

2. Add the melted butter and toss until the nuts are evenly coated. Add the remaining ingredients, toss to coat, and serve.

Panelle

YIELD: 8 SERVINGS / **ACTIVE TIME:** 40 MINUTES / **TOTAL TIME:** 1 HOUR AND 30 MINUTES

5½ CUPS CHICKPEA FLOUR

6 CUPS WATER

1½ TEASPOONS KOSHER SALT

BLACK PEPPER, TO TASTE

2 TABLESPOONS CHOPPED FRESH PARSLEY

EXTRA-VIRGIN OLIVE OIL, AS NEEDED

1. Place the chickpea flour in a saucepan and gradually add the water, whisking to prevent lumps from forming. Stir in the salt, season the mixture with pepper, and cook over low heat, stirring continually, until the mixture starts to pull away from the side of the pan, 30 to 40 minutes.

2. Stir in the parsley and remove the pan from heat.

3. Coat a baking dish with olive oil, spoon the mixture into it, and level the surface with a rubber spatula. You want the mixture to be about ½ inch thick. Let the mixture cool completely.

4. Cut the mixture into squares. Add olive oil to a narrow, deep, heavy-bottomed saucepan with high edges until it is about 2 inches deep and warm it to 350°F. Gently slip the squares into the hot oil and fry until they are crispy and brown, turning as necessary.

5. Remove the panelle from the hot oil and transfer them to a paper towel–lined plate to drain. Serve once the panelle have drained and cooled slightly.

Sicilian Bar Nuts
SEE PAGE 18

Scagliuòzzi

YIELD: 4 SERVINGS / ACTIVE TIME: 40 MINUTES / TOTAL TIME: 2 HOURS

9 OZ. INSTANT POLENTA

4 CUPS WATER

1 TEASPOON KOSHER SALT, PLUS MORE FOR TOPPING

EXTRA-VIRGIN OLIVE OIL, AS NEEDED

1. Line a loaf pan with parchment paper. Place the polenta, water, and salt in a saucepan and cook over medium heat, stirring frequently, until the polenta is thick and creamy, 10 to 15 minutes.

2. Transfer the polenta to the loaf pan and let it cool completely.

3. Turn the polenta out onto a cutting board and cut it into ½-inch-thick slices. Cut each slice in half diagonally, forming 2 triangles.

4. Add olive oil to a narrow, deep, and heavy-bottomed saucepan until it is about 2 inches deep and warm it to 350°F. Gently slip the polenta triangles into the hot oil and fry until they are a light golden brown, turning as necessary.

5. Remove the fried polenta from the hot oil, transfer them to a paper towel–lined plate to drain, and season them with salt. Serve once the fried polenta has drained and cooled slightly.

Rustico Napoletano

YIELD: 15 TO 20 RUSTICI / **ACTIVE TIME:** 30 MINUTES / **TOTAL TIME:** 1 HOUR AND 15 MINUTES

2 CUPS RICOTTA CHEESE

5 EGGS

SALT AND PEPPER, TO TASTE

10½ OZ. BUFFALO MOZZARELLA CHEESE, CUBED AND DRAINED IN THE REFRIGERATOR FOR 2 HOURS

10½ OZ. SMOKED PROVOLA CHEESE, CUBED

6 OZ. ITALIAN SALAMI, CHOPPED

1 CUP PLUS 1 TABLESPOON GRATED PARMESAN CHEESE

PASTA FROLLA AL LARDO (SEE PAGE 490), AT ROOM TEMPERATURE

1 EGG YOLK, BEATEN

1. Preheat the oven to 350°F and coat 2 muffin tins with nonstick cooking spray. Place the ricotta in a mixing bowl, add the eggs, and season the mixture with salt and pepper. Whisk to combine, add the mozzarella, provola, salami, and Parmesan, and stir until well combined.

2. Beat the frolla with a rolling pin to soften it and roll it out until it is about ¼ inch thick. Using a pastry cutter or mason jar, cut the dough into rounds that are large enough to cover the wells of the muffin tins.

3. Place the rounds in the muffin tins and fill them with a generous spoonful of the cheese mixture.

4. Roll the remaining dough into a slightly thinner sheet and cut it into rounds that are large enough to use as lids for the rustici. Place them over the filling, fold the bottom layers over them, and gently press down on the seams to seal the rustici.

5. Brush the rustici with the egg yolk and place them in the oven. Cook until the rustici are golden brown, which will depend on the depth of the wells in the muffin tins. For deeper molds, bake for approximately 40 minutes. For shallower molds, bake for approximately 25 minutes. Also, do not worry if the lids of the rustici come off, as they will be reattached as the rustici cool.

6. Remove the rustici from the oven and let them cool for 5 minutes. Place a large heatproof tray over each of the muffin tins and invert the muffin tins, making sure the rustici do not come out of the tins quite yet. Let the rustici cool until they are slightly warm before removing them from the tins and enjoying.

Crocchè

YIELD: 20 CROCCHÈ / **ACTIVE TIME:** 40 MINUTES / **TOTAL TIME:** 24 HOURS

SALT AND PEPPER, TO TASTE

2.2 LBS. POTATOES, PEELED AND CHOPPED

4 EGGS, SEPARATED

½ CUP GRATED PARMESAN CHEESE

2 HANDFULS OF FRESH PARSLEY, FINELY CHOPPED

1⅓ CUPS MOZZARELLA CHEESE, CUT INTO STRIPS AND DRAINED IN THE REFRIGERATOR FOR 1 HOUR

2 CUPS BREAD CRUMBS

EXTRA-VIRGIN OLIVE OIL, AS NEEDED

1. Bring salted water to a boil in a large saucepan. Add the potatoes and boil until they are tender, 15 to 20 minutes. Drain the potatoes and place them in a bowl.

2. Mash the potatoes until they are smooth. Add the egg yolks, Parmesan, and parsley to the potatoes, season the mixture with salt and pepper, and knead the mixture until it feels smooth and well combined.

3. Line two baking sheets with parchment paper. To shape the crocchè, take a dollop of the potato mixture, place it in the palm of your hand, and flatten it. Place a piece of mozzarella in the center, form the mixture over the cheese, and then shape it into a 2-inch-long cylinder. Repeat until all of the potato mixture has been used.

4. Place the egg whites in a bowl, add a pinch of salt, and beat the egg whites slightly. Place the bread crumbs in a separate bowl and then dredge the croquettes in the egg whites and then in the bread crumbs until they are coated. Place the crocchè on the baking sheets, cover them with kitchen towels, and let them chill in the refrigerator overnight.

5. Remove the crocchè from the refrigerator and let them warm up at room temperature for 20 minutes.

6. Add olive oil to a narrow, deep, heavy-bottomed saucepan with high edges until it is about 2 inches deep and warm it to 350°F. Working in batches of 2 or 3, slip the crocchè into the hot oil and fry until they are golden brown, turning as necessary.

7. Remove the crocchè from the hot oil and transfer them to a paper towel–lined plate to drain. Serve once all of the crocchè have drained and cooled slightly.

Roasted & Stuffed Sardines

YIELD: 2 SERVINGS / **ACTIVE TIME:** 20 MINUTES / **TOTAL TIME:** 45 MINUTES

5 WHOLE, FRESH SARDINES

3 TABLESPOONS EXTRA-VIRGIN OLIVE OIL

½ WHITE ONION, CHOPPED

¼ CUP CHOPPED CELERY

1 TEASPOON KOSHER SALT

1 TABLESPOON PAPRIKA

PINCH OF CUMIN

2 GARLIC CLOVES, MINCED

2 TABLESPOONS WATER

¼ CUP CHOPPED FRESH PARSLEY

1 CUP DAY-OLD BREAD PIECES

TAHINI SAUCE (SEE PAGE 500), FOR SERVING

1. Clean the sardines: Make an incision in the belly of each one from head to tail. Remove the guts and carefully snap the spines at the neck and tail. This will leave the sardines intact enough to hold their shape when roasted. Rinse the sardines and set them aside.

2. Place 2 tablespoons of the olive oil in a medium skillet and warm it over medium-high heat. Add the onion, celery, salt, paprika, cumin, and garlic and cook, stirring frequently, until the onion is translucent, about 3 minutes.

3. Add the water and simmer for 3 or 4 minutes. Add the parsley and bread and cook, stirring frequently, allowing the bread to absorb the liquid and brown a bit. After 5 minutes, remove the pan from heat.

4. Preheat the oven to 450°F. Place the sardines in a cast-iron skillet, keeping them nestled against each other so as to hold their shape better. Fill the sardines' bellies with the stuffing, drizzle the remaining olive oil over them, and place the pan in the oven.

5. Roast the stuffed sardines until they reach an internal temperature of 145°F, 15 to 20 minutes. Remove the sardines from the oven and serve with the Tahini Sauce.

Roasted & Stuffed Sardines
SEE PAGE 25

Pomegranate-Glazed Figs & Cheese

YIELD: 4 SERVINGS / **ACTIVE TIME:** 35 MINUTES / **TOTAL TIME:** 1 HOUR

2 CUPS POMEGRANATE JUICE

1 TEASPOON FENNEL SEEDS

1 TEASPOON BLACK PEPPERCORNS

1 BAY LEAF

PINCH OF KOSHER SALT, PLUS MORE TO TASTE

½ CUP RICOTTA CHEESE

½ CUP MASCARPONE CHEESE

⅛ TEASPOON BLACK PEPPER

12 FRESH FIGS

1 TEASPOON CASTER (SUPERFINE) SUGAR

POMEGRANATE ARILS, FOR GARNISH

1. Place the pomegranate juice, fennel seeds, peppercorns, bay leaf, and salt in a small saucepan and simmer the mixture over medium-high heat until it has been reduced to ⅓ cup.

2. Strain and let the glaze cool completely.

3. In a bowl, combine the cheeses. Add 1 tablespoon of the glaze and season the mixture with salt and the pepper. Place the mixture in a pastry bag that has been fitted with a plain ½-inch tip and set it aside.

4. Preheat the broiler in the oven. Cut the figs in half from tip to stem and place them in a heatproof dish, cut side up. Brush the cut sides with some of the glaze and dust with the caster sugar.

5. Pipe a ½-inch-wide and 6-inch-long strip of the cheese mixture on four plates.

6. Place the figs under the broiler until glazed and just warmed through, about 5 minutes.

7. To serve, arrange six fig halves on top of each strip of cheese, garnish with pomegranate arils, and drizzle any remaining glaze over the top.

Whipped Feta with Za'atar

YIELD: 2 CUPS / **ACTIVE TIME:** 5 MINUTES / **TOTAL TIME:** 5 MINUTES

2 CUPS CRUMBLED FETA CHEESE

2 TABLESPOONS ZA'ATAR (SEE PAGE 501)

¼ CUP EXTRA-VIRGIN OLIVE OIL

1 TEASPOON RED PEPPER FLAKES

JUICE FROM ½ LEMON

1. Place the feta and Za'atar in a food processor and puree until smooth.

2. With the mixer running, slowly drizzle in the olive oil until the mixture becomes smooth.

3. Transfer the whipped feta to a bowl and stir in the red pepper flakes and lemon juice. Use immediately or store in the refrigerator.

Mozzarella in Carrozza

YIELD: 6 SERVINGS / **ACTIVE TIME:** 20 MINUTES / **TOTAL TIME:** 2 HOURS AND 40 MINUTES

1 LB. FRESH MOZZARELLA CHEESE (BUFALA IS PREFERRED)

8 SLICES OF SANDWICH BREAD, CRUSTS REMOVED

3 EGGS

KOSHER SALT AND PEPPER, TO TASTE

2 CUPS BREAD CRUMBS

EXTRA-VIRGIN OLIVE OIL, AS NEEDED

1. Cut the mozzarella into ½-inch-thick slices and place them in a colander. Set the colander in a bowl and let the mozzarella drain in the refrigerator for 2 hours.

2. Top 4 of the slices of bread with the mozzarella, making sure it is distributed evenly. Cover the cheese with the remaining slices of bread.

3. Place the eggs in a bowl, season them with salt and pepper, and beat them lightly. Place the bread crumbs in a separate bowl and then dredge the sandwiches in the eggs and then in the bread crumbs until they are coated. Set the breaded sandwiches aside.

4. Add olive oil to a narrow, deep, heavy-bottomed saucepan with high edges until it is about 2 inches deep and warm it to 350°F. Working with one sandwich at a time, slip it into the hot oil and fry until golden brown, turning as necessary.

5. Remove the sandwich from the hot oil, transfer it to a paper towel–lined plate to drain, and season it with salt. Serve once all of the sandwiches have drained and cooled slightly.

Whipped Feta with Za'atar
SEE PAGE 28

Calamari Fritti

YIELD: 4 SERVINGS / **ACTIVE TIME:** 30 MINUTES / **TOTAL TIME:** 50 MINUTES

2.2 LBS. SQUID, CLEANED (SEE PAGE 199)

3 CUPS ALL-PURPOSE FLOUR

EXTRA-VIRGIN OLIVE OIL, AS NEEDED

KOSHER SALT, TO TASTE

LEMON WEDGES, FOR SERVING

1. Cut the squid into 1-inch-wide rings.

2. Place the flour in a shallow bowl, add the squid, and toss them until completely coated. Place the squid in a fine-mesh sieve and gently shake to remove any excess flour.

3. Add olive oil to a narrow, deep, heavy-bottomed saucepan with high edges until it is about 2 inches deep and warm it to 350°F. Working in batches to avoid crowding the pot, slip the squid into the hot oil and fry until they are cooked through and golden brown, turning as necessary.

4. Remove the calamari from the hot oil, transfer them to a paper towel–lined plate to drain, and season them with salt. Serve with lemon wedges once all of the calamari have drained and cooled slightly.

Cipollina Catanese

YIELD: 8 CIPOLLINE / **ACTIVE TIME:** 30 MINUTES / **TOTAL TIME:** 1 HOUR

¼ CUP EXTRA-VIRGIN OLIVE OIL

2 LARGE WHITE OR RED ONIONS, SLICED VERY THIN

1 CUP CRUSHED TOMATOES

SALT AND PEPPER, TO TASTE

2 SHEETS OF FROZEN PUFF PASTRY, THAWED

8 THIN SLICES OF HAM

3 OZ. PROVOLA CHEESE, CUT INTO STRIPS AND DRAINED IN THE REFRIGERATOR FOR 2 HOURS

1 EGG, BEATEN

1. Preheat the oven to 370°F and line a baking sheet with parchment paper. Place the olive oil in a large skillet and warm it over low heat. Add the onions and cook, stirring occasionally, until they have softened and slightly caramelized, 10 to 15 minutes.

2. Stir in the tomatoes, season the mixture with salt and pepper, and remove the pan from heat.

3. Cut each sheet of puff pastry into 4 squares.

4. Place a slice of ham on each square and top it with the tomato sauce and cheese. Bring the 4 corners of the squares to the center and press down on the seams to seal them. Brush the cipolline with the egg and place them on the baking sheet.

5. Place the cipolline in the oven and bake until they are golden brown, about 15 minutes.

6. Remove the cipolline from the oven and let them cool slightly before serving.

Panzerotti

YIELD: 6 TO 8 PANZEROTTI / **ACTIVE TIME:** 1 HOUR / **TOTAL TIME:** 3 HOURS

FOR THE DOUGH

1½ PACKETS OF ACTIVE DRY YEAST

1 TEASPOON SUGAR

7 OZ. LUKEWARM WATER (90°F)

3½ OZ. WHOLE MILK

7.4 OZ. FINELY GROUND SEMOLINA FLOUR

10.2 OZ. BREAD OR "00" FLOUR, PLUS MORE AS NEEDED

2 TABLESPOONS EXTRA-VIRGIN OLIVE OIL

2 TEASPOONS FINE SEA SALT

FOR THE FILLING

1 HEAPING CUP WHOLE PEELED TOMATOES, CRUSHED

1 TABLESPOON EXTRA-VIRGIN OLIVE OIL

DRIED OREGANO, TO TASTE

KOSHER SALT AND PEPPER, TO TASTE

4½ OZ. MOZZARELLA OR SCAMORZA CHEESE, CUBED

2 TABLESPOONS GRATED PECORINO CHEESE

EXTRA-VIRGIN OLIVE OIL, AS NEEDED

1. To begin preparations for the dough, place the yeast, sugar, and water in a large bowl, gently stir to combine, and let the mixture sit until it starts to foam, about 10 minutes.

2. Add the milk and the flours and work the mixture until it just comes together as a dough.

3. Add the olive oil and salt and knead the dough until it is smooth and elastic.

4. Shape the dough into a round, place it in a clean bowl, and cover it with plastic wrap. Let the dough rest at room temperature until it has almost doubled in size, about 1½ hours.

5. Place the dough on a flour-dusted work surface and divide it into 6 pieces. Shape the pieces into rounds, cover them with a kitchen towel, and let them rest for 45 minutes.

6. Roll each round into a 16-inch disk and set them aside.

7. To begin preparations for the filling, place the tomatoes and olive oil in a bowl, season the mixture with oregano, salt, and pepper, and stir to combine.

8. Place 2 tablespoons of the tomato mixture, 2 tablespoons mozzarella, and 1 teaspoon pecorino in the center of each round and then fold the round over itself. Press down on the edges to seal the rounds, first with your fingers and then with a fork.

9. Add olive oil to a large skillet until it is about 1 inch deep and warm it to 350°F. Working with 1 panzerotto at a time, add them to the hot oil and fry until they are golden brown, turning as necessary, making sure to spoon hot oil over the tops of the panzerotti as they cook to prevent them from exploding.

10. Remove the panzerotti from the hot oil and transfer them to a paper towel–lined plate to drain. Serve once all of the panzerotti have drained and cooled slightly.

Lahmacun

YIELD: 1 FLATBREAD / **ACTIVE TIME:** 10 MINUTES / **TOTAL TIME:** 30 MINUTES

FOR THE FLATBREAD

1 BALL OF PIZZA DOUGH

JUICE OF 1 LEMON WEDGE

SUMAC, TO TASTE

¼ SMALL RED ONION, SLICED

3 SLICES OF TOMATO

¼ CUCUMBER, PEELED AND JULIENNED

1 TABLESPOON CRUMBLED FETA CHEESE

EXTRA-VIRGIN OLIVE OIL, TO TASTE

FRESH MINT LEAVES, FOR GARNISH

FOR THE SPREAD

¾ LB. GROUND BEEF

½ LARGE ONION, CHOPPED

½ GREEN BELL PEPPER, CHOPPED

1 TOMATO, CHOPPED

1 BUNCH OF FRESH PARSLEY

1½ TEASPOONS TAHINI PASTE

1 TABLESPOON TOMATO PASTE

¼ TEASPOON RED PEPPER FLAKES

¼ TEASPOON BLACK PEPPER

¼ TEASPOON GROUND NUTMEG

½ TEASPOON CINNAMON

½ TEASPOON ALLSPICE

½ TEASPOON SUMAC

½ TEASPOON DRIED THYME

SALT, TO TASTE

JUICE OF 1 LEMON WEDGE

1. Preheat the oven to 410°F and place a baking stone in the oven as it warms. To begin preparations for the flatbread, place the dough on a piece of parchment paper and gently stretch it into a very thin round.

2. To prepare the spread, place all of the ingredients in a food processor or blender and puree until the mixture is a smooth paste.

3. Cover the dough with the spread. Using a peel or a flat baking sheet, transfer the flatbread to the heated baking stone in the oven. Bake for about 10 minutes, until the crust is golden brown and starting to char.

4. Remove and top with the lemon juice, sumac, onion, tomato, cucumber, and feta. Drizzle olive oil over the top, garnish with fresh mint leaves, and enjoy.

Sweet Potato Börek

YIELD: 24 SERVINGS / **ACTIVE TIME:** 45 MINUTES / **TOTAL TIME:** 2 HOURS

1 SWEET POTATO, PEELED AND CUBED

1 TABLESPOON EXTRA-VIRGIN OLIVE OIL

1½ CUPS CHOPPED ONIONS

4 GARLIC CLOVES, MINCED

1 TEASPOON GRATED FRESH GINGER

1 CUP WHITE WINE

7 EGGS

1 TEASPOON KOSHER SALT

½ TEASPOON BLACK PEPPER

¾ LB. FONTINA CHEESE, GRATED

1 CUP FULL-FAT GREEK YOGURT

⅓ CUP HEAVY CREAM

½ CUP CHOPPED FRESH MINT

ZEST OF 1 LEMON

½ CUP MILK

1 LB. FROZEN PHYLLO DOUGH, THAWED

2 TEASPOONS POPPY SEEDS

1. Place the sweet potato in a small saucepan and cover it with water. Bring to a boil, reduce the heat, and simmer until the sweet potato is very tender, 15 to 20 minutes. Drain and let the sweet potato cool.

2. Place the olive oil in a large skillet and warm it over medium heat. Add the onions and cook, stirring occasionally, until they have softened, about 5 minutes. Add the garlic and ginger and cook for 1 minute. Add the white wine and cook until it has evaporated, about 8 minutes. Remove the pan from heat and let the mixture cool.

3. Preheat the oven to 400°F. In a food processor, combine the sweet potato, onion mixture, 6 of the eggs, the salt, and pepper and blitz until smooth.

4. Place the Fontina, yogurt, heavy cream, mint, and lemon zest in a bowl and stir to combine. Place the milk and remaining egg in a separate bowl and whisk until combined.

5. In a deep 13 x 9–inch baking pan, spread ¾ cup of the sweet potato puree evenly over the bottom. Place 5 sheets of phyllo on top and press down gently on them. Brush the top sheet of phyllo with the egg wash.

6. Repeat with the puree, phyllo, and egg wash and then sprinkle half of the cheese mixture over the phyllo. Top with another 5-sheet layer of phyllo and press down gently on it.

7. Repeat Steps 5 and 6.

8. Brush the top sheet of phyllo with the egg wash. Sprinkle the poppy seeds over the börek and place it in the oven. Bake until the top is puffy and golden brown, about 45 minutes.

9. Remove the börek from the oven and let it cool slightly before cutting and enjoying.

Lavash Crackers

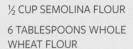

YIELD: 4 SERVINGS / **ACTIVE TIME:** 45 MINUTES / **TOTAL TIME:** 2 HOURS AND 30 MINUTES

½ CUP SEMOLINA FLOUR

6 TABLESPOONS WHOLE WHEAT FLOUR

½ CUP PLUS 2 TABLESPOONS ALL-PURPOSE FLOUR, PLUS MORE AS NEEDED

1 TEASPOON FINE SEA SALT

3 TABLESPOONS EXTRA-VIRGIN OLIVE OIL

1 TEASPOON INSTANT YEAST

½ CUP WARM WATER (105°F)

1 TABLESPOON ZA'ATAR (SEE PAGE 501)

1 TABLESPOON TOASTED SESAME SEEDS

1 TABLESPOON POPPY SEEDS

1. Place the flours, ½ teaspoon of the salt, 2 tablespoons of the olive oil, the yeast, and water in the work bowl of a stand mixer fitted with the dough hook and work the mixture on low until it comes together as a dough. Increase the speed to medium and work the dough until it no longer sticks to the side of the work bowl, about 10 minutes.

2. Cover the bowl with a linen towel and let the dough rise in a naturally warm place until it has doubled in size, about 1 hour.

3. Line two baking sheets with parchment paper. Dust a work surface with all-purpose flour. Divide the dough into two pieces, place one piece on the work surface, and roll it out into a rectangle that is about ⅛ inch thick. Place the rolled-out dough on one of the baking sheets and repeat with the other ball of dough. Don't be overly concerned with the shape of the dough, a rustic look is what we are looking for in these crackers.

4. Brush the pieces of dough with the remaining olive oil. Sprinkle the remaining salt over them.

5. Place the Za'atar, sesame seeds, and poppy seeds in a bowl and stir to combine. Sprinkle the mixture over the dough and press down gently to help the mixture adhere. Place the dough in a naturally warm place and let it rest for 30 minutes.

6. Preheat the oven to 425°F. Place the baking sheets in the oven and bake until the crackers are a deep golden brown, about 15 minutes. Remove the crackers from the oven and let them cool.

7. Break the crackers into pieces and enjoy.

Taramasalata

YIELD: 4 SERVINGS / **ACTIVE TIME:** 15 MINUTES / **TOTAL TIME:** 45 MINUTES

10 OZ. PANKO, PLUS MORE
AS NEEDED

½ CUP WATER

10 OZ. TARAMA CARP ROE

½ RED ONION, CHOPPED

JUICE OF ½ LEMON

½ CUP EXTRA-VIRGIN OLIVE
OIL, PLUS MORE AS NEEDED

SALT AND PEPPER, TO TASTE

FRESH PARSLEY, CHOPPED,
FOR GARNISH

1. Place the panko and water in a mixing bowl. Let the panko soak for 5 minutes.

2. Place the soaked panko, roe, onion, and lemon juice in a food processor and blitz until smooth.

3. With the food processor running, slowly drizzle in the olive oil until it has been incorporated and the mixture is smooth. If the taramasalata is thinner than you'd like, incorporate more panko. If it is too thick, incorporate a little more olive oil.

4. Season the dip with salt and pepper, garnish with parsley, and serve.

Roasted Tomato Caprese

YIELD: 2 SERVINGS / **ACTIVE TIME:** 25 MINUTES / **TOTAL TIME:** 45 MINUTES

½ CUP FRESH BASIL

½ CUP FRESH SPINACH

2 GARLIC CLOVES

½ CUP EXTRA-VIRGIN OLIVE OIL

½ CUP GRATED PARMESAN CHEESE

½ CUP BALSAMIC VINEGAR

2 TOMATOES

6 OZ. FRESH MOZZARELLA CHEESE, TORN

1. Preheat the oven to 450°F. Place the basil, spinach, garlic, 7 tablespoons of the olive oil, and Parmesan cheese in a food processor and blitz until smooth. Set the mixture aside.

2. Place the vinegar in a small saucepan and bring it to a simmer over medium-high heat. Reduce the heat to medium and cook the vinegar until it has been reduced by half, 6 to 8 minutes. Remove the pan from heat and let the reduction cool completely.

3. Cut the tomatoes into ½-inch-thick slices and place them on a baking sheet in a single layer. Drizzle the remaining olive oil over the top.

4. Distribute the mozzarella around the tomatoes, place the pan in the oven, and bake until the cheese and tomatoes start to brown, about 10 minutes. Remove the pan from the oven and let the tomatoes and mozzarella cool.

5. To serve, arrange the tomatoes and mozzarella on a plate, spoon the pesto over them, and drizzle the balsamic reduction over the top.

Tzatziki

YIELD: 2 CUPS / **ACTIVE TIME:** 5 MINUTES / **TOTAL TIME:** 1 HOUR AND 5 MINUTES

1 CUP FULL-FAT GREEK YOGURT

¾ CUP SEEDED AND MINCED CUCUMBER

1 GARLIC CLOVE, MINCED

JUICE FROM 1 LEMON WEDGE

SALT AND WHITE PEPPER, TO TASTE

FRESH DILL, FINELY CHOPPED, TO TASTE

1. Place the yogurt, cucumber, garlic, and lemon juice in a mixing bowl and stir to combine. Taste and season with salt, pepper, and dill.

2. Place in the refrigerator and chill for 1 hour before serving.

Stuffed Avocados

YIELD: 2 SERVINGS / **ACTIVE TIME:** 45 MINUTES / **TOTAL TIME:** 1 HOUR AND 30 MINUTES

1 CUP FINELY DICED BUTTERNUT SQUASH

2 TABLESPOONS EXTRA-VIRGIN OLIVE OIL

1 TEASPOON KOSHER SALT

1 TEASPOON BLACK PEPPER

2 RIPE AVOCADOS

½ CUP CRUMBLED FETA CHEESE

2 TABLESPOONS SMOKED EGG AIOLI (SEE PAGE 516)

1. Preheat the oven to 450°F. In a bowl, combine the squash with 1 tablespoon of the olive oil, the salt, and pepper. Transfer the squash to a baking sheet, place it in the oven, and roast until lightly browned and soft enough to mash, 15 to 20 minutes. Remove the squash from the oven and set it aside.

2. Halve the avocados and remove their pits, reserving the skins. Using a spoon, remove the avocado flesh and place it in a bowl. Add the feta and roasted squash and mash the mixture until it is smooth and well combined.

3. Fill the avocado skins with the mixture and lightly brush the top of each one with the remaining oil. Place them on a baking sheet and place them in the oven.

4. Roast until the tops of the avocados are browned, 10 to 15 minutes. Remove from the oven, drizzle the aioli over the tops, and enjoy.

Pecan Muhammara

YIELD: 4 SERVINGS / **ACTIVE TIME:** 15 MINUTES / **TOTAL TIME:** 30 MINUTES

2 RED BELL PEPPERS

¼ CUP PECANS

1 TEASPOON KOSHER SALT

1 TEASPOON ALEPPO PEPPER

½ CUP EXTRA-VIRGIN OLIVE OIL

JUICE OF 1 LEMON

1 TABLESPOON POMEGRANATE MOLASSES

¼ CUP BREAD CRUMBS

FRESH PARSLEY, CHOPPED, FOR GARNISH

1. Warm a cast-iron skillet over medium-high heat. Place the peppers in the pan and cook until they are charred all over, turning them as needed.

2. Place the peppers in a bowl, cover it with plastic wrap, and let them steam for 15 minutes.

3. Remove the stems, skins, and seed pods from the peppers and place the peppers in a blender.

4. Add the pecans, salt, Aleppo pepper, olive oil, lemon juice, and molasses and puree until smooth.

5. Add the bread crumbs and fold to incorporate them. Sprinkle some parsley on top and enjoy.

Pecan Muhammara
SEE PAGE 43

Stuffed Grape Leaves

YIELD: 4 SERVINGS / **ACTIVE TIME:** 30 MINUTES / **TOTAL TIME:** 1 HOUR AND 30 MINUTES

1 (1 LB.) JAR OF GRAPE LEAVES

¼ CUP EXTRA-VIRGIN OLIVE OIL, PLUS MORE TO TASTE

1 RED ONION, CHOPPED

1 CUP LONG-GRAIN RICE, RINSED WELL

¼ CUP RAISINS, FINELY CHOPPED

¼ CUP CHOPPED FRESH MINT, PLUS MORE FOR GARNISH

¼ CUP CHOPPED FRESH DILL

ZEST OF 1 LEMON

PINCH OF CINNAMON

SALT AND PEPPER, TO TASTE

1 LEMON, SLICED, FOR SERVING

1. Remove the grape leaves from the jar and rinse off all of the brine. Pick out 16 of the largest leaves and lay them on a baking sheet. Cover them with plastic wrap and set them aside.

2. Place half of the olive oil in a medium saucepan and warm it over medium heat. Add the onion and cook, stirring occasionally, until it has softened, about 5 minutes.

3. Add the rice and cook, stirring frequently, for 2 minutes. Add 1½ cups water and bring it to a boil. Reduce the heat to low, cover the pan, and simmer for about 15 minutes.

4. Remove the pan from heat, fluff the rice with a fork, and let it cool.

5. Add the raisins, mint, dill, lemon zest, and cinnamon to the rice and fold to combine. Season the mixture with salt and pepper and form it into 16 balls.

6. Lay down a grape leaf and remove the stem. Fold in the edges of the leaf. Place a ball of the rice mixture at the bottom of the leaf, fold the bottom of the leaf over the filling, and then roll the leaf up tightly. Place the stuffed grape leaf on a baking sheet, seam side down, and repeat with the remaining grape leaves and rice mixture.

7. Place the remaining olive oil in a large saucepan and warm it over medium-high heat. Add the stuffed grape leaves to the pan in a single layer, seam side down, and cook for 1 minute.

8. Reduce the heat to the lowest setting and carefully add 1½ cups water to the pan. Cover the pan and cook for 30 minutes, adding more water if the pan starts to look dry. You should finish with very little water in the pan.

9. Drizzle more olive oil over the grape leaves, garnish with additional mint, and serve with the slices of lemon.

Arancini

YIELD: 8 SERVINGS / **ACTIVE TIME:** 30 MINUTES / **TOTAL TIME:** 1 HOUR AND 30 MINUTES

5 CUPS CHICKEN STOCK
(SEE PAGE 482)

½ CUP UNSALTED BUTTER

2 CUPS ARBORIO RICE

1 SMALL WHITE ONION,
GRATED

1 CUP WHITE WINE

4 OZ. FONTINA CHEESE,
GRATED, PLUS MORE FOR
GARNISH

SALT AND PEPPER, TO TASTE

CANOLA OIL, AS NEEDED

6 LARGE EGGS, BEATEN

5 CUPS PANKO

TOMATO SAUCE (SEE PAGE
504), FOR SERVING

1. Bring the stock to a simmer in a large saucepan. In a large skillet, melt the butter over high heat. Add the rice and onion to the skillet and cook until the rice has a toasty fragrance, about 3 minutes. Deglaze the skillet with the white wine and cook until the rice has almost completely absorbed the wine.

2. Reduce the heat to medium-high and begin adding the stock ¼ cup at a time, stirring until it has been absorbed by the rice. Continue adding the stock until the rice is al dente.

3. Turn off the heat, stir in the cheese, and season the risotto with salt and pepper. Pour it onto a rimmed baking sheet and let it cool.

4. Add canola oil to a Dutch oven until it is 2 inches deep and warm it to 350°F. When the risotto is cool, form it into golf ball–sized spheres. Dredge them in the eggs and then the panko until completely coated.

5. Gently slip the arancini into the hot oil and fry until warmed through and golden brown, 3 to 5 minutes. Transfer the arancini to a paper towel–lined plate to drain and let them cool slightly.

6. To serve, garnish the arancini with additional Fontina and serve with Tomato Sauce.

Arancini
SEE PAGE 47

Couscous Arancini

YIELD: 2 SERVINGS / **ACTIVE TIME:** 40 MINUTES / **TOTAL TIME:** 1 HOUR AND 30 MINUTES

2 CUPS COUSCOUS

1 TABLESPOON PAPRIKA

1 TABLESPOON GARLIC POWDER

2 TEASPOONS KOSHER SALT

1 TEASPOON CUMIN

1 CUP CRUMBLED FETA CHEESE

CANOLA OIL, AS NEEDED

1. Place 2½ cups water in a saucepan and bring it to a boil.

2. Place the couscous and the seasonings in a mixing bowl and stir until well combined. Add the boiling water to the couscous and cover the bowl with plastic wrap. After 10 minutes, use a fork to fluff the couscous.

3. Add ½ cup of feta to the couscous and stir to incorporate it.

4. Add canola oil to a Dutch oven until it is about 2 inches deep and warm it to 350°F. Using your hands, form 1 oz. portions of the couscous into balls. Press into each ball with your thumb and make a depression. Fill this with some of the remaining feta and then close the ball over it.

5. Working in batches of 4 to avoid crowding the pot, gently slip the balls into the hot oil and fry until golden brown, about 4 minutes. Transfer the fried arancini to a paper towel–lined plate to drain and cool and enjoy once all of them have been cooked.

Caponata

YIELD: 6 SERVINGS / **ACTIVE TIME:** 1 HOUR / **TOTAL TIME:** 2 HOURS

1 LARGE EGGPLANT (ABOUT 1½ LBS.)

2 TABLESPOONS EXTRA-VIRGIN OLIVE OIL

1 ONION, CHOPPED

2 CELERY STALKS, PEELED AND CHOPPED

3 LARGE GARLIC CLOVES, MINCED

2 RED BELL PEPPERS, STEMS AND SEEDS REMOVED, CHOPPED

SALT AND PEPPER, TO TASTE

1 LB. ROMA TOMATOES, PEELED, SEEDED, AND FINELY CHOPPED; OR 1 (14 OZ.) CAN OF CRUSHED TOMATOES

2 TABLESPOONS PLUS 1 PINCH SUGAR

3 TABLESPOONS (HEAPING) CAPERS, RINSED AND DRAINED

3 TABLESPOONS CHOPPED GREEN OLIVES

3 TABLESPOONS RED WINE VINEGAR

1. Preheat the oven to 425°F. Place the eggplant on a baking sheet, place it in the oven, and roast until it has collapsed and is starting to char, about 25 minutes. Remove from the oven and let the eggplant cool. When cool enough to handle, roughly chop the eggplant.

2. Place 1 tablespoon of the olive oil in a large skillet and warm it over medium heat. Add the onion and celery and cook, stirring, until the onion starts to soften, about 5 minutes. Stir in the garlic, cook for 1 minute, and then add the peppers. Season with salt and cook, stirring frequently, until the peppers are tender, about 8 minutes.

3. Add the remaining olive oil and the eggplant and cook, stirring occasionally, until the eggplant begins to fall apart and the other vegetables are tender. Stir in the tomatoes and the pinch of sugar, season the mixture with salt, and cook, stirring frequently, until the tomatoes start to collapse and smell fragrant, about 7 minutes.

4. Stir in the capers, olives, remaining sugar, and the vinegar. Reduce the heat to medium-low and cook, stirring often, until the mixture is quite thick, sweet, and fragrant, 20 to 30 minutes. Taste, season with salt and pepper, and remove the pan from heat.

5. Let the caponata cool to room temperature before serving. If time allows, chill it in the refrigerator overnight and let it return to room temperature before serving.

Caponata
SEE PAGE 51

Crispy Lemon & Chickpea Cakes

YIELD: 4 SERVINGS / **ACTIVE TIME:** 15 MINUTES / **TOTAL TIME:** 45 MINUTES

3 TABLESPOONS EXTRA-VIRGIN OLIVE OIL

1 LEEK, TRIMMED, HALVED, RINSED WELL, AND SLICED THIN

2 GARLIC CLOVES, MINCED

½ CUP PINE NUTS, TOASTED

1 (14 OZ.) CAN OF CHICKPEAS, DRAINED AND RINSED

1 EGG

1 TABLESPOON FRESH LEMON JUICE

ZEST OF 1 LEMON

1 TABLESPOON DIJON MUSTARD

¼ CUP PANKO

SALT AND PEPPER, TO TASTE

¼ CUP ALL-PURPOSE FLOUR

LEMON WEDGES, FOR SERVING

1. Place 1 tablespoon of the olive oil in a medium saucepan and warm it over medium heat. Add the leek and cook, stirring occasionally, until it has softened, about 5 minutes. Add the garlic and cook, stirring continually, for 1 minute.

2. Remove the pan from heat, stir in the toasted pine nuts, and set the mixture aside.

3. Place the chickpeas in a food processor and pulse until they are minced. Add them to the leek mixture, fold in the egg, lemon juice, lemon zest, mustard, and panko, and season the mixture with salt and pepper.

4. Place the flour in a shallow bowl. Working with wet hands, form the chickpea mixture into 8 patties. Dredge the patties in the flour until coated and gently brush off any excess.

5. Place the remaining olive oil in a skillet and warm it over medium heat. Working in batches, place the patties in the skillet and cook until crispy and golden brown on each side, 8 to 10 minutes.

6. Let the cakes cool briefly before serving with lemon wedges.

Spanakopita

YIELD: 8 SERVINGS / **ACTIVE TIME:** 1 HOUR / **TOTAL TIME:** 1 HOUR AND 30 MINUTES

½ LB. BABY SPINACH, STEMS REMOVED

1 CUP CRUMBLED FETA CHEESE

6 TABLESPOONS FULL-FAT GREEK YOGURT

2 SCALLIONS, TRIMMED AND CHOPPED

1 EGG, BEATEN

2 TABLESPOONS CHOPPED FRESH MINT

2 GARLIC CLOVES, MINCED

ZEST AND JUICE OF ½ LEMON

½ TEASPOON FRESHLY GRATED NUTMEG

PINCH OF CAYENNE PEPPER

SALT AND PEPPER, TO TASTE

½ LB. FROZEN PHYLLO DOUGH, THAWED

6 TABLESPOONS UNSALTED BUTTER, MELTED

1 CUP GRATED PECORINO CHEESE

1 TABLESPOON SESAME SEEDS

1 TABLESPOON CHOPPED FRESH DILL

1. Prepare an ice bath. Fill a large saucepan three-quarters of the way with water and bring it to a boil. Add the spinach and boil for 2 minutes, making sure it is all submerged. Drain the spinach, plunge it in the ice bath, and let it cool.

2. Place the spinach in a linen towel and wring the towel to remove as much water from the spinach as possible. Chop the spinach, place it in a bowl, and add the feta, yogurt, scallions, egg, mint, garlic, lemon zest, lemon juice, nutmeg, and cayenne. Stir to combine, season the mixture with salt and pepper, and set the filling aside.

3. Preheat the oven to 425°F. Line a baking sheet with parchment paper. Place a piece of parchment paper on a work surface, place a sheet of phyllo on it, and brush it with some of the butter. Lay another sheet of phyllo on top, gently press down, and brush it with butter. Sprinkle a thin layer of the Pecorino over the second sheet. Repeat so that you have another layer of Pecorino sandwiched between two 2-sheet layers of phyllo. Make sure you keep any phyllo that you are not working with covered so that it does not dry out.

4. Working from the top of the rectangle, find the center point and cut down, as though you were cutting an open book in half. Cut these halves in two, so that you have four strips. Place 2 tablespoons of the filling on the bottom of each strip and shape the filling into a triangle.

5. Maintaining the triangle shape of the filling, fold the strips up into triangles, as if you were folding a flag. Crimp the pastries to seal, and place the spanakopita on the baking sheet, seam side down.

6. Repeat Steps 3, 4, and 5, giving you 8 spanakopita. Sprinkle the sesame seeds over each spanakopita, place them in the oven, and bake until golden brown, about 20 minutes.

7. Remove the spanakopita from the oven, sprinkle the dill over them, and enjoy.

Swordfish Crudo

YIELD: 2 SERVINGS / **ACTIVE TIME:** 15 MINUTES / **TOTAL TIME:** 30 MINUTES

4 OZ. SUSHI-GRADE SWORDFISH, SKIN REMOVED

SALT, TO TASTE

1 TEASPOON BLACK PEPPER

JUICE OF ½ LEMON

1 TABLESPOON EXTRA-VIRGIN OLIVE OIL

1 TABLESPOON SLICED SCALLIONS

4 SLICES OF JALAPEÑO CHILE PEPPER

3 SLICES OF TOMATO

1. Chill a plate in the refrigerator for 10 minutes.

2. Slice the swordfish thin against the grain and arrange the slices on the chilled plate, making sure they do not overlap.

3. Season the fish generously with salt, then sprinkle the pepper and lemon juice over it. Drizzle the olive oil over the top and sprinkle the scallions over the fish.

4. Arrange the jalapeño and tomato on the side of the plate and chill in the refrigerator until ready to serve.

Turmeric & Ginger Shrimp Cocktail

YIELD: 6 SERVINGS / **ACTIVE TIME:** 30 MINUTES / **TOTAL TIME:** 2 HOURS AND 30 MINUTES

1½ LBS. SHRIMP

1 TABLESPOON GRATED FRESH GINGER

2 GARLIC CLOVES, MINCED

1 TABLESPOON GRATED FRESH TURMERIC

2 TABLESPOONS CHOPPED SCALLIONS

1 SHALLOT, MINCED

JUICE OF 1 LIME

1 SCALLION, MINCED

1 TABLESPOON KOSHER SALT

1 TEASPOON HONEY

1 TABLESPOON EXTRA-VIRGIN OLIVE OIL

1. Peel the shrimp, leaving only the tails, and devein them. Set them aside.

2. Place the remainder of the ingredients in a mixing bowl, stir until well combined, and then add the peeled shrimp. Cover the bowl with plastic wrap and chill in the refrigerator for at least 2, and no more than 6, hours.

3. Warm a large skillet over medium-high heat. Working in batches to avoid crowding the pan, add the shrimp and the marinating liquid to the pan and cook until the shrimp have turned pink, 3 to 5 minutes. Remove the cooked shrimp from the pan and let them cool.

4. Serve at room temperature or chilled.

Sweet Potato & Tahini Dip

YIELD: 1 CUP / **ACTIVE TIME:** 15 MINUTES / **TOTAL TIME:** 1 HOUR

EXTRA-VIRGIN OLIVE OIL, AS NEEDED

1 SWEET POTATO, HALVED

1 YELLOW ONION, QUARTERED

2 LARGE GARLIC CLOVES

¼ CUP TAHINI PASTE

1 TEASPOON FRESH LEMON JUICE

½ TEASPOON KOSHER SALT

2 TABLESPOONS HONEY

½ TEASPOON ANCHO CHILE POWDER

1 TABLESPOON MINCED PISTACHIOS, FOR GARNISH

1. Preheat the oven to 400°F and coat a baking sheet with olive oil. Place the sweet potato, cut side down, and the onion on the baking sheet. Place the garlic cloves in a small piece of aluminum foil, place a few drops of oil on them, wrap them up, and place on the baking sheet.

2. Place the baking sheet in the oven and roast for about 20 minutes, then remove the garlic. Roast the sweet potato and onion until the sweet potato is very tender, another 10 minutes or so. Remove from the oven and let cool.

3. Scoop the sweet potato's flesh into a food processor. Add the roasted onion and garlic, tahini, lemon juice, and salt. Pulse until the mixture is a smooth paste. Taste and adjust the seasoning as necessary.

4. Place the honey in a very small pot and warm it over low heat. Add the ancho chile powder, remove the pan from heat, and let sit for a few minutes.

5. Place the puree in a shallow bowl and make a well in the center. Pour some of spiced honey in the well, garnish with the chopped pistachios, and enjoy.

Swordfish Crudo
SEE PAGE 56

Falafel

YIELD: 4 SERVINGS / **ACTIVE TIME:** 30 MINUTES / **TOTAL TIME:** 2 HOURS

1 (14 OZ.) CAN OF CHICKPEAS, DRAINED AND RINSED

½ RED ONION, CHOPPED

1 CUP FRESH PARSLEY, CHOPPED

1 CUP FRESH CILANTRO, CHOPPED

3 BUNCHES OF SCALLIONS, TRIMMED AND CHOPPED

1 JALAPEÑO CHILE PEPPER, STEM AND SEEDS REMOVED, CHOPPED

3 GARLIC CLOVES

1 TEASPOON CUMIN

1 TEASPOON KOSHER SALT, PLUS MORE TO TASTE

½ TEASPOON CARDAMOM

¼ TEASPOON BLACK PEPPER

2 TABLESPOONS CHICKPEA FLOUR

½ TEASPOON BAKING SODA

CANOLA OIL, AS NEEDED

1. Line a baking sheet with parchment paper. Place all of the ingredients, except for the canola oil, in a food processor and blitz until pureed.

2. Scoop ¼-cup portions of the puree onto the baking sheet and place it in the refrigerator for 1 hour.

3. Add canola oil to a Dutch oven until it is 2 inches deep and warm it to 320°F over medium heat.

4. Working in batches, add the falafel to the oil and fry, turning occasionally, until they are golden brown, about 6 minutes. Transfer the cooked falafel to a paper towel–lined plate to drain.

5. When all of the falafel have been cooked, serve with your favorite dipping sauces.

Tuna Kibbeh Nayeh

YIELD: 2 SERVINGS / **ACTIVE TIME:** 30 MINUTES / **TOTAL TIME:** 45 MINUTES

1 CUP BULGUR

½ LB. SUSHI-GRADE TUNA

2 FRESH BASIL LEAVES, CHIFFONADE

2 FRESH MINT LEAVES, CHIFFONADE

JUICE OF 1 LIME

JUICE OF 1 LEMON

1 TEASPOON KOSHER SALT

PINCH OF BLACK PEPPER

¼ CUP FINELY DICED RED ONION

2 TABLESPOONS SMOKED EGG AIOLI (SEE PAGE 516)

FLESH FROM 1 AVOCADO

PITA BREAD (SEE PAGE 338), TOASTED, FOR SERVING

1. Place the bulgur in a small saucepan, cover it with water, and cook over medium heat until tender, 15 to 20 minutes. Drain and run the bulgur under cold water until it has cooled.

2. Using a sharp knife, cut the tuna into slices and then dice it into ¼-inch cubes.

3. Place the fresh herbs, lime and lemon juices, salt, and pepper in a mixing bowl and stir until well combined. Stir in the tuna, making sure to cover it with the liquid as much as possible. Let the mixture sit for 5 minutes.

4. Stir in the bulgur, red onion, and aioli.

5. Cut the avocado into ¼-inch cubes and gently fold these into the mixture, taking care to mash them up as little as possible. Serve with toasted pitas.

Marinated Artichokes

YIELD: 4 SERVINGS / **ACTIVE TIME:** 30 MINUTES / **TOTAL TIME:** 1 HOUR

2 CUPS EXTRA-VIRGIN OLIVE OIL, PLUS MORE AS NEEDED

4 TO 8 GLOBE ARTICHOKES, PEELED AND QUARTERED

JUICE OF 1 LEMON

6 GARLIC CLOVES

¼ TEASPOON RED PEPPER FLAKES

2 SPRIGS OF FRESH THYME

1 SHALLOT, SLICED THIN

FRESH BASIL, CHOPPED, FOR GARNISH

1. Place the olive oil and artichokes in a medium saucepan. The artichokes need to be completely covered by the oil, as any contact with the air will cause them to turn brown. Add more oil to cover the artichokes, if necessary.

2. Add the remaining ingredients, except for the basil, and bring the mixture to a simmer over medium heat. Reduce the heat to the lowest setting and cook the artichokes until they are tender, about 30 minutes.

3. Remove the pan from heat and let the artichokes cool. Remove them from the oil, garnish with basil, and enjoy.

Falafel
SEE PAGE 60

Fried Artichokes

YIELD: 8 SERVINGS / **ACTIVE TIME:** 1 HOUR AND 15 MINUTES / **TOTAL TIME:** 2 HOURS

5 LEMONS, HALVED	AVOCADO OIL, AS NEEDED
4 LARGE ARTICHOKES	SALT AND PEPPER, TO TASTE

1. Prepare an ice bath in a large bowl. Squeeze two lemons into the ice bath, stir, and then throw the spent lemon halves into the ice bath. This lemon water will keep the artichokes fresh and green until you're ready to fry them. Keep a couple of fresh lemon halves on hand as you prep.

2. Rinse the artichokes under cold water. Pat them dry with a linen towel or paper towels. Using kitchen shears, remove the thorny tips from the leaves. For each artichoke, remove the bitter, fibrous end of the stem with a knife, leaving about 1½ inches of stem attached to each artichoke.

3. Using a serrated knife, peel the outer skin from the remaining stem. As the stem is more bitter than the rest of the artichoke, removing the skin tempers the bitterness. Rub the peeled stem with fresh lemon to keep it from browning.

4. Peel off 5 or 6 layers of external leaves from each artichoke, snapping off the leaves and setting them aside, until you reach inner leaves that are fresh looking and white at their base.

5. Using a serrated knife or sharp chef's knife, slice each artichoke horizontally, about ¾ inch above the base (aka the heart), and remove the pointy top of the artichoke, leaving a flat crown of leaves at the base of the artichoke while exposing the purple inner leaves.

6. Slice the artichokes in half lengthwise, splitting the stem and heart to reveal the fuzzy choke.

7. Scoop out the white spines and purple leaves from each artichoke half with a melon baller, leaving two hollowed-out halves of the heart with a small crown of flat leaves.

8. Rub the artichokes with lemon and place them in the ice bath as you clean each one. When done, pour the water from the ice bath into a large saucepan and add the spent lemon halves. You will need about 1½ inches of water to steam the artichokes, so add more water if needed.

9. Place a steaming tray inside the pan and bring the water to a boil. Place the cleaned artichoke halves in the steaming tray and cover the pan. Reduce the heat to medium and steam the artichokes until the thickest part of the stem is just tender, 15 to 20 minutes. You want the artichokes to still be a bit firm—they should only be partially cooked.

10. Place the steamed artichokes on a paper towel–lined plate and let them dry completely.

11. Add avocado oil to a cast-iron skillet until it is 1 inch deep and warm it to 325°F. Season the artichokes with salt and pepper, making sure to season between the layers of leaves as well. Gently slip the artichokes into the hot oil and fry them until the leaves are crispy and golden brown, about 15 minutes, turning the artichokes as needed. Remove the artichokes from the oil, transfer to a paper towel–lined plate, and let them drain before serving.

Couscous-Stuffed Tomatoes

YIELD: 4 SERVINGS / **ACTIVE TIME:** 30 MINUTES / **TOTAL TIME:** 1 HOUR AND 30 MINUTES

4 TOMATOES

2 TEASPOONS SUGAR

SALT AND PEPPER, TO TASTE

2 TABLESPOONS PLUS 1 TEASPOON EXTRA-VIRGIN OLIVE OIL

¼ CUP PANKO

1 CUP GRATED MANCHEGO CHEESE

1 ONION, CHOPPED

2 GARLIC CLOVES, MINCED

¼ TEASPOON RED PEPPER FLAKES

4 CUPS BABY SPINACH

¾ CUP COUSCOUS

1½ CUPS CHICKEN STOCK (SEE PAGE 482)

2 TABLESPOONS CHOPPED KALAMATA OLIVES

2 TEASPOONS RED WINE VINEGAR

1. Preheat the oven to 350°F. Cut the top ½ inch off the tomatoes and scoop out their insides. Sprinkle the sugar and some salt into the tomatoes, turn them upside down, and place them on a wire rack. Let the tomatoes drain for 30 minutes.

2. Place 1 teaspoon of the olive oil in a large skillet and warm it over medium heat. Add the panko and cook, stirring continually, until golden brown, about 3 minutes. Remove the panko from the pan, place it in a bowl, and let it cool.

3. Stir half of the cheese into the cooled panko and set the mixture aside.

4. Place 1 tablespoon of the olive oil in a clean large skillet and warm it over medium-high heat. Add the onion and cook, stirring occasionally, until it has softened, about 5 minutes. Add the garlic and red pepper flakes and cook, stirring continually, for 1 minute.

5. Add the spinach and cook until it has wilted, about 2 minutes. Add the couscous and stock and bring the mixture to a simmer. Cover the pan, remove it from heat, and let it sit until the couscous is tender, about 7 minutes.

6. Fluff the couscous with a fork, add the olives, vinegar, and remaining cheese, and fold until incorporated. Season the stuffing with salt and pepper and set it aside.

7. Place the remaining olive oil in a baking dish. Add the tomatoes, cavities facing up, and fill them with the stuffing. Top with the toasted panko mixture and place the tomatoes in the oven. Roast until the tomatoes are tender, about 20 minutes.

8. Remove the tomatoes from the oven and let them cool slightly before enjoying.

Keftes de Espinaca

YIELD: 12 SERVINGS / **ACTIVE TIME:** 15 MINUTES / **TOTAL TIME:** 30 MINUTES

½ CUP PLUS 1 TABLESPOON AVOCADO OIL

1 ONION, MINCED

½ TEASPOON GRATED GARLIC

10 OZ. FRESH SPINACH

1 LARGE EGG

1 CUP LEFTOVER MASHED POTATOES

½ CUP BREAD CRUMBS

1 TEASPOON KOSHER SALT

¼ TEASPOON BLACK PEPPER

PINCH OF CAYENNE PEPPER

1. Place the tablespoon of avocado oil in a large skillet and warm it over medium heat. Add the onion and cook, stirring frequently, until it starts to soften, about 5 minutes.

2. Add the garlic and cook until fragrant, about 1 minute. Add half of the spinach, cover the pan, and cook until the spinach has wilted. Add the remaining spinach, cover the pan again, and cook until all of the spinach has wilted.

3. Transfer the mixture to a fine-mesh strainer and gently press down on the mixture to remove excess moisture. Transfer the mixture to a cutting board and roughly chop it.

4. Place the mixture in a mixing bowl. Add the remaining ingredients and stir until thoroughly combined. Form ¼-cup portions of the mixture into patties and place them on a parchment-lined baking sheet.

5. Place the remaining avocado oil in the skillet and warm it to 365°F. Working in batches to avoid crowding the pan, slip the patties into the hot oil and fry until brown on both sides, about 8 minutes. Transfer the keftes to a paper towel–lined plate to drain before serving.

Labneh

YIELD: 8 SERVINGS / **ACTIVE TIME:** 10 MINUTES / **TOTAL TIME:** 2 DAYS

4 CUPS FULL-FAT GREEK YOGURT

½ TEASPOON KOSHER SALT

1 TABLESPOON EXTRA-VIRGIN OLIVE OIL

2 TEASPOONS ZA'ATAR (SEE PAGE 501)

1. Place the yogurt in a large bowl and season it with the salt; the salt helps pull out excess whey, giving you a creamier, thicker labneh.

2. Place a fine-mesh strainer on top of a medium-sized bowl. Line the strainer with cheesecloth or a linen towel, letting a few inches hang over the side of the strainer. Spoon the seasoned yogurt into the cheesecloth and gently wrap the sides over the top of the yogurt, protecting it from being exposed to air in the refrigerator.

3. Store everything in the refrigerator for 24 to 48 hours, discarding the whey halfway through if the bowl beneath the strainer becomes too full.

4. Remove the labneh from the cheesecloth and store it in an airtight container.

5. To serve, drizzle the olive oil over the labneh and sprinkle the Za'atar on top.

Scallop Ceviche

YIELD: 2 SERVINGS / **ACTIVE TIME:** 15 MINUTES / **TOTAL TIME:** 30 MINUTES

1 TEASPOON HONEY

½ TEASPOON POMEGRANATE MOLASSES

JUICE OF 1 LIME

SPLASH OF WHITE VINEGAR

PINCH OF KOSHER SALT

½ SHALLOT, DICED

1 TABLESPOON SLICED SCALLIONS

1 TEASPOON DICED JALAPEÑO CHILE PEPPER

6 LARGE SEA SCALLOPS, RINSED, FEET REMOVED

1. In a mixing bowl, combine the honey, pomegranate molasses, lime juice, and white vinegar. Add the salt, shallot, scallions, and jalapeño to the bowl, mix well, and let the mixture rest for 15 minutes.

2. Using a sharp knife, cut the scallops into ⅛-inch-thick slices. Add the scallops to the marinade and gently stir to coat. In a minute or two, the scallops will cure and turn fully white. Enjoy immediately.

Labneh
SEE PAGE 67

Tiropitakia

YIELD: 6 SERVINGS / **ACTIVE TIME:** 45 MINUTES / **TOTAL TIME:** 1 HOUR AND 15 MINUTES

½ LB. FETA CHEESE

1 CUP GRATED KEFALOTYRI CHEESE

¼ CUP FINELY CHOPPED FRESH PARSLEY

2 EGGS, BEATEN

BLACK PEPPER, TO TASTE

1 (1 LB.) PACKAGE OF FROZEN PHYLLO DOUGH, THAWED

1 CUP UNSALTED BUTTER, MELTED

1. Place the feta in a mixing bowl and break it up with a fork. Add the kefalotyri, parsley, eggs, and pepper and stir to combine. Set the mixture aside.

2. Place one sheet of the phyllo dough on a large sheet of parchment paper. Gently brush the sheet with some of the melted butter, place another sheet on top, and brush this with more of the butter. Cut the phyllo dough into 2-inch-wide strips, place 1 teaspoon of the filling at the end of the strip closest to you, and fold one corner over to make a triangle. Fold the strip up until the filling is completely covered. Repeat with the remaining sheets of phyllo dough and filling.

3. Preheat the oven to 350°F and coat a baking sheet with some of the melted butter. Place the pastries on the baking sheet and bake in the oven until golden brown, about 15 minutes. Remove the tiropitakia from the oven and let cool briefly before serving.

Baba Ghanoush

YIELD: 12 SERVINGS / **ACTIVE TIME:** 15 MINUTES / **TOTAL TIME:** 1 HOUR AND 15 MINUTES

2 LARGE EGGPLANTS, HALVED

4 GARLIC CLOVES, SMASHED

4 TEASPOONS FRESH LEMON JUICE, PLUS MORE TO TASTE

1½ TEASPOONS KOSHER SALT, PLUS MORE TO TASTE

½ CUP TAHINI PASTE

¼ CUP POMEGRANATE ARILS

2 TEASPOONS FINELY CHOPPED FRESH PARSLEY

¼ CUP EXTRA-VIRGIN OLIVE OIL

PITA BREAD (SEE PAGE 338), FOR SERVING

1. Preheat the oven to 400°F. Place the eggplants on a baking sheet, cut side up, and roast until they have collapsed, about 50 minutes. Remove the eggplants from the oven and let them cool for 10 minutes.

2. Scoop the flesh of the eggplants into a food processor and discard the skins. Add the garlic, lemon juice, salt, and tahini and blitz until the mixture is smooth and creamy, about 1 minute. Taste and add more lemon juice and salt as necessary.

3. Transfer to a bowl, top with the pomegranate arils, parsley, and olive oil, and serve with Pita Bread.

Marinated Olives

YIELD: 8 SERVINGS / **ACTIVE TIME:** 20 MINUTES / **TOTAL TIME:** 2 HOURS AND 20 MINUTES

1½ LBS. ASSORTED OLIVES

2 TEASPOONS LIGHTLY CRACKED CORIANDER SEEDS

1 TEASPOON LIGHTLY CRACKED FENNEL SEEDS

¾ CUP EXTRA-VIRGIN OLIVE OIL

2 TABLESPOONS RED WINE VINEGAR

4 GARLIC CLOVES, SLICED THIN

1½ TEASPOONS CHOPPED FRESH ROSEMARY

1½ TEASPOONS FRESH THYME

4 BAY LEAVES, TORN

1 SMALL DRIED RED CHILE PEPPER, STEM AND SEEDS REMOVED, CHOPPED

2 STRIPS OF LEMON ZEST

1. Rinse any dark olives under cold water so their juices don't discolor the other olives. Place all of the olives in a colander and drain them. Transfer the olives to a wide-mouthed jar and set them aside.

2. Warm a dry skillet over medium-high heat. Add the coriander and fennel seeds and toast until very fragrant, about 2 minutes, stirring occasionally. Add the olive oil and vinegar and cook for 1 minute.

3. Remove the pan from heat and add the remaining ingredients. Stir to combine and let the mixture cool completely.

4. Pour the marinade over the olives, cover, and shake the jar so that the olives are evenly coated.

5. Chill the olives in the refrigerator for 2 hours before serving. If preparing the olives a few days ahead of time, shake the jar daily to redistribute the seasonings.

Salata Mechouia

YIELD: 6 SERVINGS / **ACTIVE TIME:** 1 HOUR AND 15 MINUTES / **TOTAL TIME:** 3 HOURS AND 15 MINUTES

1 JALAPEÑO CHILE PEPPER

6 LARGE PLUM TOMATOES

3 GREEN BELL PEPPERS

2 GARLIC CLOVES, UNPEELED

2 TEASPOONS KOSHER SALT

¼ TEASPOON BLACK PEPPER

¼ CUP FRESH LEMON JUICE

3 TABLESPOONS EXTRA-VIRGIN OLIVE OIL

PITA BREAD (SEE PAGE 338), FOR SERVING

1. Preheat the oven to 375°F. Use a knife to cut a small slit in the jalapeño.

2. Place the tomatoes, bell peppers, jalapeño, and garlic on an aluminum foil–lined baking sheet. Place it in the oven and roast until the vegetables are well browned and just tender, about 30 minutes for the garlic and 1 hour for the peppers and tomatoes.

3. Remove the vegetables from the oven. Place the garlic cloves on a plate and let them cool. Place the other roasted vegetables in a large bowl and cover it with plastic wrap. Let them rest for about 15 minutes.

4. Peel the garlic cloves and set them aside. Remove the charred skins from the other vegetables, place the vegetables in a colander, and let them drain.

5. Using a fork, mash the roasted garlic.

6. Transfer the drained vegetables to a cutting board. Remove the seeds from the bell peppers and the jalapeño. Finely chop all of the vegetables and place them in a mixing bowl. Add the mashed garlic, salt, pepper, lemon juice, and olive oil and stir well until combined.

7. Enjoy immediately with the Pita Bread.

Baba Ghanoush
SEE PAGE 72

Beet Chips with Spicy Honey Mayonnaise

YIELD: 8 SERVINGS / **ACTIVE TIME:** 30 MINUTES / **TOTAL TIME:** 1 HOUR

4 CUPS CANOLA OIL

3 BEETS, RINSED WELL AND DRIED

SALT AND PEPPER, TO TASTE

SPICY HONEY MAYONNAISE (SEE PAGE 493), FOR SERVING

1. Place the canola oil in a Dutch oven and warm it to 375°F. Line a baking sheet with paper towels and set a cooling rack in it.

2. Cut the root end from the beets and use a mandoline to cut the beets into ⅛-inch-thick slices.

3. Working in batches to avoid crowding the pot, gently slip the beets into the hot oil and fry until they are browned and stop bubbling and sizzling, 3 to 4 minutes. Remove the chips with a slotted spoon, season them with salt and pepper, and let them cool—they will crisp up as they do.

4. When all of the beets have been fried, serve the chips with the spicy mayo.

Eggplant & Chorizo Bourekas

YIELD: 6 SERVINGS / **ACTIVE TIME:** 30 MINUTES / **TOTAL TIME:** 1 HOUR

1½ CUPS AVOCADO OIL

1 EGGPLANT, CUBED

1 TEASPOON KOSHER SALT, PLUS MORE TO TASTE

1 TEASPOON BLACK PEPPER, PLUS MORE TO TASTE

1 LARGE ONION, SLICED THIN

2 GARLIC CLOVES, MINCED

1 TEASPOON CUMIN SEEDS

7 OZ. CHORIZO, FINELY DICED

HANDFUL OF FRESH PARSLEY, CHOPPED

½ LB. FROZEN PUFF PASTRY, THAWED

6 EGGS

1. Place ¼ cup of the avocado oil in a large skillet and warm it over medium-high heat. Season the eggplant with the salt and pepper and place the eggplant in the hot oil. Cook, tossing the eggplant until it has absorbed all of the oil, and then reduce the heat and gently fry the eggplant until it is soft and the oil has been released back into the pan. Using a slotted spoon, transfer the eggplant to a paper towel–lined plate.

2. Add the onion to the pan and cook, stirring occasionally, until it starts to brown, about 10 minutes. Add the garlic and cumin and cook, stirring frequently, until fragrant, about 1 minute. Transfer the mixture to a bowl, add the eggplant, and stir to combine.

3. Add the chorizo to the pan and fry until it has browned and is starting to crisp up, about 10 minutes. Transfer it to a paper towel–lined plate to drain and then stir the chorizo into the eggplant-and-onion mixture. Stir the parsley into the mixture, season it with salt and pepper, and let it cool.

4. Place the remaining avocado oil in a large skillet and warm it to 350°F. Fill a bowl with water and place it beside your work surface.

5. Cut the puff pastry into six 5-inch squares. Divide the filling among the squares, placing it in the center. Make wells in the center of the filling and crack an egg into each one. Dip your fingers in the water and moisten the edges of the squares, then fold in half vertically to form triangles. Pinch the edges to seal the pockets.

6. Gently slip the bourekas into the hot oil, working in batches to avoid crowding the pan. Spoon the hot oil over the bourekas and fry until golden brown on the bottom, about 30 seconds. Turn them over, cook until golden brown on this side, and then transfer to a paper towel–lined plate to drain.

Bourekas

YIELD: 12 SERVINGS / **ACTIVE TIME:** 1 HOUR / **TOTAL TIME:** 1 HOUR AND 50 MINUTES

3 YUKON GOLD POTATOES, PEELED AND CUT INTO 1-INCH CUBES

2 TABLESPOONS EXTRA-VIRGIN OLIVE OIL

1 SMALL ONION, CHOPPED

1 GARLIC CLOVE, MINCED

⅛ TEASPOON FRESHLY GRATED NUTMEG

1 CUP RICOTTA CHEESE

1 CUP GRATED KASHKAVAL CHEESE

SALT AND PEPPER, TO TASTE

2 LARGE EGGS

½ LB. FROZEN PUFF PASTRY, THAWED

SESAME SEEDS, TOASTED, FOR TOPPING

1. Place the potatoes in a stockpot and cover them by 1 inch with cold water. Bring to a boil over medium-high heat and cook until the potatoes are fork-tender, 20 to 25 minutes. Drain the potatoes, place them in a bowl, and mash them. Let them cool.

2. Place the olive oil in a large skillet and warm it over medium-high heat. Add the onion and cook, stirring occasionally, until it is starting to brown, about 7 minutes. Add the garlic and cook, stirring frequently, until fragrant, about 1 minute. Remove the pan from heat and set it aside.

3. Place the nutmeg and cheeses in a bowl and stir until combined.

4. Add the onion mixture and the cheese mixture to the mashed potatoes and stir until well combined. Season the mixture with salt and pepper and set it aside.

5. In a bowl, beat one of the eggs. While stirring the cool potato mixture, slowly incorporate the beaten egg.

6. Preheat the oven to 375°F and line a large baking sheet with parchment paper. Fill a bowl with water and place it beside your work surface.

7. Cut the puff pastry into 5-inch squares. Place a heaping tablespoon of filling in the center of each square. Dip your fingers in the water and moisten the edges of the squares, then fold in half vertically to form triangles. Pinch the edges to seal the pockets.

8. Beat the second egg and brush it over the tops of the bourekas. Sprinkle the sesame seeds on top.

9. Place the bourekas in the oven and bake until puffy and golden brown, about 30 minutes.

10. Remove from the oven and let the bourekas cool slightly before enjoying.

Handrajo

YIELD: 16 SERVINGS / **ACTIVE TIME:** 1 HOUR / **TOTAL TIME:** 1 HOUR AND 45 MINUTES

¼ CUP SUNFLOWER OIL

2 TABLESPOONS EXTRA-VIRGIN OLIVE OIL

2 MEDIUM EGGPLANTS, PEELED, WASHED, AND CUT INTO ½-INCH CUBES

1 TEASPOON KOSHER SALT, PLUS MORE TO TASTE

1 GARLIC CLOVE

2 ONIONS, FINELY DICED

3 TOMATOES, HALVED, PEELED, AND GRATED

1½ TEASPOONS SUGAR

½ TEASPOON SWEET PAPRIKA

½ TEASPOON BLACK PEPPER

2 (28 OZ.) PACKAGES OF PUFF PASTRY, THAWED (PREFERABLY BUTTER-BASED)

1 EGG, BEATEN

LABNEH (SEE PAGE 67), FOR SERVING

1. Place the oils in a large skillet and warm over high heat. Add the eggplants to the pan in an even layer, season with ½ teaspoon of the salt, and cook, undisturbed, until the eggplants start to brown, about 5 minutes.

2. Add the garlic and onions and stir to combine. Cover the pan with a lid, reduce the heat to medium, and cook until the vegetables are soft, about 10 minutes. Remove the lid and cook for 5 more minutes, until all of the liquid has evaporated.

3. Stir in the tomatoes, sugar, paprika, pepper, and the remaining salt and cook until the flavors have melded, 5 to 7 minutes. As the mixture cooks, break up any large chunks with a wooden spoon.

4. Remove the pan from heat, discard the garlic clove, and let the mixture cool completely.

5. Preheat the oven to 425°F and position a rack in the middle. Line a baking sheet with parchment paper. Spread the sheets of puff pastry on a clean work surface and cut each sheet in half lengthwise; you should end up with four 10 x 7–inch rectangles.

6. Divide the filling among the pieces of puff pastry, spreading it on one half of their length and leaving about 1 inch of pastry uncovered at the edge. Fold the other half of the dough over the filling, bringing the edges of the rectangles together. Using a fork, press down along each edge of the rectangles to seal the pastry together. Carefully transfer each pastry to the prepared baking sheet and brush them with the beaten egg.

7. Place in the oven and bake the handrajo until they are golden brown and crispy, 20 to 25 minutes.

8. Remove from the oven, cut the handrajo into pieces, and serve with the Labneh.

Eggplant Rings

YIELD: 4 SERVINGS / ACTIVE TIME: 40 MINUTES / TOTAL TIME: 1 HOUR

1 LARGE EGGPLANT, TRIMMED AND SLICED

2 EGGS, BEATEN

1 CUP ALL-PURPOSE FLOUR

1 CUP PANKO

1 TABLESPOON KOSHER SALT

1 TABLESPOON BLACK PEPPER

CANOLA OIL, AS NEEDED

¼ CUP RED ZHUG (SEE PAGE 499)

¼ CUP KETCHUP

1. Cut the centers out of the slices of eggplant, creating rings that have about an inch of eggplant left inside.

2. Place the eggs, flour, and panko in separate bowls. Add the salt and pepper to the bowl of panko and stir to combine. Dredge an eggplant ring in the flour, then the eggs, followed by the panko, repeating until all of the rings are coated. Place the coated rings on a baking sheet.

3. Add canola oil to a cast-iron skillet until it is about 1 inch deep and warm to 375°F over medium-high heat. Working in batches to avoid crowding the pan, gently lay the eggplant rings in the oil and fry until browned and crispy all over, about 4 minutes, turning as necessary. Place the cooked rings on a paper towel–lined plate to drain.

4. Place the zhug and ketchup in a small bowl, stir to combine, and serve alongside the eggplant rings.

Fried Eggplant with Garlic & Ras el Hanout

YIELD: 4 SERVINGS / ACTIVE TIME: 30 MINUTES / TOTAL TIME: 1 HOUR

1 MEDIUM EGGPLANT, CUT INTO ½-INCH-THICK SLICES

½ TEASPOON KOSHER SALT

AVOCADO OIL, AS NEEDED

4 GARLIC CLOVES, MINCED

1 TEASPOON RAS EL HANOUT (SEE PAGE 505)

2 TABLESPOONS SALSA VERDE (SEE PAGE 505)

1. Sprinkle both sides of the eggplant with the salt, place the slices on a baking sheet in a single layer, and let them rest for 30 minutes.

2. Add avocado oil to a Dutch oven until it is 1 inch deep and warm it over high heat. Pat the eggplant dry with paper towels.

3. When the oil is sizzling, gently slip about 5 eggplant slices into the pan and fry until golden brown on both sides, 7 to 10 minutes, turning as needed. Transfer the fried eggplant to a paper towel–lined baking sheet and then repeat with the remaining slices.

4. Arrange the fried eggplant on a large platter, sprinkle the garlic and Ras el Hanout on top, drizzle the Salsa Verde over it, and enjoy.

Chickpea Poutine

YIELD: 4 SERVINGS / **ACTIVE TIME:** 45 MINUTES / **TOTAL TIME:** 2 HOURS

1 CUP CHICKPEA FLOUR

2 TEASPOONS KOSHER SALT

1 TEASPOON GARLIC POWDER

2 TABLESPOONS DRIED PARSLEY

PINCH OF CUMIN

2 CUPS BOILING WATER

CANOLA OIL, AS NEEDED

½ LB. LEFTOVER SHORT RIB OR BRISKET

½ CUP CRUMBLED FETA CHEESE

1. Place the flour, salt, garlic powder, parsley, and cumin in a mixing bowl and stir to combine. Add the boiling water and beat until the batter is smooth. Pour the batter into a small baking dish (small enough that the batter is about 1 inch deep), cover with plastic wrap, and refrigerate for 1 hour.

2. Turn the mixture out onto a cutting board and cut it into wide strips.

3. Add canola oil to a Dutch oven until it is about 3 inches deep and warm it to 350°F over medium heat. Add the chickpea fries and turn them as they cook until they are crispy and golden brown, 3 to 4 minutes. Place them on a paper towel–lined plate to drain.

4. Place the short rib in a small saucepan, add about ½ cup of water, and bring it to a simmer. Cook until the liquid has reduced by half.

5. Arrange the fries on a platter and spoon the gravy from the short rib over them. Top with the short rib, sprinkle the feta over the fries, and serve.

Chickpea Poutine
SEE PAGE 81

Fried Feta

YIELD: 2 SERVINGS / **ACTIVE TIME:** 25 MINUTES / **TOTAL TIME:** 25 MINUTES

1 CUP ALL-PURPOSE FLOUR

1 TEASPOON KOSHER SALT

1 TEASPOON BAKING POWDER

1 CUP WATER

CANOLA OIL, AS NEEDED

1 BLOCK OF FETA CHEESE (½-INCH THICK)

1 TEASPOON EXTRA-VIRGIN OLIVE OIL

1 CUP GRAPE TOMATOES

LEAVES FROM ½ HEAD OF ROMAINE LETTUCE

1 TABLESPOON BALSAMIC GLAZE (SEE PAGE 508)

1. Place the flour, salt, baking powder, and water in a small bowl and whisk until the mixture is smooth.

2. Add canola oil to a small saucepan until it is about 1 inch deep and warm it over medium-high heat.

3. Carefully dip the block of feta in the batter until it is completely coated.

4. Submerge half of the feta in the canola oil for 5 seconds, then release it so that it floats. Fry for 1½ minutes on each side, while keeping a close eye on the feta; if the batter doesn't seal, the feta will ooze out, and this won't work. Once the feta has browned, remove from the oil and set it on a cooling rack.

5. Place the olive oil in a medium skillet and warm it over high heat. Add the tomatoes and cook until they start to blister, 2 to 3 minutes. Add the lettuce leaves and brown them for about 1 minute. Remove the pan from heat.

6. To serve, place the lettuce in a shallow bowl, scatter the tomatoes on top, and nestle the fried block of feta on top. Drizzle the Balsamic Glaze over the cheese and enjoy.

Fire-Roasted Oysters

YIELD: 4 SERVINGS / **ACTIVE TIME:** 20 MINUTES / **TOTAL TIME:** 40 MINUTES

20 FRESH OYSTERS

3 TABLESPOONS UNSALTED BUTTER

½ CUP MINCED FRESH GARLIC

½ CUP GRATED PARMESAN CHEESE

¼ CUP CHOPPED FRESH PARSLEY, FOR GARNISH

1. Prepare a charcoal or gas grill for medium-high heat (about 450°F). Rinse and shuck the oysters, making sure to separate them from the shell at the tendon.

2. Put a small dollop of butter, a pinch of garlic, and a pinch of Parmesan into each oyster's shell.

3. Place the oysters on the grill and cover it. Cook until the butter and cheese turn golden brown, about 2 minutes.

4. Garnish with the parsley and enjoy.

Mussels Escabeche

YIELD: 2 TO 4 SERVINGS / **ACTIVE TIME:** 30 MINUTES / **TOTAL TIME:** 1 HOUR

1 TABLESPOON EXTRA-VIRGIN OLIVE OIL

2 SHALLOTS, 1 CHOPPED; 1 SLICED INTO RINGS

2 GARLIC CLOVES, MINCED

½ CUP WHITE WINE

½ CUP WATER

ZEST AND JUICE OF 1 LEMON

2 SPRIGS OF FRESH THYME

1 TEASPOON DIJON MUSTARD

2 LBS. MUSSELS, RINSED WELL AND DEBEARDED

1 TEASPOON PAPRIKA

2 TABLESPOONS CHOPPED FRESH PARSLEY

SALT AND PEPPER, TO TASTE

1. Place the olive oil in a medium saucepan and warm it over medium heat. Add the chopped shallot and cook, stirring frequently, until it starts to soften, about 2 minutes.

2. Add the garlic and cook for 1 minute. Add the white wine and cook until the alcohol has been cooked off, about 2 minutes.

3. Add the water, lemon zest, lemon juice, thyme, and mustard and bring the mixture to a boil. Add the mussels and cover the pan. Cook until the majority of the mussels have opened, about 5 minutes. Discard any mussels that do not open.

4. Using a slotted spoon, remove the mussels from the liquid and place them in a bowl.

5. Boil the remaining liquid until about ¼ cup remains.

6. When the mussels are cool enough to handle, remove the meat from the shells. Discard the shells and place the mussels in a bowl.

7. Strain the reduction into a clean pan and bring to a simmer. Add the shallot rings and cook for 1 minute. Stir in the paprika and parsley and season with salt and pepper.

8. Remove the pan from heat and let it cool. Fold in the mussels and enjoy.

Fire-Roasted Oysters
SEE PAGE 84

Goat Cheese, Olive & Fennel Phyllo Triangles

YIELD: 16 SERVINGS / **ACTIVE TIME:** 30 MINUTES / **TOTAL TIME:** 1 HOUR AND 30 MINUTES

1 TABLESPOON EXTRA-VIRGIN OLIVE OIL

½ FENNEL BULB, TRIMMED, CORED, AND CHOPPED

2 GARLIC CLOVES, MINCED

6 TABLESPOONS WHITE WINE

1 TABLESPOON PERNOD

1 TABLESPOON MINCED RAISINS

6 GREEN OLIVES, PITS REMOVED, MINCED

1 CUP CRUMBLED GOAT CHEESE

1 TABLESPOON FINELY CHOPPED FRESH CHIVES

1 TEASPOON LEMON ZEST

1 TEASPOON LEMON JUICE

SALT AND PEPPER, TO TASTE

½ LB. FROZEN PHYLLO DOUGH, THAWED

6 TABLESPOONS UNSALTED BUTTER, MELTED

1 TABLESPOON BLACK SESAME SEEDS

1. Place the olive oil in a medium saucepan and warm it over medium heat. Add the fennel and cook, stirring occasionally, until it has softened and is starting to brown, about 8 minutes.

2. Add the garlic and cook, stirring continually, until fragrant, about 1 minute. Add the white wine, Pernod, and raisins and cook until the liquid has evaporated, about 5 minutes. Remove the pan from heat and let it cool for 5 minutes.

3. Place the olives, goat cheese, chives, lemon zest, and lemon juice in a mixing bowl and stir to combine. Add the fennel mixture, fold to combine, and season the mixture with salt and pepper. Set the filling aside.

4. Preheat the oven to 425°F. Line a baking sheet with parchment paper. Place a piece of parchment paper on a work surface. Lay one sheet of phyllo on the parchment and brush it with some of the butter. Lay another sheet of phyllo on top and gently press down. Brush the phyllo with butter and then cut the rectangle into 2-inch-wide strips. Make sure to cover the rest of the phyllo dough so that it does not dry out.

5. Place 2 teaspoons of the filling at the bottom of each strip and shape the filling into a triangle. Taking care to maintain that triangle shape, roll up the strip, as if you were folding a flag. Crimp the folded-up pastries to seal them and place them, seam side down, on the baking sheet.

6. Repeat Steps 4 and 5 until you have 16 filled pastries.

7. Sprinkle the sesame seeds over the pastries, place them in the oven, and bake until golden brown, about 10 minutes.

8. Remove from the oven and let the pastries cool before serving.

ENTREES

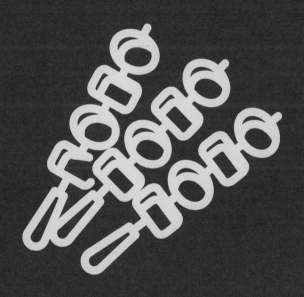

Stuffed Mackerel

YIELD: 2 SERVINGS / **ACTIVE TIME:** 30 MINUTES / **TOTAL TIME:** 1 HOUR AND 15 MINUTES

2 TABLESPOONS EXTRA-VIRGIN OLIVE OIL

½ RED ONION, CHOPPED

½ RED BELL PEPPER, CHOPPED

½ GREEN BELL PEPPER, CHOPPED

2 GARLIC CLOVES, MINCED

1 TEASPOON FRESH THYME

¼ CUP CHOPPED GREEN OLIVES

ZEST AND JUICE OF 1 LEMON

1 TABLESPOON CHOPPED FRESH PARSLEY

¼ CUP PANKO, TOASTED

SALT AND PEPPER, TO TASTE

2 (10 OZ.) MACKEREL, GUTTED, CLEANED, AND BUTTERFLIED

BRAISED GREEN BEANS (SEE PAGE 382), FOR SERVING

1. Preheat the oven to 450°F. Place 1 tablespoon of the olive oil in a large skillet and warm it over medium-high heat. Add the onion and peppers and cook, stirring occasionally, until they are browned, about 8 minutes.

2. Add the garlic and thyme and cook, stirring constantly, for 1 minute. Remove the pan from heat and fold in the olives, lemon zest, lemon juice, parsley, and panko. Season the stuffing with salt and pepper and set it aside.

3. Coat a baking sheet with the remaining olive oil. Place the mackerel on the baking sheet and season the insides of the fish with salt and pepper. Fill the fish with the stuffing and then use kitchen twine to tie the fish closed.

4. Sprinkle salt and pepper over the fish, place them in the oven, and roast until they are cooked through (internal temperature of about 135°F), about 10 minutes.

5. Remove the fish from the oven, cut off the kitchen twine, and serve with the Braised Green Beans.

Risi e Bisi

YIELD: 4 SERVINGS / **ACTIVE TIME:** 30 MINUTES / **TOTAL TIME:** 1 HOUR

2 TABLESPOONS EXTRA-VIRGIN OLIVE OIL

6 OZ. THINLY SLICED PROSCIUTTO, CUT INTO ¼-INCH-WIDE STRIPS

2 SHALLOTS, MINCED

1 GARLIC CLOVES, MINCED

1 CUP ARBORIO RICE

½ CUP WHITE WINE

CHICKEN STOCK (SEE PAGE 482), WARMED, AS NEEDED

1 LB. FROZEN PEAS

1 CUP GRATED PARMESAN CHEESE

JUICE OF ½ LEMON

SALT AND PEPPER, TO TASTE

FRESH PARSLEY, CHOPPED, FOR GARNISH

1. Place the olive oil in a large saucepan and warm it over medium-high heat. Add the prosciutto and cook, stirring frequently, until it is golden brown and crispy, about 5 minutes. Using a slotted spoon, transfer the prosciutto to a paper towel–lined plate and let it drain.

2. Add the shallots to the saucepan and cook, stirring occasionally, until they start to soften, about 3 minutes.

3. Add the garlic and rice and cook, stirring frequently, for 2 minutes. Add the white wine and cook, stirring frequently, until the rice has absorbed the wine.

4. While stirring continually, add stock ¼ cup at a time, waiting until each addition has been fully absorbed before adding more. Continue adding stock until the rice is tender, about 15 minutes.

5. Add the frozen peas and cook, stirring frequently, until warmed through, 4 to 5 minutes.

6. Stir in the Parmesan and lemon juice. Season the dish with salt and pepper, garnish with the crispy prosciutto and parsley, and enjoy.

Toasted Pasta with Crab

YIELD: 4 SERVINGS / **ACTIVE TIME:** 15 MINUTES / **TOTAL TIME:** 45 MINUTES

¼ CUP EXTRA-VIRGIN OLIVE OIL

½ LB. ANGEL HAIR PASTA, BROKEN INTO 2-INCH PIECES

1 ONION, CHOPPED

3 GARLIC CLOVES, MINCED

¼ CUP WHITE WINE

4 CUPS CHICKEN STOCK (SEE PAGE 482)

1 BAY LEAF

1 (14 OZ.) CAN OF DICED TOMATOES, DRAINED

1 TEASPOON PAPRIKA

SALT AND PEPPER, TO TASTE

1 LB. LUMP CRABMEAT

FRESH PARSLEY, CHOPPED, FOR GARNISH

1. Preheat the oven to 425°F. Place 1 tablespoon of the olive oil and the pasta in a large cast-iron skillet and toast the pasta over medium-high heat until it is browned, about 8 minutes. Transfer the pasta to a bowl.

2. Wipe out the skillet, add the remaining olive oil, and warm it over medium heat. Add the onion and cook, stirring occasionally, until it has softened, about 5 minutes. Add the garlic and cook, stirring continually, for 1 minute.

3. Add the wine and cook until the alcohol has been cooked off, 2 to 3 minutes. Add the stock, bay leaf, tomatoes, and paprika and bring the mixture to a boil. Reduce the heat, add the pasta, and simmer until the pasta is tender, about 10 minutes.

4. Season the dish with salt and pepper, add the crab, place the pan in the oven, and bake until the pasta is crispy, about 5 minutes.

5. Remove the pan from the oven, garnish the dish with parsley, and enjoy.

Spaghetti alla Nerano

YIELD: 4 SERVINGS / **ACTIVE TIME:** 15 MINUTES / **TOTAL TIME:** 30 MINUTES

½ CUP PLUS 3 TABLESPOONS EXTRA-VIRGIN OLIVE OIL

1½ LBS. ZUCCHINI, SLICED THIN

SALT AND PEPPER, TO TASTE

14 OZ. SPAGHETTI

2 GARLIC CLOVES

7 OZ. PROVOLONE CHEESE, GRATED

2 OZ. PARMESAN CHEESE, GRATED

20 FRESH BASIL LEAVES

1. Place ½ cup of olive oil in a large, deep skillet and warm it to 350°F. Add the zucchini to the hot oil and fry until they are starting to brown, turning as necessary. Transfer the fried zucchini to a paper towel–lined plate to drain and season it with salt.

2. Bring water to a boil in a large saucepan. Add salt, let the water return to a full boil, and add the pasta. Cook until the pasta is very al dente. Reserve 1½ cups pasta water and drain the spaghetti.

3. Place the remaining olive oil in a large skillet and warm it over medium heat. Add the garlic, cook for 2 minutes, and then remove it from the pan.

4. Add the pasta to the garlic oil and toss to combine.

5. Add some of the pasta water and the cheeses and toss until well combined and the pasta is al dente.

6. Add the fried zucchini, half of the basil, and more pasta water if it is needed and gently toss to combine. Stir in the remaining basil, season the dish with black pepper, and enjoy.

Toasted Pasta with Crab
SEE PAGE 94

Ratatouille with Poached Eggs

YIELD: 6 SERVINGS / **ACTIVE TIME:** 30 MINUTES / **TOTAL TIME:** 1 HOUR

¼ CUP EXTRA-VIRGIN OLIVE OIL

1 CUP CHOPPED ONION

4 GARLIC CLOVES, MINCED

2 TABLESPOONS TOMATO PASTE

1 CUP CHOPPED RED BELL PEPPER

1 CUP CHOPPED YELLOW BELL PEPPER

1 CUP CHOPPED ZUCCHINI

½ CUP WATER

2 TABLESPOONS DRIED HERBES DE PROVENCE

SALT AND PEPPER, TO TASTE

6 EGGS

¼ CUP FRESH BASIL LEAVES

½ CUP SHAVED PARMESAN CHEESE

1. Place the olive oil in a Dutch oven and warm it over medium heat. Add the onion and cook, stirring occasionally, until it has softened, about 5 minutes. Add the garlic and tomato paste and cook, stirring continually, for 1 minute.

2. Add the bell peppers and cook, stirring occasionally, until they have softened, about 5 minutes.

3. Add the zucchini, water, and herbes de Provence, cover the pot, and cook for 10 minutes. Remove the cover and cook until the liquid has reduced, about 5 minutes.

4. Season the ratatouille with salt and pepper. Using the back of a wooden spoon, make six wells in the ratatouille. Gently crack an egg into each well, reduce the heat so that the ratatouille simmers, and cover the pot. Cook until the egg whites are set, 6 to 8 minutes.

5. Spoon the ratatouille and poached eggs into bowls, top each portion with the basil and Parmesan, and enjoy.

Gnocchi alla Sorrentina

YIELD: 4 SERVINGS / **ACTIVE TIME:** 10 MINUTES / **TOTAL TIME:** 20 MINUTES

2 LBS. GNOCCHI DI PATATE (SEE PAGE 243)

3 CUPS TOMATO SAUCE (SEE PAGE 504)

¾ LB. FRESH MOZZARELLA CHEESE, DRAINED AND TORN

⅔ CUP GRATED PARMESAN CHEESE

1. Bring water to a boil in a large saucepan. Add the gnocchi and cook until they are floating on the surface.

2. Drain the gnocchi, place them in a large bowl with the tomato sauce, and gently stir to combine.

3. Transfer half of the gnocchi to a deep baking dish with high edges and cover them with half of the mozzarella and Parmesan. Repeat with the remaining gnocchi, mozzarella, and Parmesan.

4. Set the oven's broiler to high. Place the baking dish in the oven and broil until the mozzarella has melted, 5 to 8 minutes. Remove the gnocchi from the oven and serve immediately.

Spaghetti alla Puttanesca

YIELD: 4 SERVINGS / **ACTIVE TIME:** 10 MINUTES / **TOTAL TIME:** 25 MINUTES

1.1 LBS. TOMATOES

¼ CUP EXTRA-VIRGIN OLIVE OIL

1 GARLIC CLOVE, CHOPPED

8 ANCHOVIES PACKED IN KOSHER SALT, RINSED AND CHOPPED

RED PEPPER FLAKES, TO TASTE

1 (HEAPING) CUP PITTED GAETA OLIVES, CHOPPED

1 TABLESPOON CAPERS PACKED IN KOSHER SALT, SOAKED, DRAINED, SQUEEZED DRY, AND CHOPPED

2 TABLESPOONS FINELY CHOPPED FRESH ITALIAN PARSLEY

SALT, TO TASTE

14 OZ. SPAGHETTI

1. Bring water to a boil in a large saucepan. Add the tomatoes and boil them for 2 minutes. Drain the tomatoes and let them cool. When they are cool enough to handle, peel the tomatoes, remove the seeds, and chop the remaining flesh. Set the tomatoes aside.

2. Place the olive oil in a large skillet and warm it over medium-low heat. Add the garlic and cook for 2 minutes. Add the anchovies and red pepper flakes and cook for 1 minute.

3. Stir in the olives and capers and cook, stirring frequently, for 3 minutes.

4. Add the tomatoes and half of the parsley and cook, stirring occasionally, until the tomatoes start to break down, about 20 minutes.

5. Bring water to a boil in a large saucepan. Add salt, let the water return to a full boil, and add the pasta. Cook until the pasta is very al dente. Reserve ¼ cup of pasta water and drain the spaghetti.

6. Add the spaghetti and pasta water to the skillet, raise the heat to medium-high, and toss to combine. Cook until the pasta is al dente.

7. Stir in the remaining parsley and serve.

Shakshuka

YIELD: 4 SERVINGS / **ACTIVE TIME:** 30 MINUTES / **TOTAL TIME:** 1 HOUR

2 TABLESPOONS EXTRA-VIRGIN OLIVE OIL

1 ONION, CHOPPED

2 GREEN BELL PEPPERS, STEMS AND SEEDS REMOVED, CHOPPED

2 GARLIC CLOVES, MINCED

1 TEASPOON CORIANDER

1 TEASPOON SWEET PAPRIKA

½ TEASPOON CUMIN

1 TEASPOON TURMERIC

PINCH OF RED PEPPER FLAKES

2 TABLESPOONS TOMATO PASTE

5 RIPE TOMATOES, CHOPPED

SALT AND PEPPER, TO TASTE

6 EGGS

1 CUP CRUMBLED FETA CHEESE

¼ CUP CHOPPED FRESH PARSLEY, FOR GARNISH

¼ CUP CHOPPED FRESH MINT, FOR GARNISH

1. Place the olive oil in a large cast-iron skillet and warm it over medium heat. Add the onion and cook, stirring occasionally, until it has softened, about 5 minutes. Add the bell peppers and cook, stirring occasionally, until they have softened, about 5 minutes.

2. Add the garlic, coriander, paprika, cumin, turmeric, red pepper flakes, and tomato paste and cook, stirring continually, for 1 minute. Add the tomatoes and bring the mixture to a boil. Reduce the heat, cover the pan, and simmer for 15 minutes.

3. Remove the cover and cook until the shakshuka has reduced slightly, about 5 minutes.

4. Season the shakshuka with salt and pepper. Using the back of a wooden spoon, make six wells in the mixture. Crack an egg into each well and sprinkle the feta over the dish.

5. Reduce the heat to a simmer, cover the pan, and cook until the egg whites are set, 6 to 8 minutes. Remove the pan from heat, garnish with the parsley and mint, and enjoy.

Spaghetti allo Scoglio

YIELD: 4 SERVINGS / **ACTIVE TIME:** 1 HOUR / **TOTAL TIME:** 2 HOURS

¼ CUP EXTRA-VIRGIN OLIVE OIL

2 GARLIC CLOVES

2 LBS. CLAMS, RINSED WELL

2 LBS. MUSSELS, RINSED WELL AND DEBEARDED

10 OZ. SQUID, CLEANED (SEE PAGE 199) AND CUT INTO RINGS

SALT, TO TASTE

1 CUP DRY WHITE WINE

1 CUP CHERRY TOMATOES, HALVED

10 OZ. SHRIMP, DEVEINED

1 LB. SPAGHETTI

FRESH PARSLEY, CHOPPED, FOR GARNISH

1. Place half of the olive oil in a large skillet and warm it over medium heat. Add 1 garlic clove and cook, stirring occasionally, for 2 minutes.

2. Add the clams and mussels, raise the heat to medium-high, and cover the pan with a lid. Cook until the majority of the clams and mussels have opened, about 5 minutes.

3. Discard any clams and/or mussels that did not open. Remove the remaining clams and mussels from the pan, remove the meat from most of the shells, and set it aside. Leave the meat in some of the mussels and clams and reserve them for garnish. Strain any liquid in the pan and set it aside.

4. Add the remaining olive oil to the pan and warm it over medium heat. Add the remaining garlic clove and cook, stirring occasionally, for 2 minutes. Add the squid, season it lightly with salt, and cook for 2 minutes.

5. Add the wine and cook until it has evaporated. Remove the garlic clove, discard it, and add the tomatoes. Cook for 5 minutes.

6. Add the shrimp and cook until they turn pink, 2 to 3 minutes. Peel the shrimp, pressing down on their heads to release the juices. Reserve these juices.

7. Add the shrimp, their juices, mussels, and clams to the sauce, season it with salt, and remove the pan from heat.

8. Bring water to a boil in a large saucepan. Add salt, let the water return to a full boil, and add the pasta. Cook until the pasta is very al dente. Drain the spaghetti and add it to the skillet.

9. Cook the pasta and sauce over medium-high heat, tossing to combine and gradually adding the reserved liquid from cooking the mussels and clams.

10. When the pasta is al dente, garnish the dish with the parsley and reserved mussels and clams and enjoy.

Shakshuka
SEE PAGE 100

Pasta e Patate

YIELD: 4 SERVINGS / **ACTIVE TIME:** 15 MINUTES / **TOTAL TIME:** 1 HOUR

2 OZ. LARD, DICED

2 TABLESPOONS EXTRA-VIRGIN OLIVE OIL

½ MEDIUM WHITE ONION, FINELY DICED

1 LARGE CARROT, PEELED AND FINELY DICED

1 CELERY STALK, FINELY DICED

1 CUP CHERRY TOMATOES, DICED

1⅓ LBS. POTATOES, PEELED AND DICED

2 CUPS VEGETABLE STOCK (SEE PAGE 484)

2 PARMESAN RINDS

1½ CUPS WATER

6 OZ. SHORT-FORMAT PASTA

KOSHER SALT, TO TASTE

5 OZ. PROVOLA CHEESE, CUBED (OPTIONAL)

1. Place the lard and olive oil in a medium saucepan and warm the mixture over low heat. Add the onion, carrot, celery, and tomatoes and cook, stirring occasionally, until they have softened, about 6 minutes.

2. Add the potatoes and cook, stirring occasionally, for 6 minutes.

3. Add the broth, raise the heat to medium, and bring to a boil. Reduce the heat to low, cover the pan, and cook until the potatoes are tender, about 40 minutes, gently stirring occasionally.

4. Add the Parmesan rinds, water, and pasta, raise the heat to medium, and cook until the pasta is al dente. If there is too much liquid, raise the heat to reduce it to the desired amount.

5. Remove the Parmesan rinds, discard them, season the dish with salt, and remove the pan from heat.

6. Stir in the provola (if desired) and enjoy.

Cicelievitati

YIELD: 4 SERVINGS / **ACTIVE TIME:** 1 HOUR / **TOTAL TIME:** 3 HOURS

17.6 OZ. ALL-PURPOSE FLOUR

1 PACKET OF ACTIVE DRY YEAST

2 EGGS

2 PINCHES OF FINE SEA SALT, PLUS MORE TO TASTE

1 CUP WATER

SEMOLINA FLOUR, AS NEEDED

2 CUPS TOMATO SAUCE (SEE PAGE 504) OR RAGÙ NAPOLETANO (SEE PAGE 206)

2 OZ. PECORINO CHEESE, GRATED

1. Place the flour, yeast, and eggs in the work bowl of a stand mixer fitted with the dough hook and work the mixture until combined. Add the salt, work the mixture until it has been incorporated, and then add the water, 1 tablespoon at a time. Work the mixture until it comes together as a dry dough.

2. Cover the work bowl with plastic wrap and let the dough rise until it has doubled in size, about 1½ hours.

3. Dust a work surface with semolina flour, place the dough on it, and tear off a small piece of it. Roll the small piece of dough into a 3-inch-long stick that is about the thickness of a ballpoint pen. Repeat with the remaining dough.

4. Bring water to a boil in a large saucepan. Add salt, let the water return to a full boil, and add the pasta. Cook until the pasta has the consistency of properly cooked gnocchi, light and slightly chewy.

5. Drain the pasta and place it in a serving dish. Top with the sauce and pecorino and serve.

Honey-Glazed Tuna with Romesco & Warm Asparagus Salad

YIELD: 2 TO 4 SERVINGS / **ACTIVE TIME:** 30 MINUTES / **TOTAL TIME:** 1 HOUR AND 30 MINUTES

1 TABLESPOON HONEY

5 TABLESPOONS EXTRA-VIRGIN OLIVE OIL

1 LB. TUNA STEAK

SALT AND PEPPER, TO TASTE

2 GARLIC CLOVES, MINCED

10 OZ. CHERRY TOMATOES, HALVED

1 LB. ASPARAGUS, TRIMMED

½ CUP KALAMATA OLIVES, PITS REMOVED, CHOPPED

2 TABLESPOONS CHOPPED FRESH BASIL

¼ CUP GRATED PARMESAN CHEESE

ROMESCO SAUCE (SEE PAGE 496), FOR SERVING

1. Place the honey and 3 tablespoons of the olive oil in a mixing bowl and whisk to combine. Add the tuna, season it with salt and pepper, and place the bowl in the refrigerator. Let the tuna marinate for 1 hour, flipping it over every 15 minutes.

2. While the tuna is marinating, place 1 tablespoon of olive oil in a large skillet and warm it over medium heat. Add the garlic and tomatoes and cook, stirring continually, until the tomatoes start to collapse, about 3 minutes. Transfer the mixture to a bowl and set it aside.

3. Place the remaining olive oil in the skillet and warm it over medium heat. Add the asparagus in a single layer, cover the pan, and cook until the asparagus is bright green, about 5 minutes. Uncover the pan and cook until the asparagus is well browned on one side, about 5 minutes.

4. Add the asparagus to the garlic and tomatoes and season the mixture with salt and pepper. Add the olives, toss to combine, top the dish with the basil and Parmesan, and set it aside.

5. Warm a medium skillet over high heat. Add the marinade and then place the tuna in the center of the pan. Reduce the heat to medium and cook the tuna until browned on each side, about 1 minute per side.

6. Remove the tuna from the pan and let it rest for 2 minutes before slicing it and serving alongside the asparagus salad and Romesco Sauce.

Pasta alla Genovese

YIELD: 4 SERVINGS / **ACTIVE TIME:** 40 MINUTES / **TOTAL TIME:** 5 HOURS

2½ LBS. BEEF FOR BRAISING (BEST TO USE A MIX OF DIFFERENT CUTS)

⅔ CUP EXTRA-VIRGIN OLIVE OIL

5 LBS. YELLOW OR WHITE ONIONS, SLICED THIN

KOSHER SALT, TO TASTE

14 OZ. ZITI SPEZZATI OR RIGATONI

2 OZ. PECORINO CHEESE, GRATED

1. Leave one piece of beef as is and cut the rest of it into chunks.

2. Place some of the olive oil in a large saucepan and warm it over medium-high heat. Working in batches to avoid crowding the pan, add the beef and sear until it is browned all over, turning it as necessary. Add more of the olive oil if the pan starts to look dry.

3. Place all of the beef in the pan and cover it with the onions. Reduce the heat to low, cover the pan, and cook, stirring occasionally, until the onions start to soften.

4. Uncover the pan and cook until the meat is tender but not yet falling apart, 2 to 3 hours.

5. Season the mixture with salt, remove the biggest piece of beef from the pan, and set it aside. Cover the pan and continue cooking the sauce until the onions have almost dissolved and the sauce becomes juicy, 1 to 2 hours.

6. Bring water to a boil in a large saucepan. Add salt, let the water return to a full boil, and add the pasta. Cook until the pasta is al dente.

7. Drain the pasta, place it in a serving dish, and add some of the sauce and half of the pecorino. Toss to combine and top with the remaining pecorino.

8. Pour the remaining sauce over the large piece of beef and serve it following the pasta dish.

Pasta al Forno Napoletana

YIELD: 6 SERVINGS / **ACTIVE TIME:** 40 MINUTES / **TOTAL TIME:** 1 HOUR AND 30 MINUTES

FOR THE MEATBALLS

½ LB. GROUND PORK

½ LB. GROUND BEEF

4 EGGS

½ LB. FRESH BREAD CRUMBS

1 CUP GRATED PECORINO OR PARMESAN CHEESE

SALT AND PEPPER, TO TASTE

EXTRA-VIRGIN OLIVE OIL, AS NEEDED

FOR THE PASTA

SALT, TO TASTE

1 LB. ZITI OR RIGATONI

1 LB. RICOTTA CHEESE

6 CUPS RAGÙ NAPOLETANO (SEE PAGE 206)

9 OZ. PROVOLA CHEESE, CUBED

3 HARD-BOILED EGGS, SLICED (OPTIONAL)

4 OZ. ITALIAN SALAMI, CHOPPED (OPTIONAL)

1 LB. FRESH MOZZARELLA CHEESE, DRAINED AND TORN

1⅓ CUPS GRATED PECORINO OR PARMESAN CHEESE

1. To begin preparations for the meatballs, place all of the ingredients, except for the olive oil, in a mixing bowl and work the mixture until it is well combined. Form the mixture into small, walnut-sized meatballs.

2. Add olive oil to a large, deep skillet until it is about 1 inch deep and warm it over medium heat. Add the meatballs and cook until they are browned all over, turning them as necessary. Place the meatballs on paper towel–lined plates and let them drain.

3. Preheat the oven to 360°F. To begin preparations for the pasta, bring water to a boil in a large saucepan. Add salt, let the water return to a full boil, and add the pasta. Cook until the pasta is al dente. Drain the pasta and set it aside.

4. Place the ricotta and 1 cup of the ragù in a large mixing bowl and stir to combine. Add the mixture to the pasta along with 2 more cups of ragù and stir to combine.

5. Spread some ragù over the bottom of a 13 x 9–inch baking dish. Arrange half of the pasta, half of the provola, half of the meatballs, half of the eggs and salami (if desired), half of the mozzarella, and half of the pecorino in separate layers. Repeat the layering process with the remaining ingredients.

6. Place the dish in the oven and bake until the top is crispy, about 30 minutes.

7. Remove the dish from the oven and let it rest for 10 to 15 minutes before serving.

Pasta alla Genovese
SEE PAGE 108

Pasta allo Scarpariello

YIELD: 4 SERVINGS / **ACTIVE TIME:** 10 MINUTES / **TOTAL TIME:** 20 MINUTES

¼ CUP EXTRA-VIRGIN OLIVE OIL

1 GARLIC CLOVE

½ MILD CHILE PEPPER, STEM AND SEEDS REMOVED, MINCED

1 LB. CHERRY TOMATOES, HALVED

SALT, TO TASTE

14 OZ. SPAGHETTI

LARGE HANDFUL OF FRESH BASIL

6 TABLESPOONS GRATED PECORINO CHEESE

6 TABLESPOONS GRATED PARMESAN CHEESE

1. Bring water to a boil in a large saucepan.

2. Place the olive oil in a large skillet and warm it over medium-low heat. Add the garlic and cook for 2 minutes. Add the chile and cook for 1 minute.

3. Add the tomatoes, raise the heat to medium, and cook, stirring occasionally, until the tomatoes start to collapse, about 10 minutes.

4. Add salt to the boiling water, let the water return to a full boil, and add the pasta. Cook until the pasta is very al dente. Reserve 2 cups of pasta water and drain the spaghetti.

5. Add the basil and some of the pasta water to the skillet, season the sauce with salt, and remove the garlic clove.

6. Add the pasta and more pasta water (if desired) and toss until combined and the pasta is al dente. Turn off the heat, add the cheeses, and toss to combine. Serve immediately.

Pasta Fagioli e Cozze

YIELD: 4 SERVINGS / **ACTIVE TIME:** 20 MINUTES / **TOTAL TIME:** 24 HOURS

SALT AND PEPPER, TO TASTE

¾ LB. DRIED CANNELLINI BEANS, SOAKED OVERNIGHT AND DRAINED

¼ CUP EXTRA-VIRGIN OLIVE OIL

2 GARLIC CLOVES

½ RED CHILE PEPPER, STEM AND SEEDS REMOVED, MINCED

2 LBS. MUSSELS, RINSED WELL AND DEBEARDED

8 CHERRY TOMATOES

¾ LB. SHORT-FORMAT PASTA

FRESH PARSLEY, CHOPPED, FOR GARNISH

1. Bring water to a boil in a large saucepan. Add salt and the beans and cook until they are tender, about 45 minutes. Drain the beans, reserving the cooking liquid. Strain the cooking liquid and set it and the beans aside.

2. Place half of the olive oil in a large skillet and warm it over medium heat. Add half of the garlic and chile and cook, stirring occasionally, for 2 minutes.

3. Add the mussels, raise the heat to medium-high, and cover the pan with a lid. Cook until the majority of the mussels have opened, about 5 minutes. Discard any mussels that did not open. Remove the remaining mussels from the pan, remove the meat from most of the shells, and set it aside. Leave the meat in some of the mussels and reserve them for garnish. Strain any liquid in the pan and set it aside.

4. Add the remaining olive oil to the pan and warm it over medium heat. Add the remaining garlic clove and chile and cook, stirring occasionally, for 2 minutes. Add the tomatoes and cook, stirring occasionally, for 5 minutes.

5. Add the beans, half of their cooking liquid, and half of the liquid reserved from cooking the mussels. Add the pasta, cover the pan, and cook until the pasta has absorbed most of the liquid, stirring occasionally.

6. Add the remaining cooking liquid from the mussels and some more of the cooking liquid from the beans. Cook until the pasta is al dente and the sauce is creamy.

7. Add the meat from the mussels, remove the pan from heat, and season the dish with salt and pepper. Garnish the dish with parsley and the reserved mussels and enjoy.

Scialatielli all'Amalfitana

YIELD: 4 SERVINGS / **ACTIVE TIME:** 40 MINUTES / **TOTAL TIME:** 1 HOUR AND 15 MINUTES

¼ CUP EXTRA-VIRGIN OLIVE OIL

1 GARLIC CLOVE, MINCED

5 MEDIUM TOMATOES, CHOPPED

HANDFUL OF FRESH BASIL

1 LB. MUSSELS, RINSED WELL AND DEBEARDED

½ LB. CLAMS, RINSED WELL

½ LB. SQUID, CLEANED (SEE PAGE 199) AND CHOPPED

½ LB. SHRIMP, SHELLS REMOVED, DEVEINED

KOSHER SALT, TO TASTE

½ CUP DRY WHITE WINE

1 LB. SCIALATIELLI (SEE PAGE 229)

FRESH PARSLEY, CHOPPED, FOR GARNISH

1. Place the olive oil in a large skillet and warm it over medium-high heat. Add the garlic and cook for 1 minute.

2. Add the tomatoes and basil and cook, stirring occasionally, for 10 minutes.

3. Add the seafood, season the dish with salt, and cook until the majority of the clams and mussels have opened, about 5 minutes.

4. Remove the mussels and clams from the pan and set them aside. Discard any mussels and/or clams that did not open.

5. Add the wine, cook until it has evaporated, and remove the pan from heat.

6. Bring water to a boil in a large saucepan. Add salt, let the water return to a full boil, and add the pasta. Cook until the pasta is al dente.

7. While the pasta water is coming to a boil, remove the meat from two-thirds of the mussels and clams and reserve the remaining one-third for garnish.

8. Drain the pasta and add it to the sauce along with the mussels and clams. Cook over medium-high heat until everything is warmed through, tossing to combine.

9. Garnish the dish with parsley and the reserved mussels and clams and enjoy.

Paella

YIELD: 4 TO 6 SERVINGS / **ACTIVE TIME:** 30 MINUTES / **TOTAL TIME:** 1 HOUR AND 30 MINUTES

2 TABLESPOONS EXTRA-VIRGIN OLIVE OIL

1½ LBS. BONELESS, SKINLESS CHICKEN THIGHS, CHOPPED INTO 1-INCH CUBES

9 OZ. CHORIZO, CHOPPED

1 ONION, CHOPPED

1 RED BELL PEPPER, STEM AND SEEDS REMOVED, CHOPPED

6 GARLIC CLOVES, MINCED

1 (14 OZ.) CAN OF DICED TOMATOES, DRAINED

2 CUPS BOMBA RICE

4 CUPS CHICKEN STOCK (SEE PAGE 482)

⅓ CUP WHITE WINE

½ TEASPOON SAFFRON

1 TEASPOON PAPRIKA

2 BAY LEAVES

SALT AND PEPPER, TO TASTE

16 MUSSELS, RINSED WELL AND DEBEARDED

1 LB. JUMBO SHRIMP, SHELLS REMOVED, DEVEINED

FRESH PARSLEY, CHOPPED, FOR GARNISH

LEMON WEDGES, FOR SERVING

1. Preheat the oven to 350°F. Place the olive oil in a Dutch oven and warm it over medium-high heat. Add the chicken and cook until browned all over, about 6 minutes, stirring as necessary. Remove the chicken with a slotted spoon and place it in a bowl.

2. Add the chorizo to the pot and cook, stirring occasionally, until it is browned all over, about 6 minutes. Transfer to the bowl with the chicken.

3. Add the onion to the pot and cook, stirring occasionally, until it has softened, about 5 minutes. Add the bell pepper and cook, stirring occasionally, for 3 minutes.

4. Add the garlic and cook, stirring frequently, for 1 minute. Stir in the tomatoes and cook until the mixture thickens slightly, about 3 minutes. Add the rice and cook for 2 minutes.

5. Stir in the stock, wine, saffron, paprika, and bay leaves and bring the mixture to a boil, stirring frequently. Return the chicken and chorizo to the pot, season the mixture with salt and pepper, cover the pot, and place it in the oven.

6. Bake until all the liquid has evaporated, about 15 minutes, stirring occasionally.

7. Remove the pot from the oven and place the mussels and shrimp on top of the rice. Make sure to put the mussels in with their hinge down. Cover the pot and return it to the oven. Bake until the shrimp is cooked through and the majority of the mussels have opened, about 10 minutes.

8. Remove the paella from the oven, discard the bay leaves and any mussels that did not open, and garnish with parsley. Serve with lemon wedges and enjoy.

Pasta alla Mugnaia

YIELD: 4 SERVINGS / **ACTIVE TIME:** 40 MINUTES / **TOTAL TIME:** 2 HOURS

¼ CUP EXTRA-VIRGIN OLIVE OIL

1 GREEN BELL PEPPER, STEM AND SEEDS REMOVED, FINELY DICED

1 ONION, SLICED THIN

½ CARROT, PEELED AND DICED

½ LB. PIECE OF BONE-IN BEEF OR PORK

SALT, TO TASTE

1 RED BELL PEPPER, STEM AND SEEDS REMOVED, FINELY DICED

1 EGGPLANT, CUBED

1 LB. WHOLE PEELED TOMATOES, PUREED

1 CUP WATER

1 LB. TAGLIATELLE OR FETTUCCINE

PECORINO CHEESE, GRATED, FOR GARNISH

1. Place the olive oil in a large skillet and warm it over medium heat. Add the green bell pepper, onion, and carrot and cook, stirring occasionally, until they have softened, about 5 minutes.

2. Season the beef with salt, add it to the pan, and sear it until it is browned all over, turning it as necessary. Add the red bell pepper and eggplant and cook until they are browned.

3. Reduce the heat to low, add the tomatoes and water, and season the sauce with salt. Cover the pan and cook the sauce until the meat is tender, about 1 hour. Remove the sauce from heat and set it aside.

4. Bring water to a boil in a large saucepan. Add salt, let the water return to a full boil, and add the pasta. Cook until the pasta is al dente. Drain the pasta and place it in a serving dish.

5. Add the sauce to the pasta and toss to combine. Garnish the dish with pecorino and enjoy.

Timballo Abruzzese

YIELD: 8 SERVINGS / **ACTIVE TIME:** 1 HOUR AND 30 MINUTES / **TOTAL TIME:** 3 HOURS AND 30 MINUTES

FOR THE FILLING

1 TABLESPOON UNSALTED BUTTER

2 TABLESPOONS EXTRA-VIRGIN OLIVE OIL

½ CELERY STALK, FINELY DICED

½ CARROT, PEELED AND FINELY DICED

½ WHITE ONION, FINELY DICED

1 LB. GROUND BEEF

1 LB. GROUND VEAL

1 LB. GROUND PORK

1 CUP WHITE WINE

4 OZ. PARMESAN CHEESE, GRATED

FOR THE SAUCE

3 TABLESPOONS EXTRA-VIRGIN OLIVE OIL

½ CELERY STALK, FINELY DICED

½ CARROT, PEELED AND FINELY DICED

½ WHITE ONION, PEELED AND FINELY DICED

½ LB. BONE-IN PORK

4 CUPS CRUSHED TOMATOES

SALT, TO TASTE

1 EGG

½ CUP MILK

UNSALTED BUTTER, AS NEEDED

2 LBS. SCRIPPELLE

1.2 LBS. MOZZARELLA CHEESE, DRAINED AND CUBED

1. To begin preparations for the filling, place the butter and olive oil in a large skillet and warm the mixture over medium heat. Add the celery, carrot, and onion and cook, stirring occasionally, until the onion has softened, about 5 minutes.

2. Add the beef, veal, and pork and cook until they have browned, breaking the meats up with a wooden spoon as they cook.

3. Deglaze the pan with the wine, scraping up any browned bits from the bottom. Cook until the wine has evaporated, stir in the Parmesan, and set the filling aside.

4. To begin preparations for the sauce, place the olive oil in a large skillet and warm it over medium heat. Add the celery, carrot, and onion and cook, stirring occasionally, until the onion has softened, about 5 minutes.

5. Add the pork and sear until it is browned all over, turning it as needed.

6. Add the tomatoes, season the sauce with salt, and cook for about 1½ hours, letting the sauce thicken.

7. Preheat the oven to 320°F. Place the egg and milk in a bowl and whisk to combine. Set the mixture aside.

8. Coat a 13 x 9–inch baking pan with butter and line it with some of the scrippelle. Cover them with a little sauce, some of the filling, and some of the mozzarella, and drizzle 1 tablespoon of the egg mixture over everything. If desired, dot the mixture with some pieces of butter. Repeat the layering process with the scrippelle, sauce, filling, mozzarella, egg mixture, and butter (if desired).

9. Top the dish with 2 or 3 scrippelle and a few pats of butter. Place the timballo in the oven and bake for about 2 hours, taking care to not let the top burn. If the top is browning too quickly, cover the timballo with aluminum foil.

10. Remove the timballo from the oven and let it rest for 10 minutes. Invert the timballo onto a cutting board, slice it, and serve.

Pides

YIELD: 4 PIDES / **ACTIVE TIME:** 45 MINUTES / **TOTAL TIME:** 1 HOUR AND 30 MINUTES

1. To begin preparations for the dough, place all of the ingredients in the work bowl of a stand mixer fitted with the dough hook attachment and work the mixture on low until it comes together as a smooth dough. Increase the speed to medium and work the dough until it no longer sticks to the side of the bowl.

2. Coat a bowl with olive oil. Place the dough on a flour-dusted work surface and knead it for 2 minutes. Form the dough into a ball and place it, seam side down, in the greased bowl. Cover the bowl with a linen towel and let the dough rise in a naturally warm spot until it has doubled in size, about 1 hour.

3. To begin preparations for the filling, place 2 tablespoons of the olive oil in a large saucepan and warm it over medium heat. Add the eggplant and cook, stirring occasionally, until it has browned and is soft, about 5 minutes. Remove the pan from heat and set the eggplant aside.

4. Place 1 tablespoon of the olive oil in a clean large saucepan and warm it over medium heat. Add the onion and pepper and cook, stirring occasionally, until they have softened, about 5 minutes. Add the garlic, red pepper flakes, and paprika and cook, stirring continually, for 1 minute.

5. Add the tomatoes and bring the mixture to a boil. Reduce the heat and simmer the mixture until the tomatoes start to collapse, about 10 minutes, mashing the tomatoes with a wooden spoon as they cook.

6. Stir in the eggplant and cook until warmed through. Season the mixture with salt and pepper, remove the pan from heat, and let the mixture cool.

7. Preheat the oven to 450°F. Line two baking sheets with parchment paper. Cut four 12 x 4–inch strips of parchment paper. Divide the dough into four pieces and place each one on a piece of parchment paper. Roll out the dough until each piece extends ½ inch over the strips of parchment on all sides.

8. Spread the eggplant mixture over the pieces of dough, leaving a 1-inch border on the sides. Sprinkle the crumbled feta over the eggplant mixture and brush the border of dough with some of the remaining olive oil.

9. Pinch the tops of the pides to secure them. Fold each side toward the center, leaving about 1 inch of the filling exposed. Pinch the bottoms of the pides to secure them, brush the dough with some of the remaining olive oil, and sprinkle the Maldon sea salt over the top.

10. Place the pides in the oven and bake until the edges are crispy and golden brown, about 12 minutes.

11. Remove the pides from the oven and let them cool slightly before garnishing with mint and enjoying.

THE ENCYCLOPEDIA OF MEDITERRANEAN

FOR THE DOUGH

2 CUPS PLUS 2 TABLESPOONS BREAD FLOUR, PLUS MORE AS NEEDED

1 TEASPOON SUGAR

¼ TEASPOON INSTANT YEAST

⅔ CUP PLUS 2 TABLESPOONS WARM WATER (105°F)

1 TEASPOON FINE SEA SALT

2 TEASPOONS EXTRA-VIRGIN OLIVE OIL, PLUS MORE AS NEEDED

FOR THE FILLING

¼ CUP EXTRA-VIRGIN OLIVE OIL

4 CUPS DICED EGGPLANT (¼-INCH CUBES)

1 ONION, CHOPPED

½ RED BELL PEPPER, DICED

2 GARLIC CLOVES, MINCED

⅛ TEASPOON RED PEPPER FLAKES

½ TEASPOON PAPRIKA

1 (28 OZ.) CAN OF WHOLE PEELED SAN MARZANO TOMATOES, DRAINED

SALT AND PEPPER, TO TASTE

1 CUP CRUMBLED FETA CHEESE

1 TEASPOON MALDON SEA SALT

FRESH MINT, CHOPPED, FOR GARNISH

Brodetto all'Abruzzese

YIELD: 6 SERVINGS / **ACTIVE TIME:** 1 HOUR / **TOTAL TIME:** 3 HOURS

5 OZ. CLAMS

KOSHER SALT, TO TASTE

5 OZ. MUSSELS, RINSED WELL AND DEBEARDED

2 TABLESPOONS EXTRA-VIRGIN OLIVE OIL

2 GARLIC CLOVES

1 CUP WHITE WINE VINEGAR

4 CUPS WHOLE PEELED TOMATOES, CRUSHED

1 CHILE PEPPER, STEM AND SEEDS REMOVED, MINCED

11 OZ. SQUID, CLEANED (SEE PAGE 199) AND SLICED INTO RINGS

1½ LBS. MONKFISH FILLETS, CUT INTO 2 TO 3 PIECES

1½ LBS. TURBOT FILLETS, CUT INTO 2 TO 3 PIECES

1 LB. COD FILLETS, CUT INTO 2 TO 3 PIECES

5 OZ. SOLE FILLETS, CUT INTO 2 TO 3 PIECES

4 LANGOUSTINES

4 MANTIS SHRIMP OR OTHER LARGE SHRIMP, LEGS AND ANTENNAE REMOVED, DEVEINED

1 BUNCH OF FRESH PARSLEY, CHOPPED

1 BUNCH OF FRESH BASIL, CHOPPED

CRUSTY BREAD, FOR SERVING

1. Place the clams in a large bowl, cover them with cold water, and stir in 4 handfuls of salt. Let them soak for 2 hours to remove the sand.

2. Drain the clams, place them in a pot, and add the mussels. Cover the pot and cook them over high heat until the majority of the clams and mussels have opened, about 5 minutes. Transfer them to a plate and set them aside. Strain the cooking liquid and set it aside. Discard any clams and mussels that did not open.

3. Place the olive oil in a large saucepan and warm it over medium heat. Add the garlic and cook, stirring occasionally, for 2 minutes. Add the vinegar and cook until it has evaporated.

4. Add the tomatoes and chile, season the sauce with salt, and cook for about 20 minutes.

5. Add the squid and monkfish and cook for 10 minutes.

6. Add the turbot and cod, top with the sole, langoustines, and shrimp, cover the pan, and reduce the heat to medium-low. Cook for 10 minutes, gently shaking the pan occasionally.

7. Turn off the heat, taste the sauce, and adjust the seasoning as necessary.

8. Top the dish with the mussels, clams, reserved liquid, parsley, and basil, serve with toasted bread, and enjoy.

Bucatini with Asparagus & Sausage

YIELD: 4 SERVINGS / **ACTIVE TIME:** 30 MINUTES / **TOTAL TIME:** 50 MINUTES

10 OZ. FRESH ASPARAGUS, TRIMMED

SALT AND PEPPER, TO TASTE

¼ CUP EXTRA-VIRGIN OLIVE OIL

1 ONION, FINELY DICED

11 OZ. ITALIAN SAUSAGE, CASINGS REMOVED, CRUMBLED

1 CUP WHITE WINE

1 LB. BUCATINI

¼ CUP GRATED PECORINO CHEESE

1. Bring water to a boil in a medium saucepan. Separate the stems from the tips of the asparagus and add salt and the asparagus stems to the boiling water. Cook until the asparagus stems are tender, about 4 minutes, drain, and set them aside.

2. Place 2 tablespoons of olive oil in a large skillet and warm it over medium heat. Add the onion and cook, stirring occasionally, until it has softened, about 5 minutes.

3. Add the sausage and cook, stirring occasionally, until it has browned, about 8 minutes.

4. Add the wine, reduce the heat to low, and cook for 15 minutes.

5. Place the remaining olive oil in a large skillet and warm it over medium heat. Add the asparagus tips and cook, stirring frequently, until they are tender, 3 to 4 minutes. Season the asparagus tips with salt and pepper, remove the pan from heat, and set the asparagus tips aside.

6. Bring water to a boil in a large saucepan. Chop the asparagus stems, add them to the sauce, and cook for 10 minutes.

7. Add salt, let the water return to a full boil, and add the pasta. Cook until the pasta is al dente. Drain the pasta, add it to the sauce, and toss to combine.

8. Top the dish with the asparagus tips and pecorino and enjoy.

Cavatelli alla Ventricina

YIELD: 4 SERVINGS / **ACTIVE TIME:** 10 MINUTES / **TOTAL TIME:** 50 MINUTES

3 TABLESPOONS EXTRA-VIRGIN OLIVE OIL

½ ONION, FINELY DICED

2 GARLIC CLOVES, HALVED

1 LB. WHOLE PEELED TOMATOES, CRUSHED

SALT, TO TASTE

¼ CUP CHOPPED VENTRICINA

1 LB. CAVATELLI (SEE PAGE 203)

HANDFUL OF FRESH BASIL, TORN

2 OZ. PECORINO CHEESE, GRATED

1. Place the olive oil in a large skillet and warm it over medium heat. Add the onion and garlic and cook, stirring frequently, until the onion has softened, about 5 minutes.

2. Add the tomatoes, reduce the heat to low, and cook for 20 minutes.

3. Remove the garlic, season the sauce with salt, and stir in the ventricina. Cook for 20 minutes, stirring occasionally.

4. Bring water to a boil in a large saucepan. Add salt, let the water return to a full boil, and add the pasta. Cook until the pasta is al dente.

5. Drain the pasta and place it in a serving dish.

6. Stir the basil into the sauce. Top the pasta with the sauce and pecorino and serve.

Friarielli e Salsiccia

YIELD: 4 SERVINGS / **ACTIVE TIME:** 30 MINUTES / **TOTAL TIME:** 1 HOUR

SALT, TO TASTE

2.2 LBS. TURNIP GREENS, RINSED WELL, WOODY STEMS REMOVED

6 TABLESPOONS EXTRA-VIRGIN OLIVE OIL

4 GARLIC CLOVES, HALVED

1 CHILE PEPPER, STEM AND SEEDS REMOVED, CHOPPED

8 ITALIAN SAUSAGES

1. Bring salted water to a boil in a large saucepan. Add the turnip greens and cook until just tender, about 5 minutes. Drain the turnip greens and set them aside.

2. Place 5 tablespoons of olive oil in a large skillet and warm it over medium-low heat. Add the garlic and chile and cook for 2 minutes. Remove the pan from heat and season the mixture with salt.

3. Place the remaining olive oil in a large skillet and warm it over medium heat. Poke holes in the sausages, place them in the pan, and cook until they are browned all over and nearly cooked through, about 10 minutes.

4. Stir in the garlic mixture and turnip greens and cook until the sausages are completely cooked through, 3 to 4 minutes. Serve immediately.

Pasta al Pesto Calabrese

YIELD: 4 SERVINGS / **ACTIVE TIME:** 20 MINUTES / **TOTAL TIME:** 1 HOUR

¼ CUP EXTRA-VIRGIN OLIVE OIL

1 RED ONION, FINELY DICED

2 RED BELL PEPPERS, STEMS AND SEEDS REMOVED, SLICED THIN

5 OZ. WHOLE PEELED TOMATOES, CRUSHED

RED PEPPER FLAKES, TO TASTE

SALT, TO TASTE

½ CUP RICOTTA CHEESE

⅔ CUP GRATED CACIOCAVALLO OR PECORINO CHEESE

1 LB. FUSILLI OR PENNE

1. Place the olive oil in a large skillet and warm it over medium-low heat. Add the onion and cook, stirring occasionally, until it has softened, about 6 minutes.

2. Add the peppers, cover the pan, and cook, stirring occasionally, until they are tender, about 20 minutes.

3. Add the tomatoes and season the sauce with red pepper flakes and salt. Cover the pan and cook the sauce, stirring occasionally, for 20 minutes.

4. Stir in the ricotta and caciocavallo and use an immersion blender to puree the sauce until it is smooth.

5. Bring water to a boil in a large saucepan. Add salt, let the water return to a full boil, and add the pasta. Cook until the pasta is al dente.

6. Reserve 1 cup pasta water, drain the pasta, and stir it into the sauce.

7. Toss to combine, adding pasta water as needed to get the right consistency. Serve immediately.

Culurgiones al Pomodoro

YIELD: 4 SERVINGS / **ACTIVE TIME:** 10 MINUTES / **TOTAL TIME:** 20 MINUTES

2 CUPS TOMATO SAUCE (SEE PAGE 504)

SALT, TO TASTE

1 LB. CULURGIONES (SEE PAGE 211)

½ CUP GRATED PECORINO CHEESE, FOR GARNISH

1. Place the tomato sauce in a medium saucepan and warm it over medium heat.

2. Bring water to a boil in a large saucepan. Add salt, let the water return to a full boil, and add the Culurgiones. Cook until they are al dente.

3. Drain the Culurgiones and add them to the sauce. Toss to combine, garnish with the pecorino, and serve.

Culurgiones al Pomodoro

SEE PAGE 125

Fusilli alla Silana

YIELD: 6 SERVINGS / **ACTIVE TIME:** 10 MINUTES / **TOTAL TIME:** 50 MINUTES

¼ CUP EXTRA-VIRGIN OLIVE OIL

1 SMALL ONION, FINELY DICED

2 OZ. GUANCIALE, HARD SKIN REMOVED, CUT INTO STRIPS

5 OZ. SOPPRESSATA, SLICED

1 CHILE PEPPER, STEM AND SEEDS REMOVED, CHOPPED

1 OZ. COGNAC OR WHISKEY

1 LB. WHOLE PEELED TOMATOES, CRUSHED

SALT AND PEPPER, TO TASTE

1 LB. DRIED FUSILLI

7 OZ. CACIOCAVALLO CHEESE, CUBED

HANDFUL OF FRESH PARSLEY, CHOPPED

⅔ CUP GRATED PECORINO CHEESE

1. Place the olive oil in a large, deep skillet and warm it over medium heat. Add the onion, guanciale, soppressata, and chile and cook, stirring occasionally, until the guanciale's fat starts to render and the onion has softened, about 5 minutes.

2. Remove the pan from heat, add the Cognac, and place the pan over medium-low heat. Cook until the Cognac has evaporated.

3. Add the tomatoes and cook for 30 minutes, stirring occasionally.

4. Bring water to a boil in a large saucepan. Add salt, let the water return to a full boil, and add the pasta. Cook until the pasta is al dente.

5. Drain the pasta and stir it into the sauce.

6. Add the caciocavallo and parsley, cover the pan, and cook until the caciocavallo has melted.

7. Top the dish with the pecorino, season it with salt and pepper, and serve.

THE ENCYCLOPEDIA OF MEDITERRANEAN

Maccheroni with 'Nduja & Soppressata

YIELD: 4 SERVINGS / **ACTIVE TIME:** 20 MINUTES / **TOTAL TIME:** 24 HOURS

½ LB. DRIED CHICKPEAS, SOAKED OVERNIGHT

1 SPRIG OF FRESH ROSEMARY

1 GARLIC CLOVE

2 TABLESPOONS EXTRA-VIRGIN OLIVE OIL

1 RED ONION, FINELY DICED

4 OZ. SOPPRESSATA, FINELY DICED

1 LB. WHOLE PEELED TOMATOES, CRUSHED

2 TABLESPOONS 'NDUJA

KOSHER SALT, TO TASTE

1 LB. MACCHERONI AL FERRETTO (SEE PAGE 188)

⅔ CUP GRATED PECORINO CHEESE

1. Drain the chickpeas, place them in a large saucepan, and cover them with cold water. Add the rosemary and garlic, bring to a boil, and cook until the chickpeas are tender, about 45 minutes. Drain the chickpeas, reserve the cooking liquid, and set both aside.

2. Place the olive oil in a large, deep skillet and warm it over medium heat. Add the onion and soppressata and cook, stirring occasionally, until the onion has softened, about 5 minutes.

3. Add the tomatoes, reduce the heat to medium-low, and cook for 20 minutes, stirring occasionally.

4. Stir in the 'nduja and cook for 20 minutes.

5. Place half of the chickpeas in a blender and puree until smooth. Add the puree and remaining chickpeas to the sauce, season it with salt, and stir to combine.

6. Bring water to a boil in a large saucepan. Add salt, let the water return to a full boil, and add the pasta. Cook until the pasta is al dente.

7. Drain the pasta and stir it into the sauce along with some of the reserved cooking liquid. Toss to combine, top the dish with the pecorino, and enjoy.

Chicken Tagine with Warm Couscous Salad

YIELD: 6 SERVINGS / **ACTIVE TIME:** 25 MINUTES / **TOTAL TIME:** 40 MINUTES

2 TABLESPOONS EXTRA-VIRGIN OLIVE OIL

8 BONE-IN, SKIN-ON CHICKEN DRUMSTICKS OR THIGHS

SALT AND PEPPER, TO TASTE

1 ONION, MINCED

4 GARLIC CLOVES, MINCED

1 TEASPOON GRATED FRESH GINGER

ZEST OF 1 LEMON

1 TEASPOON PAPRIKA

½ TEASPOON CUMIN

⅛ TEASPOON CAYENNE PEPPER

½ TEASPOON CORIANDER

¼ TEASPOON CINNAMON

½ CUP WHITE WINE

2 CUPS CHICKEN STOCK (SEE PAGE 482)

1 CARROT, PEELED AND CUT INTO THIN HALF-MOONS

1 TABLESPOON HONEY

¾ CUP HALVED DRIED APRICOTS

1 (14 OZ.) CAN OF CHICKPEAS, DRAINED AND RINSED

FRESH MINT, CHOPPED, FOR GARNISH

WARM COUSCOUS SALAD (SEE PAGE 377), FOR SERVING

1. Place the olive oil in a Dutch oven and warm it over medium-high heat. Season the chicken with salt and pepper, add it to the pot, and cook, stirring occasionally, until it has browned, about 6 minutes. Remove the chicken from the pot and set it aside.

2. Reduce the heat to medium, add the onion, and cook, stirring occasionally, until it has softened, about 5 minutes. Add the garlic, ginger, lemon zest, paprika, cumin, cayenne, coriander, and cinnamon and cook, stirring continually, for 1 minute.

3. Add the white wine and cook until the alcohol has been cooked off, about 3 minutes, scraping up any browned bits from the bottom of the pot.

4. Add the stock, carrot, honey, and apricots and bring the mixture to a simmer. Nestle the chicken into the mixture and cook until it is cooked through (internal temperature of 165°F), about 10 minutes.

5. Add the chickpeas, cover the pot, and cook until they are heated through, about 5 minutes.

6. Garnish the tagine with mint and serve it over the couscous salad.

Maccheroni with Sausage

YIELD: 4 SERVINGS / **ACTIVE TIME:** 15 MINUTES / **TOTAL TIME:** 1 HOUR AND 30 MINUTES

¼ CUP EXTRA-VIRGIN OLIVE OIL

1 RED ONION, FINELY DICED

4 ITALIAN SAUSAGES WITH FENNEL, CASINGS REMOVED, CRUMBLED

1 LB. WHOLE PEELED TOMATOES, CRUSHED

1 MILD CHILE PEPPER, STEM AND SEEDS REMOVED, CHOPPED

SALT, TO TASTE

1 LB. MACCHERONI AL FERRETTO (SEE PAGE 188)

HANDFUL OF FRESH BASIL

⅔ CUP SMOKED AGED RICOTTA CHEESE, GRATED

1. Place the olive oil in a large skillet and warm it over medium-low heat. Add the onion and cook, stirring occasionally, until it has softened, about 6 minutes.

2. Add the sausages and cook, stirring occasionally, until they are browned, 8 to 10 minutes.

3. Add the tomatoes and chile, season the sauce with salt, and reduce the heat to low. Cover the pan and cook the sauce until the flavor has developed to your liking, about 1 hour.

4. Bring water to a boil in a large saucepan. Add salt, let the water return to a full boil, and add the pasta. Cook until the pasta is al dente.

5. Drain the pasta and stir it into the sauce along with the basil. Toss to combine, top the dish with the smoked ricotta, and serve.

Garlic & Lime Calamari

YIELD: 4 SERVINGS / **ACTIVE TIME:** 10 MINUTES / **TOTAL TIME:** 20 MINUTES

1½ LBS. SQUID, CLEANED (SEE PAGE 199) AND SLICED INTO RINGS

2 TABLESPOONS EXTRA-VIRGIN OLIVE OIL

1 TABLESPOON UNSALTED BUTTER

10 GARLIC CLOVES, CHOPPED

3 TABLESPOONS WHITE WINE

JUICE OF 1½ LIMES

SALT AND PEPPER, TO TASTE

PINCH OF CAYENNE PEPPER

3 TABLESPOONS CHOPPED FRESH DILL

1. Pat the squid rings dry and set aside. Place the olive oil and butter in a large cast-iron skillet and warm over medium- high heat. When the butter starts to foam, add the garlic and cook, stirring continuously, until fragrant, about 1 minute.

2. Add the squid to the pan, cook for 2 minutes, and then stir in the wine and lime juice. Cook for another 30 seconds, until warmed through, and remove the pan from heat.

3. Season with salt and pepper, stir in the cayenne and dill, and enjoy.

Spaghetti all'Aragosta

YIELD: 4 SERVINGS / **ACTIVE TIME:** 30 MINUTES / **TOTAL TIME:** 1 HOUR

KOSHER SALT, TO TASTE

2 MEDIUM LOBSTERS

¼ CUP EXTRA-VIRGIN OLIVE OIL

1 WHITE ONION, FINELY DICED

1 GARLIC CLOVE

1 LB. WHOLE PEELED TOMATOES, LIGHTLY CRUSHED

1 LB. SPAGHETTI

FRESH PARSLEY, CHOPPED, FOR GARNISH

1. Bring water to a boil in a large pot. Add salt and then the lobsters, making sure they are head down, which will minimize their pain. Cover the pot, reduce the heat to low, and cook the lobsters for 15 minutes.

2. Drain the lobsters and let them cool. When they are cool enough to handle, extract the meat from the lobsters, chop it, and set it aside.

3. Place the olive oil in a large, deep skillet and warm it over medium heat. Add the onion and garlic and cook, stirring frequently, until the onion has softened, about 5 minutes.

4. Remove the garlic and discard it. Add the tomatoes, season with salt, and cook, stirring occasionally, for 20 minutes.

5. Bring water to a boil in a large saucepan. Add salt, let the water return to a full boil, and add the pasta. Cook until the pasta is very al dente.

6. Add the lobster to the sauce. Drain the pasta, add it to the sauce, and raise the heat to medium-high. Cook for 2 to 3 minutes, tossing to combine.

7. Garnish the dish with parsley and enjoy.

Anelletti al Forno

YIELD: 4 SERVINGS / **ACTIVE TIME:** 1 HOUR / **TOTAL TIME:** 2 HOURS AND 30 MINUTES

1 CUP EXTRA-VIRGIN OLIVE OIL, PLUS MORE AS NEEDED

1 RED ONION, FINELY DICED

9 OZ. GROUND PORK

1 OZ. GROUND BEEF

1 CUP RED WINE

9 OZ. WHOLE PEELED TOMATOES, LIGHTLY CRUSHED

9 OZ. PEAS

SALT AND PEPPER, TO TASTE

1 LARGE EGGPLANT, CUBED

1 LB. ANELLETTI OR OTHER SHORT-FORMAT PASTA

3½ OZ. CACIOCAVALLO CHEESE, CUBED

3 HARD-BOILED EGGS, SLICED

7 OZ. TOMINO OR PECORINO CHEESE, GRATED

2 TABLESPOONS BREAD CRUMBS

1. Place 2 tablespoons of olive oil in a large, deep skillet and warm it over medium-low heat. Add the onion and cook, stirring occasionally, until it has softened, about 6 minutes.

2. Add the pork and beef, raise the heat to medium-high, and cook, breaking the meat up with a wooden spoon, until it is browned, about 8 minutes.

3. Add the wine and cook until it has evaporated.

4. Add the tomatoes and peas, season with salt and pepper, and reduce the heat to medium-low. Partially cover the pan and cook the sauce for about 40 minutes.

5. Place the eggplant in a colander and season it with salt. Fill a large saucepan with water and place the pan on top of the eggplant. Let the eggplant drain for 30 minutes.

6. Rinse the eggplant and squeeze it to remove as much water as possible. Place the eggplant on a kitchen towel and let it dry.

7. Place the remaining olive oil in a large skillet and warm it over medium-high heat. Add the eggplant and cook, stirring occasionally, until it is golden brown, 5 to 7 minutes. Transfer the eggplant to a paper towel–lined plate to drain.

8. Bring water to a boil in a large saucepan. Add salt, let the water return to a full boil, and add the pasta. Cook until the pasta is very al dente.

9. Drain the pasta and place it in a bowl. Add half of the sauce to the bowl and toss to combine. Preheat the oven to 360°F. Coat a 13 x 9–inch baking pan with olive oil and place half of the pasta on the bottom. Top the pasta with a layer consisting of half of the eggplant, one-third of the caciocavallo, one-third of the eggs, a few tablespoons of the sauce, and one-third of the tomino. Repeat this layering process and then top with a layer of the remaining caciocavallo and tomino.

10. Place the anelletti al forno in the oven and bake until the cheese is melted and bubbling, about 35 minutes.

11. Remove the anelletti al forno from the oven and let it rest for 10 minutes before serving.

Pasta 'Ncasciata

YIELD: 4 SERVINGS / **ACTIVE TIME:** 1 HOUR / **TOTAL TIME:** 2 HOURS AND 30 MINUTES

1 CUP EXTRA-VIRGIN OLIVE OIL, PLUS MORE AS NEEDED

1 WHITE ONION, FINELY DICED

6½ OZ. GROUND BEEF

6½ OZ. GROUND PORK

½ CUP DRY WHITE WINE

1½ LBS. WHOLE PEELED TOMATOES, LIGHTLY CRUSHED

2 HANDFULS OF FRESH BASIL LEAVES

KOSHER SALT AND PEPPER, TO TASTE

2 LARGE EGGPLANTS, CUT INTO ½-INCH-THICK SLICES

1 LB. SHORT-FORMAT PASTA

9 OZ. CACIOCAVALLO CHEESE, CUBED

1 CUP GRATED PECORINO CHEESE

1. Place 2 tablespoons of olive oil in a large, deep skillet and warm it over medium-low heat. Add the onion and cook, stirring occasionally, until it has softened, about 6 minutes.

2. Add the beef and pork, raise the heat to medium-high, and cook, breaking the meat up with a wooden spoon, until it is browned, about 8 minutes.

3. Add the wine and cook until it has evaporated.

4. Add the tomatoes and basil, season with salt and pepper, and reduce the heat to medium-low. Partially cover the pan and cook the sauce for about 40 minutes.

5. Place the eggplants in a colander and season them with salt. Fill a large saucepan with water and place the pan on top of the eggplants. Let the eggplants drain for 30 minutes.

6. Rinse the eggplants and squeeze them to remove as much water as possible. Place the eggplants on kitchen towels and let them dry.

7. Place the remaining olive oil in a large skillet and warm it over medium-high heat. Add the eggplants and cook, stirring occasionally, until they are golden brown, 5 to 7 minutes. Transfer the eggplants to a paper towel–lined plate to drain.

8. Bring water to a boil in a large saucepan. Add salt, let the water return to a full boil, and add the pasta. Cook until the pasta is very al dente.

9. Drain the pasta and place it in a bowl. Add half of the sauce to the bowl and toss to combine.

10. Preheat the oven to 360°F. Coat a 13 x 9–inch baking pan with olive oil and place one-half of the pasta on the bottom. Top the pasta with a layer consisting of half of the eggplant, one-third of the caciocavallo, a few tablespoons of sauce, and one-third of the pecorino. Repeat this layering process and then top with a layer of the remaining caciocavallo and pecorino. Place the 'ncasciata in the oven and bake until the cheese is melted and bubbling, about 20 minutes. Remove the 'ncasciata from the oven and let it rest for 10 minutes before serving.

Frittata di Zucchine

YIELD: 4 SERVINGS / **ACTIVE TIME:** 20 MINUTES / **TOTAL TIME:** 30 MINUTES

6 TABLESPOONS EXTRA-VIRGIN OLIVE OIL

2 LARGE ONIONS, SLICED THIN

1¼ LBS. ZUCCHINI, TRIMMED AND CHOPPED

5 EGGS

SALT AND PEPPER, TO TASTE

3½ OZ. PECORINO OR PARMESAN CHEESE, GRATED

3 TABLESPOONS BREAD CRUMBS

1 TABLESPOON CHOPPED FRESH PARSLEY

1. Place half of the olive oil in a skillet and warm it over medium heat. Add the onions and cook, stirring occasionally, until they are translucent, about 3 minutes.

2. Add the zucchini and cook, stirring occasionally, until it is tender, about 10 minutes. Remove the pan from heat and let the mixture cool.

3. Place the eggs in a bowl, season them with salt and pepper, and whisk until scrambled. Add the pecorino, bread crumbs, and parsley and whisk to combine.

4. Add the cooled vegetable mixture and fold to incorporate.

5. Place the remaining olive oil in a large skillet and warm it over medium-low heat. Add the egg mixture, cover the pan, and cook until the bottom is set, 5 to 8 minutes.

6. Gently lift the frittata on one side and check to see if it is golden brown. When it is, use a large plate to invert the pan and flip the frittata over. Cook until the frittata is browned on the other side, 3 to 4 minutes. Serve immediately.

Pampanella Molisana

YIELD: 4 SERVINGS / **ACTIVE TIME:** 15 MINUTES / **TOTAL TIME:** 2 HOURS AND 20 MINUTES

2 TABLESPOONS CHILI POWDER

2 TABLESPOONS SWEET PAPRIKA

4 GARLIC CLOVES, MINCED

SALT, TO TASTE

2 LBS. PORK TENDERLOIN

2 TABLESPOONS WHITE WINE VINEGAR

1. Preheat the oven to 350°F. Place the chili powder, paprika, and garlic in a bowl, season the mixture with salt, and stir to combine.

2. Cut the pork every ½ inch, taking care not to cut all the way through so that the tenderloin remains together. Rub the seasoning blend over every part of the pork, place it in a roasting pan, and cover it with aluminum foil.

3. Place the pan in the oven and roast the pork for 2 hours.

4. Remove the pork from the oven, drizzle the vinegar over it, and return the pork to the oven, uncovered. Roast until it is nicely browned, about 10 minutes.

5. Remove the pork from the oven and let it rest for a few minutes before serving.

Pasta con Mollica e Pepe Rosso

YIELD: 4 SERVINGS / **ACTIVE TIME:** 15 MINUTES / **TOTAL TIME:** 25 MINUTES

¼ CUP EXTRA-VIRGIN OLIVE OIL

3 GARLIC CLOVES, HALVED

CAYENNE PEPPER, TO TASTE

7 OZ. STALE BREAD, CRUSTS REMOVED, CRUMBLED

SALT, TO TASTE

1 LB. SPAGHETTI

1. Place three-quarters of the olive oil in a large skillet and warm it over medium heat. Add the garlic and cook, stirring frequently, for 2 minutes.

2. Stir in a generous amount of cayenne pepper, remove the pan from heat, and set it aside.

3. Place the remaining olive oil in a large skillet and warm it over medium heat. Add the bread crumbs and cook, stirring, until they are browned.

4. Bring water to a boil in a large saucepan. Add salt, let the water return to a full boil, and add the pasta. Cook until the pasta is al dente.

5. Drain the pasta and place it in a serving dish. Add the infused oil and bread crumbs, quickly toss to combine, and serve.

Agnello Cacio e Ova

YIELD: 4 SERVINGS / **ACTIVE TIME:** 20 MINUTES / **TOTAL TIME:** 1 HOUR AND 20 MINUTES

¼ CUP EXTRA-VIRGIN OLIVE OIL

1 YELLOW ONION, SLICED THIN

5 JUNIPER BERRIES

2.2 LBS. BONELESS LEG OF LAMB, TRIMMED AND CUT INTO 1-INCH CUBES

SALT AND PEPPER, TO TASTE

1 SPRIG OF FRESH ROSEMARY

1 SPRIG OF FRESH THYME

1 BAY LEAF

½ CUP WHITE WINE

7 EGGS

2 CUPS GRATED PECORINO CHEESE

1. Place the olive oil in a large skillet and warm it over medium heat. Add the onion and juniper berries and cook, stirring occasionally, until the onion has softened, about 5 minutes.

2. Season the lamb with salt and pepper and add it to the pan along with the rosemary, thyme, and bay leaf. Sear until the lamb is browned, turning it as necessary.

3. Add the wine, scraping up any browned bits from the bottom of the pan. Cook until the wine has nearly evaporated and then add enough water to cover the lamb. Cover the pan and braise the lamb until it is tender, about 40 minutes.

4. Uncover the pan and let the sauce reduce. Remove the rosemary, thyme, and bay leaf and discard the herbs. Reduce the heat to low.

5. Place the eggs in a bowl, whisk until scrambled, and then whisk in the pecorino. Add the egg mixture to the lamb and cook until it has set, 3 to 4 minutes. Serve immediately.

Octopus Braised in Red Wine

YIELD: 4 SERVINGS / **ACTIVE TIME:** 30 MINUTES / **TOTAL TIME:** 2 HOURS

1 OCTOPUS (ABOUT 4 LBS.)

2 TABLESPOONS EXTRA-VIRGIN OLIVE OIL

1 ONION, CHOPPED

2 TABLESPOONS TOMATO PASTE

3 GARLIC CLOVES, MINCED

3 CUPS CLAM JUICE

1 SPRIG OF FRESH ROSEMARY

1 SPRIG OF FRESH THYME

1 BAY LEAF

2 CINNAMON STICKS

1 CUP DRY RED WINE

2 TABLESPOONS RED WINE VINEGAR

SALT AND PEPPER, TO TASTE

FRESH PARSLEY, CHOPPED, FOR GARNISH

BULGUR-STUFFED EGGPLANTS (SEE PAGE 371), FOR SERVING

1. Place the octopus in a medium saucepan, cover it with water by 2 inches, and bring to a boil. Reduce the heat, cover the pan, and simmer for 1 hour.

2. Remove the octopus from the pan, cut off the tentacles, and set them aside.

3. Place the olive oil in a medium saucepan and warm it over medium heat. Add the onion and cook, stirring occasionally, until it has softened, about 5 minutes. Add the tomato paste and garlic and cook, stirring continually, for 1 minute. Add all of the remaining ingredients, except for the parsley and stuffed eggplants, and bring to a boil. Reduce the heat and simmer for 20 minutes.

4. Strain the liquid into a clean saucepan. Add the octopus and simmer until it is tender and the braising liquid has thickened, about 20 minutes.

5. Divide the octopus among the serving plates, ladle some of the braising liquid over it, and garnish with the parsley. Serve with the stuffed eggplants and enjoy.

Sarde a Beccaficu

YIELD: 4 SERVINGS / **ACTIVE TIME:** 20 MINUTES / **TOTAL TIME:** 1 HOUR

7 TABLESPOONS EXTRA-VIRGIN OLIVE OIL, PLUS MORE AS NEEDED

1 CUP BREAD CRUMBS

JUICE OF ½ ORANGE

½ CUP RAISINS

⅓ CUP PINE NUTS

7 ANCHOVIES IN OLIVE OIL, DRAINED AND CHOPPED

2 TABLESPOONS CHOPPED FRESH PARSLEY

1 GARLIC CLOVE, MINCED

1 TABLESPOON SUGAR

SALT AND PEPPER, TO TASTE

2.2 LBS. FRESH SARDINES, CLEANED, DEBONED, AND RINSED

4 BAY LEAVES

½ ORANGE, SLICED

1. Preheat the oven to 350°F and coat a baking dish with olive oil. Place 2 tablespoons of olive oil in a large skillet and warm it over medium-high heat. Add the bread crumbs and cook, stirring occasionally, until they are golden brown, 5 to 7 minutes.

2. Set 2 tablespoons of the toasted bread crumbs aside and place the rest in a bowl. Add the orange juice, raisins, pine nuts, anchovies, parsley, garlic, sugar, and 2 tablespoons of olive oil and stir to combine. Season the mixture with salt and pepper.

3. Top the sardines with the bread crumb mixture, roll them up from head to tail, and arrange them in the baking dish, packing them together tightly so that they do not open.

4. Put the bay leaves and orange slices between the sardines, drizzle the remaining olive oil over them, and sprinkle the reserved bread crumbs on top.

5. Place the baking dish in the oven and bake until the sardines are cooked through and starting to brown, about 10 to 15 minutes. Remove the sardines from the oven and enjoy.

Spaghetti al Tonno

YIELD: 4 TO 6 SERVINGS / **ACTIVE TIME:** 20 MINUTES / **TOTAL TIME:** 1 HOUR

2 TABLESPOONS AVOCADO OIL

3 GARLIC CLOVES, MINCED

1 SMALL YELLOW ONION, MINCED

⅛ TEASPOON RED PEPPER FLAKES

3 CUPS TOMATO PASSATA (STRAINED TOMATOES)

SALT AND PEPPER, TO TASTE

1 LB. SPAGHETTI

6 OZ. TUNA IN OLIVE OIL, DRAINED

4 SPRIGS OF FRESH PARSLEY, CHOPPED

1. Place the avocado oil in a medium saucepan and warm it over medium-low heat. Add the garlic and onion and cook, stirring frequently, until the onion just starts to soften, about 5 minutes.

2. Add the red pepper flakes and passata, season with salt and pepper, and stir until well combined.

3. Add about 2 cups of water to the sauce and bring it to a boil. Cover the pan, reduce the heat to medium-low, and cook until the sauce has thickened, about 45 minutes.

4. While the sauce is simmering, bring a large pot of water to boil.

5. Salt the water, add the pasta, and cook until al dente, 6 to 8 minutes.

6. Add the drained tuna to the tomato sauce and continue to simmer for about 5 minutes.

7. Drain the pasta and toss it with some of the tomato sauce. To serve, top each portion of pasta with more sauce and some of the parsley.

Scurdijata

YIELD: 4 SERVINGS / **ACTIVE TIME:** 20 MINUTES / **TOTAL TIME:** 30 MINUTES

6 TABLESPOONS EXTRA-VIRGIN OLIVE OIL

1 LB. STALE BREAD, CHOPPED

2 GARLIC CLOVES

½ HOT CHILE PEPPER, MINCED

1½ LBS. COOKED CHICKPEAS OR PEAS

2 LBS. COOKED LEAFY VEGETABLES (CHICORY, BEET GREENS, TURNIP GREENS, OR BROCCOLI RABE RECOMMENDED)

SALT AND PEPPER, TO TASTE

1. Place the olive oil and bread in a large skillet and cook over medium heat, stirring occasionally, until the bread is golden brown. Remove the bread with a slotted spoon and place it on a paper towel–lined plate to drain.

2. Add the garlic and chile to the pan and cook, stirring frequently, for 2 minutes.

3. Remove the garlic and chile and discard them. Add the chickpeas and vegetables, season with salt and pepper, and cook, stirring vigorously and mashing the chickpeas slightly, for 10 minutes.

4. Stir in the fried bread and serve warm or cold.

Chicken B'stilla

YIELD: 4 TO 6 SERVINGS / **ACTIVE TIME:** 1 HOUR / **TOTAL TIME:** 2 HOURS AND 30 MINUTES

1. Place 1 tablespoon of the olive oil in a medium saucepan and warm it over medium heat. Add the onions and salt and cook, stirring occasionally, until the onions start to soften, about 5 minutes.

2. Add the garlic, ginger, turmeric, and paprika and cook, stirring continually, until fragrant, about 1 minute. Add the water and bring the mixture to a boil.

3. Reduce the heat so that the mixture simmers and add the chicken. Cook until the chicken can be shredded, about 15 minutes. Remove the chicken, shred it, and let it cool.

4. Reduce the heat to low, add the eggs in a slow drizzle, and cook until they are just set, 2 to 3 minutes.

5. Remove the pan from heat, fold in the shredded chicken, cilantro, and parsley, and let the mixture cool.

6. Preheat the oven to 375°F. Place the almonds, 1½ tablespoons of the confectioners' sugar, and half of the cinnamon in a bowl and stir until combined.

7. Brush a medium cast-iron skillet with some of the remaining olive oil. Lay 1 sheet of the phyllo in the pan, letting it hang over the sides, and brush it with olive oil. Lay another sheet on top, 2 inches to the right of where you laid the first one. Brush it with olive oil and repeat with 8 more sheets of phyllo. Make sure to keep any sheets of phyllo that you are not working with covered so that they do not dry out.

8. Spread the almond mixture over the last layer of phyllo. Pour the chicken mixture on top of that and use a rubber spatula to spread it into an even layer.

9. Place a piece of parchment paper on a work surface. Place a sheet of phyllo in the center of the parchment and brush it with olive oil. Repeat with 3 more sheets of phyllo dough. After brushing the top sheet with olive oil, fold the stack of phyllo like a book.

10. Lay this stack of phyllo on top of the filling and fold any overhanging phyllo over the top. Combine the remaining confectioners' sugar and cinnamon and sprinkle this mixture over the phyllo.

11. Place the pan in the oven and bake until the b'stilla is crispy and golden brown, about 40 minutes. Remove the b'stilla from the oven and let it cool briefly before serving.

¼ CUP EXTRA-VIRGIN OLIVE OIL

1 CUP CHOPPED ONIONS

½ TEASPOON KOSHER SALT

1 GARLIC CLOVE, MINCED

2 TEASPOONS GRATED FRESH GINGER

¼ TEASPOON TURMERIC

½ TEASPOON PAPRIKA

2 CUPS WATER

1 LB. BONELESS, SKINLESS CHICKEN THIGHS, CUT INTO ½-INCH-WIDE STRIPS

4 EGGS, BEATEN

2 TABLESPOONS CHOPPED FRESH CILANTRO

2 TABLESPOONS CHOPPED FRESH PARSLEY

¾ CUP SLIVERED ALMONDS, TOASTED

2 TABLESPOONS CONFECTIONERS' SUGAR

2 TEASPOONS CINNAMON

½ LB. FROZEN PHYLLO DOUGH, THAWED

Braised Pork with Horiatiki Salad & Skordalia

YIELD: 6 SERVINGS / **ACTIVE TIME:** 45 MINUTES / **TOTAL TIME:** 3 HOURS

2 TABLESPOONS EXTRA-VIRGIN OLIVE OIL

2 LBS. BONELESS PORK SHOULDER, CUT INTO 1-INCH CUBES

SALT AND PEPPER, TO TASTE

2 ONIONS, CHOPPED

1 CELERY STALK, CHOPPED

1 CARROT, PEELED AND CUT INTO THIN HALF-MOONS

1 TEASPOON FRESH THYME

2 GARLIC CLOVES, MINCED

¾ CUP WHITE WINE

1 (14 OZ.) CAN OF DICED TOMATOES, DRAINED

½ CUP KALAMATA OLIVES, PITS REMOVED

4 CUPS CHICKEN STOCK (SEE PAGE 482)

1 BAY LEAF

1 TABLESPOON DRIED OREGANO

SKORDALIA (SEE PAGE 509), FOR SERVING

HORIATIKI SALAD (SEE PAGE 394), FOR SERVING

1. Preheat the oven to 300°F. Place 1 tablespoon of the olive oil in a Dutch oven and warm it over medium heat. Season the pork with salt and pepper. Working in batches to avoid crowding the pot, add the pork and cook until it is browned all over, about 8 minutes, turning it as necessary. Transfer the browned pork to a paper towel–lined plate to drain.

2. Add the remaining olive oil and the onions to the pot and cook, stirring occasionally, until they have softened, about 5 minutes. Add the celery and carrot and cook, stirring occasionally, for 3 minutes.

3. Add the thyme and garlic and cook, stirring continually, for 1 minute. Add the white wine and cook until the alcohol has been cooked off, about 3 minutes. Add the tomatoes, olives, stock, bay leaf, and oregano, return the pork to the pot, and bring the mixture to a simmer.

4. Cover the Dutch oven and place it in the oven. Braise the pork until it is extremely tender and almost falling apart, about 2 hours.

5. Remove the pork from the oven and serve it alongside the Skordalia and Horiatiki Salad.

Tiella Barese

YIELD: 4 SERVINGS / **ACTIVE TIME:** 50 MINUTES / **TOTAL TIME:** 2 HOURS

7 TABLESPOONS EXTRA-VIRGIN OLIVE OIL

2.2 LBS. MUSSELS, RINSED WELL AND DEBEARDED

3 ONIONS, SLICED THIN

6 POTATOES, PEELED AND SLICED THIN

1 LB. CHERRY TOMATOES, QUARTERED

1 GARLIC CLOVE, MINCED

6 TABLESPOONS FINELY CHOPPED FRESH PARSLEY

SALT AND PEPPER, TO TASTE

¾ LB. ARBORIO RICE

3½ OZ. GRATED PECORINO CHEESE

3 TABLESPOONS BREAD CRUMBS

1. Place 3 tablespoons of olive oil in a deep pot and warm it over medium heat. Add the mussels, cover the pot, and cook until the majority of the mussels have opened, about 5 minutes. Discard any mussels that did not open. Strain the remaining mussels, reserving the liquid. Strain the liquid and set it aside.

2. Split the mussels in half, reserving the halves containing the mussels. Set them aside.

3. Coat a Dutch oven with 2 tablespoons of olive oil and cover the bottom of the pot with the onions. Arrange half of the potatoes, half of the tomatoes, the garlic, and half of the parsley in layers on top, and season the dish with salt and pepper.

4. Add the mussels, making sure the insides of their shells are facing upwards.

5. Cover the mussels with the rice, making sure that it fills both the mussels and the empty spaces in the dish. Season the dish with salt and pepper and drizzle the remaining olive oil and the reserved liquid over the dish.

6. Arrange the remaining potatoes and tomatoes on top in layers. Top with the remaining parsley, season the dish with salt and pepper, and sprinkle the pecorino and bread crumbs over the top.

7. Pour water into the pot until the rice is covered, making sure the liquid does not reach the top layer.

8. Preheat the oven to 360°F. Cover the pot and bring it to a boil over medium heat. Place the pot in the oven and bake for 40 minutes.

9. Uncover the pot and bake for another 20 minutes so that the top becomes crunchy.

10. Remove the tiella Barese from the oven and serve.

Pasta al Ragù di Polpo

YIELD: 4 SERVINGS / **ACTIVE TIME:** 50 MINUTES / **TOTAL TIME:** 1 HOUR AND 20 MINUTES

2 LBS. FRESH OCTOPUS

¼ CUP EXTRA-VIRGIN OLIVE OIL

1 GARLIC CLOVE

½ YELLOW ONION, FINELY DICED

⅓ HOT CHILE PEPPER, MINCED

½ CUP DRY WHITE WINE

2 LBS. WHOLE PEELED TOMATOES, LIGHTLY CRUSHED

1 BAY LEAF

SALT, TO TASTE

1 LB. SCIALATIELLI (SEE PAGE 229)

FRESH PARSLEY, CHOPPED, FOR GARNISH

1. Rinse the octopus thoroughly under cold water and let it drain. Cut the octopus into large pieces, leaving 4 tentacles whole.

2. Place the olive oil in a large, deep skillet and warm it over medium heat. Add the garlic, onion, and chile and cook, stirring frequently, for 5 minutes.

3. Add the octopus and cook, stirring frequently, until it is browned. Add the white wine, raise the heat to medium-high, and cook until the wine has evaporated.

4. Remove the garlic and discard it. Add the tomatoes and bay leaf, reduce the heat to low, and season the sauce with salt. Cook until the sauce has thickened and the octopus is tender, 30 to 35 minutes.

5. Bring water to a boil in a large saucepan. Add salt, let the water return to a full boil, and add the pasta. Cook until the pasta is al dente.

6. Drain the pasta, add it to the sauce, and toss to combine.

7. To serve, top each portion with a long octopus tentacle and chopped parsley.

Orecchiette con Cime di Rapa

YIELD: 4 SERVINGS / **ACTIVE TIME:** 40 MINUTES / **TOTAL TIME:** 1 HOUR

SALT, TO TASTE

2.2 LBS. TURNIP GREENS, RINSED WELL, WOODY STEMS REMOVED

¼ CUP EXTRA-VIRGIN OLIVE OIL, PLUS MORE AS NEEDED

2 GARLIC CLOVES, HALVED

1 HOT CHILE PEPPER, STEM AND SEEDS REMOVED, CHOPPED

8 ANCHOVIES IN OLIVE OIL, DRAINED AND CHOPPED

¼ CUP BREAD CRUMBS

1 LB. ORECCHIETTE (SEE PAGE 221)

1. Bring salted water to a boil in a large saucepan. Add the turnip greens and cook until just tender, about 5 minutes. Drain the turnip greens and set them aside.

2. Place the olive oil in a large, deep skillet and warm it over medium heat. Add the garlic, chile, and anchovies and cook, stirring frequently, for 2 minutes. Remove the pan from heat and set it aside.

3. Lightly coat a small skillet with olive oil and warm it over medium heat. Add the bread crumbs and cook, stirring occasionally, until they are browned, about 5 minutes.

4. Bring water to a boil in a large saucepan. Add salt, let the water return to a full boil, and add the pasta. Cook until the pasta is al dente.

5. Add the turnip greens to the garlic mixture and cook over medium heat for 2 to 3 minutes, tossing to combine.

6. Drain the pasta, add it to the sauce, and toss to combine. Top the dish with the toasted bread crumbs and serve.

Pasta al Ragù di Polpo
SEE PAGE 148

Spaghetti alla Bottarga

YIELD: 4 SERVINGS / **ACTIVE TIME:** 10 MINUTES / **TOTAL TIME:** 30 MINUTES

SALT AND PEPPER, TO TASTE

1 LB. SPAGHETTI

¼ CUP EXTRA-VIRGIN OLIVE OIL

2 GARLIC CLOVES

3½ OZ. MULLET BOTTARGA, GRATED

¼ CUP CHOPPED FRESH PARSLEY

1. Bring water to a boil in a large saucepan. Add salt, let the water return to a full boil, and add the pasta. Cook until the pasta is very al dente.

2. Place the olive oil in a large skillet and warm it over medium heat. Add the garlic and cook, stirring frequently, for 2 minutes.

3. Add two-thirds of the bottarga and parsley, and a few tablespoons of the pasta water to the pan. Cook, gently stirring, for 2 minutes.

4. Reserve 1 cup of pasta water, drain the pasta, add it to the pan, and raise the heat to medium-high. Cook for 2 to 3 minutes, tossing to combine and adding pasta water as necessary to get the desired texture.

5. Top with the remaining bottarga and parsley, season with salt and pepper, and serve.

Fregola con le Vongole

YIELD: 4 SERVINGS / **ACTIVE TIME:** 30 MINUTES / **TOTAL TIME:** 50 MINUTES

2 LBS. CLAMS

SALT AND PEPPER, TO TASTE

¼ CUP EXTRA-VIRGIN OLIVE OIL

1 GARLIC CLOVE

¾ LB. FREGOLA (SEE PAGE 201)

1 LB. WHOLE CANNED PEELED TOMATOES, CRUSHED

FRESH PARSLEY, FINELY CHOPPED, FOR GARNISH

1. Place the clams in a large bowl, cover them with cold water, and stir in 4 handfuls of salt. Let them soak for 2 hours to remove the sand.

2. Drain the clams, rinse them, and set them aside.

3. Place 2 tablespoons of olive oil in a large, deep skillet and warm it over medium-low heat. Add the garlic and cook for 2 minutes.

4. Add the clams, cover the pan with a lid, and cook until the majority of the clams have opened, about 5 minutes. Discard any clams that did not open. Drain the clams and reserve the liquid they release. Strain the liquid and set it and the clams aside.

5. Place the remaining olive oil in the pan and warm it over medium heat. Add the Fregola and cook, stirring continually, for 2 minutes.

6. Add the tomatoes and the reserved liquid and cook for 20 minutes.

7. Remove half of the clams from their shells. Add these and the clams in their shells to the pan, season with salt and pepper, and stir to combine. Garnish the dish with parsley and serve.

Seared Shrimp Skewers

YIELD: 4 SERVINGS / **ACTIVE TIME:** 30 MINUTES / **TOTAL TIME:** 2 HOURS

⅓ CUP EXTRA-VIRGIN OLIVE OIL

5 GARLIC CLOVES, MINCED

ZEST AND JUICE OF 1 LIME

1 TEASPOON PAPRIKA

½ TEASPOON GROUND GINGER

½ TEASPOON CUMIN

½ TEASPOON KOSHER SALT

¼ TEASPOON CAYENNE PEPPER

1 LB. LARGE SHRIMP, SHELLS REMOVED, DEVEINED

FRESH CILANTRO, CHOPPED, FOR GARNISH

ROASTED GARLIC AIOLI (SEE PAGE 516), FOR SERVING

CAULIFLOWER CAKES (SEE PAGE 340), FOR SERVING

LIME WEDGES, FOR SERVING

1. Place the olive oil, garlic, lime zest, lime juice, paprika, ginger, cumin, salt, and cayenne in a mixing bowl and whisk to combine.

2. Thread the shrimp onto skewers. Place the skewers in a large resealable bag, add the marinade, and marinate in the refrigerator for 1 hour.

3. Warm a cast-iron skillet over medium-high heat. Place the shrimp skewers in the pan and cook until just browned on both sides, 3 to 4 minutes.

4. Divide the skewers among the serving plates, garnish with cilantro, and serve with the aioli, Cauliflower Cakes, and lime wedges.

Pasta alla Norma

YIELD: 4 SERVINGS / **ACTIVE TIME:** 50 MINUTES / **TOTAL TIME:** 2 HOURS

2 LARGE EGGPLANTS, CUT INTO CHUNKS

¼ CUP COARSE KOSHER SALT

2 LBS. TOMATOES

6 TABLESPOONS EXTRA-VIRGIN OLIVE OIL

1 GARLIC CLOVE, HALVED

SALT AND PEPPER, TO TASTE

1 LB. RIGATONI

¼ CUP COARSELY GRATED RICOTTA SALATA CHEESE, FOR GARNISH

HANDFUL OF FRESH BASIL, TORN, FOR GARNISH

1. Place the eggplants in a colander and season them with the coarse salt. Fill a large saucepan with water and place the pan on top of the eggplants. Let the eggplants drain for 1 hour.

2. Rinse the eggplants and squeeze them to remove as much water as possible. Place the eggplants on kitchen towels and let them dry.

3. Bring water to a boil in a large saucepan. Add the tomatoes and cook for 1 minute. Remove the tomatoes, peel them, and remove the seeds. Chop the remaining flesh and set them aside.

4. Place 2 tablespoons of olive oil in a medium saucepan and warm it over medium heat. Add the garlic and cook, stirring frequently, for 2 minutes.

5. Remove the garlic and discard it. Add the tomatoes, season with salt and pepper, and cook until the sauce starts to thicken, 20 to 30 minutes.

6. Place the remaining olive oil in a large skillet and warm it over medium-high heat. Add the eggplants and cook, stirring occasionally, until they are golden brown, 5 to 7 minutes. Transfer the eggplants to a paper towel–lined plate to drain.

7. Add the eggplants to the sauce and cook for a few minutes, stirring occasionally.

8. Bring water to a boil in a large saucepan. Add salt, let the water return to a full boil, and add the pasta. Cook until the pasta is very al dente. Drain the pasta, add it to the sauce, and cook for 2 to 3 minutes, tossing to combine.

9. Garnish the dish with the ricotta salata and basil and serve.

Lamb Shanks with Pomegranate Sauce

YIELD: 4 SERVINGS / **ACTIVE TIME:** 30 MINUTES / **TOTAL TIME:** 2 HOURS AND 30 MINUTES

4 LAMB SHANKS (ABOUT 1 LB. EACH)

SALT AND PEPPER, TO TASTE

2 TABLESPOONS AVOCADO OIL

1 LARGE ONION, SLICED

6 GARLIC CLOVES, SMASHED

1 TEASPOON CINNAMON

1 TEASPOON CORIANDER

½ TEASPOON GROUND GINGER

1 TEASPOON CUMIN

24 JUNIPER BERRIES

2 TABLESPOONS TOMATO PASTE

1 CUP SWEET RED WINE

2 CUPS BEEF STOCK (SEE PAGE 484)

1 CUP POMEGRANATE JUICE

1. Preheat the oven to 350°F. Season the lamb shanks with salt and pepper.

2. Place the avocado oil in a Dutch oven and warm it over medium-high heat. Add the lamb shanks and cook until they are browned on all sides, taking care to stand them on their edges and brown those sides as well.

3. Remove the lamb shanks from the pot and set them aside. Add the onion and garlic, reduce the heat to medium, and cook, stirring frequently, until the onion has softened slightly, about 5 minutes. Add the spices, tomato paste, wine, and stock and cook, stirring continuously, for 5 minutes.

4. Return the lamb shanks to the pot, cover it, and place it in the oven. Roast the lamb shanks for 2 hours, checking them every 30 minutes and turning them over in the sauce each time you check them.

5. When the lamb is nearly done cooking, about 1½ hours, stir in the pomegranate juice. Cook for another 30 minutes longer, until the meat on the shanks is very tender, to the point of nearly falling off the bone.

6. The sauce will be thick and concentrated; if desired, thin it with a little water. Spoon the sauce over the lamb shanks and serve with rice or couscous.

Pasta con le Sarde

YIELD: 4 SERVINGS / **ACTIVE TIME:** 50 MINUTES / **TOTAL TIME:** 2 HOURS

1 LB. FRESH SARDINES

SALT AND PEPPER, TO TASTE

7 OZ. WILD FENNEL, RINSED WELL

PINCH OF SAFFRON THREADS

¼ CUP EXTRA-VIRGIN OLIVE OIL

1 LARGE WHITE ONION, FINELY DICED

5 ANCHOVIES IN OLIVE OIL, DRAINED, RINSED, AND CHOPPED

3 TABLESPOONS RAISINS, SOAKED IN WARM WATER

3 TABLESPOONS BREAD CRUMBS

1 LB. BUCATINI

3 TABLESPOONS PINE NUTS

3 TABLESPOONS BLANCHED ALMONDS, FINELY CHOPPED

1. Clean the sardines: Scrub them, remove the heads, entrails, and spines, and open them completely. Rinse the sardines under running water and pat them dry with paper towels.

2. Bring water to a boil in a large saucepan. Add salt and the fennel and cook until the fennel is tender, about 10 minutes. Remove the fennel from the boiling water with a strainer or slotted spoon and set it aside. When the fennel has cooled slightly, chop it. Keep the water at a gentle boil.

3. Place the saffron in ½ cup water and let it steep.

4. Place the olive oil in a large skillet and warm it over medium heat. Add the onion and anchovies and cook, stirring occasionally, until the onion has softened and the anchovies have dissolved, about 5 minutes.

5. Add the saffron, saffron water, sardines, and fennel. Drain the raisins, squeeze them to remove any excess liquid, and add them to the pan. Cook until the sardines are cooked through and the sauce has thickened, about 10 minutes.

6. While the sauce is cooking, place the bread crumbs in a skillet and toast them over medium heat until they are browned, shaking the pan occasionally.

7. Add the pasta to the boiling water and cook until it is al dente.

8. Drain the pasta and add it to the sauce along with the bread crumbs, pine nuts, and almonds. Toss to combine, season with salt and pepper, remove the pan from heat, and let the dish sit for a few minutes before serving.

Moroccan Cornish Hens with Pine Nut Couscous

YIELD: 8 SERVINGS / **ACTIVE TIME:** 25 MINUTES / **TOTAL TIME:** 2 HOURS AND 40 MINUTES

2 CUPS COUSCOUS

4 OZ. PINE NUTS

3 TABLESPOONS AVOCADO OIL

SALT, TO TASTE

2 ONIONS, HALVED AND SLICED

1 TEASPOON GRATED FRESH GINGER

4 GARLIC CLOVES, CRUSHED

1 TABLESPOON CHOPPED FRESH MINT

1 TABLESPOON CHOPPED FRESH CILANTRO

1 TEASPOON CUMIN

1 TEASPOON PAPRIKA

1 TABLESPOON HONEY

1 (14 OZ.) CAN OF DICED TOMATOES, WITH THEIR LIQUID

1 TEASPOON RED PEPPER FLAKES

1 TEASPOON DRIED OREGANO

8 CORNISH GAME HENS

1 TEASPOON BLACK PEPPER

1. Preheat the oven to 350°F. Prepare the couscous according to the instructions on the package.

2. Place the pine nuts on a rimmed baking sheet, place them in the oven, and toast until golden brown, 8 to 10 minutes. Remove from the oven and set them aside.

3. When the couscous is ready, reserve ½ cup and combine it with 2 tablespoons of the avocado oil. Add the pine nuts to the remaining couscous and fold to incorporate. Season the mixture with salt and set it aside.

4. Place the remaining avocado oil in a large skillet and warm it over medium-high heat. Add the onions and cook, stirring occasionally, until translucent, about 3 minutes. Add the ginger, garlic, mint, cilantro, cumin, paprika, honey, tomatoes, red pepper flakes, and oregano and simmer, stirring occasionally, until the liquid from the tomatoes has reduced slightly.

5. Season the Cornish game hens with the pepper and stuff them with the pine nut–and–couscous mixture, making sure to pack it quite firmly. Place the stuffed Cornish hens in large baking dishes.

6. Cover the hens with the warm onion-and-herb sauce and sprinkle the reserved couscous over the top. Cover the baking dishes with aluminum foil, place the Cornish hens in the oven, and roast for 1½ hours.

7. Remove the foil from the baking dishes and roast the Cornish game hens until they are cooked through and the couscous on top is crispy, about 45 minutes, basting them on occasion.

8. Remove the Cornish game hens from the oven and let them rest for 5 to 10 minutes before serving.

Chicken in Walnut Sauce with Vegetable Kebabs

YIELD: 4 SERVINGS / **ACTIVE TIME:** 30 MINUTES / **TOTAL TIME:** 1 HOUR AND 15 MINUTES

2 TABLESPOONS EXTRA-VIRGIN OLIVE OIL

1½ LBS. BONELESS, SKINLESS CHICKEN BREASTS, POUNDED THIN AND CUT INTO 1-INCH CUBES

SALT AND PEPPER, TO TASTE

1 ONION, CHOPPED

3 GARLIC CLOVES, MINCED

½ CUP WHITE WINE

4 CUPS CHICKEN STOCK (SEE PAGE 482), PLUS MORE AS NEEDED

1 TABLESPOON PAPRIKA

¼ TEASPOON CAYENNE PEPPER

1 CUP DAY-OLD BREAD PIECES

2 CUPS WALNUTS, TOASTED

FRESH CHIVES, CHOPPED, FOR GARNISH

2 PIECES OF PITA BREAD (SEE PAGE 338), CUT INTO TRIANGLES, FOR SERVING

VEGETABLE KEBABS (SEE PAGE 368), FOR SERVING

1. Place the olive oil in a Dutch oven and warm it over medium-high heat. Season the chicken with salt and pepper, add it to the pot, and cook, stirring occasionally, until it has browned, about 6 minutes.

2. Reduce the heat to medium, add the onion, and cook, stirring occasionally, until it has softened, about 5 minutes. Add the garlic and cook, stirring continually, for 1 minute. Add the white wine and cook until the alcohol has been cooked off, about 3 minutes, scraping up any browned bits from the bottom of the pot.

3. Add the stock, paprika, and cayenne and bring the mixture to a boil. Cover the pot, reduce the heat, and simmer until the chicken is very tender, 10 to 15 minutes.

4. Remove the pot from heat and strain the braising liquid into a bowl. Place the chicken on a cutting board and shred it with a fork.

5. Place the braising liquid, bread, and walnuts in a food processor and blitz until the sauce is smooth and thick, adding stock as needed to get the desired consistency.

6. Place the sauce in the Dutch oven, add the chicken, and cook until warmed through. Garnish the dish with chives and serve with the pita and Vegetable Kebabs.

Pasta con Noci e Pangrattato

YIELD: 4 SERVINGS / **ACTIVE TIME:** 15 MINUTES / **TOTAL TIME:** 35 MINUTES

¼ CUP EXTRA-VIRGIN OLIVE OIL

1 GARLIC CLOVE, MINCED

5½ OZ. WALNUTS, GROUND

2 TABLESPOONS CHOPPED FRESH PARSLEY

1 CUP BREAD CRUMBS

SALT AND PEPPER, TO TASTE

1 LB. MALLOREDDUS (SEE PAGE 212)

1. Place the olive oil in a large skillet and warm it over medium-low heat. Add the garlic and cook for 2 minutes.

2. Add the walnuts and parsley to the skillet and cook, stirring frequently, for 2 minutes. Remove the pan from heat and set it aside.

3. Place the bread crumbs in a small skillet and toast over low heat until they are browned, shaking the pan occasionally. Remove the pan from heat and set it aside.

4. Bring water to a boil in a large saucepan. Add salt, let the water return to a full boil, and add the malloreddus pasta. Cook until the pasta is al dente.

5. Reserve 1 cup of pasta water, drain the pasta, and add it to the skillet containing the walnut mixture. Stir in the toasted bread crumbs, place the pan over medium-high heat, and cook for 2 to 3 minutes, tossing to combine and adding pasta water as needed to achieve the desired texture. Season with salt and pepper and serve immediately.

THE ENCYCLOPEDIA OF MEDITERRANEAN

Frutti di Mare with Penne

YIELD: 6 SERVINGS / **ACTIVE TIME:** 30 MINUTES / **TOTAL TIME:** 1 HOUR AND 30 MINUTES

¼ CUP EXTRA-VIRGIN OLIVE OIL

½ LB. LARGE SHRIMP, SHELLS REMOVED AND RESERVED, DEVEINED

1 CUP WHITE WINE

1 ONION, SLICED THIN

4 GARLIC CLOVES, MINCED

2 TABLESPOONS TOMATO PASTE

¼ TEASPOON RED PEPPER FLAKES

PINCH OF SAFFRON

1 (28 OZ.) CAN OF CHOPPED TOMATOES, WITH THEIR LIQUID

2 CUPS CLAM JUICE

SALT AND PEPPER, TO TASTE

1 LB. PENNE

½ LB. MUSSELS, RINSED WELL AND DEBEARDED

8 SCALLOPS, FEET REMOVED

½ LB. SQUID, CLEANED (SEE PAGE 199) AND SLICED

¼ CUP CHOPPED FRESH PARSLEY, FOR GARNISH

1 CUP PANKO, TOASTED, FOR GARNISH

1. Place 2 tablespoons of the olive oil in a medium saucepan and warm it over medium heat. Add the reserved shrimp shells and cook for 4 minutes. Add the wine, reduce the heat, and simmer for 4 minutes, scraping up any browned bits from the bottom of the pan. Strain the stock into a bowl and set it aside.

2. Place the remaining olive oil in a large skillet and warm it over medium heat. Add the onion and cook, stirring occasionally, until it has softened, about 5 minutes. Add the garlic, tomato paste, red pepper flakes, and saffron and cook, stirring continually, for 1 minute.

3. Add the stock, tomatoes, and clam juice and bring the mixture to a boil. Reduce the heat and simmer the sauce for 20 minutes.

4. Bring water to a boil in a large saucepan. Add salt and the penne and cook until the pasta is al dente, 6 to 8 minutes. Reserve ½ cup of the pasta water and drain the pasta.

5. Add the mussels, hinges facing down, to the sauce and cover the pan. Cook until the majority of the mussels have opened, about 5 minutes. Remove the mussels using a slotted spoon, discarding any that didn't open.

6. Add the scallops and shrimp to the sauce and cook until cooked through, about 2 minutes. Remove the pan from heat, add the squid, and cover the pan. Let the pan sit until the squid is cooked through, about 2 minutes.

7. Add the mussels and penne to the sauce and toss to combine, adding the reserved pasta water as needed to get the desired consistency. Season with salt and pepper, garnish with the parsley and toasted panko, and enjoy.

Moussaka

YIELD: 4 SERVINGS / ACTIVE TIME: 1 HOUR AND 15 MINUTES / TOTAL TIME: 2 HOURS

FOR THE FILLING

4 CUPS COLD WATER

¼ CUP KOSHER SALT, PLUS MORE TO TASTE

3 LARGE EGGPLANTS, TRIMMED, CUT INTO CUBES

5 TABLESPOONS EXTRA-VIRGIN OLIVE OIL

2 LBS. GROUND LAMB

2 ONIONS, DICED

3 GARLIC CLOVES, MINCED

½ CUP DRY WHITE WINE

1 CUP TOMATO SAUCE (SEE PAGE 504)

2 TABLESPOONS CHOPPED FRESH PARSLEY

1 TEASPOON DRIED OREGANO

½ TEASPOON CINNAMON

BLACK PEPPER, TO TASTE

FRESHLY GRATED NUTMEG, TO TASTE

FOR THE CRUST

5 EGGS

6 TABLESPOONS UNSALTED BUTTER

⅓ CUP ALL-PURPOSE FLOUR

2½ CUPS MILK

⅔ CUP GRATED KEFALOTYRI CHEESE

⅓ CUP FRESH DILL OR PARSLEY, CHOPPED

1. Preheat the oven to 350°F. To begin preparations for the filling, place the cold water in a bowl, add the salt, and stir. When the salt has dissolved, add the eggplant cubes and let the cubes soak for about 20 minutes. Drain the eggplants and rinse with cold water. Squeeze the cubes to remove as much water as you can, place them on a pile of paper towels, and blot them dry. Set aside.

2. While the eggplants are soaking, add 1 tablespoon of the olive oil to a large cast-iron skillet and warm it over medium-high heat. When the oil starts to shimmer, add the lamb and cook, using a wooden spoon to break it up, until it is browned, about 8 minutes. Transfer the cooked lamb to a bowl and set it aside.

3. Add 2 tablespoons of the olive oil and the eggplant cubes to the skillet and cook, stirring frequently until they start to brown, about 5 minutes. Transfer the cooked eggplant to the bowl containing the lamb and add the remaining olive oil, the onions, and garlic to the skillet. Cook, stirring frequently, until the onions are translucent, about 3 minutes, return the lamb and eggplant to the skillet, and stir in the wine, Tomato Sauce, parsley, oregano, and cinnamon. Reduce the heat to low and simmer for about 15 minutes, stirring occasionally. Season with salt, pepper, and nutmeg and transfer the mixture to a 13 x 9–inch baking dish.

4. To begin preparations for the crust, place the eggs in a large bowl and beat them lightly. Place a saucepan over medium heat and melt the butter. Reduce the heat to medium-low and add the flour. Stir constantly until the mixture is smooth. While stirring constantly, gradually add the milk and bring the mixture to a boil. When the mixture reaches a boil, remove the pan from heat. Stir approximately half of the mixture in the saucepan into the beaten eggs. Stir the tempered eggs into the saucepan and then add the cheese and dill or parsley. Stir to combine and pour the mixture over the lamb mixture in the baking dish.

5. Place the baking dish in the oven and bake the moussaka until the crust is set and golden brown, about 35 minutes. Remove from the oven and let the moussaka rest for 5 minutes before serving.

Pan-Roasted Monkfish with Braised Fennel

YIELD: 4 SERVINGS / **ACTIVE TIME:** 30 MINUTES / **TOTAL TIME:** 1 HOUR

6 TABLESPOONS EXTRA-VIRGIN OLIVE OIL

1 TABLESPOON DRIED OREGANO

2 TABLESPOONS RED WINE VINEGAR

½ ONION, FINELY DICED

2 TEASPOONS DIJON MUSTARD

2 TABLESPOONS MINCED KALAMATA OLIVES

2 TABLESPOONS MINCED GREEN OLIVES

1 TABLESPOON MINCED CAPERS

1 TABLESPOON CHOPPED FRESH PARSLEY

SALT AND PEPPER, TO TASTE

1½ LBS. MONKFISH FILLETS, CUT INTO 2-INCH CUBES

PINE NUTS, TOASTED AND CHOPPED, FOR GARNISH

PARMESAN CHEESE, SHAVED, FOR GARNISH

BRAISED FENNEL (SEE PAGE 345), FOR SERVING

LEMON WEDGES, FOR SERVING

1. Place ¼ cup of the olive oil in a small saucepan and warm it over low heat. Add the oregano, remove the pan from heat, and cover it. Let the oil steep for 5 minutes.

2. Add the vinegar, onion, mustard, olives, capers, and parsley, season the relish with salt and pepper, and stir to combine. Transfer the relish to a bowl and set it aside.

3. Place the remaining olive oil in a large cast-iron skillet and warm it over medium-high heat. Pat the monkfish dry with paper towels and season it with salt and pepper. Place the monkfish in the pan and cook until golden brown, 3 to 4 minutes. Turn it over and cook until it is cooked through (internal temperature of 160°F), another 3 to 4 minutes.

4. Transfer the monkfish to a serving platter, garnish it with the pine nuts and Parmesan, and serve with the olive relish, Braised Fennel, and lemon wedges.

Moussaka
SEE PAGE 164

Fregola con Salsiccia

YIELD: 4 SERVINGS / **ACTIVE TIME:** 30 MINUTES / **TOTAL TIME:** 50 MINUTES

¼ CUP EXTRA-VIRGIN OLIVE OIL

1 ONION, FINELY DICED

5 OZ. ITALIAN SAUSAGE, CASING REMOVED, CRUMBLED

¾ LB. FREGOLA (SEE PAGE 201)

3 CUPS VEGETABLE STOCK (SEE PAGE 484), WARMED

PINCH OF SAFFRON THREADS

SALT, TO TASTE

½ CUP GRATED SARDINIAN CHEESE

FRESH PARSLEY, CHOPPED, FOR GARNISH

1. Place the olive oil in a large skillet and warm it over medium-low heat. Add the onion and cook until it has softened, about 5 minutes.

2. Add the sausage and cook, stirring frequently, until it has browned, about 8 minutes.

3. Add the Fregola to the pan and lightly toast it. Add the broth and cook, stirring frequently, until the broth has evaporated and the dish is moist but not soupy, about 20 minutes.

4. Stir in the saffron, season the dish with salt, and cook for 1 minute. Add the grated cheese and fold to incorporate it. Garnish the dish with parsley and serve.

Spinach, Fennel & Apple Salad with Smoked Trout

YIELD: 4 SERVINGS / **ACTIVE TIME:** 15 MINUTES / **TOTAL TIME:** 30 MINUTES

2 TABLESPOONS WHITE WINE VINEGAR

1 TABLESPOON FRESH LEMON JUICE

1 TABLESPOON WHOLE-GRAIN MUSTARD

1 TEASPOON HONEY

½ CUP EXTRA-VIRGIN OLIVE OIL

1 SHALLOT, MINCED

2 TEASPOONS CHOPPED FRESH TARRAGON

SALT AND PEPPER, TO TASTE

4 CUPS BABY SPINACH

2 GRANNY SMITH APPLES, HALVED, CORES REMOVED, SLICED THIN

1 FENNEL BULB, TRIMMED, CORE REMOVED, AND SLICED THIN

½ LB. SMOKED TROUT, SKIN REMOVED, FLAKED

1. Place the vinegar, lemon juice, mustard, and honey in a salad bowl and whisk to combine.

2. While whisking continually, slowly drizzle in the olive oil until it has emulsified. Stir in the shallot and tarragon and season the vinaigrette with salt and pepper.

3. Add the spinach, apples, and fennel to the salad bowl and toss to coat.

4. To serve, plate the salad, top each portion with some of the smoked trout, and enjoy.

THE ENCYCLOPEDIA OF MEDITERRANEAN

Pitta di Patate

YIELD: 6 SERVINGS / **ACTIVE TIME:** 40 MINUTES / **TOTAL TIME:** 1 HOUR AND 30 MINUTES

¼ CUP EXTRA-VIRGIN OLIVE OIL

3 LARGE YELLOW OR RED ONIONS, SLICED THIN

1 LB. WHOLE PEELED TOMATOES, CRUSHED

½ CUP PITTED BLACK OLIVES, CHOPPED

1 TABLESPOON CAPERS IN BRINE, RINSED AND DRAINED

4 FRESH MINT LEAVES, FINELY CHOPPED

SALT AND PEPPER, TO TASTE

DRIED OREGANO, TO TASTE

2½ LBS. POTATOES

2 EGGS

1 CUP GRATED PECORINO CHEESE

3½ TABLESPOONS WHOLE MILK

BUTTER, AS NEEDED

¼ CUP BREAD CRUMBS

1. Place half of the olive oil in a large skillet and warm it over medium-low heat. Add the onions and cook, stirring occasionally, until they have softened, about 6 minutes.

2. Add the tomatoes and cook, stirring occasionally, until the mixture has thickened.

3. Stir in the olives, capers, and mint, season the mixture with salt and oregano, and cook for about 2 minutes. Remove the pan from heat and let the mixture cool.

4. Bring salted water to a boil in a large pot. Add the potatoes and boil until they are tender, about 40 minutes.

5. Preheat the oven to 390°F. Drain the potatoes and run them under cold water. Peel the potatoes, mash them, and season them with salt and pepper.

6. Add the remaining olive oil, the eggs, pecorino, and milk and stir to combine.

7. Coat a deep baking dish with butter. Sprinkle half of the bread crumbs over the bottom and then spread half of the potato mixture on top. Top with the tomato mixture, spread the remaining potato mixture over the top, and sprinkle the remaining bread crumbs over it.

8. Place the baking dish in the oven and bake for 35 minutes.

9. Set the oven's broiler to high and place the baking dish directly below it. Broil until the top is golden brown.

10. Turn off the broiler and let the dish cool in the oven, which will allow it to become firmer when you serve it.

Spinach, Fennel & Apple Salad with Smoked Trout
SEE PAGE 168

Affunniatella Molisana

YIELD: 4 SERVINGS / ACTIVE TIME: 10 MINUTES / TOTAL TIME: 30 MINUTES

¼ CUP EXTRA-VIRGIN OLIVE OIL

1 ONION, FINELY DICED

13 OZ. SWEET ITALIAN PEPPERS, STEMS AND SEEDS REMOVED, CUT INTO STRIPS

½ CHILE PEPPER, STEM AND SEEDS REMOVED, MINCED

1 TABLESPOON CHOPPED FRESH PARSLEY

3 TOMATOES, CHOPPED

SALT, TO TASTE

4 EGGS, LIGHTLY BEATEN

⅔ CUP GRATED PECORINO CHEESE

1. Place the olive oil in a large skillet and warm it over medium heat. Add the onion and cook, stirring occasionally, until it has softened, about 5 minutes.

2. Add the sweet peppers and cook, stirring occasionally, until they have softened, about 5 minutes.

3. Add the chile, parsley, and tomatoes, season with salt, and reduce the heat to low. Cook until the sauce has thickened, 15 to 20 minutes.

4. Add the eggs and scramble until they are almost set.

5. Sprinkle the pecorino over the eggs and cook until it has melted. Serve immediately.

Pasta with Halibut & Artichokes

YIELD: 4 TO 6 SERVINGS / ACTIVE TIME: 40 MINUTES / TOTAL TIME: 1 HOUR

2 TABLESPOONS AVOCADO OIL

½ LB. HALIBUT FILLETS, CHOPPED

SALT AND PEPPER, TO TASTE

3 GARLIC CLOVES, MINCED

1 SMALL YELLOW ONION, MINCED

⅛ TEASPOON RED PEPPER FLAKES

¼ CUP PANKO

1 LB. SPAGHETTI

JUICE OF 2 LEMONS

MARINATED ARTICHOKES (SEE PAGE 61)

FRESH BASIL, CHOPPED, FOR GARNISH

1. Place the avocado oil in a large skillet and warm it over medium-high heat. Season the halibut with salt, add it to the pan, and cook, stirring occasionally, until it is browned on both sides and just cooked through, about 4 minutes. Remove the halibut from the pan and set it aside.

2. Add the garlic and onion to the pan, reduce the heat to medium-low, and cook, stirring frequently, until the onion just starts to soften, about 5 minutes.

3. Add the red pepper flakes and panko, season with salt and pepper, and stir until well combined. Remove the pan from heat and set it aside.

4. Bring a large pot of water to a boil. Salt the water, add the pasta, and cook until it is al dente, 6 to 8 minutes. Drain the pasta and set it aside.

5. Place the skillet over medium heat. Add the halibut, lemon juice, artichokes, and pasta and cook until everything is warmed through, tossing to combine. Garnish the dish with basil and enjoy.

Monkfish Tagine

YIELD: 4 SERVINGS / **ACTIVE TIME:** 15 MINUTES / **TOTAL TIME:** 45 MINUTES

2 TABLESPOONS EXTRA-VIRGIN OLIVE OIL

1 ONION, CHOPPED

2 CARROTS, PEELED AND CHOPPED

1 TABLESPOON TOMATO PASTE

1 TEASPOON PAPRIKA

1 TEASPOON CUMIN

¼ TEASPOON SAFFRON

4 GARLIC CLOVES, MINCED

ZEST AND JUICE OF 1 ORANGE

1 CUP CLAM JUICE

1 (14 OZ.) CAN OF CHICKPEAS, DRAINED AND RINSED

2 LBS. MONKFISH FILLETS

SALT AND PEPPER, TO TASTE

¼ CUP SLICED KALAMATA OLIVES

2 TABLESPOONS TORN FRESH MINT

1 TEASPOON WHITE WINE VINEGAR

1. Place the olive oil in a Dutch oven and warm it over medium-high heat. Add the onion and carrots and cook, stirring occasionally, until they are lightly browned, 8 to 10 minutes.

2. Add the tomato paste, paprika, cumin, saffron, garlic, and orange zest and cook, stirring continually, for 1 minute. Stir in the orange juice, clam juice, and chickpeas and bring to a simmer.

3. Pat the monkfish dry with paper towels and season it with salt and pepper. Nestle the monkfish into the pot and spoon some liquid over it. Cover the pot and simmer until the monkfish is cooked through (internal temperature of 160°F), about 10 minutes.

4. Add the olives, mint, and vinegar and gently stir to incorporate. Taste, adjust the seasoning as necessary, and enjoy.

Gattò di Patate

YIELD: 6 SERVINGS / **ACTIVE TIME:** 40 MINUTES / **TOTAL TIME:** 1 HOUR AND 30 MINUTES

SALT AND PEPPER, TO TASTE

2½ LBS. POTATOES

2 TABLESPOONS EXTRA-VIRGIN OLIVE OIL

2 EGGS

⅓ CUP GRATED PARMESAN CHEESE

3½ TABLESPOONS WHOLE MILK

BUTTER, AS NEEDED

¼ CUP BREAD CRUMBS

7 OZ. SMOKED PROVOLA OR SMOKED SCAMORZA CHEESE, DICED

3½ OZ. SALAMI, CHOPPED

3½ OZ. HAM, DICED

1. Preheat the oven to 390°F. Bring salted water to a boil in a large pot. Add the potatoes and boil until they are tender, about 40 minutes.

2. Drain the potatoes and run them under cold water. Peel the potatoes, mash them, and season them with salt and pepper.

3. Add the olive oil, eggs, Parmesan, and milk and stir to combine.

4. Coat a deep baking dish with butter. Sprinkle half of the bread crumbs over the bottom and then spread half of the potato mixture on top.

5. Top with the provola, salami, and ham, spread the remaining potato mixture over the top, and sprinkle the remaining bread crumbs over it.

6. Place the baking dish in the oven and bake for 35 minutes.

7. Set the oven's broiler to high and place the baking dish directly below it. Broil until the top is golden brown.

8. Turn off the broiler and let the gattò cool in the oven, which will allow it to become firmer when you serve it.

Chermoula Sea Bass

YIELD: 8 SERVINGS / **ACTIVE TIME:** 20 MINUTES / **TOTAL TIME:** 45 MINUTES

8 SEA BASS FILLETS, SKIN REMOVED

3 TABLESPOONS CHERMOULA SAUCE (SEE PAGE 504)

LEMON WEDGES, FOR SERVING

1. Preheat the oven to 425°F. Rub the sea bass with the chermoula. Place a 2-inch sheet of parchment paper on a work surface and fold it in half lengthwise.

2. Arrange four of the fillets along one edge of the seam. Fold the parchment over the fillets and fold in the edges to make a pouch. Repeat with a second sheet of parchment and the remaining fillets.

3. Carefully transfer the pouches to a rimmed baking sheet. Place the pan in the oven and bake until the fish is cooked through and flakes easily at the touch of a fork, 10 to 12 minutes.

4. Remove from the oven and carefully open the pouches; be careful of the steam that escapes. Serve the sea bass immediately with lemon wedges.

Cornbread & Crab–Stuffed Branzino

YIELD: 6 SERVINGS / **ACTIVE TIME:** 1 HOUR / **TOTAL TIME:** 1 HOUR AND 45 MINUTES

CORNBREAD STUFFING (SEE PAGE 357)

1 LB. LUMP CRABMEAT

1 LEMON, SLICED THIN

4 SPRIGS OF FRESH THYME

4 BAY LEAVES

2 (1 LB.) WHOLE BRANZINO, CLEANED, SCALES REMOVED

SALT AND PEPPER, TO TASTE

1 TABLESPOON EXTRA-VIRGIN OLIVE OIL

CHARRED SCALLION SAUCE (SEE PAGE 517), FOR SERVING

WHITE RICE, COOKED, FOR SERVING

1. Preheat the oven to 400°F. Place a wire rack in a rimmed baking sheet. Layer the stuffing, crabmeat, slices of lemon, thyme, and bay leaves inside the branzino and tie the fish closed with kitchen twine. Season them with salt and pepper.

2. Place the olive oil in a large skillet and warm it over medium-high heat. Place the branzino in the pan, one at a time, and sear on each side for 3 to 4 minutes.

3. Place the branzino on the wire rack set in the baking sheet, place them in the oven, and roast until cooked through (internal temperature of 120°F).

4. Remove the branzino from the oven, cut off the kitchen twine, and serve them with the Charred Scallion Sauce and rice.

Fried Fish with Agristada Sauce

YIELD: 6 SERVINGS / **ACTIVE TIME:** 30 MINUTES / **TOTAL TIME:** 1 HOUR

2 LBS. COD OR RED MULLET FILLETS

½ CUP FRESH LEMON JUICE

¾ TEASPOON KOSHER SALT

AVOCADO OIL, AS NEEDED

1 CUP ALL-PURPOSE FLOUR

2 EGGS

AGRISTADA SAUCE (SEE PAGE 518), FOR SERVING

1. Place the fish in a shallow dish, pour the lemon juice over it, and sprinkle ¼ teaspoon of the salt over the top. Turn the fish in the lemon juice until it is well coated. Let the fish soak for 30 minutes, turning it once or twice.

2. Transfer the fish to a colander and rinse well. Pat it dry and cut it into 1-inch cubes.

3. Add avocado oil to a Dutch oven until it reaches about halfway up the side. Warm it to 350°F over medium-high heat.

4. In a shallow bowl, combine the flour with ¼ teaspoon of the salt. Place the eggs in a separate shallow bowl with the remaining ¼ teaspoon of salt and beat until scrambled.

5. Dredge the fish in the flour mixture until coated, shake off any excess, and then dredge it in the eggs until completely coated.

6. Working in batches to avoid crowding the pot, gently slip the fish into the hot oil and fry until cooked through and golden brown, about 10 minutes, turning as necessary. Transfer the fried fish to a paper towel–lined plate.

7. When all of the fish has been fried, serve with the Agristada Sauce.

Leg of Lamb with Garlic & Rosemary

YIELD: 8 SERVINGS / **ACTIVE TIME:** 30 MINUTES / **TOTAL TIME:** 2 HOURS AND 30 MINUTES

EXTRA-VIRGIN OLIVE OIL, AS NEEDED

1 (7 LB.) SEMI-BONELESS LEG OF LAMB

4 GARLIC CLOVES

1 TABLESPOON KOSHER SALT, PLUS MORE TO TASTE

2 TABLESPOONS CHOPPED FRESH ROSEMARY

2 TABLESPOONS RAS EL HANOUT (SEE PAGE 505)

2 TABLESPOONS SUMAC

2 TABLESPOONS BERBERE SEASONING

½ TEASPOON BLACK PEPPER, PLUS MORE TO TASTE

¼ CUP DRY RED WINE OR BEEF STOCK (SEE PAGE 484)

1. Coat a roasting pan with olive oil and set it aside. Trim any fatty areas on the leg of lamb so that the fat is within approximately ¼ inch of the meat, keeping in mind that it is better to leave too much fat than too little. Pat the lamb dry and score the remaining fat with a sharp paring knife, making sure not to cut into the flesh.

2. Using a mortar and pestle, grind the garlic and salt into a paste. Add the rosemary, Ras el Hanout, sumac, berbere seasoning, and pepper and stir to combine.

3. Place the lamb in the roasting pan and rub the paste all over it. Let the lamb marinate at room temperature for 30 minutes.

4. Preheat the oven to 350°F and position a rack in the middle. Place the lamb in the oven and roast until an instant-read thermometer inserted about 2 inches into the thickest part of the meat registers 130°F, about 1½ hours.

5. Remove the lamb from the oven, transfer it to a cutting board, and let it rest 15 to 25 minutes (the internal temperature will rise to about 135°F, perfect for medium-rare).

6. Place the wine or stock in the roasting pan and place it over high heat, scraping up any browned bits from the bottom of the pan. Season the pan sauce with salt and pepper and serve it beside the lamb.

Crispy Salmon Rice

YIELD: 2 SERVINGS / **ACTIVE TIME:** 30 MINUTES / **TOTAL TIME:** 30 MINUTES

2 TABLESPOONS AVOCADO OIL

½ WHITE ONION, MINCED

¼ CUP SLICED SCALLIONS

¼ CUP CHOPPED FRESH PARSLEY

2 TEASPOONS KOSHER SALT

2 CUPS LEFTOVER WHITE RICE

6 OZ. SALMON BELLY, CHOPPED

1 TABLESPOON POMEGRANATE MOLASSES

1 TABLESPOON APPLE CIDER VINEGAR

1. Place the avocado oil in a large skillet and warm it over high heat. Add the onion, scallions, parsley, and salt and cook, stirring frequently, until the onion is translucent, about 3 minutes.

2. Add the rice and cook, stirring frequently, until the rice is crispy, 3 to 5 minutes. Add the salmon, reduce the heat to medium-high, and cook until the salmon is cooked through, about 4 minutes.

3. Place the pomegranate molasses and vinegar in a small bowl and whisk to combine. Add this mixture to the pan and stir until incorporated.

4. Remove the pan from heat and enjoy immediately.

Dogfish Chraime

YIELD: 2 SERVINGS / **ACTIVE TIME:** 30 MINUTES / **TOTAL TIME:** 30 MINUTES

2 TABLESPOONS EXTRA-VIRGIN OLIVE OIL

½ ONION, DICED

2 GARLIC CLOVES, MINCED

3 TOMATOES, DICED

PINCH OF CUMIN

PINCH OF CAYENNE PEPPER

2 TEASPOONS KOSHER SALT

¾ LB. DOGFISH FILLET

1 TEASPOON BLACK PEPPER

1. Place 1 tablespoon of the olive oil in a medium skillet and warm it over medium-high heat. Add the onion and garlic and cook, stirring frequently, until the onion is translucent, about 2 minutes.

2. Stir in the tomatoes, cumin, cayenne, and 1 teaspoon of the salt and bring the mixture to a simmer. Cook until the tomatoes start to break down, about 6 minutes.

3. Cut the fillet in half and season it with the pepper and the remaining salt.

4. Place the remaining olive oil in a clean skillet and warm it over high heat. Place the fish in the pan and cook until it is browned on both sides and cooked through, about 4 minutes.

5. To serve, spoon some of the sauce into a shallow bowl, place the fish on top, and spoon a little more sauce over the top.

Crispy Salmon Rice
SEE PAGE 179

Lamb Meatballs over Eggplant

YIELD: 4 SERVINGS / **ACTIVE TIME:** 45 MINUTES / **TOTAL TIME:** 1 HOUR

FOR THE MEATBALLS

⅓ CUP FULL-FAT GREEK YOGURT

3 TABLESPOONS BREAD CRUMBS

2 TABLESPOONS WATER

1 LB. GROUND LAMB

2 TABLESPOONS CHOPPED FRESH MINT

1 EGG YOLK

1 GARLIC CLOVE, MINCED

1 TEASPOON CUMIN

¾ TEASPOON CINNAMON

⅛ TEASPOON GROUND CLOVES

SALT AND PEPPER, TO TASTE

2 TABLESPOONS EXTRA-VIRGIN OLIVE OIL

FOR THE SAUCE

1 TABLESPOON EXTRA-VIRGIN OLIVE OIL

1 LEEK, TRIMMED, HALVED, RINSED WELL, AND SLICED THIN

2 GARLIC CLOVES, MINCED

2 CUPS CHICKEN STOCK (SEE PAGE 482)

JUICE OF 2 LEMONS

1 CUP TAHINI PASTE

½ CUP FULL-FAT GREEK YOGURT

1 TABLESPOON BLACK SESAME SEEDS

SALT AND PEPPER, TO TASTE

SMOKED & SEARED EGGPLANT (SEE PAGE 349), FOR SERVING

1. To begin preparations for the meatballs, place the yogurt, bread crumbs, and water in a mixing bowl and work the mixture with a fork until it is pasty. Add the lamb, mint, egg yolk, garlic, cumin, cinnamon, and cloves, season the mixture with salt and pepper and work the mixture with your hands until well combined. Form the mixture into 12 meatballs.

2. Place the olive oil in a large skillet and warm it over medium heat. Working in batches to avoid crowding the pan, add the meatballs and cook until browned all over, about 6 minutes, turning them as needed. Remove the meatballs from the pan and set them aside.

3. To begin preparations for the sauce, place the olive oil in a medium saucepan and warm it over medium-high heat. Add the leek and cook, stirring occasionally, until it has softened, about 5 minutes. Add the garlic and cook, stirring continually, for 1 minute.

4. Add ½ cup of the stock and bring the mixture to a boil. Reduce the heat and simmer the mixture until it has reduced, about 10 minutes. Remove the pan from heat.

5. Place the remaining stock, the lemon juice, tahini, yogurt, and sesame seeds in a mixing bowl and stir until well combined. Add the mixture to the saucepan and bring the sauce to a simmer over low heat.

6. Add the meatballs to the sauce, cover the pan, and cook until they are cooked through, 8 to 10 minutes.

7. Season the sauce with salt and pepper and serve the meatballs alongside the eggplant.

Seafood Risotto

YIELD: 4 SERVINGS / **ACTIVE TIME:** 45 MINUTES / **TOTAL TIME:** 45 MINUTES

3 TO 4 CUPS CHICKEN STOCK (SEE PAGE 482)

1 CUP CLAM JUICE

2 TABLESPOONS EXTRA-VIRGIN OLIVE OIL

2 SHALLOTS, MINCED

2 CUPS ARBORIO RICE

¼ CUP WHITE WINE

SALT AND PEPPER, TO TASTE

½ LB. SCALLOPS

½ LB. SQUID, CLEANED (SEE PAGE 199), TENTACLES LEFT WHOLE, BODIES HALVED

½ LB. LARGE SHRIMP, SHELLS REMOVED, DEVEINED

2 TABLESPOONS TOMATO PASTE

1½ CUPS GRATED PARMESAN CHEESE

½ CUP CRÈME FRAÎCHE

¼ CUP CHOPPED FRESH CHIVES, FOR GARNISH

1. Place the stock and clam juice in a saucepan, bring the mixture to a simmer, and remove the pan from heat.

2. Place 1 tablespoon of the olive oil in a large, deep skillet and warm it over medium-high heat. Add the shallots and cook, stirring occasionally, until they start to soften, about 3 minutes.

3. Add the rice and cook, stirring frequently, for 2 minutes. Add the white wine and cook, stirring frequently, until the rice has absorbed the wine.

4. While stirring continually, add the stock-and-clam juice mixture 2 tablespoons at a time, waiting until each addition has been fully absorbed before adding more. Continue to add the mixture until the rice is al dente, about 15 minutes.

5. Place the remaining oil in another skillet and warm it over medium-high heat. Season the scallops, squid, and shrimp with salt, place them in the pan, and sear until cooked through, about 1½ minutes on each side. If the scallops are large, sear those separately. Transfer the seafood to a plate and set it aside.

6. Stir the tomato paste, Parmesan, and 2 tablespoons of the crème fraîche into the risotto. Season it with salt and pepper and ladle it into warmed bowls. Top each portion with the seafood, chives, and remaining crème fraîche and enjoy.

Lasagne alla Napoletana

YIELD: 6 SERVINGS / **ACTIVE TIME:** 1 HOUR / **TOTAL TIME:** 2 HOURS

FOR THE MEATBALLS

5½ OZ. GROUND BEEF

5½ OZ. GROUND PORK

2 EGGS

4 OZ. FRESH BREAD CRUMBS

2 OZ. PECORINO OR
PARMESAN CHEESE, GRATED

SALT AND PEPPER, TO TASTE

EXTRA-VIRGIN OLIVE OIL, AS
NEEDED

FOR THE LASAGNA

SALT, TO TASTE

1½ LBS. LASAGNA SHEETS

1 LB. RICOTTA CHEESE

4 CUPS RAGÙ NAPOLETANO
(SEE PAGE 206), PLUS MORE

FOR TOPPING

14 OZ. PROVOLA CHEESE,
CUBED

3 HARD-BOILED EGGS,
SLICED (OPTIONAL)

3 OZ. PECORINO OR
PARMESAN CHEESE,
GRATED, PLUS MORE FOR
TOPPING

1. To begin preparations for the meatballs, place all of the ingredients, except for the olive oil, in a mixing bowl and work the mixture until it is well combined. Form the mixture into small, walnut-sized meatballs.

2. Add olive oil to a large, deep skillet until it is about 1 inch deep and warm it over medium heat. Add the meatballs and cook until they are browned all over, turning them as necessary. Place the meatballs on paper towel–lined plates and let them drain.

3. Preheat the oven to 360°F. To begin preparations for the lasagna, bring water to a boil in a large saucepan. Add salt, let the water return to a full boil, and add a few of the lasagna sheets at a time to avoid overcrowding the pot. Cook until the lasagna sheets are al dente. Drain the lasagna sheets and set them on kitchen towels to dry.

4. Place the ricotta and 1 cup of the ragù in a large mixing bowl and stir to combine.

5. Spread some ragù over the bottom of a 13 x 9–inch baking dish. Arrange one-third of the lasagna sheets, one-third of the ricotta mixture, one-third of the provola, one-third of the meatballs, one-third of the eggs (if desired), and half of the pecorino in separate layers. Repeat the layering process two more times with the remaining ingredients.

6. Top the lasagna with additional ragù and pecorino, place it in the oven, and bake for 50 minutes.

7. Remove the lasagna from the oven and let it rest for 10 to 15 minutes before serving.

Maccheroni al Ferretto

YIELD: 1½ LBS. / **ACTIVE TIME:** 1 HOUR / **TOTAL TIME:** 1 HOUR AND 30 MINUTES

15.8 OZ. FINELY GROUND DURUM WHEAT FLOUR, PLUS MORE AS NEEDED

7.9 OZ. WATER, AT ROOM TEMPERATURE

PINCH OF FINE SEA SALT, PLUS MORE AS NEEDED

1. Place all of the ingredients in a large bowl and work the mixture until it starts to come together as a dough.

2. Transfer the dough to a flour-dusted work surface and knead it energetically until it is a smooth and homogeneous dough, about 10 minutes.

3. Cover the dough with plastic wrap and let it rest at room temperature for 30 minutes.

4. Tear the dough into small pieces and form them into logs that are about ⅓ inch thick. Cut the logs into 2-inch-long pieces.

5. Coat a long, thin metal rod or a wooden skewer with flour. Working with one piece of pasta at a time, press the implement into the center of the log, creating a hollow. Roll the implement back and forth until the pasta closes around it. Gently remove the maccheroni from the implement, taking care not to unfold it. Transfer the maccheroni to a flour-dusted baking sheet and let them dry.

6. To cook the maccheroni, bring water to a boil in a large saucepan. Add salt, let the water return to a boil, and add the maccheroni. Let them float to the surface and cook for another 5 minutes.

Eggplant Parmesan alla Napoletana

YIELD: 4 SERVINGS / **ACTIVE TIME:** 1 HOUR / **TOTAL TIME:** 2 HOURS AND 30 MINUTES

4 LARGE EGGPLANTS

SALT, TO TASTE

EXTRA-VIRGIN OLIVE OIL, AS NEEDED

4 EGGS

ALL-PURPOSE FLOUR, AS NEEDED

3½ CUPS TOMATO SAUCE (SEE PAGE 504)

9 OZ. FRESH MOZZARELLA CHEESE, DRAINED AND SLICED

2 HANDFULS OF FRESH BASIL

1⅓ CUPS GRATED PARMESAN CHEESE, PLUS MORE FOR TOPPING

1. Slice the eggplants thin lengthwise; if you have a mandoline available, use it on a rather thick setting. Layer the sliced eggplants in a colander, seasoning each layer with coarse salt. Fill a large saucepan with water and place the pan on top of the eggplants. Let the eggplants drain for 1 hour.

2. Rinse the eggplants and squeeze them to remove as much water as possible. Place the eggplants on kitchen towels and let them dry.

3. Preheat the oven to 375°F. Add olive oil to a narrow, deep, heavy-bottomed saucepan with high edges until it is about 2 inches deep and warm it to 350°F.

4. Place the eggs in a bowl, season them lightly with fine salt, and whisk until scrambled. Place flour in a shallow bowl and dredge the eggplants in the flour and then the egg until they are completely coated.

5. Gently slip the eggplants into the hot oil and fry until they are golden brown, working in batches to avoid crowding the pot. Transfer the fried eggplants to a paper towel–lined plate to drain.

6. Cover the bottom of a 13 x 9–inch baking dish with some of the tomato sauce. Arrange the eggplants, mozzarella, basil, Parmesan, and tomato sauce in individual layers in the dish, continuing the layering process until everything has been used up.

7. Top the dish with additional Parmesan, place it in the oven, and bake until the cheese and sauce start to bubble, about 25 minutes.

8. Remove the dish from the oven and let it rest for at least 30 minutes before slicing and serving.

Mahshi Laban

YIELD: 6 SERVINGS / **ACTIVE TIME:** 1 HOUR AND 30 MINUTES / **TOTAL TIME:** 2 HOURS AND 30 MINUTES

2½ TEASPOONS KOSHER SALT

1 CUP BASMATI RICE, RINSED AND DRAINED

9 ZUCCHINI

¾ CUP CANNED CHICKPEAS, DRAINED AND RINSED

½ CUP SALTED BUTTER, SOFTENED AND CUT INTO ½-INCH CUBES

¼ TEASPOON BLACK PEPPER

2 CUPS WATER

JUICE OF 1 LARGE LEMON

LABNEH (SEE PAGE 67), FOR SERVING

CUCUMBERS, SLICED, FOR SERVING

1. Bring water to a boil in a small saucepan and add 1 teaspoon of the salt and the rice. Cook the rice for 5 minutes and drain; the rice will only be partially cooked. Transfer the rice to a large mixing bowl and set it aside.

2. Trim about ½ inch from each end of the zucchini. Partially peel the zucchini with a striped pattern and then cut them in half crosswise. Using a zucchini or apple corer, carefully hollow out the inside of the zucchini, leaving a wall that is about ¼ inch thick. Set the hollowed-out zucchini aside and reserve the pulp for another preparation.

3. Add the chickpeas, half of the butter cubes, 1 teaspoon of the salt, and the pepper to the rice and stir until well combined, making sure the butter is evenly distributed.

4. Preheat the oven to 350°F. Using your hands, fill each piece of zucchini three-quarters of the way with the rice mixture. Once each zucchini is filled, place them side by side in one layer in the bottom of a large Dutch oven. Sprinkle the remaining salt over the zucchini.

5. Distribute the remaining butter over the stuffed zucchini and then fill in any empty gaps with the remaining rice mixture. Place a small plate or saucepan lid (the lid should be small enough to fit) over the stuffed zucchini to weigh them down. Cover the pot with its own lid, place it over low heat, and cook for about 10 minutes, until the zucchini release some water.

6. In a bowl, combine the water with the lemon juice. Remove the lid of the Dutch oven and add the mixture to the pot until the water reaches the level of the small plate or saucepan lid that is weighing down the zucchini. Place the lid back on the Dutch oven and transfer the pot to the oven. Cook for 1 hour or until the liquid is absorbed.

7. Remove the Dutch oven's lid and the small plate or saucepan lid. Set the oven to broil, or 500°F, and cook until the tops of the zucchini are golden brown. Remove from the oven and enjoy with Labneh and cucumbers.

Sumac & Lime Mahimahi

YIELD: 2 SERVINGS / **ACTIVE TIME:** 25 MINUTES / **TOTAL TIME:** 3 HOURS

JUICE OF 2 LIMES

1 TABLESPOON SUMAC

1 TEASPOON HONEY

1 TEASPOON KOSHER SALT

1 GARLIC CLOVE, MINCED

2 (6 OZ.) MAHIMAHI FILLETS

1 TABLESPOON EXTRA-VIRGIN OLIVE OIL

COUSCOUS, FOR SERVING

1. In a small bowl, whisk together the lime juice, sumac, honey, salt, and garlic. Add the mahimahi and stir until the fillets are coated. Chill in the refrigerator for 2 hours.

2. Place the olive oil in a large skillet and warm it over medium heat. Add the mahimahi to the pan and cook until it is browned on both sides and flakes easily at the touch of a fork, 8 to 10 minutes.

3. Remove the mahimahi from the pan and serve over couscous.

Braised Halibut with Crispy Polenta Cakes

YIELD: 4 SERVINGS / **ACTIVE TIME:** 30 MINUTES / **TOTAL TIME:** 1 HOUR AND 30 MINUTES

3 TABLESPOONS EXTRA-VIRGIN OLIVE OIL

1½ LBS. CENTER-CUT HALIBUT FILLETS

SALT AND PEPPER, TO TASTE

1 LEEK, TRIMMED, HALVED, RINSED WELL, AND SLICED THIN

2 TEASPOONS DIJON MUSTARD

½ CUP WHITE WINE

FRESH PARSLEY, CHOPPED, FOR GARNISH

CRISPY POLENTA CAKES (SEE PAGE 361), FOR SERVING

LEMON WEDGES, FOR SERVING

1. Place the olive oil in a Dutch oven and warm it over medium-high heat. Pat the halibut dry with a paper towel and season it with salt and pepper. Place the halibut in the pan and sear it until the bottom is golden brown, about 5 minutes.

2. Gently lift the halibut and remove it from the pan. Transfer it to a plate and set it aside.

3. Add the leek and cook, stirring occasionally, until it starts to brown, about 10 minutes.

4. Stir in the mustard and white wine and bring to a simmer. Return the halibut to the pan, seared side facing up. Cover the pot and cook until the halibut is cooked through (internal temperature 140°F), about 8 minutes.

5. Remove the halibut from the pot and set it aside. Place the Dutch oven over high heat and cook until the sauce has thickened, about 2 minutes. Transfer to a serving dish, place the halibut on top, and garnish with parsley. Serve with the Crispy Polenta Cakes and lemon wedges and enjoy.

Roasted Grapes & Sausage

YIELD: 4 SERVINGS / **ACTIVE TIME:** 10 MINUTES / **TOTAL TIME:** 45 MINUTES

1½ LBS. SPICY SAUSAGE

1 BUNCH OF MUSCAT GRAPES

6 OZ. FRESH MOZZARELLA CHEESE, TORN

2 TABLESPOONS BALSAMIC GLAZE (SEE PAGE 508)

1. Preheat the oven to 500°F. Cut the sausage into ¼-inch-thick slices, place them in a baking dish, and add the grapes. Toss to evenly distribute.

2. Place the baking dish in the oven and cook until the sausage is well browned and cooked through, 15 to 20 minutes.

3. Remove from the oven and transfer the mixture to a serving platter.

4. Sprinkle the mozzarella over the sausage and grapes, drizzle the Balsamic Glaze over the top, and enjoy.

Calamari Ripieni

YIELD: 4 SERVINGS / **ACTIVE TIME:** 30 MINUTES / **TOTAL TIME:** 1 HOUR

½ CUP EXTRA-VIRGIN OLIVE OIL

8 SQUID, CLEANED (SEE PAGE 199)

½ CUP PITTED BLACK OLIVES, MINCED

1 TABLESPOON CAPERS IN BRINE, DRAINED AND RINSED

10 ANCHOVIES IN OLIVE OIL, DRAINED AND CHOPPED

3 GARLIC CLOVES, FINELY MINCED

2 TABLESPOONS FINELY CHOPPED FRESH PARSLEY, PLUS MORE FOR TOPPING

¼ CUP BREAD CRUMBS, PLUS MORE FOR TOPPING

SALT AND PEPPER, TO TASTE

1. Preheat the oven to 390°F. Place 2 tablespoons of olive oil in a large skillet and warm it over medium-low heat. Dice the squid tentacles, pat them dry, and add them to the pan. Cook, stirring frequently, until they are cooked through, about 2 minutes. Remove the tentacles from the pan and place them in a bowl.

2. Add 2 tablespoons of olive oil, the olives, capers, anchovies, garlic, parsley, and bread crumbs to the bowl, season the mixture with salt and pepper, and stir to combine.

3. Place the mixture on the squid bodies, roll them up, and secure them with toothpicks.

4. Coat a baking dish with some of the remaining olive oil. Place the squid in the dish, season with salt, top with additional parsley and bread crumbs, and drizzle the remaining olive oil over the top.

5. Place the squid in the oven and bake until they just start to brown, 15 to 20 minutes. Take care not to overcook the squid, as they will harden. Remove the squid from the oven and serve immediately.

Sumac & Lime Mahimahi
SEE PAGE 192

Fusilli al Ferro

YIELD: 1½ LBS. / **ACTIVE TIME:** 1 HOUR / **TOTAL TIME:** 1 HOUR AND 30 MINUTES

15.8 OZ. FINELY GROUND DURUM WHEAT FLOUR, PLUS MORE AS NEEDED

7.9 OZ. WATER, AT ROOM TEMPERATURE

PINCH OF FINE SEA SALT, PLUS MORE AS NEEDED

1. Place all of the ingredients in a large bowl and work the mixture until it starts to come together as a dough.

2. Transfer the dough to a flour-dusted work surface and knead it energetically until it is a smooth and homogeneous dough, about 10 minutes.

3. Cover the dough with plastic wrap and let it rest at room temperature for 30 minutes.

4. Tear the dough into small pieces and form them into logs that are about ⅕ inch thick. Cut the logs into 3-inch-long pieces.

5. Coat a long, thin metal rod or a wooden skewer with flour. Working with 1 piece of pasta at a time, wrap it around the implement to form it into a spiral. Gently remove the fusilli from the implement, taking care not to undo the spiral. Transfer the fusilli to a flour-dusted baking sheet and let them dry.

6. To cook the fusilli, bring water to a boil in a large saucepan. Add salt, let the water return to a boil, and add the fusilli. Let them float to the surface and cook for another 3 minutes.

Roasted Eggplant Pitas

YIELD: 6 SERVINGS / **ACTIVE TIME:** 30 MINUTES / **TOTAL TIME:** 1 HOUR AND 30 MINUTES

¼ CUP EXTRA-VIRGIN OLIVE OIL

1 EGGPLANT, TRIMMED, SEEDED, AND CHOPPED INTO ½-INCH CUBES

2 GARLIC CLOVES, MINCED

SALT AND PEPPER, TO TASTE

1 CUP CHERRY TOMATOES, HALVED

3 PICKLE SPEARS, SLICED THIN

¼ CUP CHOPPED RED ONION

1 SCALLION, TRIMMED AND SLICED THIN

¼ CUP MARINATED ARTICHOKES (SEE PAGE 61), QUARTERED

1 TABLESPOON CHOPPED FRESH PARSLEY

1 TEASPOON ZA'ATAR (SEE PAGE 501)

6 PIECES OF PITA BREAD (SEE PAGE 338)

1 CUP HUMMUS (SEE PAGE 15)

6 HARD-BOILED EGGS

½ CUP TAHINI & YOGURT SAUCE (SEE PAGE 495)

½ CUP GREEN ZHUG (SEE PAGE 500)

1. Place 2 tablespoons of the olive oil in a large saucepan and warm it over medium heat. Add the eggplant and cook, stirring occasionally, until it has browned and softened, about 10 minutes. Add the garlic and cook, stirring continually, for 1 minute.

2. Season the mixture with salt and pepper and remove the pan from heat. Let the mixture cool.

3. Place the tomatoes, pickles, onion, scallion, artichokes, parsley, Za'atar, and remaining olive oil in a bowl and stir to combine. Refrigerate the mixture for at least 30 minutes.

4. Build your desired sandwich from the eggplant, tomato-and-artichoke mixture, and any or all of the remaining ingredients.

Smoked Pork Belly in Pickled Applesauce

YIELD: 2 SERVINGS / **ACTIVE TIME:** 30 MINUTES / **TOTAL TIME:** 11 HOURS

APPLEWOOD CHIPS, AS NEEDED

½ CUP SHAWARMA SEASONING (SEE PAGE 199)

1 TABLESPOON BROWN SUGAR

6 OZ. CENTER-CUT PORK BELLY

½ CUP PICKLED APPLESAUCE (SEE PAGE 519)

1. Preheat your smoker to 225°F, using the applewood chips.

2. In a small bowl, combine the Shawarma Seasoning and brown sugar. Rub the mixture all over the pork belly and place it on a rack in the smoker, fat side up. Smoke until the pork belly is crispy and tender, about 10 hours.

3. Remove the pork belly from the smoker and let it rest for 30 minutes.

4. Divide the Pickled Applesauce between the serving plates. Slice the pork belly, arrange the slices on top of the applesauce, and enjoy.

Seppie con i Piselli

YIELD: 4 SERVINGS / **ACTIVE TIME:** 30 MINUTES / **TOTAL TIME:** 1 HOUR AND 10 MINUTES

2.2 LBS. SQUID

¼ CUP EXTRA-VIRGIN OLIVE OIL

1 WHITE ONION, FINELY DICED

1 CUP VEGETABLE STOCK (SEE PAGE 484)

SALT AND PEPPER, TO TASTE

¼ CUP WHITE WINE

1 LB. PEAS

1 LB. WHOLE PEELED TOMATOES, CRUSHED

2 TABLESPOONS CHOPPED FRESH PARSLEY

1. To clean the squid, find the bone and make a transversal cut to eliminate it. Remove the internal organs of the squid and the ink sac (if present). Separate the head from the body and remove the innards of the head. Remove the tentacles and the beak that is positioned in the center of the tentacles. Make a small incision on the back and remove the skin. Remove the eyes, rinse the squid, and cut the body into wide strips. Set the strips and tentacles aside.

2. Place the olive oil in a large skillet and warm it over low heat. Add the onion and cook, stirring occasionally, until it has softened, about 6 minutes.

3. Add half of the broth and the squid, season with salt and pepper, and raise the heat to medium. Cook until the liquid has evaporated.

4. Add the wine and cook until it has evaporated.

5. Add the peas, tomatoes, and remaining broth, cover the pan, and reduce the heat to low. Cook for 15 minutes.

6. Stir in the parsley and serve.

Agnello alla Gallurese

YIELD: 5 SERVINGS / **ACTIVE TIME:** 20 MINUTES / **TOTAL TIME:** 1 HOUR AND 20 MINUTES

7 TABLESPOONS UNSALTED BUTTER

3 LBS. BONELESS LEG OF LAMB, TRIMMED AND CUT INTO 2-INCH CUBES

SALT AND PEPPER, TO TASTE

2 GARLIC CLOVES

2 JUNIPER BERRIES

2 SPRIGS OF FRESH ROSEMARY

2 SPRIGS OF FRESH THYME

4 BAY LEAVES

6 POTATOES, PEELED AND CUBED

½ CUP PITTED GREEN OLIVES

1. Place the butter in a large skillet and melt it over medium heat. Season the lamb with salt and pepper and add it to the pan with the garlic and juniper berries. Sear the lamb until it is browned all over, turning it as necessary.

2. Add the rosemary, thyme, bay leaves, and potatoes, season the dish with salt and pepper, and cook, stirring occasionally, for 5 minutes.

3. Add water until the lamb is covered and bring to a simmer. Reduce the heat to medium-low, cover the pan, and cook for 30 minutes.

4. Remove the rosemary, thyme, and bay leaves and discard them. Add the olives and cook until the lamb and potatoes are tender, about 20 minutes, stirring occasionally. Serve immediately.

Mussels Zafferano

YIELD: 4 SERVINGS / **ACTIVE TIME:** 20 MINUTES / **TOTAL TIME:** 40 MINUTES

7 TABLESPOONS EXTRA-VIRGIN OLIVE OIL

½ ONION, CHOPPED

1 BAY LEAF

4½ LBS. MUSSELS, RINSED WELL AND DEBEARDED

1 TABLESPOON SAFFRON THREADS

1 TEASPOON CORNSTARCH (OPTIONAL)

SALT, TO TASTE

FRESH PARSLEY, FINELY CHOPPED, FOR GARNISH

1. Place 2 tablespoons of olive oil in a Dutch oven and warm it over medium heat. Add the onion and bay leaf and cook, stirring occasionally, until the onion has softened, about 5 minutes.

2. Add the mussels, cover the pot, and cook until the majority of the mussels have opened, 5 to 7 minutes. Discard any mussels that did not open. Strain the mussels through a fine-mesh sieve, reserving any liquid.

3. Place the reserved liquid in a large saucepan and bring it to a boil. Add the saffron and remaining olive oil and whisk until the mixture has emulsified. If desired, add the cornstarch to thicken the emulsion.

4. Season the emulsion with salt, drizzle it over the mussels, garnish with parsley, and enjoy.

Stuffed Acorn Squash

YIELD: 2 SERVINGS / **ACTIVE TIME:** 40 MINUTES / **TOTAL TIME:** 2 HOURS AND 30 MINUTES

1 ACORN SQUASH

2 TABLESPOONS MOLASSES

1 TABLESPOON KOSHER SALT

2 TABLESPOONS EXTRA-VIRGIN OLIVE OIL

¼ CUP SPLIT PEAS

½ CUP COOKED BASMATI RICE

1 TEASPOON CINNAMON

½ TEASPOON GROUND CLOVES

½ TEASPOON FRESHLY GRATED NUTMEG

PINCH OF CAYENNE PEPPER

1 TABLESPOON UNSALTED BUTTER

1. Preheat the oven to 425°F. Halve the squash and remove the top and seeds from it. Discard the top and set the seeds aside.

2. Rub the cut sides of the squash with the molasses and sprinkle half of the salt over them. Rub the outside of the squash with some of the olive oil and place the squash on a baking sheet, cut sides up. Place it in the oven and roast until tender, about 40 minutes.

3. While the squash is in the oven, clean the seeds, rinse them, and pat them dry. Place on a baking sheet, drizzle the remaining olive oil over them, and season with the remaining salt. Place the seeds in the oven and roast until golden brown, about 20 minutes, stirring halfway through.

4. Bring approximately 2 cups of water to a boil in a small saucepan. Add the split peas and boil them until tender, about 30 minutes. Drain and stir the peas into the rice. Add the cinnamon, cloves, nutmeg, cayenne, and butter and stir to combine.

5. Remove the squash and seeds from the oven. Fill the squash's cavities with the rice mixture, garnish each portion with the roasted seeds, and enjoy.

Fregola

YIELD: 5 SERVINGS / **ACTIVE TIME:** 1 HOUR / **TOTAL TIME:** 1 HOUR AND 30 MINUTES

¾ TEASPOON SAFFRON

9½ OZ. LUKEWARM WATER (90°F)

15.8 OZ. COARSE DURUM WHEAT FLOUR

1. Line a baking sheet with parchment paper. Place the saffron and water in a bowl and let it steep for 30 minutes.

2. Place 2 tablespoons of flour and a tablespoon of saffron water in a terracotta dish or shallow, ceramic bowl. Rub the moistened flour continuously against the bottom of the dish until it comes together in ⅛-inch balls. Transfer the fregola to the baking sheet.

3. Repeat Steps 1 and 2 until all of the flour has been used up.

4. To cook the fregola, preheat the oven to 390°F. Place it in the oven and bake until it is lightly browned, about 20 minutes.

Lamb Kebabs

YIELD: 2 TO 4 SERVINGS / **ACTIVE TIME:** 30 MINUTES / **TOTAL TIME:** 2 HOURS

¾ CUP EXTRA-VIRGIN OLIVE OIL

¼ CUP FRESH MINT LEAVES

2 TEASPOONS CHOPPED FRESH ROSEMARY

2 GARLIC CLOVES, SMASHED

1 TEASPOON KOSHER SALT, PLUS MORE TO TASTE

ZEST AND JUICE OF 1 LEMON

¼ TEASPOON BLACK PEPPER, PLUS MORE TO TASTE

2 LBS. BONELESS LEG OF LAMB, TRIMMED AND CUT INTO 1-INCH CUBES

1 ZUCCHINI, CUT INTO 1-INCH CUBES

1 SUMMER SQUASH, CUT INTO 1-INCH CUBES

1 RED BELL PEPPER, STEM AND SEEDS REMOVED, CUT INTO 1-INCH SQUARES

1 GREEN BELL PEPPER, STEM AND SEEDS REMOVED, CUT INTO 1-INCH SQUARES

2 RED ONIONS, CUT INTO 1-INCH CUBES

1. Place ½ cup of the olive oil, the mint, rosemary, garlic, salt, lemon zest, lemon juice, and pepper in a blender and blitz until smooth.

2. Place the lamb in a bowl, add half of the marinade, and toss to coat. Cover the bowl with plastic wrap, place the lamb in the refrigerator, and marinate for 1 hour, stirring every 15 minutes.

3. Place the vegetables in another bowl, add the remaining marinade, and toss to coat. Cover the bowl with plastic wrap and let the vegetables marinate at room temperature for 1 hour.

4. Preheat the oven to 350°F. Thread the lamb onto skewers, making sure to leave a bit of space between each piece. Thread the vegetable mixture onto skewers, making sure to alternate between the vegetables.

5. Place the skewers in a 13 x 9–inch baking dish and pour the marinade over them. Cover the dish and let the skewers marinate at room temperature for 30 minutes.

6. Remove the skewers from the marinade and pat them dry. Place 2 tablespoons of the olive oil in a large skillet and warm it over medium-high heat. Add the vegetable skewers to the pan and cook until golden brown all over, about 5 minutes, turning them as necessary.

7. Place the vegetable skewers on a baking sheet, place them in the oven, and roast until the vegetables are tender, 8 to 10 minutes. Remove the skewers from the oven and set them aside.

8. Place the remaining olive oil in a large, clean skillet and warm it over medium-high heat. Add the lamb kebabs and cook until they are browned all over and medium-rare (internal temperature of 120°F), about 8 minutes, turning them as necessary.

9. Let the cooked lamb rest for 5 minutes before serving.

Cavatelli

YIELD: 1½ LBS. / **ACTIVE TIME:** 1 HOUR / **TOTAL TIME:** 1 HOUR AND 30 MINUTES

15.8 OZ. FINELY GROUND DURUM WHEAT FLOUR, PLUS MORE AS NEEDED

7.9 OZ. WATER, AT ROOM TEMPERATURE

PINCH OF FINE SEA SALT, PLUS MORE AS NEEDED

1. Place all of the ingredients in a large bowl and work the mixture until it starts to come together as a dough.

2. Transfer the dough to a flour-dusted work surface and knead it energetically until it is a smooth and homogeneous dough, about 10 minutes.

3. Cover the dough with plastic wrap and let it rest at room temperature for 30 minutes.

4. Tear the dough into small pieces and form them into logs that are about ¼ inch thick. Cut the logs into 1-inch-long pieces.

5. Press down on one side of the cavatelli with the tips of your index and middle fingers, making a movement that first pushes it forward and then comes back, rolling the pasta so that it forms a hollow in the middle. Transfer the cavatelli to a flour-dusted baking sheet and let them dry.

6. To cook the cavatelli, bring water to a boil in a large saucepan. Add salt, let the water return to a boil, and add the cavatelli. Cook until they are al dente, about 8 minutes.

Lamb Kebabs
SEE PAGE 202

Pasta al Ragù Napoletano

YIELD: 6 SERVINGS / **ACTIVE TIME:** 1 HOUR / **TOTAL TIME:** 7 TO 8 HOURS

1 CUP EXTRA-VIRGIN OLIVE OIL

2 YELLOW ONIONS, FINELY DICED

3 (1 LB.) PIECES OF STEW BEEF

6 PORK RIBS

1 CUP RED WINE

1 TABLESPOON TOMATO PASTE

4 LBS. WHOLE PEELED TOMATOES, LIGHTLY CRUSHED

SALT, TO TASTE

1½ LBS. ZITI OR RIGATONI

2 OZ. PECORINO OR PARMESAN CHEESE, GRATED

HANDFUL OF FRESH BASIL

1. Place the olive oil in a large saucepan and warm it over medium heat. Add the onions, beef, and pork ribs and cook until the onions have caramelized and the meat is browned all over, about 1½ hours. You will need to stay close to the pan, turning the meat as needed and increasing or decreasing the heat accordingly.

2. Add the wine and cook until it has nearly evaporated. Remove the meat from the pan and set it aside.

3. Reduce the heat to low, add the tomato paste, and cook, stirring occasionally, for 2 minutes.

4. Add the tomatoes, season with salt, partially cover the pan, and cook, stirring every 15 minutes, for 3 hours.

5. Return the meat to the pan and cook the sauce until it changes from bright red to a deep maroon and the flavor develops to your liking, 3 to 4 hours.

6. Bring water to a boil in a large saucepan. Add salt, let the water return to a full boil, and add the pasta. Cook until the pasta is al dente.

7. Drain the pasta, place it in a serving dish, and add some of the sauce and the smaller pieces of meat along with half of the pecorino and the basil. Toss to combine and top with the remaining pecorino.

8. Serve the larger pieces of meat and remaining sauce following the pasta.

Scarola Mbuttunat

YIELD: 4 SERVINGS / **ACTIVE TIME:** 30 MINUTES / **TOTAL TIME:** 1 HOUR

SALT, TO TASTE

4 SMALL HEADS OF ESCAROLE

5 TABLESPOONS EXTRA-VIRGIN OLIVE OIL, PLUS MORE FOR TOPPING

1 GARLIC CLOVE, MINCED

RED PEPPER FLAKES, TO TASTE

5 ANCHOVIES IN OLIVE OIL, DRAINED AND CHOPPED

½ CUP PITTED BLACK OLIVES, CHOPPED

½ CUP PITTED GREEN OLIVES, CHOPPED

2 TABLESPOONS CAPERS, RINSED IF PACKED IN SALT OR DRAINED IF PACKED IN BRINE

½ CUP RAISINS, SOAKED IN WARM WATER FOR 10 MINUTES, DRAINED, AND SQUEEZED

3 TABLESPOONS PINE NUTS

2 TABLESPOONS CHOPPED WALNUTS

2 TABLESPOONS CHOPPED FRESH PARSLEY

2 OZ. PECORINO CHEESE, SHAVED

½ CUP BREAD CRUMBS, PLUS MORE FOR TOPPING

1. Preheat the oven to 480°F. Bring salted water to a boil in a large saucepan. Remove the core and outer leaves from the heads of escarole and rinse them under cold water. Tie the heads of escarole tightly with kitchen twine, place them in the boiling water, and boil for 2 minutes. Drain the escarole and let it cool.

2. Place the olive oil in a large skillet and warm it over medium heat. Add the garlic and red pepper flakes and cook for 1 minute. Add the anchovies, olives, capers, raisins, pine nuts, walnuts, and parsley, season with salt, and cook for 5 minutes.

3. Add the pecorino and bread crumbs and cook for 2 minutes.

4. Gently open the heads of escarole and fill them with the olive mixture. Tie the stuffed escarole closed with kitchen twine and place it in a baking dish.

5. Drizzle olive oil over the stuffed escarole and sprinkle bread crumbs on top. Place the stuffed escarole in the oven and roast until it is golden brown, about 20 minutes.

6. Remove the stuffed escarole from the oven and let it cool slightly before serving.

Busiate

YIELD: 1½ LBS. / **ACTIVE TIME:** 1 HOUR / **TOTAL TIME:** 1 HOUR AND 30 MINUTES

15.8 OZ. FINELY GROUND DURUM WHEAT FLOUR, PLUS MORE AS NEEDED

7.9 OZ. WATER, AT ROOM TEMPERATURE

PINCH OF FINE SEA SALT, PLUS MORE AS NEEDED

1. Place all of the ingredients in a large bowl and work the mixture until it starts to come together as a dough.

2. Transfer the dough to a flour-dusted work surface and knead it energetically until it is a smooth and homogeneous dough, about 10 minutes.

3. Cover the dough with plastic wrap and let it rest at room temperature for 30 minutes.

4. Place the dough on a flour-dusted work surface, tear small pieces from it, and shape them into ¼-inch-thick logs. Cut the logs into 6-inch-long strands.

5. Coat a long, thin metal rod or a wooden skewer with flour. Working with one piece of pasta at a time, wrap it around the implement to form it into a long spiral. Gently remove the busiate from the implement, taking care not to undo the spiral. Transfer it to a flour-dusted baking sheet and let it dry.

6. To cook the busiate, bring water to a boil in a large saucepan. Add salt, let the water return to a boil, and add the busiate. Cook until they are al dente, 7 to 8 minutes.

Pizza di Scarola

YIELD: 6 SERVINGS / **ACTIVE TIME:** 40 MINUTES / **TOTAL TIME:** 4 HOURS

FOR THE DOUGH

1 SACHET OF ACTIVE DRY YEAST

15.8 OZ. LUKEWARM WATER (90°F)

1 TABLESPOON SUGAR

28.2 OZ. ALL-PURPOSE FLOUR, PLUS MORE AS NEEDED

2 TABLESPOONS EXTRA-VIRGIN OLIVE OIL

⅔ OZ. FINE SEA SALT

FOR THE FILLING

5 TABLESPOONS EXTRA-VIRGIN OLIVE OIL, PLUS MORE AS NEEDED

1 GARLIC CLOVE, MINCED

3 ANCHOVIES IN OLIVE OIL, DRAINED AND CHOPPED

RED PEPPER FLAKES, TO TASTE

1 LARGE HEAD OF ESCAROLE, RINSED WELL AND CHOPPED

½ CUP PITTED BLACK OLIVES

2 TABLESPOONS CAPERS, RINSED IF PACKED IN SALT OR DRAINED IF PACKED IN BRINE

SALT, TO TASTE

1. To begin preparations for the dough, place the yeast, water, and sugar in a large bowl, gently stir to combine, and let the mixture sit until it starts to foam, about 10 minutes.

2. Add the flour and work the mixture until it just comes together as a dough.

3. Add the olive oil and salt and knead the dough until it is smooth and elastic.

4. Shape the dough into a round, place it in a clean bowl, and cover it with plastic wrap. Let the dough rest at room temperature until it has almost doubled in size, about 3 hours.

5. To begin preparations for the filling, place the olive oil in a large skillet and warm it over medium-low heat. Add the garlic and anchovies, season with red pepper flakes, and cook for 2 minutes.

6. Add the escarole, cover the pan with a lid, and cook until the escarole has wilted, about 15 minutes.

7. Add the olives and capers, lightly season the mixture with salt, and cook for 5 more minutes. Remove the pan from heat and let the filling cool.

8. Preheat the oven to 430°F. Place the dough on a flour-dusted work surface and divide it into 2 pieces, one larger than the other. Roll out the larger piece into a ¼-inch-thick, 10-inch round.

9. Coat a 9-inch pie plate with olive oil and place the 10-inch round over it. Place the filling on top of the dough, roll out the remaining piece of dough, and place it on top of the filling. Fold the bottom crust down over the top crust and press down on the seam to seal. Brush the top crust with olive oil and place the scarola in the oven.

10. Bake until the scarola is golden brown, about 30 minutes. Remove it from the oven and enjoy warm or at room temperature.

THE ENCYCLOPEDIA OF MEDITERRANEAN

Culurgiones

YIELD: 40 CULURGIONES / **ACTIVE TIME:** 2 HOURS / **TOTAL TIME:** 24 HOURS

FOR THE FILLING

2 TABLESPOONS EXTRA VIRGIN OLIVE OIL

2 GARLIC CLOVES, PEELED

KOSHER SALT, TO TASTE

1½ LBS. POTATOES, PEELED

20 FRESH MINT LEAVES

1½ CUPS GRATED PECORINO CHEESE

FOR THE DOUGH

8.8 OZ. FINELY GROUND DURUM WHEAT FLOUR, PLUS MORE AS NEEDED

4½ OZ. ALL-PURPOSE FLOUR

5.8 OZ. LUKEWARM WATER (90°F)

1 TABLESPOON EXTRA VIRGIN OLIVE OIL

¼ TEASPOON FINE SEA SALT, PLUS MORE AS NEEDED

1. The day before you are going to prepare the culurgiones, prepare the filling. Place the olive oil and garlic in an airtight container and let the mixture steep for 6 hours.

2. Bring water to a boil in a large saucepan. Add salt and the potatoes and cook until they are tender. Drain the potatoes, place them in a bowl, and mash until they are smooth. Add the mint and pecorino and stir to incorporate. Strain the olive oil into the filling and stir to incorporate. Chill the filling in the refrigerator over night.

3. Remove the filling from the refrigerator and let it rest at room temperature.

4. To begin preparations for the dough, place all of the ingredients in a large bowl and work the mixture until it starts to come together as a dough.

5. Transfer the dough to a flour-dusted work surface and knead it energetically until it is a smooth and homogeneous dough, about 10 minutes.

6. Cover the dough with plastic wrap and let it rest at room temperature for 30 minutes.

7. Place the dough on a flour-dusted work surface and roll it into a ⅒-inch-thick sheet (you can also use a pasta maker to do this). Cut the dough into 5-inch rounds.

8. Form tablespoons of the filling into patties and place them in the center of the rounds. Fold the dough over the filling to form half-moons.

9. To seal the culurgiones and give them the correct shape, it's best to watch a video, of which there are many online. You want to fold in one end of each one, and then fold one side over the other, making pleats as you do to seal in the filling.

10. To cook the culurgiones, bring water to a boil in a large saucepan. Add salt, let the water return to a boil, and add the culurgiones. Cook for about 6 minutes.

Malloreddus

YIELD: 1½ LBS. / **ACTIVE TIME:** 1 HOUR / **TOTAL TIME:** 3 HOURS

15.8 OZ. FINELY GROUND DURUM WHEAT FLOUR, PLUS MORE AS NEEDED

7.9 OZ. LUKEWARM WATER (90°F)

PINCH OF FINE SEA SALT, PLUS MORE AS NEEDED

1. Place all of the ingredients in a large bowl and work the mixture until it starts to come together as a dough.

2. Transfer the dough to a flour-dusted work surface and knead it energetically until it is a smooth and homogeneous dough, about 10 minutes.

3. Cover the dough with plastic wrap and let it rest at room temperature for 15 minutes.

4. Divide the dough into 3 pieces. Cover 2 pieces with plastic wrap and place the other on a flour-dusted work surface.

5. Shape the dough into a ⅖-inch-thick log and cut it into ⅖-inch-long pieces.

6. Roll the pieces over a gnocchi board or a fork while gently pressing down on them to shape the malloreddus. Place them on a flour-dusted baking sheet, cover with a kitchen towel, and let them rest for 1 hour.

7. Repeat Steps 5 and 6 with the remaining pieces of dough.

8. To cook the malloreddus, bring water to a boil in a large saucepan. Add salt, let the water return to a boil, and add the malloreddus. Let them rise to the surface and cook for 1 more minute.

Short Ribs with Braised Cauliflower & Stuffed Tomatoes

YIELD: 4 SERVINGS / **ACTIVE TIME:** 45 MINUTES / **TOTAL TIME:** 4 HOURS

2 TABLESPOONS EXTRA-VIRGIN OLIVE OIL

3 LBS. BONE-IN SHORT RIBS

SALT AND PEPPER, TO TASTE

1 ONION, CHOPPED

1 CARROT, PEELED AND CHOPPED

2 CELERY STALKS, CHOPPED

4 GARLIC CLOVES, MINCED

1 TABLESPOON TOMATO PASTE

1 TABLESPOON RAS EL HANOUT (SEE PAGE 505)

1 TEASPOON FRESH THYME

½ CUP RED WINE

2 CUPS PRUNE JUICE

2 CUPS BEEF STOCK (SEE PAGE 484)

1 BAY LEAF

1 CUP PRUNES

2 TEASPOONS RED WINE VINEGAR

FRESH CILANTRO, CHOPPED, FOR GARNISH

SESAME SEEDS, TOASTED, FOR GARNISH

BRAISED CAULIFLOWER (SEE PAGE 378), FOR SERVING

COUSCOUS-STUFFED TOMATOES (SEE PAGE 65), FOR SERVING

1. Preheat the oven to 300°F. Place the olive oil in a Dutch oven and warm it over medium-high heat. Season the short ribs with salt and pepper, add them to the pot, and sear them for 1 minute on each side. Remove the short ribs from the pot and set them aside.

2. Reduce the heat to medium, add the onion, carrot, and celery, and cook, stirring occasionally, until they have softened, about 5 minutes. Add the garlic, tomato paste, Ras el Hanout, and thyme and cook, stirring continually, for 1 minute.

3. Add the red wine and cook until the alcohol has been cooked off, about 3 minutes, scraping up any browned bits from the bottom of the pan.

4. Add the prune juice, stock, bay leaf, and prunes and bring the mixture to a boil. Return the short ribs to the pot, cover the pot, and place it in the oven. Braise the short ribs until they are extremely tender, 3 to 4 hours.

5. Remove the pot from the oven, remove the cooked short ribs, bay leaf, and half of the prunes, and set them aside. Transfer the mixture remaining in the Dutch oven to a food processor and blitz until smooth.

6. Return the sauce to the Dutch oven, add the reserved prunes and short ribs, and stir in the vinegar. Bring the dish to a simmer, taste, and adjust the seasoning as necessary.

7. Garnish with cilantro and sesame seeds and serve with the Braised Cauliflower and Couscous-Stuffed Tomatoes.

Stuffed Zucchini

YIELD: 4 SERVINGS / **ACTIVE TIME:** 25 MINUTES / **TOTAL TIMVE:** 45 MINUTES

4 ZUCCHINI, TRIMMED AND HALVED, SEEDS SCOOPED OUT WITH A SPOON

3 TABLESPOONS EXTRA-VIRGIN OLIVE OIL

SALT AND PEPPER, TO TASTE

½ LB. GROUND LAMB

4 SHALLOTS, MINCED

4 GARLIC CLOVES, MINCED

1 TABLESPOON RAS EL HANOUT (SEE PAGE 505)

1 CUP CHICKEN STOCK (SEE PAGE 482)

½ CUP COUSCOUS

½ CUP DRIED APRICOTS, CHOPPED

3 TABLESPOONS PINE NUTS, TOASTED AND CHOPPED

2 TABLESPOONS CHOPPED FRESH PARSLEY

1. Preheat the oven to 400°F. Place the zucchini on a baking sheet, cut side down, brush with 1 tablespoon of the olive oil, and season them with salt and pepper. Place the zucchini in the oven and roast until their skins start to wrinkle, about 7 minutes. Remove the zucchini from the oven and set them aside. Leave the oven on.

2. Place 1 tablespoon of the olive oil in a medium saucepan and warm it over medium-high heat. Add the lamb, season it with salt and pepper, and cook, breaking up the meat with a wooden spoon, until it is browned, about 5 minutes. Using a slotted spoon, transfer the lamb to a bowl and set it aside.

3. Drain the fat from the saucepan, add the remaining olive oil and the shallots and cook, stirring occasionally, until they are translucent, about 3 minutes. Add the garlic and Ras el Hanout and cook, stirring continually, for 1 minute.

4. Add the stock, couscous, and apricots and bring the mixture to a boil. Remove the pan from heat, cover it, and let it stand for 5 minutes.

5. Fluff the couscous mixture with a fork, stir in the pine nuts, parsley, and lamb, and season it with salt and pepper.

6. Turn the roasted zucchini over and distribute the filling between their cavities. Place them in the oven and roast until warmed through, about 5 minutes. Remove from the oven and let the stuffed zucchini cool slightly before enjoying.

24-Hour Focaccia Dough

YIELD: DOUGH FOR 1 LARGE FOCACCIA / **ACTIVE TIME:** 30 MINUTES / **TOTAL TIME:** 24 HOURS

¾ TEASPOON (SCANT) INSTANT YEAST OR 1 TEASPOON (SCANT) ACTIVE DRY YEAST

21.1 OZ. BREAD FLOUR OR "00" FLOUR, PLUS MORE AS NEEDED

13 OZ. WATER

2½ TEASPOONS FINE SEA SALT

2 TABLESPOONS EXTRA-VIRGIN OLIVE OIL

1. If using active dry yeast, warm 3½ tablespoons of the water until it is about 105°F. Add the water and yeast to a bowl and gently stir. Let it sit until it starts to foam. Instant yeast does not need to be proofed.

2. In a large bowl, combine the flour, yeast, and water. Work the mixture until it just comes together as a dough. Transfer it to a flour-dusted work surface and knead the dough until it is compact, smooth, and elastic.

3. Add the salt and knead until the dough is developed, elastic, and extensible, about 5 minutes. Add the olive oil and knead the dough until the oil has been incorporated. Form the dough into a ball, place it in an airtight container that is at least three times bigger, cover, and refrigerate for 24 hours.

4. Remove the dough from the refrigerator and let it warm to room temperature before making focaccia.

Falsomagro

YIELD: 6 SERVINGS / **ACTIVE TIME:** 40 MINUTES / **TOTAL TIME:** 2 HOURS

1½ LBS. LEAN BEEF, IN 1 LARGE AND THIN SLICE

5 OZ. GROUND BEEF

2 TABLESPOONS GRATED PECORINO CHEESE

¼ CUP BREAD CRUMBS

SALT AND PEPPER, TO TASTE

1 OZ. GUANCIALE, CUT INTO STRIPS

2 OZ. CACIOCAVALLO CHEESE, CUT INTO STRIPS

2 OZ. MORTADELLA, CUT INTO STRIPS

3 HARD-BOILED EGGS, CHOPPED

½ CUP EXTRA-VIRGIN OLIVE OIL

1 CARROT, PEELED AND FINELY CHOPPED

1 CELERY STALK, FINELY DICED

1 ONION, FINELY DICED

¼ CUP RED WINE

1½ LBS. WHOLE PEELED TOMATOES, CRUSHED

1 TABLESPOON TOMATO PASTE

1. Beat the slice of beef with a meat tenderizer to ensure that it is uniformly thick.

2. Place the ground beef, pecorino, and bread crumbs in a large bowl and stir to combine. Season the mixture with salt and pepper and then spread it over the slice of beef, leaving a ½ inch border around the edge.

3. Layer the guanciale, caciocavallo, and mortadella on top and then place the hard-boiled eggs in the center.

4. Roll up the slice of beef, starting from a short side, and tie it with kitchen twine.

5. Place ¼ cup of olive oil in a large skillet and warm it over medium heat. Add the slice of beef and sear it until it is browned all over, turning it as necessary. Remove the pan from heat and set it aside.

6. Place the remaining olive oil in a Dutch oven and warm it over medium heat. Add the carrot, celery, and onion and cook, stirring occasionally, until the vegetables have softened, about 5 minutes.

7. Add the seared beef to the pot and cook for about 5 minutes.

8. Add the red wine and cook until it has almost evaporated, scraping up any browned bits from the bottom of the pot.

9. Stir in the tomatoes and tomato paste, season the dish with salt and pepper, and reduce the heat to low. Cover the pan and cook, stirring occasionally, until the beef is tender, about 1 hour.

10. Cut the twine off of the beef and let it rest for 5 minutes before slicing and serving.

Braciole Napoletane

YIELD: 6 SERVINGS / **ACTIVE TIME:** 20 MINUTES / **TOTAL TIME:** 40 MINUTES

8 THIN SLICES OF LEAN BEEF (EACH ABOUT 5 OZ.)

KOSHER SALT AND PEPPER, TO TASTE

4 GARLIC CLOVES, 2 MINCED; 2 HALVED

6 TABLESPOONS RAISINS, CHOPPED

¼ CUP PINE NUTS, CHOPPED

3 TABLESPOONS CHOPPED FRESH PARSLEY

1 CUP GRATED PECORINO CHEESE

3 TABLESPOONS EXTRA-VIRGIN OLIVE OIL

1 CUP RED WINE

TOMATO SAUCE (SEE PAGE 504)

1. Beat the slices of beef with a meat tenderizer to ensure that they are uniformly thick. Season them with salt and pepper and set them aside.

2. Place the minced garlic, raisins, pine nuts, and parsley in a bowl and stir to combine. Evenly distribute the mixture and the pecorino over the slices of beef.

3. Starting from a short side, roll up the slices of beef and then secure them with skewers or large toothpicks.

4. Place the olive oil in a large skillet and warm it over medium heat. Add the remaining garlic and cook for 1 minute.

5. Add the slices of stuffed beef and sear until they are browned all over, turning them as necessary.

6. Remove the garlic from the pan and add the red wine. Cook until it has nearly evaporated, about 5 minutes.

7. Add the sauce, stir to combine, and cover the pan. Reduce the heat to low and cook until the slices of stuffed beef are just cooked through, 10 to 15 minutes. Serve immediately.

Pollo alla Pizzaiola

YIELD: 4 SERVINGS / **ACTIVE TIME:** 20 MINUTES / **TOTAL TIME:** 1 HOUR

4 LARGE BONE-IN, SKIN-ON CHICKEN THIGHS

SALT AND PEPPER, TO TASTE

¼ CUP EXTRA-VIRGIN OLIVE OIL

2 GARLIC CLOVES, MINCED

⅔ CUP WHITE WINE

1½ LBS. WHOLE PEELED TOMATOES, CRUSHED

½ CUP PITTED BLACK OLIVES, SLICED

2 TABLESPOONS CAPERS, RINSED IF PACKED IN SALT OR DRAINED IF PACKED IN BRINE

6 OZ. FRESH MOZZARELLA CHEESE, DRAINED AND SLICED

DRIED OREGANO, TO TASTE

1. Trim the fattiest parts from the chicken, season it with salt and pepper, and set it aside.

2. Place the olive oil in a large skillet and warm it over low heat. Add the garlic and cook until it starts to brown, about 2 minutes.

3. Add the chicken, skin side down, raise the heat to medium-high, and sear until it is browned all over, turning it as necessary.

4. Add the wine and cook until it has nearly evaporated.

5. Add the tomatoes, reduce the heat to low, and cover the pan. Cook until the chicken is tender, about 30 minutes.

6. Add the olives and capers, season the dish with salt and pepper, and cook, uncovered, until the sauce has thickened, about 10 minutes.

7. Add the mozzarella, season the dish with oregano, and cover the pan. Cook until the mozzarella has melted, about 5 minutes, and serve immediately.

Orecchiette

YIELD: 1½ LBS. / **ACTIVE TIME:** 1 HOUR / **TOTAL TIME:** 1 HOUR AND 30 MINUTES

15.8 OZ. FINELY GROUND DURUM WHEAT FLOUR, PLUS MORE AS NEEDED

7.9 OZ. WATER, AT ROOM TEMPERATURE

2 PINCHES OF FINE SEA SALT, PLUS MORE AS NEEDED

1. Place all of the ingredients in a large bowl and work the mixture until it starts to come together as a dough. Transfer the dough to a flour-dusted work surface and knead it energetically until it is a smooth and homogeneous dough, about 10 minutes.

2. Cover the dough with plastic wrap and let it rest at room temperature for 30 minutes.

3. Divide the dough into 3 pieces. Cover 2 pieces with plastic wrap and place the other on a flour-dusted work surface.

4. Shape the dough into a ⅖-inch-thick log and cut it into ⅖-inch-long pieces. Using a knife with a smooth blade, shape the pieces into orecchiette by running the knife over their tops to drag them toward you. Use your thumb to turn the orecchiette over. Transfer them to flour-dusted baking sheets. Repeat with the remaining pieces of dough.

5. To cook the orecchiette, bring water to a boil in a large saucepan. Add salt, let the water return to a full boil, and add the orecchiette. Cook until they are al dente, about 5 minutes.

Rianata

YIELD: 1 LARGE FOCACCIA / **ACTIVE TIME:** 40 MINUTES / **TOTAL TIME:** 4 HOURS AND 45 MINUTES

2½ TEASPOONS ACTIVE DRY YEAST OR 2 TEASPOONS INSTANT YEAST

14.8 OZ. WATER

1 LB. BREAD FLOUR, PLUS MORE AS NEEDED

8.8 OZ. FINE SEMOLINA FLOUR

1 TABLESPOON PLUS 1 TEASPOON EXTRA-VIRGIN OLIVE OIL, PLUS MORE AS NEEDED

1 TABLESPOON FINE SEA SALT, PLUS MORE TO TASTE

8 ANCHOVIES IN OLIVE OIL, DRAINED

30 CHERRY TOMATOES, HALVED

½ LB. PECORINO CHEESE, GRATED

DRIED OREGANO, TO TASTE

1. If using active dry yeast, warm 3½ tablespoons of the water until it is about 105°F. Add the water and yeast to a bowl and gently stir. Let the mixture sit until it starts to foam. Instant yeast does not need to be proofed.

2. In a large bowl, combine the flours, olive oil, yeast, and water until the mixture comes together as a dough. Transfer it to a flour-dusted work surface and knead the dough until it is compact, smooth, and elastic.

3. Add the salt and knead until the dough is developed, elastic, and extensible, about 5 minutes. Form the dough into a ball and place it in an airtight container that has been coated with olive oil. Let the dough rest at room temperature until it has doubled in size, about 2 hours.

4. Coat an 18 x 13–inch baking sheet with olive oil, place the dough on it, and brush the dough with more olive oil. Cover with a linen towel and let the dough rest for 30 minutes.

5. Gently stretch the dough until it covers the entire pan. Let it rest for another hour.

6. Preheat the oven to 430°F. Press the anchovies and tomatoes into the dough, sprinkle the pecorino over the focaccia, season it with salt and oregano, and drizzle olive oil over everything.

7. Place the focaccia in the oven and bake for 20 to 30 minutes, until the focaccia is golden brown and crispy on the edges and the bottom.

8. Remove the focaccia from the oven and let it cool slightly before serving.

Focaccia Genovese

YIELD: 1 LARGE FOCACCIA / **ACTIVE TIME:** 2 HOURS / **TOTAL TIME:** 27 HOURS

24-HOUR FOCACCIA DOUGH (SEE PAGE 216)

ALL-PURPOSE FLOUR, AS NEEDED

2 TABLESPOONS EXTRA-VIRGIN OLIVE OIL, PLUS MORE AS NEEDED

⅔ CUP WATER

1 TEASPOON FINE SEA SALT

COARSE SEA SALT, TO TASTE

1. Place the dough on a flour-dusted work surface and form it into a loose ball, making sure not to compress the core of the dough and deflate it. Coat an 18 ×13–inch baking sheet with olive oil, place the dough on the pan, and gently flatten the dough into an oval. Cover the dough with a linen towel and let it rest at room temperature for 30 minutes to 1 hour.

2. Stretch the dough toward the edges of the baking pan. If the dough does not want to extend to the edges of the pan right away, let it rest for 15 to 20 minutes before trying again. Cover with the linen towel and let it rest for another 30 minutes to 1 hour.

3. Place the olive oil, water, and fine sea salt in a mixing bowl and stir to combine. Set the mixture aside. Lightly dust the focaccia with flour and press down on the dough with two fingers to make deep indentations. Cover the focaccia with half of the olive oil mixture and let it rest for another 30 minutes.

4. Preheat the oven to 450°F. Cover the focaccia with the remaining olive oil mixture and sprinkle the coarse sea salt over the top. Place in the oven and bake for 15 to 20 minutes, until the focaccia is a light golden brown. As this focaccia is supposed to be soft, it's far better to remove it too early as opposed to too late.

5. Remove the focaccia from the oven and let it cool briefly before serving.

Chicken Zafferano

YIELD: 4 SERVINGS / **ACTIVE TIME:** 20 MINUTES / **TOTAL TIME:** 1 HOUR

4 LB. WHOLE CHICKEN, BROKEN DOWN

SALT, TO TASTE

4 TABLESPOONS UNSALTED BUTTER

3 TABLESPOONS EXTRA-VIRGIN OLIVE OIL

½ CUP WHITE WINE

¼ CUP COGNAC OR BRANDY

1 CUP BEEF STOCK (SEE PAGE 484)

1 CUP LIGHT CREAM

1 TABLESPOON SAFFRON THREADS

2 TABLESPOONS CHOPPED FRESH PARSLEY

3 TABLESPOONS ALL-PURPOSE FLOUR

1. Trim the fattiest parts from the chicken, season it with salt, and set it aside.

2. Place the butter and olive oil in a large skillet and warm the mixture over medium-high heat. Add the chicken, skin side down, and sear until it is browned on both sides, turning it as necessary.

3. Deglaze the pan with the wine and Cognac, scraping up any browned bits from the bottom of the pan. Cook until the liquid has nearly evaporated.

4. Add two-thirds of the broth, reduce the heat to medium-low, and cover the pan. Cook for 20 minutes.

5. Uncover the pan, raise the heat to medium-high, and cook for 5 to 10 minutes. Remove the chicken from the pan, transfer it to a plate, and cover loosely with aluminum foil to keep it warm.

6. Add the remaining broth, cream, saffron, parsley, and flour, season the mixture with salt, and cook, stirring continually, until the flavor of the sauce has developed to your liking. Ladle the sauce over the chicken and enjoy.

Baked Orzo

YIELD: 4 TO 6 SERVINGS / **ACTIVE TIME:** 30 MINUTES / **TOTAL TIME:** 1 HOUR AND 30 MINUTES

2 CUPS ORZO

3 TABLESPOONS EXTRA-VIRGIN OLIVE OIL

1 EGGPLANT, SEEDS REMOVED, CHOPPED INTO ½-INCH CUBES

1 ONION, CHOPPED

4 GARLIC CLOVES, MINCED

2 TEASPOONS DRIED OREGANO

1 TABLESPOON TOMATO PASTE

3 CUPS CHICKEN STOCK (SEE PAGE 482)

1 CUP GRATED PARMESAN CHEESE

2 TABLESPOONS CAPERS, DRAINED AND CHOPPED

SALT AND PEPPER, TO TASTE

2 TOMATOES, SLICED THIN

2 ZUCCHINI, SLICED THIN

1 CUP CRUMBLED FETA CHEESE

1. Preheat the oven to 350°F. Place the orzo in a medium saucepan and toast it, stirring frequently, over medium heat until it is lightly browned, about 10 minutes. Transfer the orzo to a bowl.

2. Place 2 tablespoons of the olive oil in the saucepan and warm it over medium heat. Add the eggplant and cook, stirring occasionally, until it has browned, about 10 minutes. Remove the eggplant from the pan and place it in the bowl with the orzo.

3. Add the remaining olive oil to the saucepan and warm it over medium heat. Add the onion and cook, stirring occasionally, until it has softened, about 5 minutes. Add the garlic, oregano, and tomato paste and cook, stirring continually, for 1 minute.

4. Remove the pan from heat, add the stock, Parmesan, capers, orzo, and eggplant, season the mixture with salt and pepper, and stir to combine. Pour the mixture into a 10 x 8–inch baking dish.

5. Alternating rows, layer the tomatoes and zucchini on top of the orzo mixture. Season with salt and pepper.

6. Place the baking dish in the oven and bake until the orzo is tender, about 30 minutes. Remove the dish from the oven, sprinkle the feta on top, and enjoy.

Roasted Chicken Thighs with Pistachio & Raisin Sauce

YIELD: 4 SERVINGS / **ACTIVE TIME:** 20 MINUTES / **TOTAL TIME:** 24 HOURS

4 BONE-IN, SKIN-ON CHICKEN THIGHS

2 TEASPOONS EXTRA-VIRGIN OLIVE OIL

SALT AND PEPPER, TO TASTE

PISTACHIO & RAISIN SAUCE (SEE PAGE 512), FOR SERVING

MARINATED CAULIFLOWER & CHICKPEAS (SEE PAGE 374), FOR SERVING

1. Pat the chicken thighs dry and poke their skin all over with a skewer. Place the chicken thighs on a wire rack set in a rimmed baking sheet. Place the chicken thighs in the refrigerator and let them sit, uncovered, overnight.

2. Preheat the oven to 425°F. Remove the chicken thighs from the refrigerator and brush them with the olive oil. Season with salt and pepper and place them in the oven.

3. Roast the chicken thighs until they are cooked through (internal temperature is 160°F), 15 to 20 minutes. Remove the chicken thighs from the oven and let them rest for 10 minutes.

4. Spread some of the sauce over each of the serving plates, place a chicken thigh on each plate, and serve with the Marinated Cauliflower & Chickpeas.

Peperoni Ripieni di Tonno

YIELD: 8 SERVINGS / **ACTIVE TIME:** 20 MINUTES / **TOTAL TIME:** 2 HOURS AND 20 MINUTES

1.3 LBS. STALE BREAD, SOAKED IN WATER AND SQUEEZED DRY

1 LB. TUNA IN OLIVE OIL, DRAINED

14 ANCHOVIES IN OLIVE OIL, DRAINED AND CHOPPED

¼ CUP PITTED GREEK OLIVES, CHOPPED

3 TABLESPOONS CAPERS IN KOSHER SALT, SOAKED, DRAINED, AND SQUEEZED

2 GARLIC CLOVES, MINCED

3 TABLESPOONS FINELY CHOPPED FRESH PARSLEY

½ CUP EXTRA-VIRGIN OLIVE OIL, PLUS MORE TO TASTE

SALT AND PEPPER, TO TASTE

8 RED OR YELLOW BELL PEPPERS

1. Preheat the oven to 350°F. Place all of the ingredients, except for the peppers, in a bowl and stir until well combined.

2. Cut off the tops of the peppers and set the tops aside. Remove the seeds and ribs from the peppers, taking care not to break the peppers.

3. Stuff the peppers with the filling and place the pepper tops back on top. Place the peppers in a baking dish, on their sides so that they sit end to end, lightly season them with salt, and drizzle olive oil over them.

4. Place the peppers in the oven and bake until they start to look slightly charred, about 1 hour, turning them over halfway through.

5. Remove the peppers from the oven and let them cool completely. Chill the peppers in the refrigerator for 1 hour before serving.

Scialatielli

YIELD: 1½ LBS. / **ACTIVE TIME:** 30 MINUTES / **TOTAL TIME:** 1 HOUR

15.8 OZ. FINELY GROUND DURUM WHEAT FLOUR, PLUS MORE AS NEEDED

7 OZ. WHOLE MILK

1 LARGE EGG, LIGHTLY BEATEN

HANDFUL OF FRESH BASIL, FINELY CHOPPED

1 OZ. PECORINO CHEESE, GRATED

⅓ OZ. EXTRA-VIRGIN OLIVE OIL

1. Place the flour, milk, egg, basil, and pecorino in a large bowl and work the mixture until it starts to come together as a dough. Add the olive oil and work the dough until it has been incorporated. Transfer the dough to a flour-dusted work surface and knead it energetically until it is a smooth and homogeneous dough, about 10 minutes.

2. Cover the dough with plastic wrap and let it rest at room temperature for 30 minutes.

3. Divide the dough into 2 pieces. Cover 1 piece with plastic wrap and place the other piece on a flour-dusted work surface. Roll the dough out into a rectangle that is about ⅕ inch thick. Sprinkle flour over the dough and, working from the long sides, roll up the dough from the edges so that they meet in the center. Cut the dough into ⅖-inch-thick rings, unroll them, and dust them with flour. Let them dry until they are ready to be boiled. Repeat with the other piece of dough.

4. To cook the scialatielli, bring water to a boil in a large saucepan. Add salt, let the water return to a boil, and add the scialatielli. Cook until they are al dente, about 5 minutes.

Sfincione Palermitano

YIELD: 1 LARGE FOCACCIA / **ACTIVE TIME:** 1 HOUR / **TOTAL TIME:** 4 HOURS AND 30 MINUTES

2½ TEASPOONS ACTIVE DRY YEAST OR 2 TEASPOONS INSTANT YEAST

22½ OZ. WATER

19¾ OZ. BREAD FLOUR, PLUS MORE AS NEEDED

8.4 OZ. FINE SEMOLINA FLOUR

1 TABLESPOON FINE SEA SALT, PLUS MORE TO TASTE

2 TABLESPOONS PLUS 2 TEASPOONS EXTRA-VIRGIN OLIVE OIL

2 ONIONS, SLICED

22.9 OZ. CRUSHED TOMATOES

12 ANCHOVIES IN OLIVE OIL, DRAINED AND TORN

BLACK PEPPER, TO TASTE

1 LB. CACIOCAVALLO CHEESE, TWO-THIRDS CUBED, ONE-THIRD GRATED

FRESH OREGANO, CHOPPED, TO TASTE

BREAD CRUMBS, TO TASTE

1. If using active dry yeast, warm 3½ tablespoons of the water until it is about 105°F. Add the water and yeast to a bowl and gently stir. Let the mixture sit until it starts to foam. Instant yeast does not need to be proofed.

2. In a large bowl, combine the flours, yeast, and water until the mixture comes together as a dough. If kneading by hand, transfer the dough to a flour-dusted work surface. Work the dough until it is compact, smooth, and elastic.

3. Add the salt and work the dough until it is developed, elastic, and extensible, about 5 minutes. Form the dough into a ball, place it in a bowl, and cover the bowl with a damp linen towel. Let it rest at room temperature until it has doubled in size, about 2 hours.

4. Coat the bottom of a skillet with olive oil and warm it over medium-low heat. When the oil starts to shimmer, add the onions and cook, stirring frequently, until they are starting to brown, about 12 minutes. Add the tomatoes and 3 of the anchovies, cover the skillet, reduce the heat, and simmer until the flavor is to your liking, 20 to 30 minutes. Season with salt and pepper and let cool completely.

5. Coat an 18 x 13–inch baking pan with olive oil, place the dough on the pan, and gently stretch it until it covers the entire pan. Cover the dough with plastic wrap and let it rest for 1 hour.

6. Preheat the oven to 430°F. Top the focaccia with the cubed caciocavallo and the remaining anchovies and press down on them until they are embedded in the dough. Cover with the tomato sauce, generously sprinkle oregano over the sauce, and drizzle the olive oil over everything. Sprinkle the grated caciocavallo and a generous handful of bread crumbs over the focaccia.

7. Place it in the oven and bake for 20 minutes. Lower the temperature to 350°F and bake for another 15 to 20 minutes, until the focaccia is golden brown, both on the edges and on the bottom.

8. Remove the focaccia from the oven and let it cool slightly before serving.

Lamb Shawarma

YIELD: 8 SERVINGS / **ACTIVE TIME:** 30 MINUTES / **TOTAL TIME:** 30 HOURS

FOR THE SHAWARMA SEASONING

2 TABLESPOONS CUMIN SEEDS

2 TEASPOONS CARAWAY SEEDS

2 TEASPOONS CORIANDER SEEDS

2 RED CHILE PEPPERS, STEMS AND SEEDS REMOVED, FINELY DICED

4 GARLIC CLOVES, GRATED

½ CUP AVOCADO OIL

1 TABLESPOON PAPRIKA

½ TEASPOON CINNAMON

FOR THE LAMB

6 LB. BONE-IN LEG OF LAMB, SHANK ATTACHED, FRENCHED

SALT AND PEPPER, TO TASTE

½ TEASPOON CARAWAY SEEDS

½ TEASPOON CORIANDER SEEDS

¼ CUP AVOCADO OIL

1 LARGE ONION, SLICED THIN

1 TABLESPOON ANCHO CHILE POWDER

1 TABLESPOON CHIPOTLE CHILE POWDER

1 TEASPOON TURMERIC

½ TEASPOON CINNAMON

1 (28 OZ.) CAN OF CRUSHED TOMATOES

4 CUPS CHICKEN STOCK (SEE PAGE 482)

1. To prepare the shawarma seasoning, use a mortar and pestle or a spice grinder to grind the cumin, caraway, and coriander seeds into a fine powder. Transfer to a small bowl and stir in the chiles, garlic, avocado oil, paprika, and cinnamon.

2. To begin preparations for the lamb, trim any excess fat from the lamb and remove any silverskin. Lightly score the flesh with a paring knife and season the lamb generously with salt and pepper. Place it on a wire rack set in a rimmed baking sheet and apply the seasoning. Refrigerate for 12 to 24 hours.

3. Preheat the oven to 450°F. Place the lamb in the oven and roast until it is well browned all over, 20 to 25 minutes.

4. Remove the lamb from the oven and reduce the oven temperature to 250°F. Grind the caraway and coriander seeds into a powder and set it aside.

5. Place the avocado oil in a large Dutch oven and warm it over medium heat. Add the onion and cook, stirring occasionally, until it starts to soften, about 5 minutes. Stir in the chile powders, turmeric, and cinnamon and cook, stirring continuously, until fragrant, about 2 minutes. Add the tomatoes and stock and bring to a simmer. Season the sauce lightly with salt and pepper.

6. Place the lamb in the pot and add enough water to cover it if it is not submerged. Cover the pot, place it in the oven, and braise the lamb until the meat is very tender, about 5 hours.

7. Remove from the oven, transfer the lamb to a platter, and tent it with foil. Place the Dutch oven over medium-high heat and bring the braising liquid to a boil. Cook, stirring often, until it has reduced by half, 25 to 30 minutes. Spoon the sauce over the lamb and enjoy.

Pomegranate & Honey–Glazed Chicken

YIELD: 4 SERVINGS / **ACTIVE TIME:** 20 MINUTES / **TOTAL TIME:** 1 HOUR AND 20 MINUTES

¼ CUP AVOCADO OIL

1 LARGE ONION, CHOPPED

3 GARLIC CLOVES, MINCED

½ CUP POMEGRANATE MOLASSES

½ CUP SWEETENED POMEGRANATE JUICE

½ CUP HONEY

2 CUPS VEGETABLE OR CHICKEN STOCK (SEE PAGE 484 OR 482)

1 TEASPOON CUMIN

½ TEASPOON GROUND GINGER

⅛ TEASPOON ALLSPICE

½ TEASPOON TURMERIC

4 LBS. BONE-IN, SKIN-ON CHICKEN PIECES

SALT AND PEPPER, TO TASTE

FRESH PARSLEY, CHOPPED, FOR GARNISH

POMEGRANATE ARILS, FOR GARNISH

1. Place 2 tablespoons of the avocado oil in a large skillet and warm it over medium-high heat. Add the onion and cook, stirring occasionally, until it is soft and translucent, about 3 minutes.

2. Add the garlic and cook, stirring frequently, until fragrant, about 1 minute. Stir in the pomegranate molasses, pomegranate juice, honey, stock, and seasonings and bring the mixture to a boil. Lower the heat and simmer the sauce until it has reduced by half and thickened slightly, about 20 minutes. Taste the sauce and adjust the seasoning as necessary. Transfer the sauce to a bowl and set it aside.

3. Rinse the chicken pieces, pat them dry, and season with salt and pepper.

4. Place the remaining avocado oil in the pan. Add the chicken pieces, skin side down, and cook until browned. Turn the chicken over, pour the sauce into the pan, reduce the heat, and cover the pan. Cook the chicken until cooked through and tender, 35 to 40 minutes.

5. Transfer the cooked chicken to a platter, garnish with parsley and pomegranate arils, and enjoy.

Turmeric Chicken with Toum

YIELD: 2 TO 4 SERVINGS / **ACTIVE TIME:** 1 HOUR / **TOTAL TIME:** 24 HOURS

1 TABLESPOON GROUND TURMERIC

2 TEASPOONS GROUND DRIED ORANGE PEEL

1 TEASPOON GROUND FENNEL SEEDS

¾ TEASPOON CUMIN

1½ TEASPOONS CORIANDER

1 GARLIC CLOVE, GRATED

1-INCH PIECE OF FRESH TURMERIC, PEELED AND GRATED

1 TABLESPOON FRESH ORANGE JUICE

1 TABLESPOON PLUS 1 TEASPOON ORANGE BLOSSOM WATER

¾ CUP FULL-FAT GREEK YOGURT

3½ LB. WHOLE CHICKEN

1 TABLESPOON PLUS 2½ TEASPOONS FINE SEA SALT

1 TEASPOON BLACK PEPPER

TOUM (SEE PAGE 509), FOR SERVING

1. Place the ground turmeric, orange peel, fennel seeds, cumin, coriander, garlic, and fresh turmeric in a bowl and stir to combine. Add the orange juice, orange blossom water, and yogurt to the bowl and stir until incorporated.

2. Season the cavity of the chicken with some of the salt and pepper. Rub some of the marinade inside the cavity of the chicken.

3. Using kitchen twine, tie the legs together.

4. Evenly season the outside of the chicken with the salt and pepper. Place the chicken on a baking sheet and let it sit, uncovered, at room temperature for 30 minutes.

5. Rub the marinade all over the outside of the chicken; it may seem like a lot, but use it all. Place the chicken, uncovered, in the refrigerator and let it marinate overnight.

6. Remove the chicken from the refrigerator and let it sit at room temperature for 30 minutes prior to cooking.

7. Preheat the oven to 450°F.

8. Place the chicken, breast side up, on a rack in a roasting pan. Place it in the oven and roast for 40 to 50 minutes, until the interior of the thickest part of the thigh reaches 160° to 165°F on an instant-read thermometer. If the chicken's skin browns too quickly in the oven, lower the heat to 375°F.

9. Remove the chicken from the oven and let it rest for 15 minutes. Serve with the Toum and enjoy.

**Pomegranate &
Honey–Glazed Chicken**
SEE PAGE 232

Vegetable Tanzia

YIELD: 6 SERVINGS / **ACTIVE TIME:** 45 MINUTES / **TOTAL TIME:** 1 HOUR AND 45 MINUTES

½ CUP AVOCADO OIL

2 LBS. YELLOW ONIONS, SLICED THIN

1 TEASPOON KOSHER SALT, PLUS MORE TO TASTE

½ CUP PITTED PRUNES, HALVED

½ CUP DRIED APRICOTS, HALVED

½ CUP DRIED FIGS, STEMS REMOVED, HALVED

½ CUP SHELLED WALNUTS

2 TABLESPOONS SUGAR

1 TEASPOON CINNAMON

BLACK PEPPER, TO TASTE

1 LB. SWEET POTATOES, PEELED AND CUT INTO 2-INCH-LONG PIECES

1 LB. TURNIPS, PEELED AND CUT INTO 2-INCH-LONG PIECES

2 LBS. BUTTERNUT SQUASH, PEELED, SEEDED, AND CUT INTO 2-INCH-LONG PIECES

½ TEASPOON TURMERIC

½ CUP SLIVERED ALMONDS, FOR GARNISH

WHITE RICE, COOKED, FOR SERVING

1. Place 6 tablespoons of the avocado oil in a large skillet and warm it over medium heat. Add the onions and salt and cook, stirring frequently, until the onions are caramelized and a deep golden brown, about 30 minutes.

2. Transfer the onions to a large bowl. Add the prunes, apricots, figs, walnuts, sugar, and cinnamon and stir to combine. Season the mixture with salt and pepper.

3. Preheat the oven to 375°F. Place the sweet potatoes, turnips, and butternut squash in a roasting pan and rub them with the remaining avocado oil. Sprinkle the turmeric over the top, season the vegetables with salt and pepper, and toss to combine. Spread the vegetables in an even layer in the pan and spoon the fruit mixture over and around them.

4. Add 1½ cups of water to the pan and place it in the oven. Roast until the vegetables are well browned and cooked through, about 1 hour, stirring halfway through. Add more water if the pan starts to look dry.

5. While the vegetables are roasting, toast the almonds in a dry skillet over medium-low heat, stirring often, until lightly browned, about 6 minutes. Remove the pan from heat.

6. Remove the tanzia from the oven, sprinkle the toasted almonds on top, and serve over rice.

Chicken Souvlaki

YIELD: 6 SERVINGS / **ACTIVE TIME:** 20 MINUTES / **TOTAL TIME:** 2 HOURS AND 30 MINUTES

10 GARLIC CLOVES, CRUSHED

4 SPRIGS OF FRESH OREGANO

1 SPRIG OF FRESH ROSEMARY

1 TEASPOON PAPRIKA

1 TEASPOON KOSHER SALT

1 TEASPOON BLACK PEPPER

¼ CUP EXTRA-VIRGIN OLIVE OIL, PLUS MORE AS NEEDED

¼ CUP DRY WHITE WINE

2 TABLESPOONS FRESH LEMON JUICE

2½ LBS. BONELESS, SKINLESS CHICKEN THIGHS, CHOPPED

2 BAY LEAVES

PITA BREAD (SEE PAGE 338), WARMED, FOR SERVING

1. Place the garlic, oregano, rosemary, paprika, salt, pepper, olive oil, wine, and lemon juice in a food processor and blitz to combine.

2. Place the chicken and bay leaves in a bowl or a large resealable bag, pour the marinade over the chicken, and stir so that it gets evenly coated. Marinate in the refrigerator for 2 hours.

3. Prepare a gas or charcoal grill for medium-high heat (about 450°F). If using bamboo skewers, soak them in water.

4. Remove the chicken from the refrigerator and thread the pieces onto the skewers. Make sure to leave plenty of space between the pieces of chicken, as it will provide the heat with more room to operate, ensuring that the chicken cooks evenly.

5. Place the skewers on the grill and cook, turning as necessary, until the chicken is cooked through, 12 to 15 minutes. Remove the skewers from the grill and let them rest briefly before serving with the pita and vegetables, herbs, and condiments of your choice.

Za'atar Chicken

YIELD: 4 SERVINGS / **ACTIVE TIME:** 45 MINUTES / **TOTAL TIME:** 24 HOURS

4 LB. WHOLE CHICKEN

2 TABLESPOONS EXTRA-VIRGIN OLIVE OIL

2 TABLESPOONS ZA'ATAR (SEE PAGE 501)

HONEY-GLAZED CARROTS (SEE PAGE 386), FOR SERVING

ROASTED ROOT VEGETABLES (SEE PAGE 405), FOR SERVING

1. Place a wire rack in a rimmed baking sheet. Place the chicken, breast side down, on a cutting board. Using kitchen shears, cut out the chicken's backbone. Flip the chicken over so the breast side is facing up. Push down on the middle of the chicken to flatten it as much as possible. Pat the chicken dry and place it on the wire rack.

2. Place the chicken in the refrigerator and let it rest, uncovered, overnight.

3. Remove the chicken from the refrigerator and let it rest at room temperature for 30 minutes.

4. Preheat the oven to 425°F. Place the olive oil in a large skillet and warm it over medium heat. Add the chicken to the pan and weigh it down with a cast-iron skillet—this added weight will help the chicken cook evenly. Cook until the chicken is golden brown on each side, 15 to 20 minutes.

5. Place the chicken on a baking sheet, breast side up, sprinkle the Za'atar over the chicken, and place it in the oven. Roast the chicken until it is cooked through (internal temperature is 165°F), about 15 minutes.

6. Remove the chicken from the oven and let it rest for 10 minutes. Serve with the glazed carrots and other roasted root vegetables.

Kefta with Chickpea Salad

YIELD: 4 SERVINGS / **ACTIVE TIME:** 35 MINUTES / **TOTAL TIME:** 1 HOUR

1½ LBS. GROUND LAMB

½ LB. GROUND BEEF

½ WHITE ONION, MINCED

2 GARLIC CLOVES, GRATED

ZEST OF 1 LEMON

1 CUP FRESH PARSLEY, CHOPPED

2 TABLESPOONS CHOPPED FRESH MINT

1 TEASPOON CINNAMON

2 TABLESPOONS CUMIN

1 TABLESPOON PAPRIKA

1 TEASPOON CORIANDER

SALT AND PEPPER, TO TASTE

¼ CUP EXTRA-VIRGIN OLIVE OIL

CHICKPEA SALAD (SEE PAGE 352), FOR SERVING

1. Place all of the ingredients, except for the olive oil and the Chickpea Salad, in a mixing bowl and stir until well combined. Microwave a small bit of the mixture until cooked through. Taste and adjust the seasoning in the remaining mixture as necessary.

2. Working with wet hands, form the mixture into 18 ovals and thread 3 meatballs on each skewer.

3. Place the olive oil in a Dutch oven and warm it over medium-high heat. Working in batches, add 3 skewers to the pot and sear the kefta until they are browned all over and nearly cooked through, about 10 minutes. Transfer the browned kefta to a paper towel–lined plate to drain.

4. When the kefta have been browned, return all of the skewers to the pot, cover it, and remove from heat. Let the kefta stand until cooked through, about 10 minutes.

5. When the kefta are cooked through, remove them from the skewers. Divide the salad between the serving plates, top each portion with some of the kefta, and enjoy.

Almodrote

YIELD: 8 SERVINGS / **ACTIVE TIME:** 40 MINUTES / **TOTAL TIME:** 1 HOUR AND 45 MINUTES

5 EGGPLANTS, HALVED

1 GARLIC CLOVE, UNPEELED AND HALVED LENGTHWISE

UNSALTED BUTTER, AS NEEDED

2 TABLESPOONS ALL-PURPOSE FLOUR

1 SMALL ZUCCHINI, GRATED (OPTIONAL)

2 EGGS

3 CUPS GRATED KASHKAVAL CHEESE

½ TEASPOON KOSHER SALT

FULL-FAT GREEK YOGURT, FOR SERVING

1. Position a rack in the middle of the oven and preheat the oven to 425°F. Place the eggplants on baking sheets, cut side up, place them in the oven, and roast until they collapse, about 40 minutes. Remove from the oven and let them cool. When they are cool enough to handle, scoop the flesh into a fine-mesh sieve and let it drain.

2. Rub a baking dish with the cut sides of the garlic clove, making sure to go over the entire surface of the dish a few times. Generously coat the dish with butter and then sprinkle with the flour, making sure to coat the entire dish. Tap out any excess flour.

3. Place the eggplant in a bowl and taste them—if they are sweet, you can skip adding the zucchini; if they are a bit bitter, place the zucchini in a linen towel and wring it to remove as much liquid as possible. Add it to the bowl.

4. Add the eggs, 2½ cups of the cheese, and the salt and stir vigorously with a fork until the mixture is combined, making sure to break up the eggplant.

5. Spread the eggplant mixture evenly in the baking dish. Sprinkle the remaining cheese over the top, place the dish in the oven, and bake until well browned and crispy on top, 25 or 30 minutes.

6. Remove from the oven and serve with Greek yogurt.

Neapolitan Pizza Dough

YIELD: 4 BALLS OF DOUGH / **ACTIVE TIME:** 30 MINUTES / **TOTAL TIME:** 8 TO 12 HOURS

⅛ TEASPOON PLUS 1 PINCH ACTIVE DRY YEAST OR ⅛ TEASPOON INSTANT YEAST

14.8 OZ. WATER

23.9 OZ. BREAD FLOUR, PLUS MORE AS NEEDED

1 TABLESPOON FINE SEA SALT

1. If using active dry yeast, warm 3½ tablespoons of the water until it is about 105°F. Add the water and yeast to a bowl and gently stir. Let the mixture sit until it starts to foam. Instant yeast does not need to be proofed.

2. In a large bowl, combine the flour, yeast, and water. Work the mixture until it just comes together as a dough. Transfer it to a flour-dusted work surface and knead the dough until it is compact, smooth, and elastic.

3. Add the salt and knead until the dough is developed and elastic, meaning it pulls back energetically when pulled. Transfer the dough to an airtight container, cover it, and let it rest for 2 to 3 hours at room temperature. For a classic Neapolitan dough, room temperature should be 77°F. If your kitchen is colder, let the dough rest longer before shaping it into rounds.

4. Divide the dough into four pieces and shape them into very tight rounds, as it is important to create tension in the outer layer of dough. Place the rounds in a baking dish with high edges, leaving enough space between rounds so that they won't touch when fully risen. Cover with a linen towel and let rest for 6 to 8 hours, depending on the temperature in the room, before using it to make pizza.

THE ENCYCLOPEDIA OF MEDITERRANEAN

Gnocchi di Patate

YIELD: 8 SERVINGS / **ACTIVE TIME:** 1 HOUR / **TOTAL TIME:** 2 HOURS

2.2 LBS. STARCHY
POTATOES, PEELED

10.6 OZ. ALL-PURPOSE
FLOUR, PLUS MORE AS
NEEDED

1 MEDIUM EGG

SALT, TO TASTE

1. Place the potatoes in a large saucepan and cover them with cold water. Bring to a boil and cook until a knife inserted into the potatoes passes easily to their centers. Drain the potatoes.

2. Sift the flour onto a work surface, place the potatoes over it, and mash the potatoes.

3. Place the egg in a small bowl and season it with salt. Beat until scrambled and add it to the potato mixture. Work the mixture with your hands until it comes together as a soft, smooth dough. Be careful not to incorporate too much flour into the dough, otherwise the gnocchi will harden too much during cooking.

4. Cut the dough into pieces and form them into long, ⅗-inch-thick logs. Cut them into 1-inch-long pieces. Dust a fork or a gnocchi board with flour and roll the pieces of dough over it, gently pressing down to shape the gnocchi. Place the gnocchi on a flour-dusted baking sheet.

5. To cook the gnocchi, bring water to a boil in a large saucepan. Add salt, let the water return to a boil, and add the gnocchi. Cook until they rise to the surface.

Pizza Margherita

YIELD: 1 PIZZA / **ACTIVE TIME:** 15 MINUTES / **TOTAL TIME:** 45 MINUTES

SEMOLINA FLOUR, AS NEEDED

1 BALL OF NEAPOLITAN PIZZA DOUGH (SEE PAGE 242)

⅓ CUP PIZZA SAUCE (SEE PAGE 517)

4 OZ. FRESH MOZZARELLA CHEESE, DRAINED AND CUT INTO SHORT STRIPS

FRESH BASIL, TO TASTE

SALT, TO TASTE

EXTRA-VIRGIN OLIVE OIL, TO TASTE

1. Preheat the oven to the maximum temperature and place a baking stone or steel on the bottom of the oven as it warms. Dust a work surface with semolina flour, place the dough on the surface, and gently stretch it into a 10- to 12-inch round. Cover the dough with the sauce and top with the mozzarella and basil leaves.

2. Season the pizza with salt and drizzle olive oil over the top.

3. Dust a peel or a flat baking sheet with semolina flour and use it to transfer the pizza to the heated baking implement in the oven. Bake for about 15 minutes, until the crust is golden brown and starting to char. Remove and let cool slightly before slicing and serving.

White Shakshuka

YIELD: 4 SERVINGS / **ACTIVE TIME:** 15 MINUTES / **TOTAL TIME:** 45 MINUTES

¼ CUP AVOCADO OIL

1 LARGE YELLOW ONION, CHOPPED

4 GARLIC CLOVES, MINCED

¼ CUP CHOPPED FRESH HYSSOP LEAVES (OR A MIX OF CHOPPED FRESH MINT, OREGANO, SAGE, AND/OR THYME)

SALT AND PEPPER, TO TASTE

1 CUP TOMATO SAUCE (SEE PAGE 504)

2 CUPS LABNEH (SEE PAGE 67)

8 LARGE EGG YOLKS

PITA BREAD (SEE PAGE 338), WARMED, FOR SERVING

1. Place the avocado oil in a medium skillet and warm it over medium heat. Add the onion and cook, stirring occasionally, until golden brown, 10 to 12 minutes. Add the garlic and 3 tablespoons of the hyssop and cook, stirring frequently, until fragrant, about 1 minute. Season with salt and pepper.

2. Stir in the sauce and Labneh and spread it evenly in the pan. Cook until the sauce begins to steam and bubbles form at the edges, about 15 minutes.

3. Using the back of a spoon, create 8 depressions in the mixture and gently nestle an egg yolk in each one. Cook until the yolks begin to grow firm and opaque at the edges but remain soft at their centers, 3 to 5 minutes.

4. Sprinkle the remaining hyssop over the shakshuka, season with salt and pepper, and serve immediately with the warm pita.

Olive Oil–Poached Fluke

YIELD: 2 SERVINGS / **ACTIVE TIME:** 15 MINUTES / **TOTAL TIME:** 2 HOURS AND 15 MINUTES

½ LB. FLUKE FILLET

1¼ CUPS EXTRA-VIRGIN OLIVE OIL

1 TEASPOON KOSHER SALT

PINCH OF BLACK PEPPER

½ LEMON

FRESH PARSLEY, FOR GARNISH

1. Place the fluke and 1 cup of the olive oil in a vacuum bag and vacuum-seal it. Cook it sous vide at 145°F for 1 hour.

2. Remove the fluke from the water bath, place it in the refrigerator, and chill for 1 hour.

3. Slice the fish into 1-inch-thick pieces and arrange them on chilled serving plates. Season with the salt and pepper, drizzle the remaining olive oil around the plate, and squeeze the lemon over the pieces of fluke. Garnish with parsley and enjoy.

THE ENCYCLOPEDIA OF MEDITERRANEAN

Jerusalem Mixed Grill

YIELD: 6 SERVINGS / **ACTIVE TIME:** 45 MINUTES / **TOTAL TIME:** 1 HOUR

¼ CUP AVOCADO OIL

1 LARGE RED ONION, HALVED AND SLICED THIN

2 TEASPOONS KOSHER SALT, PLUS MORE TO TASTE

2 TEASPOONS TURMERIC

1 TEASPOON CUMIN

1 TEASPOON GROUND FENUGREEK

1 TEASPOON BAHARAT SEASONING

1 TEASPOON CINNAMON

2½ LBS. BONELESS, SKINLESS CHICKEN THIGHS (OR 1½ LBS. BONELESS, SKINLESS CHICKEN THIGHS, ½ LB. CHICKEN HEARTS, AND ½ LB. CHICKEN LIVERS), TRIMMED AND CUT INTO NICKEL-SIZE PIECES

1 LEMON, HALVED

SANDWICH BUNS OR PITA BREAD (SEE PAGE 338), FOR SERVING

PICKLES, FOR SERVING

HUMMUS (SEE PAGE 15), FOR SERVING

1. Place 2 tablespoons of the avocado oil in a large skillet and warm it over medium heat. Add the onion and a pinch of salt and cook, stirring frequently, until the onion begins to soften, about 7 minutes.

2. Lower the heat and continue to cook the onion, stirring occasionally, until the onion is deeply caramelized, which could take up to 45 minutes. Transfer the caramelized onion to a bowl and set it aside.

3. While the onion is cooking, combine the turmeric, cumin, fenugreek, baharat, cinnamon, and the 2 teaspoons salt in a large bowl. Add the chicken and toss until fully coated with the spices.

4. Place the remaining avocado oil in a large skillet and warm it over high heat. Add the chicken and spread it out in an even layer. Let the meat sear, undisturbed, for about 2 minutes, then lower the heat to medium-high and cook, stirring once or twice, until it is completely cooked through, about 6 minutes. Squeeze one of the lemon halves over the chicken.

5. Remove the chicken mixture from the skillet and stir it into the caramelized onion. Serve with sandwich buns or pita, pickles, and plenty of Hummus.

Whole Branzino

YIELD: 2 SERVINGS / **ACTIVE TIME:** 20 MINUTES / **TOTAL TIME:** 40 MINUTES

1 TO 2 LB. WHOLE BRANZINO

2 FRESH BASIL LEAVES

1 TABLESPOON KOSHER SALT

1 TABLESPOON BLACK PEPPER

2 TABLESPOONS EXTRA-VIRGIN OLIVE OIL

½ LEMON

1. Preheat the oven to 425°F. Clean the fish, remove the bones, and descale it. Pat it dry with paper towels and rub the flesh with the basil leaves. Season with the salt and pepper and close the fish back up.

2. Place the olive oil in a large cast-iron skillet and warm it over high heat. Place the fish in the pan and cook until it is browned on both sides, 8 to 10 minutes.

3. Place the pan in the oven and roast the fish until the internal temperature is 145°F, about 10 minutes.

4. Remove from the oven and transfer the branzino to a large platter. Squeeze the lemon over the top and enjoy.

Pizza Romana

YIELD: 1 PIZZA / **ACTIVE TIME:** 15 MINUTES / **TOTAL TIME:** 45 MINUTES

SEMOLINA FLOUR, AS NEEDED

1 BALL OF NEAPOLITAN PIZZA DOUGH (SEE PAGE 242)

⅓ CUP PIZZA SAUCE (SEE PAGE 517)

2½ OZ. FRESH MOZZARELLA CHEESE, DRAINED AND CUT INTO SHORT STRIPS

5 ANCHOVIES IN OLIVE OIL, DRAINED AND CHOPPED

1 TABLESPOON CAPERS, DRAINED AND RINSED

SALT, TO TASTE

DRIED OREGANO, TO TASTE

EXTRA-VIRGIN OLIVE OIL, TO TASTE

1. Preheat the oven to the maximum temperature and place a baking stone or steel on the bottom of the oven as it warms. Dust a work surface with semolina flour, place the dough on the surface, and gently stretch it into a 10- to 12-inch round. Cover the dough with the sauce and top with the mozzarella, anchovies, and capers.

2. Season the pizza with salt and oregano and drizzle olive oil over the top.

3. Dust a peel or a flat baking sheet with semolina flour and use it to transfer the pizza to the heated baking implement in the oven. Bake for about 15 minutes, until the crust is golden brown and starting to char. Remove and let cool slightly before slicing and serving.

Vegetarian Musakhan

YIELD: 4 FLATBREADS / **ACTIVE TIME:** 30 MINUTES / **TOTAL TIME:** 2 HOURS

FOR THE DOUGH

1 CUP BREAD FLOUR, PLUS MORE AS NEEDED

½ CUP WHOLE WHEAT FLOUR

2 TEASPOONS HONEY

½ TEASPOON INSTANT YEAST

¾ CUP WARM WATER (105°F)

1 TABLESPOON EXTRA-VIRGIN OLIVE OIL, PLUS MORE AS NEEDED

1 TEASPOON FINE SEA SALT

FOR THE TOPPING

5 TABLESPOONS EXTRA-VIRGIN OLIVE OIL

½ LB. PORTOBELLO MUSHROOMS, SLICED

1 CUP CHOPPED ONIONS

1 CARROT, PEELED AND GRATED

2 TABLESPOONS CHOPPED FRESH OREGANO

2 GARLIC CLOVES, MINCED

¾ TEASPOON SUMAC

⅛ TEASPOON CINNAMON

⅛ TEASPOON CARDAMOM

PINCH OF FRESHLY GRATED NUTMEG

PINCH OF SAFFRON

2 TEASPOONS LIGHT BROWN SUGAR

SALT AND PEPPER, TO TASTE

¼ CUP PINE NUTS

1. To begin preparations for the dough, place all of the ingredients in the work bowl of a stand mixer fitted with the dough hook and work the mixture on low until it comes together as a dough. Increase the speed to medium and work the dough until it no longer sticks to the side of the bowl, about 10 minutes.

2. Coat a bowl with olive oil. Place the dough on a bread flour–dusted work surface and knead it for 2 minutes. Form the dough into a ball and place it, seam side down, in the bowl. Cover the bowl with a linen towel and let the dough rise in a naturally warm spot until it has doubled in size, about 1 hour.

3. To begin preparations for the topping, place 1 tablespoon of the olive oil in a large skillet and warm it over medium heat. Add the mushrooms and sear them until browned, about 5 minutes. Turn them over and sear until browned on that side, about 5 minutes. Transfer the mushrooms to a paper towel–lined plate.

4. Place 1 tablespoon of the olive oil in the skillet and warm it over medium heat. Add the onions and cook, stirring occasionally, until they have softened, about 5 minutes. Add the carrot and cook, stirring occasionally, for 2 minutes. Add the oregano, garlic, sumac, cinnamon, cardamom, nutmeg, and saffron and cook, stirring continually, for 1 minute. Stir in the brown sugar, season the mixture with salt and pepper, and remove the pan from heat. Let the mixture cool.

5. Place the mixture in a food processor, add the remaining olive oil, and blitz until smooth. Preheat the oven to 400°F and position a baking stone on a rack in the middle. Divide the dough into 4 pieces, place them on a flour-dusted work surface, and roll each one out into a 10 x 4–inch rectangle. Spread the puree over each musakhan, leaving a ½-inch crust. Sprinkle the pine nuts and mushrooms over the puree.

6. Using a flour-dusted peel or the back of a baking sheet, slide the musakhan onto the baking stone one at a time. Bake until the crust is golden brown, about 10 minutes. Remove the musakhan from the oven and let them cool slightly before enjoying.

Whole Branzino
SEE PAGE 248

Coques

YIELD: 2 FLATBREADS / **ACTIVE TIME:** 45 MINUTES / **TOTAL TIME:** 24 HOURS

FOR THE DOUGH

½ CUP BREAD FLOUR, PLUS MORE AS NEEDED

1 CUP WHOLE WHEAT FLOUR

2 TEASPOONS SUGAR

½ TEASPOON INSTANT YEAST

½ CUP PLUS 2 TABLESPOONS WARM WATER (105°F)

1 TABLESPOON EXTRA-VIRGIN OLIVE OIL, PLUS MORE AS NEEDED

1 TEASPOON FINE SEA SALT

FOR THE TOPPING

¼ CUP EXTRA-VIRGIN OLIVE OIL

1 RED ONION, HALVED AND SLICED THIN

1¼ CUPS THINLY SLICED ROASTED RED PEPPERS

1 TABLESPOON SUGAR

1 TEASPOON DRIED OREGANO

2 GARLIC CLOVES, MINCED

PINCH OF RED PEPPER FLAKES

1 TABLESPOON SHERRY VINEGAR

⅓ CUP PINE NUTS

SALT AND PEPPER, TO TASTE

¼ CUP CHOPPED FRESH PARSLEY, FOR GARNISH

1. To begin preparations for the dough, place all of the ingredients in the work bowl of a stand mixer fitted with the dough hook and work the mixture on low until it comes together as a smooth dough. Increase the speed to medium and work the dough until it no longer sticks to the side of the bowl.

2. Coat a bowl with olive oil. Dust a work surface with bread flour. Place the dough on the work surface and knead it for 30 seconds. Form the dough into a ball and place it, seam side down, in the bowl. Cover the bowl with plastic wrap and place it in the refrigerator to chill overnight.

3. To begin preparations for the topping, place 2 tablespoons of the olive oil in a skillet and warm it over medium heat. Add the onion, peppers, and sugar and cook, stirring occasionally, until the onion is golden brown, about 10 minutes. Add the oregano, garlic, and red pepper flakes and cook, stirring continually, for 1 minute. Stir in the vinegar and pine nuts, season the mixture with salt and pepper, and remove the pan from heat. Let the mixture cool.

4. Remove the dough from the refrigerator and let it sit at room temperature for 1 hour.

5. Preheat the oven to 450°F. Line two baking sheets with parchment paper. Divide the dough in half and place it on a flour-dusted work surface. Roll them out into 12 x 4–inch rectangles or ovals. Brush the coques with olive oil and prick them all over with a fork.

6. Place the coques on the baking sheets, place them in the oven, and bake for 6 minutes. Remove the coques from the oven, brush them with the remaining olive oil, and distribute the pepper-and-onion mixture over the top.

7. Return the coques to the oven and bake until the pine nuts and edges are golden brown, about 10 minutes, rotating the pans halfway through.

8. Remove the coques from the oven and let them cool for 5 minutes. Garnish with the parsley and enjoy.

Pizza Diavola

YIELD: 1 PIZZA / **ACTIVE TIME:** 15 MINUTES / **TOTAL TIME:** 50 MINUTES

2 TABLESPOONS EXTRA-VIRGIN OLIVE OIL, PLUS MORE TO TASTE

RED PEPPER FLAKES, TO TASTE

SEMOLINA FLOUR, AS NEEDED

1 BALL OF NEAPOLITAN PIZZA DOUGH (SEE PAGE 242)

⅓ CUP PIZZA SAUCE (SEE PAGE 517)

2½ OZ. CACIOCAVALLO OR PROVOLA CHEESE, CUBED

5 SLICES OF SPICY SALAMI

SALT, TO TASTE

DRIED OREGANO, TO TASTE

1. Preheat the oven to the maximum temperature and place a baking stone or steel on the bottom of the oven as it warms. Combine the olive oil and red pepper flakes in a small bowl and set the mixture aside.

2. Dust a work surface with semolina flour, place the dough on the surface, and gently stretch it into a 10- to 12-inch round. Cover the dough with the sauce and top with the cheese and salami. Drizzle the spicy olive oil over the top and season with salt and oregano.

3. Dust a peel or a flat baking sheet with semolina flour and use it to transfer the pizza to the heated baking implement in the oven. Bake for about 15 minutes, until the crust is golden brown and starting to char. Remove and let cool slightly before slicing and serving.

Kuku Sabzi

YIELD: 4 SERVINGS / **ACTIVE TIME:** 15 MINUTES / **TOTAL TIME:** 25 MINUTES

4 EGGS

1 TEASPOON CUMIN

1 TEASPOON BLACK PEPPER

1 TEASPOON KOSHER SALT

5 SCALLIONS, TRIMMED AND SLICED THIN

1 CUP CHOPPED FRESH PARSLEY

1 CUP CHOPPED FRESH CILANTRO

1 CUP CHOPPED FRESH DILL

2 TABLESPOONS AVOCADO OIL

1. In a large bowl, whisk the eggs until smooth. Add the remaining ingredients, except for the avocado oil, and whisk until incorporated.

2. Place the avocado oil in a 10-inch nonstick skillet and warm it over medium-low heat. Pour the egg mixture into the pan and let it cook for 1 to 2 minutes. Reduce the heat to low, cover the pan, and cook until the frittata begins to set and the bottom is lightly golden brown, 7 to 8 minutes. Flip the frittata using a spatula (or slide it onto a plate and invert it back into the pan) and cook until set, 2 to 3 minutes more.

3. Transfer the frittata to a platter, slice, and enjoy.

Pizza Diavola
SEE PAGE 253

Fish & Crispy Rice Cake with Saffron Crust

YIELD: 6 SERVINGS / **ACTIVE TIME:** 1 HOUR / **TOTAL TIME:** 25 HOURS

FOR THE FISH

¼ CUP PAPRIKA OIL (SEE PAGE 520)

4 GARLIC CLOVES, QUARTERED

1 BUNCH OF CILANTRO, STEMS RESERVED AND LEFT WHOLE, LEAVES CHOPPED, PLUS MORE FOR GARNISH

2 BELL PEPPERS, SEEDS AND STEMS REMOVED, FINELY DICED

3 DRIED RED CHILE PEPPERS

6 (6 OZ.) GROUPER OR TILAPIA FILLETS

1 TO 2 PRESERVED LEMONS, CUT INTO SMALL PIECES

3 TABLESPOONS SAFFRON WATER (SEE PAGE 322)

1 TEASPOON KOSHER SALT

1 TEASPOON BLACK PEPPER

FOR THE RICE CAKE

2 CUPS BASMATI RICE, RINSED WELL AND DRAINED

SALT, TO TASTE

3 TABLESPOONS AVOCADO OIL

4 SAFFRON THREADS, CRUSHED

1 (HEAPING) TEASPOON SWEET PAPRIKA

1. To begin preparations for the fish, place the Paprika Oil in a large skillet and add the garlic, cilantro stems, bell peppers, and chiles. Place the fish on top and then add the preserved lemons. Pour the Saffron Water over the fish and rub it into the fish. Season with salt and pepper, cover the pan, and refrigerate overnight.

2. To begin preparations for the rice cake, bring 4 cups of water to a boil in a large saucepan. Stir in the rice and 1 teaspoon of salt, reduce the heat to medium-low, cover the pan, and cook for about 9 minutes; you don't want the rice to be fully cooked. Spoon the rice into a fine-mesh sieve placed over a bowl and let it sit until all of the liquid has drained.

3. Place the avocado oil in a large skillet and warm it over medium-high heat. Use a wooden spoon to stir the saffron and paprika into the oil. When the oil starts to sizzle, carefully spoon in the rice, pressing it into the bottom of the pan to form a cake. Reduce the heat to medium, place a few paper towels over the rice, and cover the pan. Cook until the rice cake is nicely browned and crispy, 15 to 20 minutes. Using a spatula, lift the cake occasionally to make sure the rice isn't burning. When the cake is ready, uncover the pan and let the rice cake cool for a few minutes.

4. Remove the paper towels. Carefully invert a large plate over the top of the pan, invert the plate and pan together, and then lift the pan away. Serve right away. The rice cake can also be made up to 1 hour ahead of time and left at room temperature, while covered. Reheat in a 300°F oven before serving.

5. To resume preparations for the fish, remove the pan from the refrigerator, place it over medium-high heat, and cook, covered, for 10 minutes. Reduce the heat to low, sprinkle the cilantro leaves over the fish, and cook, uncovered, until the dish looks bright and bubbly, about 10 minutes. Serve immediately.

Pizza Marinara

YIELD: 1 PIZZA / **ACTIVE TIME:** 15 MINUTES / **TOTAL TIME:** 45 MINUTES

SEMOLINA FLOUR, AS NEEDED

1 BALL OF NEAPOLITAN PIZZA DOUGH (SEE PAGE 242)

⅓ CUP PIZZA SAUCE (SEE PAGE 517)

1 GARLIC CLOVE, SLICED THIN

SALT, TO TASTE

DRIED OREGANO, TO TASTE

EXTRA-VIRGIN OLIVE OIL, TO TASTE

1. Preheat the oven to the maximum temperature and place a baking stone or steel on the bottom of the oven as it warms. Dust a work surface with semolina flour, place the dough on the surface, and gently stretch it into a 10- to 12-inch round. Cover the dough with the sauce and top with the garlic.

2. Season the pizza with salt and dried oregano and drizzle olive oil over the top.

3. Dust a peel or a flat baking sheet with semolina flour and use it to transfer the pizza to the heated baking implement in the oven. Bake for about 15 minutes, until the crust is golden brown and starting to char. Remove and let cool slightly before slicing and serving.

Za'atar-Crusted Ribeye

YIELD: 2 SERVINGS / **ACTIVE TIME:** 20 MINUTES / **TOTAL TIME:** 1 HOUR

ZA'ATAR (SEE PAGE 501)

1 LB. RIBEYE STEAK, AT ROOM TEMPERATURE

1. Prepare a gas or charcoal grill for high heat (500°F), making sure to set up the heat in a way that there is a cooler spot (400°F) available.

2. Apply the Za'atar generously to both sides of the steak.

3. Place the steak over high heat and let it cook until nicely seared, about 3 minutes. Turn the steak over and cook for another 3 minutes.

4. Move the steak over to the cooler part of the grill and cook until it is cooked to the desired level of doneness, 3 to 4 minutes for medium-rare. Remove the steak from the grill and let it rest for 2 to 3 minutes before serving.

Pizza Marinara
SEE PAGE 257

Lamb Belly Hash

YIELD: 6 SERVINGS / **ACTIVE TIME:** 1 HOUR / **TOTAL TIME:** 12 HOURS

2 LBS. LAMB BELLY

1 TEASPOON KOSHER SALT

2 TEASPOONS BLACK PEPPER

APPLEWOOD CHIPS, AS NEEDED

2 POTATOES, UNPEELED

2 TABLESPOONS TRUFFLE OIL

3 GARLIC CLOVES, MINCED

1. Preheat the oven to 250°F. Season the lamb belly with the salt and pepper and place it in a roasting pan. Add water to the pan until it is 2 inches deep, cover the pan with aluminum foil, and place it in the oven. Braise the lamb belly for 8 hours.

2. If using a smoker, preheat it to 250°F.

3. Place the applewood chips in a smoker or cast-iron skillet. If using the skillet, place the pan over high heat. When the wood chips start to smoke, place the skillet in a deep roasting pan. Set the potatoes in the roasting pan (not in the skillet) and cover the roasting pan with aluminum foil. Place the roasting pan in the oven. Smoke the potatoes for 2 hours.

4. Bring water to a boil in a medium saucepan.

5. Remove the smoked potatoes from the smoker or oven, place them in the boiling water, and boil until fork-tender, about 30 minutes. Drain and let the potatoes cool.

6. Remove the lamb from the oven and let it rest. Place the truffle oil in a large cast-iron skillet and warm it over high heat. Add the garlic and cook, stirring continuously, until fragrant, about 1 minute.

7. Add the potatoes and mash them so that they break apart. Add the lamb, trying to add as little of the excess fat from the pan as possible. Break up the potatoes and the lamb as they crisp up in the pan, stirring occasionally so that everything is evenly distributed.

8. Reduce the heat to medium and cook until the hash is crispy on both sides, 5 to 7 minutes. Serve immediately.

Marinated Lamb Heart

YIELD: 2 SERVINGS / **ACTIVE TIME:** 30 MINUTES / **TOTAL TIME:** 4 HOURS AND 30 MINUTES

½ CUP WHITE VINEGAR

2 TABLESPOONS EXTRA-VIRGIN OLIVE OIL

¼ CUP CHOPPED FRESH PARSLEY

1 TEASPOON CORIANDER

½ WHITE ONION, MINCED

3 FRESH MINT LEAVES, CHOPPED

3 FRESH BASIL LEAVES, CHOPPED

2 GARLIC CLOVES, MINCED

2 TEASPOONS KOSHER SALT

6 TO 8 OZ. LAMB HEART

1. Place all of the ingredients, except the lamb heart, in a bowl and stir until well combined.

2. Place the lamb heart on a cutting board and use a sharp knife to remove any connective tissue—it is white with a honeycomb-like texture—from the outside of the lamb heart. Place the lamb heart in the marinade and chill in the refrigerator for 2 to 4 hours.

3. Warm a large cast-iron skillet over high heat. Place the lamb heart in the skillet and cook until the lamb heart is seared on both sides and cooked to medium-rare, about 2 minutes per side. Remove from the skillet and let the lamb heart rest for a few minutes. Cut it into ½-inch-thick slices and enjoy.

Crab Roulade

YIELD: 10 SERVINGS / **ACTIVE TIME:** 25 MINUTES / **TOTAL TIME:** 40 MINUTES

1 LB. LUMP CRABMEAT

¼ CUP MINCED SHALLOTS

¼ CUP MAYONNAISE

¼ CUP CRÈME FRAÎCHE

¼ CUP CHOPPED FRESH CHIVES, PLUS MORE FOR GARNISH

SALT AND PEPPER, TO TASTE

5 AVOCADOS, HALVED, PITS REMOVED, SLICED THIN

PASSION FRUIT EMULSION (SEE PAGE 494), FOR GARNISH

1 FRESNO CHILE PEPPER, SLICED THIN, FOR GARNISH

¼ CUP SESAME SEEDS, TOASTED, FOR GARNISH

½ CUP MICROGREENS, FOR GARNISH

1. Place the crab, shallots, mayonnaise, crème fraîche, and chives in a mixing bowl, season the mixture with salt and pepper, and stir until well combined.

2. Place a piece of plastic wrap on a damp work surface. Place one-tenth of the crab salad on the plastic wrap and roll it up tightly into a cylinder, twisting the ends. Repeat until you have 10 cylinders of the crab salad. Place them in the refrigerator and chill for 15 minutes.

3. Remove the crab salad from the refrigerator and wrap each portion with the slices from half of an avocado.

4. Garnish the roulade with the Passion Fruit Emulsion, chile, sesame seeds, microgreens, and additional chives and enjoy.

Duck Breast Wellington

YIELD: 2 SERVINGS / **ACTIVE TIME:** 20 MINUTES / **TOTAL TIME:** 45 MINUTES

1 SKIN-ON DUCK BREAST

5-INCH SQUARE OF PUFF PASTRY

ALL-PURPOSE FLOUR, AS NEEDED

1 TABLESPOON WHIPPED FETA WITH ZA'ATAR (SEE PAGE 28)

UNSALTED BUTTER, AS NEEDED

1. Warm a cast-iron skillet over medium-high heat.

2. Using a sharp knife, score the skin of the duck breast in a crosshatch pattern, taking care not to cut into the breast meat.

3. Reduce the heat to medium and place the duck breast in the pan, skin side down. Use your hand to move the duck around the pan—this will prevent it from sticking as the fat renders. Cook until the skin begins to brown and duck fat starts to pool, 5 to 7 minutes. Remove the duck breast from the pan.

4. Preheat the oven to 375°F. Place the square of puff pastry on a flour-dusted work surface and roll it out until it is about ⅛ inch thick. Place the duck breast, skin side up, in the center of the square and spread the feta over the skin. Fold the dough over the duck breast and gently press down to seal.

5. Coat a baking sheet with butter, place the puff pastry on the pan, and place it in the oven.

6. Bake until the pastry is golden brown and the duck breast is cooked through, 15 to 20 minutes. Remove from the pan and enjoy, making sure to serve the pastry with the skin of the duck breast facing down.

Sweet & Sour Short Ribs

YIELD: 4 SERVINGS / **ACTIVE TIME:** 45 MINUTES / **TOTAL TIME:** 5 HOURS

2 LBS. BONE-IN SHORT RIBS

2 TABLESPOONS KOSHER SALT

3 TABLESPOONS BLACK PEPPER

¼ CUP EXTRA-VIRGIN OLIVE OIL

1 ONION, QUARTERED

8 GARLIC CLOVES, MINCED

2 APPLES, PEELED AND SLICED

1 TABLESPOON SUMAC

½ CUP WHITE VINEGAR

¼ CUP HONEY

1. Preheat the oven to 300°F. Using a sharp knife, remove the silverskin, connective tissue, and any excess fat from the short ribs.

2. In a small bowl, combine the salt and pepper. Rub the mixture over the short ribs.

3. Warm a roasting pan or a very large skillet over high heat. After 5 minutes or so, add a tablespoon of the olive oil and the short ribs to the pan. Cook until they are browned all over, about 10 minutes. Remove the ribs from the pan and set them in a large baking dish or roasting pan. Keep the first pan over high heat.

4. Add the onion, garlic, apples, remaining olive oil, and sumac to the pan over high heat and cook, stirring continuously, for 1 minute.

5. Pour the mixture over the ribs and then drizzle the vinegar and honey over them. Cover the pan with foil, place the pan in the oven, and braise for 4 hours.

6. Remove the pan from the oven and check the ribs. If the meat is very tender, to where it is just about to fall off the bone, cut the ribs between the bones. If not, return the pan to the oven and continue to braise the ribs until tender, checking every 30 minutes or so.

7. To serve, spoon some of the pan juices, apples, and onion over the ribs.

Orange Chicken with Roasted Vegetables & Olives

YIELD: 4 SERVINGS / **ACTIVE TIME:** 30 MINUTES / **TOTAL TIME:** 1 HOUR

3 CARROTS, PEELED AND CHOPPED

1 SMALL FENNEL BULB, TRIMMED AND SLICED THIN

1 CUP CHERRY TOMATOES

¼ CUP EXTRA-VIRGIN OLIVE OIL

4 GARLIC CLOVES, MINCED

2 TEASPOONS FINELY CHOPPED FRESH ROSEMARY

1 TABLESPOON ORANGE ZEST

1 TABLESPOON RED WINE VINEGAR

SALT AND PEPPER, TO TASTE

2 LBS. BONELESS, SKINLESS CHICKEN BREASTS

JUICE OF 2 ORANGES

KALAMATA OLIVES, CHOPPED, FOR GARNISH

FRESH BASIL, FINELY CHOPPED, FOR GARNISH

1. Preheat the oven to 400°F. Place the carrots, fennel, tomatoes, 2 tablespoons of the olive oil, the garlic, rosemary, orange zest, and red wine vinegar in a bowl, season the mixture with salt and pepper, and stir to combine.

2. Transfer the vegetable mixture to a baking dish, place it in the oven, and roast until the vegetables are almost completely tender, about 40 minutes. Remove the dish from the oven and set it aside. Leave the oven on.

3. While the vegetables are roasting, season the chicken with salt and pepper, place it in a bowl, and add the orange juice. Stir until the chicken is coated and let the mixture marinate.

4. Place the remaining olive oil in a skillet and warm it over medium-high heat. When the oil starts to shimmer, add the chicken and cook until browned on both sides, about 8 minutes. Remove the chicken from the pan and place it on top of the vegetable mixture in the baking dish.

5. Place the baking dish in the oven and roast until the chicken is cooked all the way through, about 16 minutes.

6. Divide the vegetables among the serving plates, top each portion with a chicken breast, and garnish with olives and basil.

Roasted Apricot Chicken with Mint & Sage Butternut Squash

YIELD: 6 SERVINGS / **ACTIVE TIME:** 30 MINUTES / **TOTAL TIME:** 2 HOURS

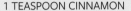

1 TEASPOON CINNAMON

½ TEASPOON CUMIN

1 TEASPOON TURMERIC

1½ TEASPOONS SMOKED SPANISH PAPRIKA

1 TABLESPOON KOSHER SALT

1 TEASPOON EXTRA-VIRGIN OLIVE OIL

4 LB. WHOLE CHICKEN

3 PLUM TOMATOES, DICED

1 CUP CHOPPED DRIED TURKISH APRICOTS

4 LARGE GARLIC CLOVES, MINCED

¼ CUP GOLDEN RAISINS

3 CUPS CHICKEN STOCK (SEE PAGE 482)

MINT & SAGE BUTTERNUT SQUASH (SEE PAGE 367), FOR SERVING

1. Preheat the oven to 375°F. Place the cinnamon, cumin, turmeric, paprika, 1 teaspoon of the salt, and the olive oil in a mixing bowl and stir until well combined. Add the chicken to the bowl and work the rub into the chicken with your hands until the entire chicken is coated.

2. Place the tomatoes, apricots, garlic, raisins, and stock in a Dutch oven and stir until combined. Place the chicken on top of the mixture and place the pot in the oven. Bake until the thickest part of the chicken's thigh reaches an internal temperature of 160°F, about 50 minutes.

3. Remove the chicken from the pot, transfer it to a cutting board, and let it rest for 15 minutes.

4. Place the Dutch oven with the veggies over medium-low heat and simmer until the liquid has been reduced by half, 10 to 15 minutes.

5. Carve the chicken and cut the meat into bite-size pieces. Stir them into the simmering sauce and serve over the Mint & Sage Butternut Squash.

Ropa Vieja

YIELD: 8 SERVINGS / **ACTIVE TIME:** 40 MINUTES / **TOTAL TIME:** 3 HOURS

2 LBS. FLANK STEAK

3 BAY LEAVES

4 GARLIC CLOVES, 3 SLICED, 1 CRUSHED

2 YELLOW ONIONS, SLICED

4 CUPS CHICKEN STOCK (SEE PAGE 482)

¼ CUP PLUS 1 TABLESPOON AVOCADO OIL

1 RED BELL PEPPER, STEM AND SEEDS REMOVED, SLICED

1 GREEN BELL PEPPER, STEM AND SEEDS REMOVED, SLICED

1 (28 OZ.) CAN OF TOMATO PUREE

1½ CUPS WHITE WINE

1 TEASPOON CUMIN

½ TEASPOON SMOKED PAPRIKA

1 TEASPOON KOSHER SALT, PLUS MORE TO TASTE

⅛ TEASPOON BLACK PEPPER

2 CUPS JASMINE RICE, RINSED AND DRAINED

SLICED AVOCADO, FOR SERVING

1. Preheat the oven to 325°F. Place the flank steak, 2 of the bay leaves, the sliced garlic cloves, 1½ of the onions, and the stock in a Dutch oven and place it in the oven. Braise until the meat is tender and easy to shred with a fork, 2 to 2½ hours.

2. Remove the pot from the oven and shred the beef with a fork. Set it aside.

3. Place ¼ cup of the avocado oil in a medium saucepan and warm it over high heat. Add the peppers and cook, stirring occasionally, until soft, about 5 minutes. Add the remaining onion and cook, stirring occasionally, until the onion is translucent, about 3 minutes. Stir in the tomato puree, wine, cumin, paprika, salt, and pepper. Cover the pan, reduce the heat to medium, and cook until the sauce has thickened, about 15 minutes.

4. Add the shredded meat and remaining bay leaf to the sauce and stir to combine. Cover the pan and cook for 5 minutes. Taste and adjust the seasoning as necessary.

5. Place the remaining avocado oil in a large saucepan with the crushed garlic clove and warm over medium heat. Add the rice and stir to coat with the oil. Add 4 cups of water and season with salt.

6. Bring to a simmer, cover the pan, reduce the heat, and let the rice simmer for 15 minutes. Turn off the heat and let the pan sit for 5 minutes. Fluff the rice before serving with the ropa vieja and avocado.

Sabich

YIELD: 6 SERVINGS / **ACTIVE TIME:** 20 MINUTES / **TOTAL TIME:** 1 HOUR

2 MEDIUM EGGPLANTS, SLICED INTO 1-INCH-THICK ROUNDS

2 TEASPOONS KOSHER SALT

AVOCADO OIL, TO TASTE

SERVE WITH ANY, OR ALL, OF THE FOLLOWING:

6 TO 8 PIECES OF PITA BREAD (SEE PAGE 338)

8 HARD-BOILED EGGS, QUARTERED

2 CUCUMBERS, CHOPPED

2 TOMATOES, CHOPPED

1 ONION, CHOPPED

1 BELL PEPPER, STEM AND SEEDS REMOVED, CHOPPED

TAHINI SAUCE (SEE PAGE 500)

FRESH PARSLEY, CHOPPED

PICKLES

OLIVES

HOT PEPPERS

RED ZHUG (SEE PAGE 499)

1. Arrange the eggplant rounds in a single layer on a wire rack set in a baking sheet. Sprinkle them on both sides with the salt and let the eggplant slices stand for at least 20 minutes and up to 1 hour.

2. Preheat the oven to 425°F. Pat the eggplant slices dry using a paper towel, brush both sides generously with oil, and place them on a baking sheet or two, being careful not to overcrowd either pan. Place the eggplants in the oven and roast until golden brown, about 20 minutes, turning the eggplants over halfway through.

3. Create your spread with your preferences among the remaining ingredients and enjoy.

Sabich
SEE PAGE 269

Slow-Roasted Lamb Shoulder with Brussels Sprouts & Crispy Kale

YIELD: 4 TO 6 SERVINGS / **ACTIVE TIME:** 30 MINUTES / **TOTAL TIME:** 3 HOURS AND 30 MINUTES

1 TABLESPOON FENNEL SEEDS

1 TABLESPOON CUMIN SEEDS

2 GARLIC CLOVES, GRATED

1 TABLESPOON FRESH OREGANO

¼ CUP BROWN SUGAR

2 TEASPOONS KOSHER SALT

¼ CUP MALT VINEGAR

¼ CUP AVOCADO OIL

4½ LB. BONE-IN LAMB SHOULDER

1 CUP WATER

1 LB. BRUSSELS SPROUTS, TRIMMED AND HALVED

½ TEASPOON BLACK PEPPER

½ CUP SMOKED ALMONDS, CHOPPED

5¼ OZ. BABY KALE LEAVES

1. Preheat the oven to 350°F. Using a mortar and pestle, grind the fennel and cumin seeds into a powder. Place that mixture, the garlic, oregano, brown sugar, 1 teaspoon of the salt, the vinegar, and 2 tablespoons of the avocado oil in a mixing bowl and stir to combine.

2. Rub the lamb with the mixture and place it in a large roasting pan. Add the water and cover the roasting pan with aluminum foil.

3. Place the lamb in the oven and roast for 2 hours. Remove from the oven, remove the foil, and spoon the cooking liquid over the lamb. Return the lamb to the oven and roast until well browned, about 40 minutes.

4. While the lamb is in the oven, place the Brussels sprouts, remaining salt, the pepper, and the remaining oil in a large bowl and toss to combine. Transfer to a parchment-lined baking sheet, place it in the oven, and roast until golden brown, 15 to 20 minutes.

5. Add the almonds and kale to the pan of Brussels sprouts, return the pan to the oven, and roast until the kale is crispy, about 5 minutes.

6. Remove the lamb and vegetables from the oven and serve them together.

Tomatoes Reinados

YIELD: 6 SERVINGS / **ACTIVE TIME:** 45 MINUTES / **TOTAL TIME:** 1 HOUR AND 15 MINUTES

10 TOMATOES

1 LOAF OF WHITE BREAD

1 LB. GROUND BEEF

1½ TEASPOONS KOSHER SALT

¼ TEASPOON BLACK PEPPER

½ CUP AVOCADO OIL

1 EGG

½ CUP ALL-PURPOSE FLOUR

1. Cut the top ¼ inch off the tomatoes. Scoop out the insides of the tomatoes and set them aside. Use the scooped-out tomato flesh for another preparation.

2. Soak the loaf of bread in water for about 10 minutes and then drain.

3. Place the ground beef, bread, salt, and pepper in a mixing bowl and stir until well combined. Stuff each tomato with about 2 tablespoons of the beef mixture, using your palms to flatten the top of the stuffing.

4. Place the oil in a saucepan and warm it to 350°F over medium-high heat. Place the egg in a small bowl and beat it. Place the flour in a separate small bowl.

5. Dip the top of a tomato into the flour, shake off any excess, and then dip the top of the tomato in the beaten egg. Place the tomato on a plate and repeat with the remaining tomatoes.

6. Place the tomatoes in the pot, top down, and fry until their tops are golden brown. Transfer the fried tomatoes into another skillet, fried side up.

7. Add water to the pan until it reaches three-quarters of the way up the tomatoes. Place the pan over medium-high heat and bring the water to a boil. Reduce the heat to low, cover the pan, and cook the tomatoes until the meat is cooked, the tomatoes are tender, and about one-quarter of the water remains, about 45 minutes.

8. Remove the tomatoes from the pan and enjoy.

Turkish Coffee–Rubbed Brisket

YIELD: 6 SERVINGS / **ACTIVE TIME:** 30 MINUTES / **TOTAL TIME:** 30 HOURS

4 LB. BEEF BRISKET

2 ONIONS, QUARTERED

2 LARGE POTATOES, SCRUBBED AND CUT INTO 1-INCH-THICK WEDGES

1 LARGE CARROT, PEELED AND CUT INTO 2-INCH-LONG PIECES

1 FENNEL BULB, TRIMMED AND CUT INTO WEDGES

1 GARLIC HEAD, HALVED CROSSWISE

2 TABLESPOONS AVOCADO OIL

1 TABLESPOON PLUS 1 TEASPOON KOSHER SALT

1½ TEASPOONS BLACK PEPPER

1 TABLESPOON VERY FINELY GROUND ARABICA COFFEE

1 TABLESPOON SMOKED CINNAMON

1 TEASPOON CARDAMOM

1. Preheat the oven to 400°F. Trim any fatty areas on the brisket so that the fat is within approximately ¼ inch of the meat, keeping in mind that it is better to leave too much fat than too little.

2. Place the onions, potatoes, carrot, fennel, and garlic in a heavy roasting pan. Add the avocado oil, 1 teaspoon of the salt, and ½ teaspoon of the pepper and toss to combine.

3. Place the coffee, cinnamon, cardamom, remaining salt, and remaining pepper in a small bowl and stir until well combined. Rub the mixture all over the brisket and nestle the brisket into the vegetables. Place the pan in the oven and roast until the vegetables are lightly browned, about 45 minutes.

4. Cover the pan tightly with aluminum foil, lower the oven's temperature to 300°F, and roast until the brisket is fork-tender, 5 to 6 hours. As the brisket cooks, check on it every 45 minutes, adding ¼ cup water to the pan if it starts to look dry.

5. Remove the roasting pan from the oven and let it cool to room temperature. Refrigerate the brisket and vegetables until the fat is solid, 8 to 24 hours.

6. Transfer the brisket to a cutting board and slice it across the grain. Skim and discard the fat in the roasting pan. Return the slices of brisket to the roasting pan with the vegetables and cooking juices.

7. Preheat the oven to 300°F. Transfer the roasting pan to the oven and heat the brisket until the liquid is starting to bubble and the brisket and vegetables are just warmed through, 15 to 20 minutes.

8. Transfer the brisket and vegetables to a serving dish, cover it with aluminum foil, and set it aside.

9. Place the roasting pan over two burners on the stovetop and simmer the liquid over medium heat until it has thickened, 10 to 15 minutes.

10. Pour the reduced liquid over the brisket and vegetables and enjoy.

Eggplant Dolma

YIELD: 6 TO 8 SERVINGS / **ACTIVE TIME:** 30 MINUTES / **TOTAL TIME:** 1 HOUR AND 30 MINUTES

3 SLICES OF WHOLE WHEAT BREAD, CRUSTS REMOVED, ROUGHLY TORN

1 CUP WATER

2 LBS. GROUND BEEF

2 TEASPOONS KOSHER SALT, PLUS MORE TO TASTE

2 TEASPOONS CUMIN

1 TEASPOON BLACK PEPPER, PLUS MORE TO TASTE

2 EGGPLANTS (PREFERABLY WITH AN ELONGATED SHAPE)

4 EGGS

¼ CUP AVOCADO OIL, PLUS MORE AS NEEDED

1 CUP TOMATO SAUCE (SEE PAGE 504)

2 TABLESPOONS TAMARIND CONCENTRATE

1 TABLESPOON SUGAR

FETA CHEESE, CRUMBLED, FOR GARNISH

FRESH PARSLEY, CHOPPED, FOR GARNISH

1. Preheat the oven to 350°F. In a large bowl, cover the torn bread with ½ cup of the water and work the mixture with your hands until it is a paste. Add the beef, salt, cumin, and pepper and work the mixture with your hands until well combined. Set the mixture aside.

2. Remove the tops and bottoms of each eggplant, then slice each one lengthwise into ¼-inch-thick slices.

3. Place the eggs in a large bowl, season with salt and pepper, and whisk until scrambled. Add the eggplant slices and dredge them until completely coated. Transfer the slices to a colander and let them drain for 5 minutes.

4. Place the avocado oil in a large skillet and warm it over medium-high heat. Line a baking sheet with paper towels and place it by the stove. Working in batches to avoid crowding the pan, add the eggplants and fry until golden brown and softened, 4 to 6 minutes, turning them over once. Transfer the fried eggplants to the lined baking sheet. Add more avocado oil to the pan as needed.

5. Place 2 tablespoons of the beef mixture at the base of each slice of eggplant and roll them up lengthwise. Place the rolls beside each other, seam side down, in a 13 x 9–inch baking dish.

6. Place the remaining water, Tomato Sauce, tamarind concentrate, and sugar in a mixing bowl and stir to combine. Season the sauce with salt and pepper and pour it over the eggplants.

7. Place the eggplants in the oven and bake until the edges are golden brown and the filling is cooked through, 35 to 40 minutes.

8. Remove from the oven, garnish with feta and chopped parsley, and enjoy.

Brisket with Pistachio Gremolata

YIELD: 8 SERVINGS / **ACTIVE TIME:** 30 MINUTES / **TOTAL TIME:** 30 HOURS

7 LB. BEEF BRISKET

2 TEASPOONS KOSHER SALT, PLUS MORE TO TASTE

1 TEASPOON FRESHLY GROUND BLACK PEPPER, PLUS MORE TO TASTE

CLOVES FROM 1 HEAD OF GARLIC

1 CUP WALNUTS

2 TABLESPOONS HONEY

3 CUPS POMEGRANATE JUICE

PISTACHIO GREMOLATA (SEE PAGE 493), FOR SERVING

1. Trim any fatty areas on the brisket so that the fat is within approximately ¼ inch of the meat, keeping in mind that it is better to leave too much fat than too little. Season the brisket all over with salt and pepper. Transfer the brisket to a large resealable plastic bag or bowl.

2. Place the garlic, walnuts, honey, and 1 cup of the pomegranate juice in a blender and puree until very smooth. Add the remaining pomegranate juice and blend until smooth. Pour the marinade over the brisket. Seal the bag or cover the bowl tightly with aluminum foil and let the brisket marinate in the refrigerator for 24 hours.

3. Transfer the brisket and marinade to a roasting pan, cover it tightly with foil, and let the brisket sit at room temperature for 1 hour.

4. Preheat the oven to 275°F. Place the covered roasting pan in the oven and braise the brisket until it is tender enough that the meat can easily be shredded with two forks, 5 to 6 hours.

5. Transfer the brisket to a cutting board and cover it loosely with aluminum foil.

6. Transfer the cooking liquid to a saucepan and spoon off as much fat as possible from the surface. Cook over medium-high heat, skimming off any fat and foam as it surfaces, until the liquid has been reduced by two-thirds, leaving you with about 2 cups of sauce. Taste and season the sauce with salt and pepper if necessary.

7. To serve, slice the brisket against the grain and transfer it to a platter. Spoon the sauce over the top and top with the gremolata.

Briam

YIELD: 4 SERVINGS / **ACTIVE TIME:** 40 MINUTES / **TOTAL TIME:** 2 HOURS

3 YUKON GOLD POTATOES, PEELED AND SLICED THIN

3 ZUCCHINI, SLICED THIN

SALT AND PEPPER, TO TASTE

1 TABLESPOON CHOPPED FRESH OREGANO

2 TEASPOONS CHOPPED FRESH ROSEMARY

½ CUP FRESH PARSLEY, CHOPPED

4 GARLIC CLOVES, MINCED

3 TABLESPOONS EXTRA-VIRGIN OLIVE OIL

4 TOMATOES, SEEDED AND CHOPPED

1 LARGE RED ONION, HALVED AND SLICED THIN

1. Preheat the oven to 400°F. Place the potatoes and zucchini in a bowl, season with salt and pepper, and then add the oregano, rosemary, parsley, garlic, and olive oil. Stir until the vegetables are evenly coated and set aside.

2. Cover the bottom of a medium cast-iron skillet with half of the tomatoes. Arrange the potatoes, zucchini, and onion in rows, working in from the edge of the pan to the center and alternating the vegetables as you go. Top with the remaining tomatoes and cover with foil.

3. Place the skillet in the oven and roast for 45 minutes. Remove from the oven, remove the foil, and roast for another 40 minutes, until the vegetables are charred and tender.

4. Remove from the oven and let the briam cool slightly before enjoying.

Pesce all'Ebraica

YIELD: 4 SERVINGS / **ACTIVE TIME:** 10 MINUTES / **TOTAL TIME:** 30 MINUTES

4 LBS. WHITEFISH

1 TEASPOON KOSHER SALT, PLUS MORE TO TASTE

BLACK PEPPER, TO TASTE

¼ CUP APPLE CIDER VINEGAR OR RED WINE VINEGAR

1 TABLESPOON HONEY

½ CUP AVOCADO OIL

¼ CUP GOLDEN RAISINS, CHOPPED

¼ CUP PINE NUTS

FRESH PARSLEY, CHOPPED, FOR GARNISH

1. Preheat the oven to 400°F. Season the fish with salt and pepper and place it in a 13 x 9–inch baking dish.

2. In a small bowl, add the vinegar, honey, oil, and 1 teaspoon of salt and stir until well combined. Pour the mixture over the fish and then sprinkle the raisins and pine nuts over the top.

3. Place the pan in the oven and bake until the fish is opaque and can be flaked easily with a fork. For a very thin piece of fish, this will only take about 10 minutes. For a thicker fillet, such as halibut, this can take up to 20 minutes. Baste the fish after 10 minutes if it is not yet ready.

4. Remove from the oven, garnish with parsley, and enjoy.

Brisket with Pistachio Gremolata
SEE PAGE 276

Aliciotti con Indivia

YIELD: 4 SERVINGS / **ACTIVE TIME:** 25 MINUTES / **TOTAL TIME:** 45 MINUTES

2 TABLESPOONS EXTRA-VIRGIN OLIVE OIL

6 GARLIC CLOVES, MINCED

2 BUNCHES OF ESCAROLE, CHOPPED

36 FRESH ANCHOVIES OR ANCHOVY FILLETS IN OIL AND VINEGAR

¼ TEASPOON KOSHER SALT

⅛ TEASPOON BLACK PEPPER

⅛ TEASPOON RED PEPPER FLAKES

1. Preheat the oven to 350°F. Coat a 13 x 9–inch baking dish with a tablespoon of the olive oil and sprinkle a teaspoon of the garlic over the dish. Place the escarole in the baking dish and sprinkle the remaining garlic over the top.

2. Slice open the anchovies from head to tail. Place a layer of anchovies, skin side up, over the escarole. Season with the salt, pepper, and red pepper flakes, drizzle the remaining olive oil over the anchovies, and cover the baking dish with aluminum foil.

3. Place the dish in the oven and bake until the escarole is tender and the anchovies have softened, about 20 minutes.

4. Remove from the oven and enjoy immediately.

Chicken with Mehshi Sfeeha

YIELD: 6 SERVINGS / **ACTIVE TIME:** 30 MINUTES / **TOTAL TIME:** 3 HOURS

1 LB. GROUND BEEF

¼ CUP SHORT-GRAIN RICE, RINSED AND DRAINED

1 TABLESPOON ALLSPICE

7 TEASPOONS KOSHER SALT, PLUS MORE TO TASTE

1 TABLESPOON WATER

12 DRIED EGGPLANT SKINS

1 EGGPLANT, SLICED INTO ½-INCH-THICK ROUNDS

¼ CUP AVOCADO OIL

3 LB. WHOLE CHICKEN

1 TABLESPOON RAS EL HANOUT (SEE PAGE 505)

1 TEASPOON PAPRIKA

4 TO 6 GARLIC CLOVES, MINCED

1. Preheat the oven to 400°F. In a large bowl, combine the beef, rice, 1 teaspoon of the allspice, 1 teaspoon of the salt, and the water and stir until well combined. Set the mixture aside.

2. To rehydrate the eggplant skins, bring 6 cups of water to a boil. Carefully place the dried eggplant skins in the water and boil until they are soft, stirring occasionally, about 5 minutes. Drain, sprinkle about ½ teaspoon of salt on each eggplant skin, and let them cool.

3. Stuff each eggplant skin with about 2 teaspoons of the meat mixture and flatten the filling at the top edge of the eggplant skins.

4. Lay the slices of fresh eggplant on paper towels and season them with salt. Let them stand for 30 minutes.

5. Pat the slices of fresh eggplant dry. Add 2 tablespoons of the avocado oil to a medium skillet and warm it over medium-high heat. Place a single layer of eggplant slices in the pan and fry until they are a deep golden brown on both sides, 4 to 8 minutes. Transfer the fried eggplant to a paper towel–lined plate and continue frying the fresh eggplant.

6. Place 1 tablespoon of oil in a Dutch oven and warm it over medium-high heat. Place the stuffed dried eggplants in a single layer on the bottom of the pot and sprinkle a teaspoon of allspice over the top. Lay the fried eggplant over the stuffed dried eggplants.

7. Place the whole chicken over the fried eggplant and rub the chicken with the remaining oil, remaining allspice, a generous amount of salt, the Ras el Hanout, paprika, and garlic. Place the chicken in the pot, breast side down. Add enough water to the pot to reach halfway up the stuffed eggplants (about ½ cup).

8. Place the Dutch oven in the oven, uncovered, and bake until the chicken is cooked through, 1½ to 2 hours. Flip the chicken over halfway through, and check to make sure that there is enough liquid in the pot.

9. Remove from the oven and let the dish rest for 15 minutes before enjoying.

Roast Chicken with Fennel & Carrots

YIELD: 4 SERVINGS / **ACTIVE TIME:** 30 MINUTES / **TOTAL TIME:** 3 HOURS

4 LB. WHOLE CHICKEN

SALT AND PEPPER, TO TASTE

2 FENNEL BULBS, EACH CUT INTO 6 WEDGES

1 LB. SMALL CARROTS, PEELED AND CUT ON A BIAS INTO 4-INCH-LONG PIECES

3 TABLESPOONS AVOCADO OIL

1. Pat the chicken dry with paper towels and season it generously with salt, inside and out. Tie the legs together with kitchen twine and let it sit at room temperature for 1 hour. If time allows, place the chicken in the refrigerator, uncovered, overnight.

2. Preheat the oven to 425°F and position a rack in the upper third of the oven. Place a large cast-iron skillet on the rack.

3. In a large bowl, combine the fennel, carrots, and 2 tablespoons of the avocado oil and toss to coat. Season the mixture with salt and pepper.

4. Pat the chicken dry with paper towels and rub it with half of the remaining oil. Drizzle the remaining oil into the hot skillet, as this helps keep the chicken from sticking. Place the chicken in the center of the skillet and arrange the vegetables around it.

5. Roast until the fennel and carrots are golden brown and an instant-read thermometer inserted into the thickest part of the breast registers 155°F, 50 to 60 minutes.

6. Remove the chicken from the oven and let it rest in the pan for 20 minutes. The internal temperature will climb to 165°F as the chicken rests.

7. Carve the chicken and serve with the vegetables.

Chicken with Turmeric Tahini, Chickpeas & Onions

YIELD: 4 SERVINGS / **ACTIVE TIME:** 25 MINUTES / **TOTAL TIME:** 1 HOUR AND 30 MINUTES

3 LBS. BONE-IN, SKIN-ON CHICKEN PIECES

SALT AND PEPPER, TO TASTE

2 CUPS TURMERIC TAHINI SAUCE

2 (14 OZ.) CANS OF CHICKPEAS, DRAINED AND RINSED

1 RED ONION, SLICED THIN

1 TABLESPOON TURMERIC

1 TEASPOON CUMIN

1 TEASPOON CORIANDER

1 TEASPOON BERBERE SEASONING

2 TABLESPOONS AVOCADO OIL

1 TABLESPOON FRESH LEMON JUICE

HOT SAUCE, TO TASTE

½ BUNCH OF FRESH CILANTRO, COARSELY CHOPPED

1. Season the chicken pieces with a generous amount of salt and pepper and place them in a large resealable plastic bag with 1 cup of the turmeric tahini sauce. Seal the bag, leaving one corner open about ½ inch. Massage the bag to coat all of the chicken pieces with sauce, then squeeze the bag to remove as much air as you can. Seal the bag and let the chicken marinate at room temperature for 30 minutes, or overnight in the refrigerator.

2. Preheat the oven to 425°F. On a large baking sheet, toss the chickpeas and half of the onion with the turmeric, cumin, coriander, and berbere. Drizzle the avocado oil over the mixture, season with salt and pepper, and toss everything to coat. Push everything to the edges of the pan and place the chicken pieces in the center in a single layer.

3. Place in the oven and roast until the onion is crispy, the chicken skin is brown, and an instant-read thermometer registers 160°F when inserted into the thickest part of a thigh, about 50 minutes.

4. While the chicken is in the oven, place the remaining onion and the lemon juice in a bowl, season with salt and pepper, and stir to combine.

5. Remove the chicken from the oven and transfer it to a serving plate along with the chickpeas and onions. Drizzle the remaining tahini sauce and hot sauce over the mixture, sprinkle the onion-and-lemon mixture and cilantro over it, and enjoy.

Cold Roast Salmon with Smashed Green Bean Salad

YIELD: 10 SERVINGS / **ACTIVE TIME:** 20 MINUTES / **TOTAL TIME:** 1 HOUR AND 45 MINUTES

1 WHOLE SIDE OF SALMON (ABOUT 3½ LBS.)

7 TABLESPOONS AVOCADO OIL, PLUS MORE FOR SERVING

BLACK PEPPER, TO TASTE

4 TEASPOONS KOSHER SALT, PLUS MORE TO TASTE

½ TEASPOON RED PEPPER FLAKES, DIVIDED

¼ CUP FRESH LEMON JUICE

2 LBS. GREEN BEANS, TRIMMED

1 BUNCH OF RADISHES (FRENCH BREAKFAST PREFERRED), TRIMMED

1 CUP SALTED AND ROASTED PISTACHIOS, SHELLED AND COARSELY CHOPPED

MALDON SEA SALT, TO TASTE

LEMON WEDGES, FOR SERVING

LEMONY YOGURT SAUCE (SEE PAGE 499), FOR SERVING

SALSA VERDE (SEE PAGE 505), FOR SERVING

1. Preheat the oven to 300°F. Place the salmon on a rimmed baking sheet and rub 2 tablespoons of avocado oil over each side. Season the salmon all over with black pepper, 2 teaspoons of the salt, and ¼ teaspoon of the red pepper flakes.

2. Place the salmon skin side down on the baking sheet and place it in the oven. Roast until a paring knife inserted into the side of the salmon meets with no resistance, 20 to 25 minutes. The fish should be opaque throughout, and you should just be able to flake it with a fork. Remove from the oven and let it cool completely.

3. While the salmon is roasting, place the lemon juice, remaining avocado oil, remaining salt, and remaining red pepper flakes in a large bowl and whisk to combine. Set the dressing aside.

4. Working in batches, place the green beans in a large resealable plastic bag. Seal the bag and whack the beans with a rolling pin to split their skins and soften their insides without completely pulverizing them. Place them in a bowl with the lemon dressing and massage the mixture with your hands to break down the beans further. Let the mixture sit at room temperature for at least 1 hour.

5. Slice the radishes thin lengthwise. Place them in a large bowl of ice water, cover, and chill until ready to serve; this will allow you to get the prep out of the way and keep the radishes crisp and firm.

6. Just before serving, drain the radishes and toss them with the green beans. Stir in the pistachios, taste, and adjust the seasoning as necessary. Transfer to a platter, drizzle avocado oil over the top, and sprinkle the Maldon sea salt on top.

7. Using two spatulas, carefully transfer the salmon to another platter, leaving the skin behind on the baking sheet. Drizzle avocado oil over it and squeeze a lemon wedge or two over the salmon. Sprinkle Maldon over the fish and serve with more lemon wedges, the Lemony Yogurt Sauce, and the Salsa Verde.

THE ENCYCLOPEDIA OF MEDITERRANEAN

SOUPS
& STEWS

Bouillabaisse

YIELD: 6 SERVINGS / **ACTIVE TIME:** 25 MINUTES / **TOTAL TIME:** 1 HOUR AND 30 MINUTES

6 TABLESPOONS EXTRA-VIRGIN OLIVE OIL

1 ONION, CHOPPED

1 CUP CHOPPED LEEKS

½ CUP SLICED CELERY

1 CUP CHOPPED FENNEL

2 GARLIC CLOVES, MINCED

BOUQUET GARNI (SEE PAGE 485)

ZEST OF 1 ORANGE

1 TOMATO, PEELED, SEEDED, AND CHOPPED

PINCH OF SAFFRON

3 CUPS FISH STOCK (SEE PAGE 482)

3 CUPS LOBSTER STOCK (SEE PAGE 483)

2 TEASPOONS PERNOD

1 TABLESPOON TOMATO PASTE

1 LB. MONKFISH, CUT INTO 1-INCH CUBES

12 SMALL SHRIMP, SHELLS REMOVED, DEVEINED

12 STEAMER CLAMS

24 MUSSELS

SALT AND PEPPER, TO TASTE

FRESH PARSLEY, CHOPPED, FOR GARNISH

CRUSTY BREAD, TOASTED, FOR SERVING

1. Place ¼ cup of the olive oil in a large saucepan and warm it over medium heat. Add the onion, leeks, celery, and fennel and cook, stirring occasionally, until the vegetables have softened, about 10 minutes.

2. Add the garlic, Bouquet Garni, orange zest, and tomato and cook, stirring continually, for 1 minute. Stir in the saffron, stocks, Pernod, and tomato paste and bring the soup to a boil. Reduce the heat and simmer the soup for 20 minutes.

3. While the soup is simmering, place the remaining olive oil in a skillet and warm it over medium heat. Add the monkfish and shrimp and cook for 2 minutes on each side. Remove the shrimp and monkfish from the pan and set them aside.

4. Add the clams to the soup and cook for 3 minutes. Add the mussels and cook until the majority of the clams and mussels have opened, 3 to 4 minutes. Discard any clams and mussels that do not open.

5. Add the monkfish and shrimp to the soup and cook until warmed through.

6. Season the soup with salt and pepper and ladle it into warmed bowls. Garnish each portion with parsley and serve with crusty bread.

Seafood & Leek Soup

YIELD: 4 TO 6 SERVINGS / **ACTIVE TIME:** 30 MINUTES / **TOTAL TIME:** 1 HOUR AND 30 MINUTES

2 TABLESPOONS EXTRA-VIRGIN OLIVE OIL

½ LB. MEDIUM SHRIMP, SHELLS REMOVED AND RESERVED, DEVEINED

¾ CUP WHITE WINE

2 CUPS CLAM JUICE

3 CUPS WATER

1 LEEK, TRIMMED, HALVED, RINSED WELL, AND SLICED THIN

6 OZ. PANCETTA, CHOPPED

2 TABLESPOONS TOMATO PASTE

1 TEASPOON GRATED FRESH GINGER

1 TEASPOON CORIANDER

1 TEASPOON PAPRIKA

½ TEASPOON TURMERIC

2 PINCHES OF RED PEPPER FLAKES

½ LB. COD, SKIN REMOVED, CUT INTO ½-INCH CUBES

10 OZ. SQUID, CLEANED (SEE PAGE 199) AND HALVED IF LARGE

1 TEASPOON FRESH LEMON JUICE

SALT AND PEPPER, TO TASTE

CRUSTY BREAD, FOR SERVING

1. Place half of the olive oil in a medium saucepan and warm over medium heat. Add the shrimp shells and cook, stirring frequently, until the bottom of the pan starts to brown, about 4 minutes. Remove the shells from the pan and discard them.

2. Add the white wine and cook until it has evaporated, scraping any browned bits up from the bottom of the pan.

3. Add the clam juice and water and bring the broth to a boil. Reduce the heat and simmer.

4. Place the remaining olive oil in a separate pan and warm it over medium-high heat. Add the leek and pancetta and cook, stirring frequently, until the leek has softened and the pancetta is lightly browned, 6 to 8 minutes.

5. Stir in the tomato paste, ginger, coriander, paprika, turmeric, and red pepper flakes and cook, stirring continually, for 1 minute. Add the mixture to the broth and simmer for 20 minutes.

6. Add the cod and cook for 2 minutes. Add the shrimp and cook for another 2 minutes.

7. Remove the pan from heat, add the squid, and cover the pan. Let the soup sit until the squid is cooked through, 4 to 6 minutes.

8. Stir in the lemon juice, season the soup with salt and pepper, and ladle it into warmed bowls. Serve with crusty bread and enjoy.

Artichoke à la Barigoule

YIELD: 4 SERVINGS / **ACTIVE TIME:** 30 MINUTES / **TOTAL TIME:** 1 HOUR AND 30 MINUTES

2 CUPS BABY ARTICHOKES IN OLIVE OIL, DRAINED AND QUARTERED, OIL RESERVED

½ LB. BUTTON MUSHROOMS, SLICED THIN

1 LEEK, TRIMMED, HALVED, RINSED WELL, AND SLICED THIN

1 GARLIC CLOVE, MINCED

2 ANCHOVIES IN OLIVE OIL, DRAINED AND FINELY CHOPPED

½ TEASPOON FRESH THYME

2 TABLESPOONS ALL-PURPOSE FLOUR

¼ CUP DRY VERMOUTH

4 CUPS CHICKEN STOCK (SEE PAGE 482), PLUS MORE AS NEEDED

½ CUP PEELED AND CHOPPED CELERIAC

1 BAY LEAF

½ CUP HEAVY CREAM

1½ TABLESPOONS CHOPPED FRESH TARRAGON

1 TEASPOON CHAMPAGNE VINEGAR

SALT AND PEPPER, TO TASTE

1. Place 2 tablespoons of the olive oil reserved from the artichokes in a medium saucepan and warm it over medium heat. Add the artichokes and cook, stirring occasionally, until they are lightly caramelized, about 5 minutes. Remove the pan from heat, transfer the artichokes to a plate, and let them cool.

2. Place the pan back over medium heat and add the mushrooms. Cover the pan and cook for 5 minutes. Remove the cover and cook until most of the liquid the mushrooms release has evaporated, about 5 minutes.

3. Add another tablespoon of the reserved oil and the leek and cook, stirring occasionally, until it has softened, about 5 minutes. Stir in the garlic, anchovies, and thyme and cook, stirring continually, for 1 minute.

4. Stir in the flour, cook for 1 minute, and then add the vermouth. Cook until the alcohol has been cooked off, 1 to 2 minutes.

5. While whisking, gradually add the stock. When all of the stock has been incorporated, add the celeriac and bay leaf along with the artichokes and bring the mixture to a boil. Reduce the heat and simmer until the celeriac is tender, 10 to 15 minutes, adding more stock if the level of liquid starts to look a bit too low.

6. Remove the pan from heat, remove the bay leaf, and discard it. Stir in the cream, tarragon, and vinegar, season the soup with salt and pepper, ladle it into warmed bowls, and enjoy.

Chicken & Tomato Stew

YIELD: 4 SERVINGS / **ACTIVE TIME:** 45 MINUTES / **TOTAL TIME:** 3 HOURS

4 BONE-IN, SKIN-ON CHICKEN LEGS

SALT, TO TASTE

¼ CUP EXTRA-VIRGIN OLIVE OIL

1 LARGE ONION, SLICED THIN

6 GARLIC CLOVES, HALVED

2 TABLESPOONS HONEY

1 TABLESPOON TOMATO PASTE

¾ TEASPOON TURMERIC

½ TEASPOON CINNAMON

1 (14 OZ.) CAN OF WHOLE PEELED TOMATOES, WITH THEIR JUICES

3 CUPS CHICKEN STOCK (SEE PAGE 482)

1 LEMON

1½ TEASPOONS SUGAR

1 TABLESPOON TOASTED SESAME SEEDS

½ CUP TORN FRESH MINT LEAVES

PITA BREAD (SEE PAGE 338), FOR SERVING

1. Pat the chicken dry and season it with salt. Let the chicken sit at room temperature for at least 15 minutes and up to 1 hour, or cover and refrigerate for up to 24 hours.

2. Place 2 tablespoons of the olive oil in a large Dutch oven and warm it over medium-high heat. Add the chicken and cook until it is a deep golden brown on both sides, about 12 minutes, adjusting the heat as necessary to avoid burning.

3. Transfer the chicken to a plate, leaving the drippings in the pan.

4. Place the onion in the pot and cook, stirring frequently, until it has softened, 6 to 8 minutes. Add the garlic and cook, stirring frequently, until the onion begins to brown around the edges, about 3 minutes. Stir in the honey, tomato paste, turmeric, and cinnamon and cook until fragrant, about 2 minutes. Add the tomatoes and their juices and smash the tomatoes with a wooden spoon until they break down into pieces no larger than 1 inch.

5. Return the chicken to the pot, add the stock (it should barely cover the chicken), and bring to a simmer. Reduce the heat to low, partially cover the pot, and simmer until the chicken is tender and the sauce has thickened, about 1 hour.

6. While the chicken is simmering, trim the top and bottom from the lemon and cut it into quarters. Remove the seeds and the white pith in the center. Slice the quarters crosswise into quarter-moons.

7. Place the lemon pieces in a medium skillet, cover them with water, and bring to a boil. Cook for 3 minutes, drain, and pat dry with paper towels. Transfer the lemon pieces to a small bowl, sprinkle the sugar over them, and toss to coat.

8. Wipe out the skillet and warm the remaining olive oil over medium-high heat. Arrange the lemon pieces in a single layer in the skillet. Cook, turning halfway through, until they are deeply browned all over, about 3 minutes. Return the lemon to the bowl and season with salt. Ladle the stew into bowls, top with the caramelized lemon, sesame seeds, and mint, and serve with pitas.

Albondigas Soup

YIELD: 4 SERVINGS / **ACTIVE TIME:** 45 MINUTES / **TOTAL TIME:** 2 HOURS

FOR THE MEATBALLS

2 CUPS DAY-OLD BREAD PIECES, CRUST REMOVED

½ CUP MILK

½ LB. GROUND PORK

½ LB. GROUND BEEF

½ CUP GRATED ZAMORANO CHEESE

¼ CUP CHOPPED FRESH PARSLEY

2 TABLESPOONS MINCED SHALLOTS

2 TABLESPOONS EXTRA-VIRGIN OLIVE OIL

1 TEASPOON KOSHER SALT

½ TEASPOON BLACK PEPPER

1 EGG

FOR THE SOUP

1 TABLESPOON EXTRA-VIRGIN OLIVE OIL

1 ONION, CHOPPED

2 CELERY STALKS, CHOPPED

2 RED BELL PEPPERS, STEMS AND SEEDS REMOVED, CUT INTO ¼-INCH-WIDE STRIPS

2 GARLIC CLOVES, MINCED

1½ TEASPOONS PAPRIKA

¼ TEASPOON SAFFRON

2 PINCHES OF RED PEPPER FLAKES

½ CUP WHITE WINE

6 CUPS CHICKEN STOCK (SEE PAGE 482)

¼ CUP CHOPPED FRESH PARSLEY

SALT AND PEPPER, TO TASTE

1. To begin preparations for the meatballs, place the bread and milk in a mixing bowl. Let the bread soak for 10 minutes.

2. Use a fork to mash the bread until it is very soft and broken down. Add the remaining ingredients and work the mixture with your hands until thoroughly combined. Cover the bowl with plastic wrap and chill it in the refrigerator for 30 minutes.

3. Line a baking sheet with parchment paper. Remove the mixture from the refrigerator and form tablespoons of it into balls. Place the meatballs on the baking sheet, cover them with plastic wrap, and refrigerate for 30 minutes.

4. To begin preparations for the soup, place the olive oil in a large saucepan and warm it over medium-high heat. Add the onion and cook, stirring frequently, for 2 minutes. Add the celery and bell peppers and cook, stirring occasionally, until the vegetables are soft, about 8 minutes.

5. Add the garlic, paprika, saffron, and red pepper flakes and cook, stirring continually, for 45 seconds. Add the wine and cook until the alcohol has been cooked off, 1 to 2 minutes. Add the stock and bring the soup to a boil.

6. Reduce the heat, add the meatballs, and simmer until they are cooked through, 15 to 20 minutes.

7. Stir in the parsley, season the soup with salt and pepper, and ladle it into warmed bowls.

Polpette di Ricotta in Brodo

YIELD: 4 SERVINGS / **ACTIVE TIME:** 40 MINUTES / **TOTAL TIME:** 1 HOUR

1½ CUPS RICOTTA CHEESE (MADE FROM SHEEP'S MILK PREFERRED), DRAINED

¼ CUP GRATED PARMESAN CHEESE

¼ CUP BREAD CRUMBS

2 HANDFULS OF FRESH PARSLEY, FINELY CHOPPED

1 EGG

SALT AND PEPPER, TO TASTE

6 CUPS VEGETABLE STOCK (SEE PAGE 484)

1. Place all of the ingredients, except for the broth, in a mixing bowl and stir until well combined. Place the mixture in the refrigerator and chill for 30 minutes.

2. Place the broth in a medium saucepan and bring it to a boil.

3. Form the mixture into 1 oz. balls and slip them into the broth. Cook the ricotta balls for 10 minutes.

4. Ladle the soup into warmed bowls and enjoy.

Zuppa Gallurese

YIELD: 4 SERVINGS / **ACTIVE TIME:** 20 MINUTES / **TOTAL TIME:** 1 HOUR

6 CUPS BEEF STOCK (SEE PAGE 484)

7 OZ. PECORINO CHEESE, GRATED

3 TABLESPOONS CHOPPED FRESH PARSLEY

1 TEASPOON CHOPPED MIXED HERBS

¼ TEASPOON CINNAMON

¼ TEASPOON FRESHLY GRATED NUTMEG

2.2 LBS. DAY-OLD BREAD, SLICED THIN

1 LB. CACIOCAVALLO CHEESE, SLICED THIN

1. Place the broth in a saucepan and warm it over medium heat.

2. Place the pecorino, parsley, herbs, cinnamon, and nutmeg in a bowl and stir to combine.

3. Preheat the oven to 350°F. Layer some of the bread on the bottom of a 13 x 9–inch baking pan. Top with some of the caciocavallo and the pecorino mixture and prick the cheese with a fork. Continue the layering process until all of these ingredients have been used up.

4. Pour the broth over the dish, place it in the oven, and bake until the gallurese is golden brown, about 30 minutes.

5. Remove the gallurese from the oven and let it rest for 20 minutes before serving.

Zuppa di Castagne Sarda

YIELD: 4 SERVINGS / **ACTIVE TIME:** 1 HOUR / **TOTAL TIME:** 3 HOURS

1 LB. CHESTNUTS

6 OZ. LARD, CHOPPED

1 ONION, FINELY DICED

6 CUPS WATER, PLUS MORE AS NEEDED

SALT, TO TASTE

¾ LB. SHORT-FORMAT PASTA

1. Preheat the oven to 160°F. Peel the chestnuts, place them on a baking sheet, and roast them for 20 minutes. Remove the chestnuts from the oven, remove the nuts, and set them aside.

2. Place the lard in a large saucepan and warm it over medium heat. Add the onion and cook, stirring occasionally, until it has softened, about 5 minutes.

3. Add the chestnuts and water, season with salt, and partially cover the pan. Bring the soup to a simmer, reduce the heat to low, and cook for 1½ hours.

4. Add the pasta and cook until it is al dente, adding more water if needed.

5. Ladle the soup into warmed bowls and enjoy.

Rutabaga & Fig Soup

YIELD: 4 SERVINGS / **ACTIVE TIME:** 20 MINUTES / **TOTAL TIME:** 1 HOUR

2 TABLESPOONS EXTRA-VIRGIN OLIVE OIL

1 ONION, CHOPPED

4 CUPS PEELED AND CHOPPED RUTABAGA

1 TABLESPOON HONEY

4 CUPS VEGETABLE STOCK (SEE PAGE 484)

1 TEASPOON FRESH THYME

16 FRESH FIGS

1 CUP BUTTERMILK

SALT AND PEPPER, TO TASTE

SPICY CHICKPEAS (SEE PAGE 360), FOR SERVING

1. Place the olive oil in a medium saucepan and warm it over medium heat. Add the onion and rutabagas and cook, stirring occasionally, until the onion is soft, about 10 minutes.

2. Stir in the honey, stock, thyme, and figs and bring the soup to a boil.

3. Reduce the heat so that the soup simmers and cook until the rutabagas are tender, about 20 minutes.

4. Transfer the soup to a food processor or blender and blitz until smooth. Place the soup in a clean saucepan, add the buttermilk, and bring to a simmer.

5. Season the soup with salt and pepper, ladle into warm bowls, and serve with the Spicy Chickpeas.

Virtù Teramane

YIELD: 4 SERVINGS / **ACTIVE TIME:** 1 HOUR AND 30 MINUTES / **TOTAL TIME:** 24 HOURS

SALT, TO TASTE

3 CUPS FRESH SPINACH

1 SMALL ZUCCHINI, CHOPPED

1 HEAD OF ENDIVE, CHOPPED

1 CARROT, PEELED AND CHOPPED

1 CELERY STALK, CHOPPED

¾ CUP DRIED CHICKPEAS, SOAKED OVERNIGHT AND DRAINED

¾ CUP LENTILS

1 CUP DRIED FAVA BEANS, SOAKED OVERNIGHT AND DRAINED

⅔ CUP DRIED SPLIT PEAS

2 OZ. LARD, CHOPPED

1 ONION, FINELY DICED

1 GARLIC CLOVE

5 OZ. PANCETTA, CUBED

1 TEASPOON CHOPPED FRESH PARSLEY

2 TOMATOES, CHOPPED

8 CUPS CHICKEN STOCK OR BEEF STOCK (SEE PAGE 482 OR 484)

½ LB. SHORT-FORMAT PASTA (MIX OF DRIED SEMOLINA PASTA AND HOMEMADE EGG PASTA RECOMMENDED)

PECORINO CHEESE, GRATED, FOR GARNISH

1. Bring water to a boil in a large saucepan. Add salt and the spinach, zucchini, endive, carrot, and celery and cook for 5 minutes. Drain the vegetables and let them cool. When they are cool enough to handle, squeeze them to remove as much water as possible and set them aside.

2. Place the chickpeas, lentils, beans, and split peas in separate saucepans, cover them with water, and cook until they just start to soften—the cook times will differ for each legume. Drain the legumes and set them aside.

3. Place the lard in a large saucepan and warm it over medium heat. Add the onion, garlic, and pancetta and cook, stirring frequently, until the pancetta's fat starts to render.

4. Remove the garlic from the pan and discard it. Add the parsley and tomatoes and cook, stirring occasionally, until the tomatoes start to collapse, about 15 minutes.

5. Add the broth and cooked vegetables to the pan and cook for 10 minutes.

6. Add the pasta and legumes and cook until they are tender, about 30 minutes.

7. Ladle the soup into warmed bowls, garnish each portion with pecorino, and enjoy.

Tomato & Eggplant Soup

YIELD: 4 SERVINGS / **ACTIVE TIME:** 30 MINUTES / **TOTAL TIME:** 1 HOUR AND 30 MINUTES

½ CUP EXTRA-VIRGIN OLIVE OIL

2 EGGPLANTS, TRIMMED AND CUT INTO ¾-INCH CUBES

1 ONION, CHOPPED

2 GARLIC CLOVES, MINCED

2 TEASPOONS RAS EL HANOUT (SEE PAGE 505)

½ TEASPOON CUMIN

4 CUPS CHICKEN STOCK (SEE PAGE 482), PLUS MORE AS NEEDED

1 (14 OZ.) CAN OF CRUSHED TOMATOES

⅓ CUP RAISINS

¼ CUP PINE NUTS, TOASTED

2 TEASPOONS FRESH LEMON JUICE

SALT AND PEPPER, TO TASTE

FRESH CILANTRO, CHOPPED, FOR GARNISH

EGGPLANT & PINE NUT RAGOUT (SEE PAGE 513), FOR SERVING

1. Place 1 tablespoon of the olive oil in a large saucepan and warm it over medium heat. Add the eggplants, cover the pan, and cook, stirring occasionally, for 5 minutes. Remove the cover and cook, stirring occasionally, until the eggplants are browned, about 10 minutes.

2. Add 2 tablespoons of the olive oil to the pan along with the onion and cook, stirring occasionally, until the onion has softened, about 5 minutes. Stir in the garlic, Ras el Hanout, and cumin and cook, stirring continually, for 1 minute.

3. Add the stock, tomatoes, raisins, and pine nuts and bring the soup to a boil. Reduce the heat and simmer the soup until the flavor has developed to your liking, about 20 minutes.

4. Remove the pan from heat and let the soup cool for 10 minutes.

5. Place the soup in a blender and puree until smooth, adding more stock if the soup seems too thick.

6. Place the soup in a clean saucepan and warm it over medium-low heat. Stir in the lemon juice and season with salt and pepper.

7. Ladle the soup into warmed bowls, drizzle some of the remaining olive oil over each portion, and garnish with cilantro. Add a dollop of the Eggplant & Pine Nut Ragout to each bowl and enjoy.

Harira

YIELD: 6 SERVINGS / **ACTIVE TIME:** 30 MINUTES / **TOTAL TIME:** 1 HOUR

3 TABLESPOONS UNSALTED BUTTER

1½ LBS. BONELESS, SKINLESS CHICKEN THIGHS

SALT AND PEPPER, TO TASTE

1 LARGE ONION, FINELY DICED

5 GARLIC CLOVES, MINCED

1-INCH PIECE OF FRESH GINGER, PEELED AND GRATED

2 TEASPOONS TURMERIC

1 TEASPOON CUMIN

½ TEASPOON CINNAMON

⅛ TEASPOON CAYENNE PEPPER

¾ CUP FINELY CHOPPED FRESH CILANTRO

½ CUP FINELY CHOPPED FRESH PARSLEY

4 CUPS CHICKEN STOCK (SEE PAGE 482)

4 CUPS WATER

1 (14 OZ.) CAN OF CHICKPEAS, DRAINED AND RINSED

1 CUP BROWN LENTILS, PICKED OVER AND RINSED

1 (28 OZ.) CAN OF CRUSHED TOMATOES

½ CUP VERMICELLI BROKEN INTO 2-INCH PIECES

2 TABLESPOONS FRESH LEMON JUICE, PLUS MORE TO TASTE

1. Place the butter in a Dutch oven and melt it over medium-high heat. Season the chicken thighs with salt and pepper, place them in the pot, and cook until browned on both sides, about 8 minutes. Remove the chicken from the pot and set it on a plate.

2. Add the onion and cook, stirring occasionally, until it starts to brown, about 8 minutes. Add the garlic and ginger and cook until fragrant, about 1 minute. Stir in the turmeric, cumin, cinnamon, and cayenne pepper and cook for 1 minute. Add ½ cup of the cilantro and ¼ cup of the parsley and cook for 1 minute.

3. Stir in the stock, water, chickpeas, and lentils and bring the soup to a simmer. Return the chicken to the pot, reduce the heat to medium-low, partially cover the Dutch oven, and gently simmer, stirring occasionally, until the lentils are just tender, about 20 minutes.

4. Add the tomatoes and vermicelli and simmer, stirring occasionally, until the pasta is tender, about 10 minutes.

5. Stir in the lemon juice and the remaining cilantro and parsley. Taste, adjust the seasoning as necessary, and enjoy.

Harira
SEE PAGE 301

Chilled White Tomato Soup with Braised Grapes

YIELD: 4 SERVINGS / **ACTIVE TIME:** 30 MINUTES / **TOTAL TIME:** 24 HOURS

10 RIPE TOMATOES, STEMS REMOVED, CHOPPED

4 CUPS DAY-OLD SOURDOUGH BREAD PIECES

2 CUPS SLIVERED BLANCHED ALMONDS, TOASTED

1 GARLIC CLOVE, MINCED

4 TEASPOONS WHITE WINE VINEGAR

PINCH OF CAYENNE PEPPER

½ CUP ALMOND OIL

SALT AND PEPPER, TO TASTE

EXTRA-VIRGIN OLIVE OIL, FOR GARNISH

BRAISED GRAPES (SEE PAGE 356), FOR SERVING

1. Place the tomatoes in a food processor and blitz them for 5 minutes.

2. Strain the puree through cheesecloth into a bowl, making sure you let gravity do its job and refrain from forcing the puree through. Strain the puree through cheesecloth again, letting it sit overnight.

3. Place 4 cups of the tomato water in a bowl. If you do not have 4 cups, add the necessary amount of water. Add the bread and let it soak for 5 minutes.

4. Place the almonds in a food processor and blitz until they are finely ground.

5. Remove the bread from the tomato water, gently squeeze the bread, and add it to the food processor.

6. Measure out 3 cups of the tomato water and set it aside.

7. Add the garlic, vinegar, and cayenne to the food processor and blitz for 1 minute. With the food processor running, slowly drizzle in the almond oil and blitz until it has been thoroughly incorporated.

8. Add the reserved tomato water and blitz the mixture for 2 minutes. Season the soup with salt and pepper, place it in the refrigerator, and chill for 4 hours.

9. Remove the soup from the refrigerator and strain it. Ladle the soup into chilled bowls, garnish each with a drizzle of olive oil, and serve with the Braised Grapes.

Riso e Verza

YIELD: 4 SERVINGS / **ACTIVE TIME:** 30 MINUTES / **TOTAL TIME:** 1 HOUR

2 TABLESPOONS EXTRA-VIRGIN OLIVE OIL

1 SMALL ONION, FINELY DICED

½ CARROT, PEELED AND FINELY DICED

½ CELERY STALK, FINELY DICED

1 SMALL HEAD OF SAVOY CABBAGE, SLICED VERY THIN

1 CUP VIALONE NANO RICE, RINSED WELL

SALT, TO TASTE

HOT WATER, AS NEEDED

⅔ CUP GRATED PECORINO CHEESE

1. Place the olive oil in a large skillet and warm it over medium heat. Add the onion, carrot, and celery and cook, stirring occasionally, until the onion has softened, about 5 minutes.

2. Add the cabbage, reduce the heat to medium-low, and cover the pan. Cook the cabbage until it is tender, 10 to 15 minutes.

3. Add the rice, season the dish with salt, and add a few ladles of hot water. Cook, stirring frequently and adding hot water as necessary, until the rice is al dente, 15 to 20 minutes.

4. Remove the pan from heat and let it rest for a few minutes.

5. Stir in the pecorino and serve.

Avgolemono

YIELD: 4 TO 6 SERVINGS / **ACTIVE TIME:** 15 MINUTES / **TOTAL TIME:** 45 MINUTES

8 CUPS CHICKEN STOCK (SEE PAGE 482)

½ CUP ORZO

3 EGGS

JUICE OF 1 LEMON

1 TABLESPOON COLD WATER

SALT AND PEPPER, TO TASTE

1 LEMON, SLICED THIN, FOR GARNISH

FRESH DILL, CHOPPED, FOR GARNISH

1. Place the stock in a large saucepan and bring it to a boil. Reduce the heat so that the stock simmers. Add the orzo and cook until tender, about 5 minutes.

2. Strain the stock and orzo over a large bowl. Set the orzo aside. Return the stock to the pan and bring it to a simmer.

3. Place the eggs in a mixing bowl and beat until scrambled and frothy. Stir in the lemon juice and cold water. While stirring constantly, add approximately ½ cup of the stock to the egg mixture. Stir another cup of stock into the egg mixture and then stir the tempered eggs into the saucepan. Reduce the heat to low and be careful not to let the stock come to boil once you add the egg mixture.

4. Return the orzo to the soup. Cook, stirring continually, until everything is warmed through, about 2 minutes. Season with salt and pepper, ladle the soup into warmed bowls, and garnish each portion with slices of lemon and dill.

Lamb & Cannellini Soup

YIELD: 4 SERVINGS / **ACTIVE TIME:** 20 MINUTES / **TOTAL TIME:** 24 HOURS

2 TABLESPOONS EXTRA-VIRGIN OLIVE OIL

1 ONION, CHOPPED

2 GARLIC CLOVES, MINCED

1½ LBS. GROUND LAMB

3 CARROTS, PEELED AND CHOPPED

3 CELERY STALKS, CHOPPED

1 (14 OZ.) CAN OF STEWED TOMATOES, DRAINED

¼ CUP FINELY CHOPPED FRESH PARSLEY

2 TABLESPOONS FINELY CHOPPED FRESH THYME

½ LB. DRIED CANNELLINI BEANS, SOAKED OVERNIGHT AND DRAINED

6 CUPS CHICKEN STOCK (SEE PAGE 482)

½ LB. BABY SPINACH

¼ CUP SLICED KALAMATA OLIVES

SALT AND PEPPER, TO TASTE

FETA CHEESE, CRUMBLED, FOR GARNISH

1. Place the olive oil in a large saucepan and warm over medium heat. Add the onion and cook, stirring frequently, until it starts to soften, about 5 minutes. Stir in the garlic, cook for 2 minutes, and then add the lamb. Cook until it starts to brown, about 5 minutes, and add the carrots and celery.

2. Cook for 5 minutes, stir in the tomatoes, herbs, cannellini beans, and stock, and bring the soup to a boil. Reduce the heat to medium-low, cover the pan, and simmer until the beans are tender, about 1 hour.

3. Add the spinach and olives and cook until the spinach wilts, about 2 minutes. Season the soup with salt and pepper, ladle it into warmed bowls, and garnish each portion with feta cheese.

Lamb & Cannellini Soup
SEE PAGE 307

Cholent

YIELD: 4 SERVINGS / **ACTIVE TIME:** 15 MINUTES / **TOTAL TIME:** 2 DAYS

1½ LBS. FATTY BEEF CHUCK, CUBED

4 MARROW BONES

2 LARGE YUKON GOLD OR RUSSET POTATOES, PEELED AND CUT INTO CHUNKS

1 ONION, PEELED

4 GARLIC CLOVES, PEELED

2 CUPS PEARL BARLEY

1 CUP DRIED KIDNEY BEANS, SOAKED OVERNIGHT AND DRAINED; SOAKING WATER RESERVED

⅓ CUP KETCHUP

1 TABLESPOON PAPRIKA

3 CUPS WATER

2 TEASPOONS KOSHER SALT

1 TEASPOON BLACK PEPPER

1 TEASPOON GARLIC POWDER

1 LB. PACKAGED KISHKE

1. Coat the inside of a slow cooker with nonstick cooking spray. Add the beef, marrow bones, and potatoes to the slow cooker, followed by the onion, garlic, barley, kidney beans, and the water the beans soaked in.

2. In a bowl, combine the ketchup, paprika, and 2½ cups of the water and add it to the slow cooker. Stir in the salt, pepper, and garlic powder and arrange the kishke on top.

3. Set the slow cooker to low and cook overnight, for 8 to 10 hours. Check it in the morning and add the remaining water if the stew seems too dry.

4. Ladle the stew into warmed bowls and enjoy.

Lamb Stew

YIELD: 10 SERVINGS / **ACTIVE TIME:** 30 MINUTES / **TOTAL TIME:** 1 HOUR

2 TABLESPOONS RED WINE

1 TABLESPOON FRESH LEMON JUICE

½ TEASPOON LEMON ZEST

1 TABLESPOON BERBERE SEASONING

1 TEASPOON SMOKED PAPRIKA

1 TEASPOON DIJON MUSTARD

3½ LBS. BONELESS LEG OF LAMB, CUBED

1 TEASPOON KOSHER SALT, PLUS MORE TO TASTE

½ TEASPOON BLACK PEPPER, PLUS MORE TO TASTE

¼ CUP EXTRA-VIRGIN OLIVE OIL

2 ONIONS, SLICED THIN

6 GARLIC CLOVES, MINCED

2 TEASPOONS CHOPPED FRESH ROSEMARY

2 TEASPOONS FRESH THYME

2 PLUM TOMATOES, DICED

1 ORANGE BELL PEPPER, STEM AND SEEDS REMOVED, DICED

1 LARGE SHALLOT, SLICED THIN

1. Place the wine, lemon juice, lemon zest, berbere, paprika, and mustard in a small bowl and stir until well combined.

2. Season the lamb with the salt and pepper. Place the olive oil in a large Dutch oven and warm it over medium-high heat. Working in two batches, add the lamb and cook until browned all over, about 8 minutes for each batch, turning it as necessary. Using a slotted spoon, transfer the browned lamb to a bowl.

3. Add the onions, garlic, rosemary, thyme, and a generous pinch of salt and pepper to the pot, reduce the heat to medium, and cook, stirring occasionally, until the onions have softened and are starting to brown, about 8 minutes.

4. Return the lamb and any juices that have accumulated to the pot along with the wine mixture, tomatoes, bell pepper, and shallot. Cook, stirring, until the bell pepper has softened and the lamb is just cooked through, about 10 minutes.

5. Taste, adjust the seasoning as necessary, and enjoy.

Lamb Sharba

YIELD: 6 SERVINGS / **ACTIVE TIME:** 30 MINUTES / **TOTAL TIME:** 2 HOURS

2 TABLESPOONS EXTRA-VIRGIN OLIVE OIL

¾ LB. BONELESS LEG OF LAMB, CUT INTO 1-INCH CUBES

1 ONION, CHOPPED

1 TOMATO, QUARTERED, SEEDED, AND SLICED THIN

1 GARLIC CLOVE, MINCED

1 TABLESPOON TOMATO PASTE

1 BUNCH OF FRESH MINT, TIED WITH TWINE, PLUS MORE FOR GARNISH

2 CINNAMON STICKS

1¼ TEASPOONS TURMERIC

1¼ TEASPOONS PAPRIKA

½ TEASPOON CUMIN

8 CUPS CHICKEN STOCK (SEE PAGE 482)

1 (14 OZ.) CAN OF CHICKPEAS, DRAINED AND RINSED

¾ CUP ORZO

SALT AND PEPPER, TO TASTE

1. Place the olive oil in a Dutch oven and warm it over medium-high heat. Add the lamb and cook, turning it as necessary, until it is browned all over, about 5 minutes. Remove the lamb with a slotted spoon and place it on a paper towel–lined plate.

2. Add the onion to the pot and cook, stirring occasionally, until it starts to soften, about 5 minutes. Add the tomato, garlic, tomato paste, mint, cinnamon sticks, turmeric, paprika, and cumin and cook, stirring continually, for 1 minute.

3. Add the stock and bring the mixture to a boil. Return the seared lamb to the pot, reduce the heat, and simmer until the lamb is tender, about 30 minutes.

4. Add the chickpeas and orzo and cook until the orzo is tender, about 10 minutes.

5. Remove the mint and discard it. Season the soup with salt and pepper and ladle it into warmed bowls. Garnish with additional mint and enjoy.

Dafina

YIELD: 4 SERVINGS / **ACTIVE TIME:** 20 MINUTES / **TOTAL TIME:** 24 HOURS

2 (14 OZ.) CANS OF CHICKPEAS, DRAINED AND RINSED

12 LARGE RED POTATOES, PEELED

2 LBS. BONE-IN FLANKEN MEAT

4 CHICKEN DRUMSTICKS

4 EGGS, LEFT WHOLE

4 PITTED DATES

1 TABLESPOON KOSHER SALT

1 TEASPOON BLACK PEPPER

1 TEASPOON PAPRIKA

1 TEASPOON CUMIN

1 TEASPOON TURMERIC

1 TEASPOON HONEY

1 TEASPOON CINNAMON

3 GARLIC CLOVES

2 TABLESPOONS AVOCADO OIL

1. Place the chickpeas on the bottom of a slow cooker. Place the potatoes against the wall of the slow cooker and then place the flanken meat, chicken, eggs, and dates in the center.

2. Place the remaining ingredients in a mixing bowl, stir to combine, and add the mixture to the slow cooker, making sure to keep all of the ingredients in their particular places. Add water until the mixture is covered by ¼ inch.

3. Set the slow cooker to low and cook for 24 hours.

4. Ladle the stew into warmed bowls and enjoy.

Short Rib & Okra Stew

YIELD: 6 SERVINGS / **ACTIVE TIME:** 30 MINUTES / **TOTAL TIME:** 3 HOURS

2¼ LBS. BONELESS SHORT RIBS

1 TEASPOON KOSHER SALT, PLUS MORE TO TASTE

½ TEASPOON BLACK PEPPER, PLUS MORE TO TASTE

¼ CUP PLUS 5 TABLESPOONS AVOCADO OIL

3 GARLIC CLOVES, SMASHED

¼ CUP TOMATO PASTE

¾ LB. TOMATOES, QUARTERED

1½ CUPS WATER

JUICE OF 1 LEMON, PLUS MORE TO TASTE

1 TEASPOON SWEET PAPRIKA

3 BAY LEAVES

1 SMALL JALAPEÑO CHILE PEPPER, STEM AND SEEDS REMOVED, SLICED THIN

1 TEASPOON SUGAR

1 LB. OKRA, TRIMMED

1 BUNCH OF FRESH MINT

1 CUP BASMATI RICE

1 TEASPOON CORIANDER SEEDS

1½ CUPS BOILING WATER

1. Preheat the oven to 350°F. Slice the short ribs into 2-inch cubes and season with the salt and pepper.

2. Place ¼ cup of the avocado oil in a Dutch oven and warm it over medium-high heat. Working in batches to avoid crowding the pot, add the short ribs and cook until browned all over, about 5 minutes, turning the meat as necessary. Transfer the browned short ribs to a plate.

3. Add the garlic to the pot and cook until it is fragrant, about 1 minute. Add the tomato paste and cook for 30 seconds, stirring constantly. Add the tomatoes a little bit at a time, crushing them in your hands before adding them to the pot. Add the water, lemon juice, paprika, 1 of the bay leaves, and 3 to 5 slices of the jalapeño. Return the short ribs to the pot and sprinkle the sugar over them. Reduce the heat to low and let the stew simmer while preparing the okra.

4. Add 3 tablespoons of avocado oil to a large skillet and warm it over high heat. Add the okra and cook, tossing it frequently, until it is bright green and lightly blistered, 1 to 2 minutes. Remove the pan from heat, season the okra with salt and lemon juice, and toss to coat. Add the okra to the stew, making sure it is evenly distributed. Add 6 to 10 mint leaves, cover the pot, and place it in the oven. Braise for 2 hours, checking the stew every 30 minutes and adding water as necessary if the liquid has reduced too much.

5. After 2 hours, the meat should be fork-tender. Turn on the broiler and broil the stew until it is dark and caramelized, about 10 minutes.

6. While the stew is in the oven, place the remaining avocado oil in a small saucepan and warm it over high heat. Add the rice and toast it, stirring continuously, until the grains are too hot to touch, about 2 minutes. Add the remaining bay leaves, the coriander seeds, and boiling water, bring the rice to a boil, and cover the pan. Reduce the heat and simmer the rice until it is tender, about 20 minutes.

7. Remove the rice from heat and let it stand, covered, for 10 minutes. Gently fluff the rice with a fork and cover until ready to serve. Remove the stew from the oven. Season with salt and pepper and sprinkle the remaining mint over it. Serve with the rice and enjoy.

Fava Bean Soup with Grilled Halloumi Cheese

YIELD: 4 SERVINGS / **ACTIVE TIME:** 30 MINUTES / **TOTAL TIME:** 24 HOURS

1½ CUPS DRIED FAVA BEANS, SOAKED OVERNIGHT

6 CUPS VEGETABLE STOCK (SEE PAGE 484)

4 GARLIC CLOVES, MINCED

5 TABLESPOONS EXTRA-VIRGIN OLIVE OIL

1 SHALLOT, MINCED

ZEST AND JUICE OF 1 LEMON

SALT AND PEPPER, TO TASTE

2 TABLESPOONS FINELY CHOPPED FRESH PARSLEY

½ LB. HALLOUMI CHEESE, CUT INTO 4 PIECES

1. Drain the fava beans and place them in a large saucepan with the stock and garlic. Bring to a boil, reduce the heat so that the soup simmers, cover, and cook until the beans are so tender that they are starting to fall apart, about 1 hour.

2. While the soup is simmering, place ¼ cup of the olive oil in a skillet and warm over medium heat. When the oil starts to shimmer, add the shallot and sauté until it starts to soften, about 5 minutes. Remove the pan from heat, stir in the lemon zest, and let the mixture sit for 1 hour.

3. Transfer the soup to a food processor and blitz until smooth. Return the soup to a clean saucepan, season with salt and pepper, and bring it to a gentle simmer. Stir in the shallot mixture, lemon juice, and parsley, cook until heated through, and remove the soup from heat.

4. Warm a skillet over medium heat. Place the remaining olive oil in a small bowl, add the cheese, and toss to coat. Place the cheese in the pan and cook until browned on both sides, about 2 minutes per side. Serve alongside the soup.

Avikas

1 TABLESPOON EXTRA-VIRGIN OLIVE OIL

1 LB. BEEF CHUCK, CUBED

1 TABLESPOON KOSHER SALT

1 YELLOW ONION, CHOPPED

1 TABLESPOON TOMATO PASTE

½ CUP DRIED CANNELLINI BEANS, SOAKED OVERNIGHT AND DRAINED

¼ TEASPOON BLACK PEPPER

LONG-GRAIN RICE, COOKED, FOR SERVING

1. Place the olive oil in a large saucepan and warm it over medium-high heat.

2. Season the meat with 1 teaspoon of the salt, place it in the pan, and cook until well browned all over, turning it as needed. Transfer the meat to a plate and set it aside.

3. Add the onion to the pan and cook, stirring occasionally, until golden brown, about 10 minutes. Add the tomato paste and cook until it has caramelized, about 2 minutes.

4. Return the meat to the pot and stir in the beans, pepper, and remaining salt. Cover with water, bring the soup to a boil, and then reduce the heat. Cover the pan and gently simmer the soup until the soup has thickened and the beans and meat are tender, about 30 minutes.

5. Ladle the soup into bowls and serve with rice.

Split Pea Soup with Smoked Ham

2 TABLESPOONS UNSALTED BUTTER

1 ONION, MINCED

1 CARROT, PEELED AND MINCED

1 CELERY STALK, MINCED

5 CUPS CHICKEN STOCK (SEE PAGE 482)

1 CUP YELLOW SPLIT PEAS

½ LB. SMOKED HAM, CHOPPED

2 TABLESPOONS FINELY CHOPPED FRESH PARSLEY, PLUS MORE FOR GARNISH

1 BAY LEAF

1 TEASPOON FINELY CHOPPED FRESH THYME

SALT AND PEPPER, TO TASTE

LEMON WEDGES, FOR SERVING

1. Place the butter in a large saucepan and melt it over medium heat. Add the onion, carrot, and celery and cook, stirring frequently, until they have softened, about 5 minutes.

2. Add the stock, split peas, ham, parsley, bay leaf, and thyme. Bring the soup to a boil, reduce the heat to medium-low, and simmer, stirring occasionally, until the peas are al dente, about 1 hour.

3. Remove the bay leaf and discard it. Season the soup with salt and pepper and ladle it into warmed bowls. Garnish with additional parsley and serve with lemon wedges.

Chamin

YIELD: 4 SERVINGS / **ACTIVE TIME:** 30 MINUTES / **TOTAL TIME:** 24 HOURS

1½ TABLESPOONS EXTRA-VIRGIN OLIVE OIL

1 SMALL ONION, CHOPPED

5 GARLIC CLOVES, MINCED

¾ CUP CHOPPED PARSNIP

2 CARROTS, PEELED AND SLICED

1 TEASPOON CUMIN

¼ TEASPOON TURMERIC

1½-INCH PIECE OF FRESH GINGER, PEELED AND MINCED

½ LB. BEEF BRISKET, TRIMMED AND CHOPPED

4 OZ. LAMB SHOULDER, TRIMMED AND CHOPPED

4 CUPS BEEF STOCK (SEE PAGE 484)

½ CUP CHICKPEAS, SOAKED OVERNIGHT AND DRAINED

1 SMALL POTATO, PEELED AND CHOPPED

1 SMALL ZUCCHINI, SLICED

½ LB. TOMATOES, CHOPPED

2 TABLESPOONS BROWN LENTILS

1 BAY LEAF

½ BUNCH OF FRESH CILANTRO, CHOPPED

SALT AND PEPPER, TO TASTE

FRESH CHILE PEPPERS, STEMS AND SEEDS REMOVED, CHOPPED, FOR GARNISH

LEMON WEDGES, FOR SERVING

LONG-GRAIN RICE, COOKED, FOR SERVING

1. Preheat the oven to 250°F. Place the olive oil in a Dutch oven and warm over medium heat. Add the onion, garlic, parsnip, carrots, cumin, turmeric, and ginger and cook, stirring continually, for 2 minutes.

2. Add the brisket and lamb and cook, stirring occasionally, until both are browned all over, about 8 minutes.

3. Add the stock and bring the soup to a simmer. Stir in the chickpeas, potato, zucchini, tomatoes, lentils, bay leaf, and cilantro. Cover the pot, place it in the oven, and cook until the meat is tender, about 2 hours.

4. Remove the stew from the oven and skim the fat from the top. Season with salt and pepper and ladle into warmed bowls. Garnish with the chiles and serve with the lemon wedges and rice.

Mansaf

YIELD: 4 SERVINGS / **ACTIVE TIME:** 30 MINUTES / **TOTAL TIME:** 1 HOUR AND 30 MINUTES

2 TABLESPOONS EXTRA-VIRGIN OLIVE OIL

1 ONION, CHOPPED

2 LBS. LAMB SHOULDER, CUBED

6 CUPS BEEF STOCK (SEE PAGE 484)

SEEDS FROM 2 CARDAMOM PODS

1 CUP FULL-FAT GREEK YOGURT

SALT AND PEPPER, TO TASTE

2 CUPS COOKED LONG-GRAIN RICE

¼ CUP PINE NUTS, TOASTED, FOR GARNISH

FRESH PARSLEY, FINELY CHOPPED, FOR GARNISH

1. Place the olive oil in a saucepan and warm over medium-high heat. Add the onion and cook, stirring frequently, until it starts to soften, about 5 minutes. Add the lamb and cook until it is browned all over, about 8 minutes.

2. Add the stock and cardamom and bring the soup to a boil. Reduce the heat to medium-low, cover the pan, and simmer until the lamb is very tender, about 1 hour.

3. Stir in the yogurt, season with salt and pepper, and remove the soup from heat. Divide the rice between the serving bowls, ladle the soup over the rice, and garnish with the pine nuts and parsley.

Pasta e Lattuga

YIELD: 4 SERVINGS / **ACTIVE TIME:** 10 MINUTES / **TOTAL TIME:** 25 MINUTES

8 CUPS WATER

SALT, TO TASTE

½ LB. MACARONI OR OTHER SHORT-FORMAT PASTA

1 HEAD OF ROMAINE LETTUCE, WASHED AND CHOPPED

2 TABLESPOONS EXTRA-VIRGIN OLIVE OIL, FOR GARNISH

1. Bring the water to a boil in a large saucepan. Add salt—less than you would for a typical pasta dish.

2. Add the pasta and lettuce and cook until the pasta is al dente.

3. Ladle the soup into warmed bowls, top each portion with some of the olive oil, and enjoy.

Eggplant & Zucchini Soup

YIELD: 4 SERVINGS / **ACTIVE TIME:** 20 MINUTES / **TOTAL TIME:** 1 HOUR AND 15 MINUTES

1 LARGE EGGPLANT, PEELED AND CHOPPED

2 LARGE ZUCCHINI, CHOPPED

1 ONION, CHOPPED

3 GARLIC CLOVES, MINCED

2 TABLESPOONS EXTRA-VIRGIN OLIVE OIL

3 CUPS CHICKEN STOCK (SEE PAGE 482)

1 TABLESPOON FINELY CHOPPED FRESH OREGANO

1 TABLESPOON CHOPPED FRESH MINT, PLUS MORE FOR GARNISH

SALT AND PEPPER, TO TASTE

TZATZIKI (SEE PAGE 42), FOR SERVING

PITA BREAD (SEE PAGE 338), FOR SERVING

MINTY PICKLED CUCUMBERS (SEE PAGE 360), FOR SERVING

1. Preheat the oven to 425°F. Place the eggplant, zucchini, onion, and garlic in a baking dish, drizzle the olive oil over the mixture, and gently stir to coat. Place in the oven and roast for 30 minutes, removing to stir occasionally.

2. Remove from the oven and let the vegetables cool briefly.

3. Place half of the roasted vegetables in a food processor. Add the stock and blitz until pureed. Place the puree in a medium saucepan, add the remaining roasted vegetables, and bring to a boil.

4. Stir in the oregano and mint and season with salt and pepper. Cook for 2 minutes and ladle into warmed bowls. Garnish with additional mint and serve with the Tzatziki, Pita Bread, and Minty Pickled Cucumbers.

Romesco de Peix

YIELD: 6 SERVINGS / **ACTIVE TIME:** 25 MINUTES / **TOTAL TIME:** 40 MINUTES

½ CUP SLIVERED ALMONDS

½ TEASPOON SAFFRON

¼ CUP BOILING WATER

½ CUP EXTRA-VIRGIN OLIVE OIL

1 LARGE YELLOW ONION, CHOPPED

2 LARGE RED BELL PEPPERS, STEMS AND SEEDS REMOVED, CHOPPED

2½ TEASPOONS SWEET PAPRIKA

1 TABLESPOON SMOKED PAPRIKA

1 BAY LEAF

2 TABLESPOONS TOMATO PASTE

½ CUP SHERRY

2 CUPS FISH STOCK (SEE PAGE 482)

1 (28 OZ.) CAN OF CHOPPED TOMATOES, WITH THEIR LIQUID

SALT AND PEPPER, TO TASTE

1½ LBS. MONKFISH FILLETS, CHOPPED INTO LARGE PIECES

1 LB. MUSSELS, RINSED WELL AND DEBEARDED

FRESH CILANTRO, FINELY CHOPPED, FOR GARNISH

1. Place the almonds in a large cast-iron skillet and toast them over medium heat until they are just browned. Transfer them to a food processor and pulse until they are finely ground.

2. Place the saffron and boiling water in a bowl and let the mixture steep.

3. Place the olive oil in a Dutch oven and warm over medium heat. Add the onion and bell peppers and cook, stirring occasionally, until the peppers are tender, about 15 minutes.

4. Add the sweet paprika, smoked paprika, bay leaf, and tomato paste and cook, stirring constantly, for 1 minute. Add the sherry and bring the mixture to a boil. Boil for 5 minutes and then stir in the stock, tomatoes, saffron, and the soaking liquid. Stir to combine, season with salt and pepper, and reduce the heat so that the soup simmers.

5. Stir in the ground almonds and cook until the mixture thickens slightly, about 8 minutes. Add the fish and mussels, stir gently to incorporate, and simmer until the fish is cooked through and a majority of the mussels have opened, about 5 minutes. Discard any mussels that do not open.

6. Ladle the mixture into warmed bowls, garnish with cilantro, and enjoy.

Tunisian Butternut Squash Soup

YIELD: 12 SERVINGS / **ACTIVE TIME:** 30 MINUTES / **TOTAL TIME:** 2 HOURS

1 LARGE BUTTERNUT SQUASH, HALVED AND SEEDED

1 TEASPOON THREE-PEPPER HARISSA SAUCE (SEE PAGE 510)

1 TEASPOON KOSHER SALT

½ TEASPOON BLACK PEPPER

¼ CUP FRESH LEMON JUICE

1 TABLESPOON LEMON ZEST

1½ TEASPOONS LIME ZEST

2 TABLESPOONS EXTRA-VIRGIN OLIVE OIL

2 PARSNIPS, PEELED AND CUBED

2 TABLESPOONS AVOCADO OIL

3 SMALL SHALLOTS, DICED

3 GARLIC CLOVES, SLICED

8 CUPS CHICKEN STOCK (SEE PAGE 482)

1. Preheat the oven to 400°F. Place the butternut squash on an aluminum foil–lined baking sheet, cut side up.

2. Place the harissa, salt, pepper, lemon juice, lemon zest, lime zest, and olive oil in a bowl and stir until combined.

3. Spread some of the mixture over the squash. Place the parsnips around the squash, drizzle the remaining harissa mixture over them, and toss to coat.

4. Place the pan in the oven and roast until the squash and parsnips are fork-tender, about 1 hour. Remove from the oven and let the vegetables cool for 20 minutes.

5. Place the avocado oil in a large saucepan and warm it over medium heat. Add the shallots and cook, stirring frequently, until they are translucent, about 3 minutes. Add the garlic and cook, stirring frequently, until fragrant, about 1 minute.

6. Scoop the squash's flesh into a food processor, add the parsnips and some of the stock, and blitz until smooth.

7. Add the puree to the saucepan, add the remaining stock, and simmer until the flavor has developed to your liking, about 25 minutes.

8. Taste, adjust the seasoning as necessary, and ladle the soup into warmed bowls.

Minestra Maritata

YIELD: 6 SERVINGS / **ACTIVE TIME:** 1 HOUR / **TOTAL TIME:** 5 HOURS

FOR THE BROTH

2 CELERY STALKS, EACH CUT INTO 2 TO 3 PIECES

2 CARROTS, PEELED AND HALVED

1 ONION, HALVED

HANDFUL OF SPRIGS OF FRESH PARSLEY, SPRIGS OF FRESH THYME, AND BAY LEAVES, TIED TOGETHER WITH KITCHEN TWINE

½ WHOLE CHICKEN

1 LB. PORK RIBS

1 LB. STEW BEEF

3 ITALIAN SAUSAGES

KOSHER SALT, TO TASTE

FOR THE VEGETABLES

KOSHER SALT, TO TASTE

1 LB. ESCAROLE OR LETTUCE, TRIMMED AND RINSED WELL

1 LB. CABBAGE, CHOPPED

1 LB. CHARD OR CHICORY, TRIMMED AND RINSED WELL

1 LB. COLLARD GREENS, TRIMMED AND RINSED WELL

½ CUP LARD, WHIPPED (OPTIONAL)

EXTRA-VIRGIN OLIVE OIL, FOR TOPPING

PARMESAN CHEESE, GRATED, FOR GARNISH

CRUSTY BREAD, FOR SERVING

1. To begin preparations for the broth, place all of the ingredients, except for salt, in a stockpot and cover with cold water. Bring to a boil, reduce the heat to low, and gently simmer the broth until the flavor has developed to your liking, 3 to 4 hours, frequently skimming off any foam that rises to the surface.

2. Season the broth with salt, strain it, and reserve the solids. Chill the broth in the refrigerator until the layer of fat has solidified. Remove the layer of fat, discard it, and strain the broth through a fine-mesh sieve. Place the broth in a large saucepan and set it aside.

3. Remove the meat from the chicken and ribs and dice it. Dice the stew beef and sausages and set all of the meat aside.

4. To begin preparations for the vegetables, bring water to a boil in a large saucepan and prepare an ice bath. Add salt to the boiling water and then add the vegetables one at a time. Boil the vegetables for 2 minutes, remove them from the boiling water, and plunge them into the ice bath.

5. Chop the blanched vegetables and add them to the broth along with the meat. Add the lard (if desired) and simmer until the flavor has developed to your liking, 30 to 40 minutes.

6. Season the dish with salt and drizzle some olive oil over the top. Garnish with Parmesan, serve with crusty bread, and enjoy.

Saffron & Mussel Soup

YIELD: 4 SERVINGS / **ACTIVE TIME:** 20 MINUTES / **TOTAL TIME:** 45 MINUTES

3 LBS. MUSSELS, RINSED WELL AND DEBEARDED

3 CUPS WHITE WINE

4 TABLESPOONS UNSALTED BUTTER

2 LEEKS, TRIMMED, RINSED WELL, AND CHOPPED

2 CELERY STALKS, CHOPPED

¾ CUP CHOPPED FENNEL

1 CARROT, PEELED AND MINCED

2 GARLIC CLOVES, MINCED

⅛ TEASPOON SAFFRON

2 CUPS HEAVY CREAM

SALT AND PEPPER, TO TASTE

3 TOMATOES, CHOPPED

FRESH PARSLEY, FINELY CHOPPED, FOR GARNISH

MICROGREENS, FOR GARNISH

RADISH, FOR GARNISH

LEMON WEDGES, FOR SERVING

1. Place the mussels and wine in a large saucepan, cover, and cook over medium heat, shaking the pan occasionally, for 4 to 5 minutes, until the majority of the mussels have opened.

2. Discard any unopened mussels. Drain, reserve the cooking liquid, and remove the meat from all but 18 of the mussels. Reserve the 18 mussels in their shells for garnish.

3. Add the butter to the saucepan and melt it over medium heat. Add the leeks, celery, fennel, carrot, and garlic and cook, stirring frequently, until the vegetables start to soften, about 5 minutes.

4. Strain the reserved liquid through a fine-mesh sieve and add it to the saucepan. Cook for 10 minutes, until the liquid has reduced by one-quarter.

5. Add the saffron and cream and bring the soup to a boil. Reduce the heat to low, season with salt and pepper, add the mussels and tomatoes, and cook gently until heated through.

6. Ladle the soup into warmed bowls, garnish with the parsley, microgreens, radish, and reserved mussels, and serve with lemon wedges.

Moroccan Lentil Stew

YIELD: 6 SERVINGS / **ACTIVE TIME:** 10 MINUTES / **TOTAL TIME:** 8 HOURS

1 CUP BROWN LENTILS

½ CUP GREEN LENTILS

4 CUPS VEGETABLE STOCK (SEE PAGE 484)

3 CARROTS, PEELED AND CHOPPED

1 LARGE YELLOW ONION, CHOPPED

3 GARLIC CLOVES, MINCED

3-INCH PIECE OF FRESH GINGER, PEELED AND GRATED

ZEST AND JUICE OF 1 LEMON

3 TABLESPOONS SMOKED PAPRIKA

2 TABLESPOONS CINNAMON

1 TABLESPOON CORIANDER

1 TABLESPOON TURMERIC

1 TABLESPOON CUMIN

1½ TEASPOONS ALLSPICE

2 BAY LEAVES

SALT AND PEPPER, TO TASTE

1 (14 OZ.) CAN OF CANNELLINI BEANS, DRAINED AND RINSED

FRESH MINT, CHOPPED, FOR GARNISH

GOAT CHEESE, CRUMBLED, FOR GARNISH

1. Place the lentils in a fine-mesh sieve, rinse them well, and pick them over to remove any debris or shriveled lentils.

2. Place all of the ingredients, except for the cannellini beans and the garnishes, in a slow cooker. Cover and cook on low for 7½ hours.

3. After 7½ hours, stir in the cannellini beans. Cover and cook on low for 30 another minutes.

4. Ladle the stew into warmed bowls and garnish with fresh mint and goat cheese.

Bone Marrow & Matzo Ball Soup

YIELD: 8 SERVINGS / **ACTIVE TIME:** 35 MINUTES / **TOTAL TIME:** 24 HOURS

4 LBS. MARROW BONES

2 TEASPOONS KOSHER SALT, PLUS MORE TO TASTE

2 EGGS, SEPARATED

2 TABLESPOONS CHOPPED FRESH PARSLEY

1 TEASPOON BLACK PEPPER

DASH OF FRESHLY GRATED NUTMEG

1 CUP MATZO MEAL

8 CUPS CHICKEN STOCK (SEE PAGE 482)

1 GARLIC CLOVE

1. Place the marrow bones in a saucepan, add a few pinches of salt, and cover the bones with cold water. Let the bones soak overnight.

2. Preheat the oven to 400°F. Pat the bones dry, arrange them on a baking sheet, and place them in the oven. Roast for 30 minutes, remove from the oven, and let the marrow bones cool slightly.

3. Using a spoon or a table knife, remove the roasted marrow from the bones and place it in a small bowl. Continue until you have about ½ cup of marrow.

4. Place half of the marrow in a mixing bowl and mash it with a fork until it is smooth. Add the egg yolks, parsley, salt, pepper, and nutmeg and stir until combined. Add the matzo and work the mixture until it comes together as a soft dough.

5. Cover the bowl with plastic wrap and chill it in the refrigerator for 2 hours.

6. Place the egg whites in a mixing bowl and whip them until they hold soft peaks. Add them to the matzo dough and gently fold to incorporate them.

7. Place the stock in a large saucepan and stir in the garlic and the remaining marrow. Bring the stock to a simmer.

8. Form the dough into small balls and drop them into the simmering stock in batches of five. Cook each batch in the simmering stock until cooked through and tender, 10 to 15 minutes. Transfer the cooked matzo balls to a serving bowl.

9. When all of the matzo balls have been cooked, divide them among the serving bowls. Ladle the stock over each portion and enjoy.

Msoki de Pesaj

YIELD: 6 SERVINGS / **ACTIVE TIME:** 45 MINUTES / **TOTAL TIME:** 3 HOURS

2½ LBS. BONELESS LAMB SHOULDER, CUT INTO 3-INCH CUBES

1 TABLESPOON KOSHER SALT, PLUS MORE TO TASTE

½ TEASPOON BLACK PEPPER, PLUS MORE TO TASTE

2 TABLESPOONS AVOCADO OIL

2 LARGE YELLOW ONIONS, CHOPPED

2 CARROTS, PEELED AND CHOPPED

1 TURNIP, PEELED AND CHOPPED

1 GARLIC CLOVE, MINCED

1 CINNAMON STICK

2 TEASPOONS THREE-PEPPER HARISSA SAUCE (SEE PAGE 510)

2 LBS. SPINACH LEAVES, FINELY CHOPPED

2 LEEKS, TRIMMED, RINSED WELL, MINCED

1 ZUCCHINI, CHOPPED

1 FENNEL BULB, TRIMMED AND CHOPPED

3 CELERY STALKS, CHOPPED

1½ CUPS FAVA BEANS

1 CUP GREEN PEAS

4 ARTICHOKE HEARTS, CUT INTO WEDGES

¼ BUNCH OF FRESH PARSLEY, CHOPPED

¼ BUNCH OF FRESH CILANTRO, CHOPPED

¼ BUNCH OF FRESH MINT LEAVES, FINELY CHOPPED

2 TEASPOONS ORANGE BLOSSOM WATER

1. Season the lamb with the salt and pepper. Place the avocado oil in a large Dutch oven and warm it over medium-high heat. Working in batches to avoid crowding the pot, add the lamb and cook until browned all over, about 8 minutes for each batch, turning it as necessary. Using a slotted spoon, transfer the browned lamb to a bowl.

2. Add the onions, carrots, turnip, and garlic to the pot and cook, stirring frequently, until the vegetables are tender, 15 to 20 minutes.

3. Add the cinnamon stick and harissa and cook, stirring frequently, for 5 minutes.

4. Add the spinach, leeks, zucchini, fennel, and celery and cook until the fennel is tender, about 15 minutes.

5. Stir in the lamb, fava beans, peas, artichoke hearts, parsley, cilantro, mint, and orange blossom water. Add water until the liquid reaches three-quarters of the way up the mixture. Bring the stew to a simmer and let it cook, stirring occasionally, until the liquid has reduced to one-quarter the original amount.

6. Season the stew with salt and pepper, ladle it into warmed bowls, and enjoy.

Tunisian Vegetable Soup

YIELD: 12 SERVINGS / **ACTIVE TIME:** 20 MINUTES / **TOTAL TIME:** 1 HOUR AND 15 MINUTES

3 CUPS CUBED CELERIAC

2 CUPS SLICED CARROTS

1 CUP CHOPPED ONION

3 GARLIC CLOVES

2 TABLESPOONS EXTRA-VIRGIN OLIVE OIL

¼ CUP TOMATO PASTE

2 TEASPOONS KOSHER SALT

2 TEASPOONS TURMERIC

1 TEASPOON CUMIN

1 TEASPOON CORIANDER

½ TEASPOON BLACK PEPPER

8 CUPS VEGETABLE STOCK (SEE PAGE 484)

1½ CUPS CUBED BUTTERNUT SQUASH

1 CUP SLICED PARSNIP

1 CUP CUBED RED BLISS POTATOES

10 OZ. ENOKI MUSHROOMS

1. Place half each of the celeriac, carrots, and onion, and all of the garlic in a food processor and pulse until the vegetables are very finely diced.

2. Place the olive oil in a large saucepan and warm it over medium-high heat. Add the vegetable mixture and cook, stirring frequently, until the onion is starting to brown, about 10 minutes.

3. Add the tomato paste, salt, turmeric, cumin, coriander, and pepper and cook, stirring frequently, for 4 minutes.

4. Add the stock, bring the soup to a boil, and then add the remaining celeriac, carrots, and onion, along with the butternut squash, parsnip, and potatoes. Reduce the heat, cover the pan, and simmer for 40 minutes.

5. Remove the pan from heat, add the mushrooms, and cover the pan. Let stand for 10 minutes before ladling the soup into warmed bowls.

Broccoli & Anchovy Soup

YIELD: 4 SERVINGS / **ACTIVE TIME:** 20 MINUTES / **TOTAL TIME:** 45 MINUTES

1 TABLESPOON EXTRA-VIRGIN OLIVE OIL

1 TABLESPOON UNSALTED BUTTER

1 ONION, CHOPPED

1 GARLIC CLOVE, MINCED

1½ CUPS CHOPPED PORTOBELLO MUSHROOMS

1 BIRD'S EYE CHILE PEPPER, STEMS AND SEEDS REMOVED, CHOPPED

2 ANCHOVIES IN OLIVE OIL, DRAINED AND MINCED

1 CUP CHOPPED TOMATO

¼ CUP WHITE WINE

4 CUPS CHICKEN STOCK OR VEGETABLE STOCK (SEE PAGE 482 OR 484)

2 CUPS BROCCOLI FLORETS

SALT AND PEPPER, TO TASTE

PARMESAN CHEESE, GRATED, FOR GARNISH

1. Place the olive oil and butter in a saucepan and warm over low heat. When the butter has melted, add the onion, garlic, mushrooms, chile, and anchovies and cook, stirring frequently, until the onion starts to soften, about 5 minutes.

2. Stir in the tomato and the white wine and simmer, stirring occasionally, for 10 minutes.

3. Add the stock, raise the heat to medium-high, and bring the soup to a boil. Reduce the heat so that the soup simmers. Add the broccoli florets and cook for 10 minutes.

4. Season with salt and pepper, ladle into warmed bowls, and garnish with Parmesan cheese.

Saffron, Tomato & Fennel Soup

YIELD: 12 TO 16 SERVINGS / **ACTIVE TIME:** 5 MINUTES / **TOTAL TIME:** 25 MINUTES

2 TABLESPOONS EXTRA-VIRGIN OLIVE OIL

½ CUP DICED ONIONS

¼ CUP DICED PARSNIPS

¼ CUP DICED CELERY

¼ CUP DICED FENNEL (RESERVE FENNEL FRONDS AND STALK)

2 TABLESPOONS SLICED GARLIC

3 BAY LEAVES

1½ TABLESPOONS KOSHER SALT, PLUS MORE TO TASTE

1 TABLESPOON BLACK PEPPER, PLUS MORE TO TASTE

1 CUP WHITE WINE

1 TEASPOON SAFFRON WATER (SEE PAGE 322)

8 CUPS HIGH-QUALITY TOMATO JUICE

1 TABLESPOON FRESH OREGANO

2 TABLESPOONS CHOPPED FRESH BASIL

2 TABLESPOONS CHOPPED FRESH PARSLEY

1 TABLESPOON FRESH LEMON JUICE

1 TABLESPOON RED WINE VINEGAR

1. Place the olive oil in a saucepan and warm it over medium heat. Add the onions, parsnips, celery, fennel, garlic, bay leaves, salt, and pepper and cook, stirring frequently, until the onions are translucent, about 3 minutes.

2. Deglaze the pan with the wine, scraping up any browned bits from the bottom of the pan. Bring the wine to a simmer and then stir in the Saffron Water, tomato juice, and all of the fresh herbs. Return the soup to a simmer and let it cook for 10 minutes.

3. Stir in the lemon juice and vinegar, season the soup with salt and pepper, ladle it into warmed bowls, and enjoy.

Chicken Stew with Potatoes & Radishes

YIELD: 4 SERVINGS / **ACTIVE TIME:** 30 MINUTES / **TOTAL TIME:** 2 HOURS AND 30 MINUTES

4 CHICKEN LEGS

SALT AND PEPPER, TO TASTE

2 TABLESPOONS EXTRA-VIRGIN OLIVE OIL, PLUS MORE TO TASTE

1 LARGE ONION, CHOPPED

5 GARLIC CLOVES, SLICED THIN

2 TABLESPOONS HUNGARIAN PAPRIKA (HOT OR SWEET), PLUS MORE TO TASTE

1 (28 OZ.) CAN OF WHOLE PEELED TOMATOES, WITH THEIR LIQUID

3 CUPS CHICKEN STOCK (SEE PAGE 482)

1½ LBS. NEW POTATOES

½ LEMON

¾ CUP SOUR CREAM, FOR SERVING

6 RADISHES, SLICED THIN, FOR SERVING

1. Season the chicken legs generously with salt. Place the olive oil in a large Dutch oven and warm it over medium-high heat. Working in two batches, add the chicken and cook until the skin is golden brown, 8 to 10 minutes. Transfer the chicken to a plate and set it aside.

2. Add the onion and cook, stirring occasionally, until it is browned, 8 to 10 minutes. Add the garlic and cook, stirring frequently, until softened, about 1 minute. Add the paprika and cook, stirring continually, until fragrant, about 30 seconds.

3. Add the tomatoes and cook, breaking them up with a wooden spoon until no pieces are bigger than ½ inch. Bring the mixture to a simmer and cook until the liquid in the pan has thickened slightly, 6 to 8 minutes.

4. Add stock, the potatoes, and chicken and return to a simmer. Cook, stirring occasionally, until the chicken is very tender and the potatoes are creamy, about 1½ hours. Add more stock to the pot as necessary to keep the potatoes submerged. Remove the pot from heat and season the stew with salt and paprika.

5. Squeeze the lemon into a small bowl and stir in the sour cream. Season the mixture with salt. In another small bowl, combine the radishes with a pinch of salt and toss to coat.

6. To serve, ladle the stew into warmed bowls, season each portion generously with pepper, and drizzle some olive oil over the top. Serve with the sour cream and radishes.

SALADS & SIDE DISHES

Pita Bread

YIELD: 8 SERVINGS / **ACTIVE TIME:** 1 HOUR / **TOTAL TIME:** 3 HOURS

1 CUP LUKEWARM WATER (90°F)

1 TABLESPOON ACTIVE DRY YEAST

1 TABLESPOON SUGAR

1¾ CUPS ALL-PURPOSE FLOUR, PLUS MORE AS NEEDED

1 CUP WHOLE WHEAT FLOUR

1 TABLESPOON KOSHER SALT

1. In a large mixing bowl, combine the water, yeast, and sugar. Let the mixture sit until it starts to foam, about 10 minutes.

2. Add the flours and salt to the mixing bowl and work the mixture until it comes together as a smooth dough. Cover the bowl with a linen towel and let it rise for about 15 minutes.

3. Preheat the oven to 500°F and place a baking stone on the floor of the oven.

4. Divide the dough into 8 pieces and form them into balls. Place the balls on a flour-dusted work surface, press them down, and roll them until they are about ¼ inch thick.

5. Working with one pita at a time, place the pita on the baking stone and bake until it is puffy and brown, about 8 minutes.

6. Remove the pita from the oven and serve warm or at room temperature.

Cauliflower Cakes

YIELD: 4 SERVINGS / **ACTIVE TIME:** 30 MINUTES / **TOTAL TIME:** 1 HOUR AND 30 MINUTES

1 HEAD OF CAULIFLOWER, TRIMMED AND CUT INTO SMALL FLORETS

¼ CUP EXTRA-VIRGIN OLIVE OIL

1 TEASPOON TURMERIC

½ TEASPOON CORIANDER

¼ TEASPOON GROUND GINGER

1 TEASPOON KOSHER SALT

¼ TEASPOON BLACK PEPPER

6 OZ. GOAT CHEESE

3 SCALLIONS, TRIMMED AND SLICED THIN

1 EGG, BEATEN

2 GARLIC CLOVES, MINCED

ZEST OF 1 LEMON

⅓ CUP ALL-PURPOSE FLOUR

1. Preheat the oven to 425°F. Place the cauliflower in a mixing bowl, add 2 tablespoons of the olive oil, the turmeric, coriander, ginger, salt, and pepper, and toss to coat. Place the cauliflower on a baking sheet in a single layer, place it in the oven, and roast until it is tender and lightly browned, about 10 minutes.

2. Remove the cauliflower from the oven, transfer it to a mixing bowl, and mash until it is smooth. Let the mashed cauliflower cool.

3. Add the goat cheese, scallions, egg, garlic, and lemon zest to the cauliflower and gently fold until they have been incorporated and evenly distributed. Add the flour and stir to incorporate.

4. Divide the mixture into four pieces and shape each one into a ½-inch-thick patty. Place the patties on a plate, cover them with plastic wrap, and refrigerate for 30 minutes.

5. Place the remaining olive oil in a large skillet and warm it over medium heat. Add the cauliflower patties and cook until golden brown on both sides, about 10 minutes. Remove the cauliflower cakes from the pan and serve immediately.

THE ENCYCLOPEDIA OF MEDITERRANEAN

Salade Niçoise

YIELD: 4 SERVINGS / **ACTIVE TIME:** 45 MINUTES / **TOTAL TIME:** 1 HOUR

1 LB. BABY RED POTATOES, QUARTERED

SALT AND PEPPER, TO TASTE

2 EGGS

2 CUPS TRIMMED GREEN BEANS

2 HEADS OF BIBB LETTUCE, SEPARATED INTO LEAVES

DIJON DRESSING (SEE PAGE 519)

2 SMALL TOMATOES, CUT INTO ½-INCH WEDGES

CONFIT TUNA (SEE PAGE 485)

½ RED ONION, SLICED THIN

¼ CUP PITTED KALAMATA OLIVES

1 TABLESPOON CAPERS, DRAINED

1. Prepare an ice bath. Place the potatoes in a large saucepan and cover them with water. Season the water with salt and bring the potatoes to a boil. Add the eggs (in their shells) and cook for 10 minutes.

2. Remove the eggs and place them in the ice bath for 5 minutes. Remove the eggs from the ice bath and peel them when you have a moment.

3. Cook the potatoes until tender and then remove them with a strainer or slotted spoon. Add the potatoes to the ice bath.

4. Add the green beans to the boiling water and cook for 3 minutes. Remove the green beans from the pot and place them in the ice bath. When the green beans are cool, drain the potatoes and green beans and pat them dry.

5. Place the lettuce in a mixing bowl and add enough of the dressing to lightly coat the lettuce. Toss to coat, season with salt and pepper, and place on a serving platter.

6. Add the tomatoes, Confit Tuna, potatoes, and blanched green beans to the bowl, add some dressing, and toss to coat.

7. Place the salad on a platter, top with the hard-boiled eggs, red onion, olives, and capers, and enjoy.

Salade Niçoise
SEE PAGE 341

Panzarella

YIELD: 4 SERVINGS / **ACTIVE TIME:** 30 MINUTES / **TOTAL TIME:** 1 HOUR

4 CUPS CUBED CRUSTY BREAD

6 TABLESPOONS EXTRA-VIRGIN OLIVE OIL

SALT AND PEPPER, TO TASTE

2 TABLESPOONS RED WINE VINEGAR

2 TABLESPOONS CHOPPED FRESH BASIL

2 TABLESPOONS CHOPPED FRESH OREGANO

1 LB. CHERRY TOMATOES, HALVED

1 (14 OZ.) CAN OF CANNELLINI BEANS, DRAINED AND RINSED

½ RED ONION, SLICED THIN

4 CUPS BABY ARUGULA

PARMESAN CHEESE, SHAVED, FOR GARNISH

1. Preheat the oven to 375°F. Place the bread and 2 tablespoons of the olive oil in a mixing bowl, season the mixture with salt and pepper, and toss to coat. Place the bread on a baking sheet, place it in the oven, and bake until it is golden brown, 8 to 10 minutes, stirring frequently. Remove the bread from the oven and let it cool.

2. Place the vinegar in a salad bowl. While whisking, slowly drizzle in the remaining olive oil. As this is a split vinaigrette, the oil will not emulsify. Add the herbs, tomatoes, beans, and onion to the vinaigrette and toss to coat.

3. Add the bread and baby arugula, stir gently until combined, and season the salad with salt and pepper. Garnish with the Parmesan and enjoy.

Insalata di Rinforzo

YIELD: 6 SERVINGS / **ACTIVE TIME:** 15 MINUTES / **TOTAL TIME:** 30 MINUTES

SALT, TO TASTE

1 HEAD OF CAULIFLOWER, CUT INTO FLORETS

8 ANCHOVIES IN OLIVE OIL, DRAINED

½ CUP CAPERS IN SALT, SOAKED, DRAINED, AND SQUEEZED

¾ CUP GREEN OLIVES, PITTED

½ CUP MIXED PICKLES, DRAINED

3½ OZ. PAPACCELLE (STUFFED PEPPERS IN OIL), HALVED

5 TABLESPOONS EXTRA-VIRGIN OLIVE OIL

3 TABLESPOONS RED WINE VINEGAR

1. Bring salted water to a boil in a large saucepan. Add the cauliflower and cook until it is al dente, about 10 minutes. Drain the cauliflower and let it cool completely.

2. Arrange the cooled cauliflower in a serving dish and top with the anchovies, capers, olives, pickles, and papacelle.

3. Place the olive oil, vinegar, and a pinch of salt in a bowl and whisk until the mixture has emulsified. Pour the dressing over the salad and enjoy.

Braised Fennel

YIELD: 4 SERVINGS / **ACTIVE TIME:** 20 MINUTES / **TOTAL TIME:** 30 MINUTES

2 TABLESPOONS EXTRA-VIRGIN OLIVE OIL

2 FENNEL BULBS, TRIMMED AND HALVED

½ CUP WHITE WINE

ZEST AND JUICE OF ½ LEMON

2 CUPS CHICKEN STOCK (SEE PAGE 482)

1 TABLESPOON HONEY

1 RADICCHIO, CORE REMOVED, SLICED THIN

SALT AND PEPPER, TO TASTE

1. Place the olive oil in a Dutch oven and warm it over medium-high heat. Add the fennel and cook until it is golden brown on both sides, 6 to 8 minutes.

2. Add the white wine and cook until it has almost evaporated, about 3 minutes, scraping up any browned bits from the bottom of the Dutch oven.

3. Add the lemon zest, lemon juice, stock, and honey, bring to a simmer, and cover the pot. Simmer until the fennel is tender, about 10 minutes. Remove the fennel from the pot with a slotted spoon and place it in a bowl.

4. Add the radicchio to the Dutch oven and cook over medium heat, stirring frequently, until it has softened, about 5 minutes. Place the radicchio on top of the fennel, season the dish with salt and pepper, and serve.

Slow-Cooked Cherry Tomatoes

YIELD: 6 SERVINGS / **ACTIVE TIME:** 10 MINUTES / **TOTAL TIME:** 1 HOUR

1½ LBS. HEIRLOOM CHERRY TOMATOES

½ HEAD OF GARLIC, TOP ½ INCH TRIMMED

2 SPRIGS OF FRESH ROSEMARY

½ CUP AVOCADO OIL

¾ TEASPOON CORIANDER SEEDS

½ TEASPOON SUGAR

¾ TEASPOON KOSHER SALT

1 TABLESPOON RED WINE VINEGAR

1. Preheat the oven to 350°F and position a rack in the middle. Place the tomatoes, garlic, rosemary, avocado oil, coriander seeds, sugar, and salt in a baking dish and toss to coat. Turn the garlic cut side down, place the dish in the oven, and then roast until the tomatoes are browned and very tender, about 50 minutes, tossing them 2 or 3 times as they cook.

2. Remove the dish from the oven and let it cool slightly.

3. Add the vinegar, stir to combine, and enjoy.

**Slow-Cooked
Cherry Tomatoes**
SEE PAGE 345

Octopus Salad

YIELD: 8 SERVINGS / **ACTIVE TIME:** 30 MINUTES / **TOTAL TIME:** 2 HOURS AND 30 MINUTES

1 WHOLE OCTOPUS

3 RADISHES, SLICED THIN

2 TEASPOONS KOSHER SALT

1 CUP WHITE VINEGAR

1 PEAR, CORED AND SLICED

1 TABLESPOON EXTRA-VIRGIN OLIVE OIL

½ CUP SALSA VERDE (SEE PAGE 505)

2 CUPS MESCLUN GREENS

1. Fill a pot large enough to fully submerge the octopus with water and bring it to a simmer. Add the octopus and cover the pot. Simmer until the octopus is very tender, 45 minutes to 1 hour. Remove the tentacles from the octopus and let them cool.

2. While the octopus is cooking, place the radishes and half of the salt in a bowl and toss to coat. Cover the radishes with some of the vinegar and let them sit.

3. Place the pear in a separate bowl, sprinkle the remaining salt over it, and toss to coat. Cover the pear with some of the vinegar and let it sit.

4. Warm a large cast-iron skillet over high heat. Brush the pan with the olive oil, pat the octopus tentacles dry, place them in the pan, and sear until slightly charred all over, 3 to 4 minutes.

5. To serve, spread some of the salsa on a plate and place a full tentacle alongside it. Put some of the greens in a small pile beside the tentacle, sprinkle the radishes and pear on top, and enjoy.

Bamies

YIELD: 4 SERVINGS / **ACTIVE TIME:** 15 MINUTES / **TOTAL TIME:** 40 MINUTES

2 TABLESPOONS EXTRA-VIRGIN OLIVE OIL

1 ONION, CHOPPED

1 LB. OKRA, RINSED WELL AND CHOPPED

1 POTATO, PEELED AND MINCED

1 GARLIC CLOVE, MINCED

2 TOMATOES, CHOPPED

3 TABLESPOONS WHITE WINE

½ CUP VEGETABLE STOCK (SEE PAGE 484)

2 TABLESPOONS CHOPPED FRESH PARSLEY

2 TEASPOONS SUGAR

SALT, TO TASTE

FETA CHEESE, CRUMBLED, FOR GARNISH

1. Place the olive oil in a medium skillet and warm it over medium heat. Add the onion and cook, stirring occasionally, until it starts to brown, about 8 minutes.

2. Add the okra and potato and cook, stirring frequently, until they start to brown, about 5 minutes.

3. Add the garlic and cook for 1 minute. Add the tomatoes, wine, stock, parsley, and sugar and stir to incorporate.

4. Cook until the tomatoes have collapsed and the okra and potato are tender, about 8 minutes.

5. Season with salt, garnish with feta, and enjoy.

Smoked & Seared Eggplant

YIELD: 4 SERVINGS / **ACTIVE TIME:** 10 MINUTES / **TOTAL TIME:** 30 MINUTES

1 CUP WOOD CHIPS

1 ONION, QUARTERED

2 TEASPOONS KOSHER SALT

¼ CUP AVOCADO OIL

1 SMALL EGGPLANT, TRIMMED AND CUBED

1 RED BELL PEPPER, STEM AND SEEDS REMOVED, DICED

¼ CUP BALSAMIC VINEGAR

1. Place the wood chips in a small cast-iron skillet and light them on fire. Place the cast-iron pan in a roasting pan and place the onion beside the skillet. Cover the roasting pan with aluminum foil and smoke the onion for 20 minutes.

2. Transfer the onion to a food processor and puree until smooth. Add 1 teaspoon of the salt, stir to combine, and set the puree aside.

3. Place the avocado oil in a large skillet and warm it over high heat. Add the eggplant, season it with the remaining salt, and sear it for 1 minute. Turn the eggplant over, add the bell pepper, and cook for another minute.

4. Add the balsamic vinegar and toss to coat. To serve, spoon the onion puree onto the serving plates and top with the vegetables.

Smoked & Seared Eggplant
SEE PAGE 349

Chickpea Salad

YIELD: 4 SERVINGS / **ACTIVE TIME:** 20 MINUTES / **TOTAL TIME:** 24 HOURS

2 CUPS DRIED CHICKPEAS, SOAKED OVERNIGHT

4 CUPS CHICKEN STOCK (SEE PAGE 482)

1 ONION, CHOPPED

1 CUP CHOPPED FRESH CILANTRO

¼ CUP EXTRA-VIRGIN OLIVE OIL

¼ CUP FRESH LEMON JUICE

¼ TEASPOON SAFFRON

1 TABLESPOON CUMIN

1 TEASPOON CINNAMON

1 TEASPOON RED PEPPER FLAKES

SALT AND PEPPER, TO TASTE

1. Drain the chickpeas, place them in a saucepan, and add the stock. Bring to a boil, reduce the heat, and simmer until the chickpeas are tender, about 45 minutes.

2. Drain the chickpeas and let them cool completely.

3. Place the chickpeas and the remaining ingredients in a mixing bowl, toss until combined, and enjoy.

Shaved Snap Pea Salad

YIELD: 2 SERVINGS / **ACTIVE TIME:** 20 MINUTES / **TOTAL TIME:** 50 MINUTES

1 LB. SNAP PEAS

1 TABLESPOON CHOPPED FRESH DILL

1 TABLESPOON CHOPPED FRESH BASIL

1 TABLESPOON CHOPPED FRESH MINT

2 TEASPOONS HONEY

¼ CUP WHITE VINEGAR

1 TEASPOON KOSHER SALT

1 TABLESPOON CRUSHED TOASTED WALNUTS

1. Using a sharp knife, stack 4 snap peas and cut them into thin slices on a bias. Transfer them to a bowl and repeat with the remaining snap peas.

2. Add the remaining ingredients and toss until well combined.

3. Chill the salad in the refrigerator for 30 minutes before serving.

THE ENCYCLOPEDIA OF MEDITERRANEAN

Broccolini Salad

YIELD: 10 SERVINGS / **ACTIVE TIME:** 15 MINUTES / **TOTAL TIME:** 15 MINUTES

2 TABLESPOONS KOSHER SALT, PLUS MORE TO TASTE

2 LBS. BROCCOLINI

1 CUP DRIED CRANBERRIES

1 CUP SLICED ALMONDS, TOASTED

½ CUP CRUMBLED FETA OR GOAT CHEESE

1 CUP BLUEBERRIES

½ CUP CHAMPAGNE VINAIGRETTE (SEE PAGE 498)

2 CUPS SLICED RED GRAPES

1 TABLESPOON BLACK PEPPER, PLUS MORE TO TASTE

¼ CUP CHOPPED FRESH HERBS (PARSLEY, MINT, BASIL, AND OREGANO RECOMMENDED)

¼ CUP EXTRA-VIRGIN OLIVE OIL

5 GARLIC CLOVES, MINCED

1. Bring salted water to a boil in a large saucepan and prepare an ice bath. Add the broccolini and cook for 4 minutes.

2. Transfer the broccolini to the ice bath and let it cool. Pat the broccolini dry and chop it into bite-size pieces.

3. Place the broccolini in a large salad bowl, add all of the remaining ingredients, except for the olive oil and garlic, and toss to combine. Set the salad aside.

4. Place the olive oil in a medium skillet and warm it over medium heat. Add the garlic and cook, stirring continuously, until it is golden brown, about 1½ minutes.

5. Pour the mixture over the salad and toss to incorporate. Taste, adjust the seasoning as necessary, and enjoy.

Candied Walnuts

YIELD: 4 SERVINGS / **ACTIVE TIME:** 20 MINUTES / **TOTAL TIME:** 30 MINUTES

1 CUP WALNUTS

1 CUP MAPLE SYRUP

2 CUPS CANOLA OIL

2 TABLESPOONS SUGAR

1 TEASPOON KOSHER SALT

1. Line a baking sheet with parchment paper. Place the walnuts and maple syrup in a small saucepan and bring to a boil. Reduce the heat and simmer for 5 minutes.

2. Transfer the walnuts to the baking sheet. Using a fork, separate the walnuts so that they don't stick together when cool. Let the walnuts cool completely.

3. Place the canola oil in a Dutch oven and warm it to 350°F. Working in batches to avoid crowding the pot, add the walnuts and fry until golden brown. Transfer the fried walnuts to a paper towel–lined plate to drain and season them with the salt as they cool.

Shaved Snap Pea Salad
SEE PAGE 352

Concia

YIELD: 4 SERVINGS / **ACTIVE TIME:** 1 HOUR / **TOTAL TIME:** 6 HOURS

3 ZUCCHINI, SLICED LENGTHWISE INTO ¼-INCH-THICK PIECES

SALT AND PEPPER, TO TASTE

AVOCADO OIL, AS NEEDED

6 GARLIC CLOVES, MINCED

½ BUNCH OF FRESH BASIL, CHOPPED

¼ CUP WHITE WINE VINEGAR

1. Season the zucchini slices with salt and pepper on both sides, place them on a paper towel–lined baking sheet, and let them rest for 10 minutes.

2. Pat the zucchini dry and replace the paper towels on the baking sheet. Add avocado oil to a large saucepan until it is ½ inch deep and warm it over medium heat. Working in batches of 6 slices, gently slip the zucchini into the hot oil, making sure that the pieces all lie flat and do not overlap. Fry the zucchini until golden brown all over, about 5 minutes, turning as necessary. Transfer the fried zucchini to the paper towel–lined baking sheet and let it drain.

3. Place all of the fried zucchini in a mixing bowl. Season it with salt and pepper, add the garlic, basil, and vinegar, and gently stir until the zucchini is evenly coated.

4. Cover the bowl with plastic wrap and chill it in the refrigerator for 5 hours before enjoying. To serve, let the concia come to room temperature.

Braised Grapes

YIELD: 4 SERVINGS / **ACTIVE TIME:** 20 MINUTES / **TOTAL TIME:** 20 MINUTES

1 TABLESPOON EXTRA-VIRGIN OLIVE OIL

2 CUPS GRAPES, STEMS REMOVED

½ CUP DRY VERMOUTH

2 STAR ANISE PODS

2 CINNAMON STICKS

SALT AND PEPPER, TO TASTE

¼ CUP SLIVERED BLANCHED ALMONDS, TOASTED

1. Place the olive oil in a medium skillet and warm it over medium heat. Add the grapes and cook, stirring frequently, until they have been browned, 5 to 10 minutes.

2. Add the vermouth, star anise, and cinnamon sticks and cook until the vermouth has evaporated, 2 to 4 minutes.

3. Season the mixture with salt and pepper, sprinkle the almonds over the top, and let the braised grapes cool completely before serving.

THE ENCYCLOPEDIA OF MEDITERRANEAN

Cornbread Stuffing

YIELD: 2½ CUPS / **ACTIVE TIME:** 30 MINUTES / **TOTAL TIME:** 1 HOUR

¼ CUP ALL-PURPOSE FLOUR

1½ TEASPOONS BAKING POWDER

¼ TEASPOON BAKING SODA

⅓ TEASPOON FINE SEA SALT, PLUS MORE TO TASTE

½ CUP YELLOW CORNMEAL

1 EGG

½ CUP PLAIN YOGURT

1½ TEASPOONS HONEY

½ CUP MILK

1½ TABLESPOONS UNSALTED BUTTER, MELTED, PLUS MORE AS NEEDED

¼ RED ONION, DICED

1 CELERY STALK, DICED

1 GARLIC CLOVE, MINCED

SALT, TO TASTE

1 TEASPOON CHOPPED FRESH SAGE

1 TEASPOON CHOPPED FRESH THYME

1. Preheat the oven to 350°F. Line 6 wells in a muffin pan with paper liners. Sift the flour, baking powder, baking soda, salt, and cornmeal into a mixing bowl and set the mixture aside.

2. Place the egg, yogurt, honey, ¼ cup of the milk, and the melted butter in a separate bowl and whisk until combined. Add the wet mixture to the dry mixture and whisk until it comes together as a smooth batter.

3. Pour the batter into the paper liners, place the pan in the oven, and bake until a cake tester inserted into the center of each muffin comes out clean, 10 to 15 minutes. Remove the muffins from the oven and let them cool completely. When the muffins are cool enough to handle, chop them into bite-size pieces.

4. Coat a small skillet with butter and warm it over medium heat. Add the onion, celery, and garlic and cook, stirring frequently, until the onion has softened, about 5 minutes. Season the mixture with salt, stir in the sage and thyme, and transfer the mixture to a bowl.

5. Add the pieces of cornbread and toss to combine. Add the remaining milk, stir until incorporated, and use immediately.

Peppery Glazed Asparagus

YIELD: 2 SERVINGS / **ACTIVE TIME:** 10 MINUTES / **TOTAL TIME:** 20 MINUTES

JUICE OF 1 LEMON

1 TABLESPOON SUGAR

1 TABLESPOON EXTRA-VIRGIN OLIVE OIL

1 TEASPOON KOSHER SALT

2 GARLIC CLOVES, MINCED

10 ASPARAGUS STALKS, TRIMMED

1 TEASPOON BLACK PEPPER

PARMESAN CHEESE, SHAVED, FOR GARNISH

1. Preheat the broiler on the oven to high. Place the lemon juice, sugar, olive oil, salt, and garlic in a bowl, stir until well combined, and then add the asparagus. Toss until the asparagus is coated.

2. Place the asparagus on a baking sheet and sprinkle the pepper over it. Place the asparagus in the oven and broil until the asparagus is beautifully browned, approximately 10 minutes.

3. Remove the asparagus from the oven, garnish with the Parmesan, and enjoy.

Spicy Chickpeas

YIELD: 4 SERVINGS / **ACTIVE TIME:** 20 MINUTES / **TOTAL TIME:** 24 HOURS

1 CUP DRIED CHICKPEAS, SOAKED OVERNIGHT AND DRAINED

2 CUPS CANOLA OIL

1 TEASPOON SMOKED PAPRIKA

½ TEASPOON ONION POWDER

½ TEASPOON BROWN SUGAR

¼ TEASPOON GARLIC POWDER

¼ TEASPOON KOSHER SALT

PINCH OF CHILI POWDER

PINCH OF CAYENNE PEPPER

1. Bring 4 cups of water to a boil in a saucepan. Add the chickpeas, reduce the heat so that the water simmers, and cook until the chickpeas are tender, 45 minutes to 1 hour. Drain the chickpeas, place them on a paper towel–lined plate, and pat them dry.

2. Place the canola oil in a Dutch oven and warm it to 350°F over medium heat.

3. Place the remaining ingredients in a bowl, stir until thoroughly combined, and set the mixture aside.

4. Place the chickpeas in the hot oil and fry until golden brown, about 3 minutes. Remove and place them in the bowl with the seasoning mixture. Toss to coat and serve.

Minty Pickled Cucumbers

YIELD: 2 CUPS / **ACTIVE TIME:** 20 MINUTES / **TOTAL TIME:** 3 HOURS

½ CUP SUGAR

½ CUP WATER

½ CUP RICE VINEGAR

2 TABLESPOONS DRIED MINT

1 TABLESPOON CORIANDER SEEDS

1 TABLESPOON MUSTARD SEEDS

2 CUCUMBERS, SLICED

1. Place all of the ingredients, except for the cucumbers, in a small saucepan and bring to a boil, stirring to dissolve the sugar.

2. Place the cucumbers in a large mason jar. Remove the pan from heat and pour the brine over the cucumbers.

3. Let cool completely before using or storing in the refrigerator, where the pickles will keep for 1 week.

THE ENCYCLOPEDIA OF MEDITERRANEAN

Crispy Polenta Cakes

YIELD: 4 SERVINGS / **ACTIVE TIME:** 30 MINUTES / **TOTAL TIME:** 1 HOUR

2 TABLESPOONS EXTRA-VIRGIN OLIVE OIL

1 SHALLOT, MINCED

1 TEASPOON FRESH THYME

2 CUPS MILK

1 CUP POLENTA

1 CUP GRATED PARMESAN CHEESE

SALT AND PEPPER, TO TASTE

1. Line a square 8-inch baking dish with plastic wrap. Place 1 tablespoon of the olive oil in a small saucepan and warm it over medium heat. Add the shallot and cook, stirring frequently, until it softens, about 3 minutes.

2. Add the thyme and cook, stirring continually, for 1 minute. Add the milk and bring to a boil. Add the polenta and cook, stirring frequently, until the mixture looks like scrambled eggs, about 10 minutes. Remove the pan from heat, add the Parmesan, and fold to incorporate.

3. Season the polenta with salt and pepper and transfer it to the baking dish, pressing down to ensure it is in an even layer. Place the polenta in the refrigerator and chill until it is firm, about 30 minutes.

4. Remove the polenta from the refrigerator and cut it into round or square cakes. Place the remaining olive oil in a large skillet and warm it over medium-high heat. Add the cakes to the pan and cook until they are golden brown on both sides, about 6 minutes. Transfer to a paper towel–lined plate to drain before serving.

Arugula Salad with Candied Walnuts

YIELD: 4 SERVINGS / **ACTIVE TIME:** 30 MINUTES / **TOTAL TIME:** 1 HOUR AND 30 MINUTES

4 OZ. PROSCIUTTO, SLICED THIN

6 CUPS ARUGULA

FIG VINAIGRETTE (SEE PAGE 508)

2 OZ. PARMESAN CHEESE, SHAVED

SALT AND PEPPER, TO TASTE

1 CUP CANDIED WALNUTS (SEE PAGE 353)

2 TABLESPOONS FIG JAM

1. Preheat the oven to 350°F. Place the prosciutto on a baking sheet lined with a Silpat mat, place it in the oven, and bake until crispy and golden brown, about 10 minutes. Remove the prosciutto from the oven and let it cool. When it is cool enough to handle, chop it into bite-size pieces.

2. Place the arugula in a salad bowl, add some of the vinaigrette, and toss to coat. Add the Parmesan, season the salad with salt and pepper, and toss to combine. Top with the Candied Walnuts and prosciutto.

3. Spread some of the fig jam on each serving plate. Top with the salad, serve with the remaining vinaigrette, and enjoy.

Fig & Goat Cheese Salad

YIELD: 2 SERVINGS / **ACTIVE TIME:** 30 MINUTES / **TOTAL TIME:** 30 MINUTES

1 CUP PINOT NOIR

¼ CUP SUGAR

4 ORANGE SLICES

6 FRESH FIGS, HALVED

2 TABLESPOONS CRUMBLED GOAT CHEESE

1. Prepare a charcoal or gas grill for high heat (about 500°F). Place the wine and sugar in a small saucepan and warm the mixture over medium-high heat, stirring until the sugar has dissolved. Simmer until the mixture has reduced to a syrupy consistency. Remove the pan from heat and set it aside.

2. Place the orange slices on the grill and cook until they're caramelized on each side, about 2 minutes. Remove them from heat and set them aside.

3. Place the figs on the grill, cut side down, and cook until they are lightly browned and soft, about 4 minutes.

4. To serve, place the orange slices on a plate, place the figs on top of the orange slices, sprinkle the goat cheese over the dish, and then drizzle the reduction over the top.

Red Cabbage, Date & Beet Salad

YIELD: 6 SERVINGS / **ACTIVE TIME:** 30 MINUTES / **TOTAL TIME:** 1 HOUR AND 30 MINUTES

2 CUPS KOSHER SALT

6 LARGE RED BEETS

½ HEAD OF RED CABBAGE, CORED AND SLICED THIN

5 DRIED MEDJOOL DATES, PITTED AND SLICED THIN LENGTHWISE

½ CUP TAHINI SAUCE (SEE PAGE 500)

⅓ CUP CHOPPED FRESH CILANTRO

⅓ CUP CHOPPED FRESH MINT

⅓ CUP CHOPPED SCALLIONS

¼ CUP EXTRA-VIRGIN OLIVE OIL

¼ CUP FRESH LEMON JUICE

1. Preheat the oven to 400°F. Line a baking sheet with parchment paper and cover it with the salt.

2. Set the beets on the bed of salt, place them in the oven, and roast them until fork-tender, 45 minutes to 1 hour.

3. Remove the beets from the oven and let them cool for 30 minutes. Discard the salt.

4. Peel the beets, cut them into 2-inch-long slices that are ⅛ inch thick, and place them in a bowl. You can also grate the beets.

5. Add all of the remaining ingredients to the bowl and stir until well combined. Taste, adjust the seasoning as necessary, and enjoy.

Insalata di Arance e Finocchio

YIELD: 4 SERVINGS / **ACTIVE TIME:** 15 MINUTES / **TOTAL TIME:** 30 MINUTES

6 ORANGES

1 SMALL ONION, SLICED THIN

1 SMALL BULB OF FENNEL, TRIMMED AND SLICED THIN

½ CUP PITTED BLACK OLIVES

¼ CUP EXTRA-VIRGIN OLIVE OIL

SALT AND PEPPER, TO TASTE

1. Peel the oranges and, using a sharp knife, remove the white pith. Slice the oranges thin and set them aside.

2. Arrange the onion and fennel on a serving platter and top with the oranges and olives.

3. Drizzle the olive oil over the salad and season it with salt and pepper.

4. Let the salad marinate for about 15 minutes before serving.

Patate al Forno alla Siciliana

YIELD: 4 SERVINGS / **ACTIVE TIME:** 25 MINUTES / **TOTAL TIME:** 1 HOUR AND 15 MINUTES

2.2 LBS. POTATOES, PEELED AND CHOPPED

¼ CUP EXTRA-VIRGIN OLIVE OIL

SALT AND PEPPER, TO TASTE

1 RED ONION, SLICED

1⅓ CUPS CHERRY TOMATOES, HALVED

½ CUP PITTED BLACK OLIVES

HANDFUL OF FRESH SAGE, CHOPPED

1 SPRIG OF FRESH ROSEMARY

3 BAY LEAVES

1. Preheat the oven to 390°F and line a baking dish with parchment paper. Rinse the potatoes and pat them dry. Place them in a large bowl with the olive oil, season them with salt and pepper, and toss to coat.

2. Add the remaining ingredients and toss to combine.

3. Place the mixture in the baking dish, place it in the oven, and roast until the potatoes are crispy, golden brown, and tender, about 50 minutes.

4. Remove the dish from the oven, remove the rosemary and bay leaves, and discard them. Stir the mixture so that the cooking juices are incorporated and serve immediately.

Chilled Calamari Salad

YIELD: 4 SERVINGS / **ACTIVE TIME:** 15 MINUTES / **TOTAL TIME:** 45 MINUTES

SALT AND PEPPER, TO TASTE

1½ LBS. SMALL SQUID, CLEANED (SEE PAGE 199), BODIES AND TENTACLES SEPARATED

3 TABLESPOONS RED WINE VINEGAR

2 TABLESPOONS THREE-PEPPER HARISSA SAUCE (SEE PAGE 510)

1½ TEASPOONS DIJON MUSTARD

⅓ CUP EXTRA-VIRGIN OLIVE OIL

2 ORANGES, PEELED AND CUT INTO SEGMENTS

1 RED BELL PEPPER, STEM AND SEEDS REMOVED, CUT INTO STRIPS

2 CELERY STALKS, CHOPPED

¼ CUP HAZELNUTS, TOASTED

¼ CUP SHREDDED FRESH MINT

1. Bring approximately 8 cups of water to a boil in a large saucepan and prepare an ice bath. Season the boiling water generously with salt, add the tentacles of the squid, and cook for 1 minute. Add the bodies, cook for another minute, and use a slotted spoon to transfer the squid to the ice bath.

2. Drain the squid, pat it dry, and chill in the refrigerator.

3. Place the red wine vinegar, harissa, and mustard in a salad bowl and whisk to combine. While whisking, slowly drizzle in the olive oil until it has emulsified.

4. Add the chilled calamari, oranges, bell pepper, and celery and gently toss until combined.

5. Season the salad with salt and pepper, top with the hazelnuts and mint, and enjoy.

Za'atar Bread

YIELD: 1 LOAF / **ACTIVE TIME:** 30 MINUTES / **TOTAL TIME:** 3 HOURS

½ CUP PLUS 1 TABLESPOON EXTRA-VIRGIN OLIVE OIL, PLUS MORE AS NEEDED

1¾ CUPS BREAD FLOUR, PLUS MORE AS NEEDED

1½ TEASPOONS INSTANT YEAST

1 TEASPOON SUGAR

½ CUP PLUS 2 TABLESPOONS WARM WATER (105°F)

1 TEASPOON FINE SEA SALT

3 TABLESPOONS ZA'ATAR (SEE PAGE 501)

1 TABLESPOON SESAME SEEDS

MALDON SEA SALT, TO TASTE

1. Coat a bowl with olive oil. Place the flour, yeast, sugar, water, 3 tablespoons of the olive oil, and the fine sea salt in the work bowl of a stand mixer fitted with the dough hook and work the mixture on low until it comes together as a smooth dough. Increase the speed to medium and work the dough until it is a tight, elastic ball.

2. Place the dough in the bowl, cover the bowl with plastic wrap, and let the dough rise in a naturally warm spot until it has doubled in size, about 1 hour.

3. Preheat the oven to 375°F. Coat a 10 x 8–inch rimmed baking sheet with 2 tablespoons of the olive oil. Place the dough on the pan and gently stretch it to the edges of the pan. Cover the pan with plastic wrap and let it rest in the naturally warm space until it has doubled in size, about 30 minutes.

4. Place the Za'atar and the remaining olive oil in a bowl and stir to combine. Spread the mixture over the dough and sprinkle the sesame seeds on top.

5. Place the pan in the oven and bake until the bread is golden brown, about 20 minutes, rotating the pan halfway through.

6. Remove the bread from the oven and sprinkle Maldon sea salt over the top. Let the bread cool slightly before slicing and serving.

Mint & Sage Butternut Squash

YIELD: 4 TO 6 SERVINGS / **ACTIVE TIME:** 10 MINUTES / **TOTAL TIME:** 25 MINUTES

1 BUTTERNUT SQUASH

1 TEASPOON AVOCADO OIL

1 TABLESPOON CHOPPED
FRESH SAGE

1 TABLESPOON CHOPPED
FRESH MINT

1. Preheat the oven to 350°F. Peel the squash, halve it, and remove the seeds. Dice the squash into small cubes and place them in a mixing bowl.

2. Add the avocado oil, sage, and mint and toss to coat.

3. Spread the squash on a baking sheet in a single layer. Place the squash in the oven and bake until it is fork-tender, about 15 minutes.

4. Remove the squash from the oven and enjoy.

Kemia de Remolachas

YIELD: 6 SERVINGS / **ACTIVE TIME:** 15 MINUTES / **TOTAL TIME:** 45 MINUTES

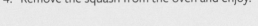

3 BEETS

1 TABLESPOON PLUS 2
TEASPOONS KOSHER SALT

1 TABLESPOON EXTRA-
VIRGIN OLIVE OIL

2 TEASPOONS CUMIN

¼ TEASPOON BLACK PEPPER

1. Place the beets and 1 tablespoon of the salt in a pot and cover with cold water. Bring to a boil and cook until the beets are fork-tender, about 30 minutes. Drain and let the beets cool slightly.

2. Peel the beets and cut them into 1-inch cubes.

3. Place the olive oil in a skillet and warm it over medium heat. Add the beets, cumin, remaining salt, and the pepper and cook, stirring frequently, for 3 minutes.

4. Transfer to a serving dish and enjoy warm or at room temperature.

Vegetable Kebabs

YIELD: 4 SERVINGS / **ACTIVE TIME:** 30 MINUTES / **TOTAL TIME:** 1 HOUR AND 30 MINUTES

¼ CUP PLUS 1 TABLESPOON EXTRA-VIRGIN OLIVE OIL

2 TEASPOONS DIJON MUSTARD

2 GARLIC CLOVES, MINCED

2 TEASPOONS RED WINE VINEGAR

2 TEASPOONS HONEY

1 TEASPOON CHOPPED FRESH ROSEMARY

SALT AND PEPPER, TO TASTE

2 PORTOBELLO MUSHROOMS, STEMS REMOVED, CUT INTO 1-INCH CUBES

2 ZUCCHINI, CUT INTO 1-INCH CUBES

1 RED BELL PEPPER, STEM AND SEEDS REMOVED, CUT INTO 1-INCH CUBES

1 GREEN BELL PEPPER, STEM AND SEEDS REMOVED, CUT INTO 1-INCH CUBES

1. Place ¼ cup of the olive oil, the mustard, garlic, vinegar, honey, and rosemary in a mixing bowl and whisk to combine. Season the dressing with salt and pepper and set it aside.

2. Thread the vegetables onto skewers and place them on a baking sheet. Pour the dressing over the skewers, cover them with plastic wrap, and let them marinate at room temperature for 1 hour, turning occasionally.

3. Place the remaining olive oil in a large skillet and warm it over medium-high heat. Remove the vegetable skewers from the dressing and reserve the dressing. Add the skewers to the pan and cook until golden brown all over and tender, about 8 minutes, turning them as necessary.

4. Place the skewers in a serving dish, pour the reserved dressing over them, and enjoy.

Kemia de Zanahorias

YIELD: 6 SERVINGS / **ACTIVE TIME:** 10 MINUTES / **TOTAL TIME:** 20 MINUTES

1 TABLESPOON PLUS 1 TEASPOON KOSHER SALT

6 CARROTS, CUT INTO ¼-INCH-THICK ROUNDS

1 TABLESPOON EXTRA-VIRGIN OLIVE OIL

5 GARLIC CLOVES, SLICED THIN

1 TEASPOON THREE-PEPPER HARISSA SAUCE (SEE PAGE 510)

1 TEASPOON PAPRIKA

1 TEASPOON CARAWAY SEEDS

1 TABLESPOON WHITE WINE VINEGAR

1. Bring a large pot of water to a boil. Add the tablespoon of salt and the carrots and cook until the carrots are fork-tender, about 5 minutes. Drain the carrots and set them aside.

2. Place the olive oil in a large skillet and warm it over medium-high heat. Add the garlic and cook, stirring frequently, until golden brown. Add the cooked carrots, harissa, and paprika and cook, stirring frequently, for 3 minutes.

3. Transfer the mixture to a serving bowl, stir in the caraway seeds, vinegar, and remaining salt, and enjoy.

Ful Medames

YIELD: 4 SERVINGS / **ACTIVE TIME:** 15 MINUTES / **TOTAL TIME:** 30 MINUTES

1 TABLESPOON AVOCADO OIL

1 ONION, CHOPPED

3 GARLIC CLOVES, MINCED

2 TOMATOES, CHOPPED

2 (14 OZ.) CANS OF FAVA BEANS, DRAINED AND RINSED; OR 3 CUPS SHELLED AND COOKED FRESH FAVA BEANS

1 TEASPOON CUMIN

1 TABLESPOON RAS EL HANOUT (SEE PAGE 505)

¼ TEASPOON CAYENNE PEPPER

3 TABLESPOONS FRESH LEMON JUICE

¼ CUP FRESH PARSLEY, CHOPPED

SALT, TO TASTE

1. Place the avocado oil in a large skillet and warm it over medium heat. Add the onion and garlic and cook, stirring frequently, until the onion is translucent, about 4 minutes.

2. Add the tomatoes and cook for another 4 minutes. Stir in the fava beans, cumin, Ras el Hanout, and cayenne pepper, reduce the heat to medium-low, and cook for 10 minutes.

3. Remove the pan from the heat and mash the fava beans lightly, right in the skillet, until most of the beans are mashed. Scoop into a serving bowl, stir in the lemon juice and parsley, season with salt, and enjoy.

THE ENCYCLOPEDIA OF MEDITERRANEAN

Bulgur-Stuffed Eggplants

YIELD: 4 SERVINGS / **ACTIVE TIME:** 30 MINUTES / **TOTAL TIME:** 1 HOUR AND 15 MINUTES

2 EGGPLANTS, HALVED LENGTHWISE

2 TABLESPOONS EXTRA-VIRGIN OLIVE OIL

SALT AND PEPPER, TO TASTE

¼ CUP BULGUR, RINSED

1 ONION, CHOPPED

2 GARLIC CLOVES, MINCED

1 TEASPOON DRIED OREGANO

¼ TEASPOON CINNAMON

4 PLUM TOMATOES, SEEDED, CHOPPED

1 CUP GRATED PARMESAN CHEESE

¾ CUP PINE NUTS, TOASTED

1 TEASPOON RED WINE VINEGAR

1. Preheat the oven to 375°F. Score the flesh of each eggplant and brush them with 1 tablespoon of the olive oil. Season the eggplants with salt and pepper, place them on a baking sheet, cut side down, and place them in the oven. Roast until they have collapsed and are tender, about 45 minutes.

2. While the eggplants are in the oven, place the bulgur in a mixing bowl and add 2 tablespoons of boiling water. Cover the bowl and let the bulgur sit until it has absorbed the water, about 30 minutes.

3. Place the remaining olive oil in a large skillet and warm it over medium-high heat. Add the onion and cook, stirring occasionally, until it has softened, about 5 minutes.

4. Add the garlic, oregano, and cinnamon and cook, stirring continually, for 1 minute. Remove the pan from heat and stir in the bulgur, tomatoes, ½ cup of the Parmesan, the pine nuts, and vinegar. Season the mixture with salt and pepper and set it aside.

5. Remove the eggplants from the oven. Leave the oven on. Using a fork, gently push the eggplants' flesh to the sides and press down on it to make a cavity for the filling.

6. Fill the eggplants with the bulgur mixture. Top with the remaining Parmesan, place the eggplants in the oven, and roast until the cheese has melted, about 8 minutes.

7. Remove the eggplants from the oven and enjoy.

Ful Medames
SEE PAGE 370

Marinated Cauliflower & Chickpeas

YIELD: 4 SERVINGS / **ACTIVE TIME:** 20 MINUTES / **TOTAL TIME:** 45 MINUTES

1 HEAD OF CAULIFLOWER, TRIMMED AND CUT INTO FLORETS

½ CUP EXTRA-VIRGIN OLIVE OIL

4 GARLIC CLOVES, MINCED

1 TEASPOON SUGAR

1 TEASPOON PAPRIKA

2 TEASPOONS CHOPPED FRESH ROSEMARY

¼ TEASPOON SAFFRON

2 TABLESPOONS WHITE WINE VINEGAR

1 (14 OZ.) CAN OF CHICKPEAS, DRAINED AND RINSED

SALT AND PEPPER, TO TASTE

FRESH PARSLEY, CHOPPED, FOR GARNISH

LEMON WEDGES, FOR SERVING

1. Prepare an ice bath. Bring salted water to a boil in a medium saucepan. Add the cauliflower and cook until it has softened, about 4 minutes. Transfer the cauliflower to the ice bath, let it cool, and drain.

2. Place 1 tablespoon of the olive oil in a large saucepan and warm it over medium heat. Add the garlic and cook, stirring continually, for 1 minute. Add the sugar, paprika, rosemary, and remaining olive oil and cook, stirring continually, for 1 minute.

3. Remove the pan from heat, stir in the saffron, and let the mixture cool.

4. Add the vinegar, chickpeas, and blanched cauliflower and stir to combine. Season the dish with salt and pepper, garnish with parsley, and serve with lemon wedges.

Onion Mahshi

YIELD: 4 SERVINGS / **ACTIVE TIME:** 30 MINUTES / **TOTAL TIME:** 1 HOUR AND 30 MINUTES

4 LARGE YELLOW ONIONS

1 LB. GROUND BEEF

1 TABLESPOON ALLSPICE

¾ CUP ARBORIO RICE

1½ TABLESPOONS PLUS 1 TEASPOON KOSHER SALT

½ CUP POMEGRANATE MOLASSES

½ CUP WATER

1 TEASPOON SUGAR

1. Fill a large saucepan halfway with water and bring it to a boil. Peel the onions and trim away the root ends. Make a lengthwise slit to reach the center of the onions, cutting only halfway through them.

2. Place the onions in the boiling water and cook until the onions start to soften and their layers start to separate, 10 to 15 minutes. Drain the onions and let them cool.

3. Place the beef, allspice, rice, and 1½ tablespoons of the salt in a mixing bowl and work the mixture until it is well combined.

4. Gently separate the onions into individual layers, making sure each layer stays intact and does not tear.

5. Spoon 1 to 2 tablespoons of the meat mixture into one end of a piece of onion and roll it up to seal. Repeat until all of the onions have been filled with the meat mixture. Pack the stuffed onions tightly into a baking dish, stacking them in two layers if necessary.

6. Preheat the oven to 350°F. Place the pomegranate molasses, water, remaining salt, and the sugar in a bowl and whisk until combined. Pour the sauce over the onions and then add water until the liquid reaches three-quarters of the way up the onions.

7. Cover the dish with aluminum foil and bake until the rice is tender and the meat is cooked through, about 30 minutes. Remove the foil and cook until the sauce thickens, 15 to 20 minutes. Transfer to a serving dish and enjoy.

THE ENCYCLOPEDIA OF MEDITERRANEAN

Warm Couscous Salad

YIELD: 4 SERVINGS / **ACTIVE TIME:** 15 MINUTES / **TOTAL TIME:** 15 MINUTES

1¾ CUPS WATER

7 TABLESPOONS EXTRA-VIRGIN OLIVE OIL

SALT AND PEPPER, TO TASTE

1½ CUPS ISRAELI COUSCOUS

1½ TABLESPOONS FRESH LEMON JUICE

1 GARLIC CLOVE, MINCED

2 TEASPOONS MUSTARD

1 TEASPOON HONEY

FRESH MINT, CHOPPED, FOR GARNISH

FRESH PARSLEY, CHOPPED, FOR GARNISH

1. Place the water and 1 tablespoon of the olive oil in a saucepan, season the mixture with salt, and bring it to a boil. Add the couscous and cook for 8 minutes.

2. Place the lemon juice, garlic, mustard, and honey in a mixing bowl and whisk until combined. While whisking continually, slowly drizzle in the remaining olive oil until it has emulsified.

3. Drain the couscous and place it in a serving bowl. Add dressing to taste, season the salad with salt and pepper, and toss to combine. Garnish with mint and parsley and enjoy.

Roasted Plums with Tahini Dressing

YIELD: 4 SERVINGS / **ACTIVE TIME:** 20 MINUTES / **TOTAL TIME:** 2 HOURS AND 30 MINUTES

2 LBS. PLUMS, HALVED AND PITS REMOVED

2 TABLESPOONS AVOCADO OIL

1½ TEASPOONS FINE SEA SALT, PLUS MORE TO TASTE

¼ TEASPOON BLACK PEPPER

1 TABLESPOON FRESH THYME OR OREGANO

3 TABLESPOONS FRESH LEMON JUICE, PLUS MORE TO TASTE

1 CUP TAHINI PASTE

1 ICE CUBE

MALDON SEA SALT, TO TASTE

1. Preheat the oven to 400°F and line a baking sheet with parchment paper. Arrange the plums, cut side up, on the baking sheet, drizzle the avocado oil over them, and sprinkle the fine sea salt, pepper, and herbs over them. Toss to coat.

2. Place the baking sheet in the oven and reduce the heat to 250°F. Roast until the plums are very soft and starting to caramelize, about 2 hours. Remove the plums from the oven and let them cool slightly.

3. Place the lemon juice, tahini, ¾ cup water, a few pinches of fine sea salt, and the ice cube in a mixing bowl and whisk vigorously until the dressing comes together. It should lighten in color and thicken enough that it holds an edge when the whisk is dragged through it. Remove the ice cube, if any of it remains, taste, and adjust the seasoning as necessary.

4. Arrange the plums on a plate, drizzle the dressing over the top, and sprinkle Maldon sea salt over the top.

Braised Cauliflower

YIELD: 4 SERVINGS / **ACTIVE TIME:** 20 MINUTES / **TOTAL TIME:** 40 MINUTES

¼ CUP EXTRA-VIRGIN OLIVE OIL

1 HEAD OF CAULIFLOWER, TRIMMED AND HALVED THROUGH THE STEM

SALT AND PEPPER, TO TASTE

2 GARLIC CLOVES, MINCED

⅛ TEASPOON RED PEPPER FLAKES

1 TEASPOON SUMAC

½ CUP WHITE WINE

1 BAY LEAF

6 TO 8 CUPS VEGETABLE STOCK (SEE PAGE 484)

2 SCALLIONS, TRIMMED AND SLICED ON A BIAS, FOR GARNISH

1. Place the olive oil in a Dutch oven and warm it over medium heat. Season the cauliflower with salt and pepper, place it in the Dutch oven, and cook until golden brown all over, about 6 minutes, turning it as necessary. Remove the cauliflower from the pot and set it aside.

2. Add the garlic, red pepper flakes, and sumac and cook, stirring continually, for 1 minute. Add the wine and cook until the alcohol has been cooked off, about 2 minutes. Add the bay leaf, return the cauliflower to the pot, and add stock until the cauliflower is covered. Bring the mixture to a simmer and cook until the stem of the cauliflower is tender, about 10 minutes.

3. Transfer the cauliflower to a serving dish, garnish with the scallions, and enjoy.

Crunchy Celery Slaw with Dates

YIELD: 8 SERVINGS / **ACTIVE TIME:** 1 HOUR / **TOTAL TIME:** 3 HOURS

¼ CUP BROWN MUSTARD SEEDS

⅓ CUP PLUS ¼ CUP RICE VINEGAR

2 TABLESPOONS PLUS 1 TEASPOON SUGAR

½ TEASPOON KOSHER SALT, PLUS MORE TO TASTE

⅓ CUP EXTRA-VIRGIN OLIVE OIL

1 SMALL SHALLOT, SLICED THIN

2 TABLESPOONS SOY SAUCE

2 PERSIAN CUCUMBERS

5 OZ. ARUGULA, STEMS REMOVED

4 CELERY STALKS, SLICED THIN ON A BIAS

10 MEDJOOL DATES, PITS REMOVED, SLICED

SESAME SEEDS, TOASTED, FOR GARNISH

1. Place the mustard seeds in a mason jar. Place ¼ cup of the vinegar, 2 tablespoons of the sugar, and the salt in a small saucepan and bring the mixture to a simmer, stirring to dissolve the sugar and salt. Pour the brine over the mustard seeds and let the mixture sit until cool, about 2 hours. Drain the mustard seeds and set them aside.

2. Place the olive oil and shallot in a small saucepan and cook over medium heat for 1 minute, making sure that the shallot doesn't take on any color. Remove the pan from heat and let the oil cool.

3. Strain the oil into a small bowl through a fine-mesh sieve. Discard the shallot or save it for another preparation.

4. Add the soy sauce and remaining vinegar and sugar to the shallot oil and whisk to combine. Season the vinaigrette with salt and set it aside.

5. Trim the cucumbers and use a mandoline to slice them into long, thin ribbons. Place the cucumbers, arugula, celery, and dates in a salad bowl and toss to combine.

6. Drizzle half of the vinaigrette over the slaw and add 2 tablespoons of the mustard seeds. Toss to coat, taste, and adjust the seasoning as necessary.

7. Garnish with the sesame seeds and serve with the remaining vinaigrette.

Charred Sweet Potatoes with Toum

YIELD: 4 SERVINGS / **ACTIVE TIME:** 1 HOUR AND 30 MINUTES / **TOTAL TIME:** 3 HOURS

1½ LBS. SMALL SWEET POTATOES, SCRUBBED

4 TABLESPOONS UNSALTED BUTTER

TOUM (SEE PAGE 509)

2 TABLESPOONS HONEY

2 TEASPOONS NIGELLA SEEDS

SALT, TO TASTE

1. Preheat the oven to 400°F and position a rack in the bottom third of the oven. Place the sweet potatoes in a large cast-iron skillet and poke them all over with a fork. Add just enough water to cover the bottom of the pan. Cover the pan tightly with aluminum foil, place it in the oven, and bake the sweet potatoes until fork-tender, 30 to 35 minutes.

2. Remove the sweet potatoes from the oven, place them on a cutting board, and let them cool.

3. Slice the sweet potatoes in half lengthwise. Return the skillet to the oven and heat it for 20 minutes.

4. Remove the skillet from the oven, add 2 tablespoons of the butter, and swirl to coat. Place the sweet potatoes in the pan, cut side down, place them in the oven, and roast until the edges are browned and crispy, 18 to 25 minutes.

5. Remove the sweet potatoes from the oven. Spoon some of the Toum into a shallow bowl and arrange the sweet potatoes on top. Place the remaining butter and the honey in the skillet and warm over medium heat. Drizzle the honey butter over the sweet potatoes, sprinkle the nigella seeds over the top, season with salt, and enjoy.

Braised Green Beans

YIELD: 2 TO 4 SERVINGS / **ACTIVE TIME:** 20 MINUTES / **TOTAL TIME:** 45 MINUTES

2 TABLESPOONS EXTRA-VIRGIN OLIVE OIL

1 ONION, CHOPPED

1 TEASPOON DRIED OREGANO

2 GARLIC CLOVES, MINCED

½ LB. GREEN BEANS, TRIMMED AND CUT INTO 2-INCH-LONG PIECES

½ LB. BABY POTATOES

1 (14 OZ.) CAN OF DICED TOMATOES, DRAINED

1 TABLESPOON TOMATO PASTE

SALT AND PEPPER, TO TASTE

1 TEASPOON FRESH LEMON JUICE

¼ CUP FRESH BASIL LEAVES, TORN, FOR GARNISH

1. Preheat the oven to 450°F. Place 1 tablespoon of the olive oil in a Dutch oven and warm it over medium-high heat. Add the onion and cook, stirring occasionally, until it has softened, about 5 minutes.

2. Add the oregano and garlic and cook, stirring continually, for 1 minute. Add the green beans, potatoes, and 1 cup water and bring to a boil. Reduce the heat and simmer for 10 minutes.

3. Stir in the tomatoes and tomato paste, cover the pot, and place it in the oven. Braise until the potatoes are tender and the sauce has thickened, 15 to 20 minutes.

4. Remove the pot from the oven, season the dish with salt and pepper, and stir in the lemon juice. Drizzle the remaining olive oil over the dish, garnish with the basil, and enjoy.

Lavash

YIELD: 10 SERVINGS / **ACTIVE TIME:** 30 MINUTES / **TOTAL TIME:** 2 HOURS

FOR THE LAVASH

7 TABLESPOONS WARM WATER (105°F)

7 TABLESPOONS MILK, WARMED

2 TEASPOONS EXTRA-VIRGIN OLIVE OIL, PLUS MORE AS NEEDED

¼ TEASPOON SUGAR

½ TEASPOON FINE SEA SALT

1½ TEASPOONS ACTIVE DRY YEAST

1¾ CUPS ALL-PURPOSE FLOUR, PLUS MORE AS NEEDED

FOR THE TOPPING

1 TABLESPOON EXTRA-VIRGIN OLIVE OIL

2 CUPS CHOPPED EGGPLANT

½ RED BELL PEPPER, SLICED THIN

2 GARLIC CLOVES, MINCED

1 TABLESPOON TOMATO PASTE

½ TEASPOON RED PEPPER FLAKES

2 CUPS ARUGULA

½ CUP PITTED GREEN OLIVES, SLICED THIN

SALT AND PEPPER, TO TASTE

½ CUP GRATED PARMESAN CHEESE

1. To begin preparations for the lavash, place all of the ingredients in the work bowl of a stand mixer fitted with the dough hook and mix on low speed until the mixture comes together as a dough. Raise the speed to medium and work the dough for about 10 minutes, until it no longer sticks to the side of the work bowl.

2. Remove the dough from the work bowl and place it on a flour-dusted work surface. Knead the dough by hand for 2 minutes. Coat a bowl with olive oil and place the dough in it, seam side down. Cover the dough with plastic wrap and let it sit in a naturally warm spot until it has doubled in size, about 1 hour.

3. Line a baking sheet with parchment paper. Divide the dough into 10 pieces, shape each one into a ball, and place the balls on the baking sheet. Cover the dough with a linen towel and let it rest for 10 minutes.

4. Warm a cast-iron skillet over medium-high heat. Working with one ball of dough at a time, place the dough on a flour-dusted work surface and roll it out into a 6-inch circle. Place the dough in the dry skillet, reduce the heat to medium, and cook until it starts to bubble and brown around the edge, about 2 minutes. Turn the lavash over and cook for another minute. Remove each cooked lavash from the pan, place on a wire rack, and let cool.

5. To begin preparations for the topping, warm a large cast-iron skillet over medium heat. Add the olive oil and eggplant and cook, stirring occasionally, until the eggplant starts to soften, about 5 minutes. Add the bell pepper and cook, stirring occasionally, for another 5 minutes.

6. Add the garlic, tomato paste, and red pepper flakes and cook, stirring continually, for 1 minute. Add the arugula and cook, stirring frequently, until it has wilted, about 2 minutes. Remove the pan from heat and fold in the olives. Season the mixture with salt and pepper and spread it over the lavash, leaving a ½-inch border around the edge. Sprinkle the Parmesan cheese over the lavash and enjoy.

THE ENCYCLOPEDIA OF MEDITERRANEAN

Koshari

YIELD: 8 SERVINGS / **ACTIVE TIME:** 1 HOUR / **TOTAL TIME:** 2 HOURS

SALT, TO TASTE

6 OZ. FARFALLE OR ELBOW PASTA

½ CUP LENTILS, PICKED OVER AND RINSED

½ CUP WHITE RICE

3½ TABLESPOONS AVOCADO OIL

2 LARGE ONIONS, SLICED

1 CUP CANNED CHICKPEAS, DRAINED AND RINSED

TOMATO SAUCE (SEE PAGE 504), FOR SERVING

1. Preheat the oven to 225°F. Bring salted water to a boil in a large saucepan. Add the pasta and cook until al dente, 6 to 8 minutes. Drain the pasta and set it aside.

2. Bring salted water to a boil in another saucepan and add the lentils. Cook until they are tender, about 20 minutes. Drain the lentils and set them aside.

3. Place the rice and 1 cup water in a small saucepan and bring it to a boil. Cover the pan, reduce the heat to low, cover, and cook until the rice is tender, 18 to 20 minutes. Remove the pan from heat but keep it covered to keep the rice warm.

4. Place 2 tablespoons of the avocado oil in a large skillet and warm it over medium-low heat. Add the onions and cook, stirring occasionally, until they are golden brown, about 30 minutes. Transfer the onions to a bowl and place it in the oven to keep warm.

5. Add ½ tablespoon of the avocado oil and the cooked pasta to the skillet and cook over medium heat, without stirring, until the bottom of the pasta is crispy, about 2 minutes. Stir and cook for another 2 minutes. Transfer the pasta to a serving dish.

6. Add ½ tablespoon of the avocado oil to the skillet. Add the lentils and cook until they are slightly crispy, 1 to 2 minutes. Spoon the lentils over the pasta. Add the rice to the serving dish.

7. Add the remaining avocado oil to the skillet. Add the chickpeas and cook until they are warmed through, about 2 minutes. Spoon the chickpeas into the serving dish.

8. Spoon the caramelized onions into the serving dish. Drizzle the sauce over the top or serve it alongside the koshari.

Honey-Glazed Carrots

YIELD: 8 SERVINGS / **ACTIVE TIME:** 15 MINUTES / **TOTAL TIME:** 30 MINUTES

5 LBS. CARROTS, PEELED

4 TABLESPOONS UNSALTED BUTTER

⅓ CUP ORANGE JUICE

1 TABLESPOON BUCKWHEAT HONEY

1½ TEASPOONS KOSHER SALT

2 TABLESPOONS FRESH LEMON JUICE

⅛ TEASPOON CAYENNE PEPPER

1. Place the carrots, butter, orange juice, honey, and salt in a saucepan, cover the pan, and cook over medium heat until the carrots are tender, about 10 minutes.

2. Uncover the pan and continue to cook the carrots, stirring occasionally, until the sauce reduces slightly, about 10 minutes.

3. Remove the pan from heat, stir in the lemon juice and cayenne, and transfer the carrots and sauce to a serving dish. Enjoy immediately.

Couscous & Shrimp Salad

YIELD: 6 SERVINGS / **ACTIVE TIME:** 40 MINUTES / **TOTAL TIME:** 50 MINUTES

¾ LB. SHRIMP, SHELLED AND DEVEINED

6 BUNCHES OF FRESH MINT

10 GARLIC CLOVES, PEELED

3½ CUPS CHICKEN STOCK (SEE PAGE 482)

3 CUPS ISRAELI COUSCOUS

1 BUNCH OF ASPARAGUS, TRIMMED

3 PLUM TOMATOES, DICED

1 TABLESPOON FINELY CHOPPED FRESH OREGANO

½ PERSIAN CUCUMBER, DICED

ZEST AND JUICE OF 1 LEMON

½ CUP DICED RED ONION

½ CUP SUN-DRIED TOMATOES IN OLIVE OIL, DRAINED AND SLICED THIN

¼ CUP PITTED AND CHOPPED KALAMATA OLIVES

⅓ CUP EXTRA-VIRGIN OLIVE OIL

SALT AND PEPPER, TO TASTE

½ CUP CRUMBLED FETA CHEESE

1. Place the shrimp, mint, and garlic in a Dutch oven and cover with water. Bring to a simmer over medium heat and cook until the shrimp are pink and cooked through, about 5 minutes after the water comes to a simmer.

2. Drain, cut the shrimp in half lengthwise, and them set aside. Discard the mint and garlic cloves.

3. Place the stock in the Dutch oven and bring to a boil. Add the couscous, reduce the heat so that the stock simmers, cover, and cook until the couscous is tender and has absorbed the stock, 7 to 10 minutes. Transfer the couscous to a salad bowl.

4. Fill the pot with water and bring it to a boil. Add the asparagus and cook until it has softened, 1 to 1½ minutes. Drain, rinse the asparagus under cold water, and chop into bite-size pieces. Pat the asparagus dry.

5. Add all of the remaining ingredients, except for the feta, to the salad bowl containing the couscous. Add the asparagus and stir to incorporate. Top with the shrimp, sprinkle the feta over the salad, and serve.

Grapefruit & Fennel Salad

YIELD: 4 SERVINGS / **ACTIVE TIME:** 20 MINUTES / **TOTAL TIME:** 20 MINUTES

½ WHITE ONION

2 FENNEL STALKS, FRONDS REMOVED AND RESERVED

1 APPLE

1 TEASPOON CHOPPED FRESH DILL

1 TEASPOON CHOPPED FRESH MINT

1 TABLESPOON CHOPPED FRESH PARSLEY

1 TABLESPOON HONEY

3 TABLESPOONS WHITE VINEGAR

1 GRAPEFRUIT

1 JALAPEÑO CHILE PEPPER, STEM AND SEEDS REMOVED, SLICED THIN

1. Using a mandoline or a sharp knife, cut the white onion, fennel stalks, and apple into very thin slices. Chop the fennel fronds. Place these items in a bowl.

2. Add the fresh herbs, honey, and white vinegar and toss to combine.

3. Trim the top and bottom from the grapefruit and then cut along the contour of the fruit to remove the pith and peel. Cut one segment, lengthwise, between the pulp and the membrane. Make a similar slice on the other side of the segment and then remove the pulp. Set aside and repeat with the remaining segments. This technique is known as "supreming," and can be used for all citrus fruits.

4. Add the segments to the salad bowl along with the jalapeño, toss to combine, and enjoy.

Turkish Eggplant Salad

YIELD: 4 SERVINGS / **ACTIVE TIME:** 30 MINUTES / **TOTAL TIME:** 1 HOUR AND 30 MINUTES

2 LARGE EGGPLANTS

2 TABLESPOONS EXTRA-VIRGIN OLIVE OIL

3 TOMATOES, DICED

1 WHITE ONION, JULIENNED

4 GARLIC CLOVES, MINCED

1 TABLESPOON PAPRIKA

1 TEASPOON KOSHER SALT

1 TEASPOON CUMIN

1 TEASPOON CAYENNE PEPPER

½ CUP CHOPPED FRESH PARSLEY

1. Preheat the oven to 450°F. Poke a few holes in the eggplants, place them on a baking sheet, and place them in the oven. Roast until completely tender and starting to collapse, 40 minutes to 1 hour. Remove the eggplants from the oven and let them cool completely.

2. Place the olive oil in a large skillet and warm it over high heat. Add the tomatoes and onion and cook until the onion is translucent, about 4 minutes. Add the remaining ingredients, except for the parsley, and cook for approximately 20 minutes, stirring occasionally. Transfer the mixture to a mixing bowl.

3. Halve the eggplants and scoop the flesh into the tomato mixture. Stir to combine, adding the parsley as you go. Let the mixture cool to room temperature before serving.

Grilled Romaine & Sweet Potato

YIELD: 2 SERVINGS / **ACTIVE TIME:** 30 MINUTES / **TOTAL TIME:** 30 MINUTES

CANOLA OIL, AS NEEDED

1 CUP SHREDDED BAKED SWEET POTATO SKINS

1 TABLESPOON KOSHER SALT

2 TEASPOONS BLACK PEPPER

½ GREEN APPLE

½ CUP WHITE VINEGAR

1 HEART OF ROMAINE LETTUCE

2 TEASPOONS EXTRA-VIRGIN OLIVE OIL

1 TABLESPOON BALSAMIC VINEGAR

2 TABLESPOONS CRUMBLED FETA CHEESE

1. Prepare a gas or charcoal grill for high heat (about 500°F). Add canola oil to a small saucepan until it is about 2 inches deep and warm it to 350°F. Add the sweet potato skins and fry until golden brown and crispy, about 1 minute. Remove the fried sweet potato skins from the oil and place them on a paper towel–lined plate. Season the potato skins with 1 teaspoon of the salt and 1 teaspoon of the pepper.

2. Cut the apple into ½-inch slices, leaving the skin on. Place the apple in a small bowl, add the white vinegar and 1 teaspoon of the salt, and toss to coat. Set the mixture aside.

3. Cut off the bottom from the heart of romaine, separate the leaves, and place them in a bowl. Add the olive oil, the remaining salt, and remaining pepper and toss to coat.

4. Place the lettuce on the grill and cook until slightly charred on both sides, but take it off before it starts to wilt, about 1 minute.

5. Arrange the lettuce on a plate, crumble the fried sweet potato skins over them, and distribute the apple on top. Drizzle the balsamic over the dish, sprinkle the feta on top, and enjoy.

Fried Brussels Sprouts with Tahini & Feta

YIELD: 4 SERVINGS / **ACTIVE TIME:** 15 MINUTES / **TOTAL TIME:** 15 MINUTES

CANOLA OIL, AS NEEDED

3 CUPS SMALL BRUSSELS SPROUTS, TRIMMED

2 TABLESPOONS TAHINI SAUCE (SEE PAGE 500)

½ CUP CRUMBLED FETA CHEESE

PINCH OF KOSHER SALT

1. Add canola oil to a Dutch oven until it is about 2 inches deep and warm it to 350°F.

2. Gently slip the Brussels sprouts into the oil, working in batches to avoid crowding the pot. Fry the Brussels sprouts until golden brown, about 4 minutes, turning them as necessary. Remove one Brussels sprout to test that it is done—let it cool briefly and see if the inside is tender enough. Transfer the fried Brussels sprouts to a paper towel–lined plate.

3. Place the sprouts, tahini, and feta in a mixing bowl and stir until combined. Sprinkle the salt over the dish and enjoy.

Mujadara

YIELD: 4 SERVINGS / **ACTIVE TIME:** 20 MINUTES / **TOTAL TIME:** 1 HOUR

4 GARLIC CLOVES, MINCED

2 BAY LEAVES

1 TABLESPOON CUMIN

SALT AND PEPPER, TO TASTE

1 CUP BASMATI RICE

1 CUP BROWN OR GREEN LENTILS

⅓ CUP EXTRA-VIRGIN OLIVE OIL

2 ONIONS, HALVED AND SLICED THIN

½ CUP SLICED SCALLIONS

½ CUP CHOPPED FRESH CILANTRO

TAHINI & YOGURT SAUCE (SEE PAGE 495), FOR SERVING

1. Place the garlic, bay leaves, cumin, and a few generous pinches of salt in a Dutch oven. Season with pepper, add 5 cups water, and bring to a boil over high heat.

2. Stir in the rice and reduce the heat to medium. Cover the pot and cook, stirring occasionally, for 10 minutes.

3. Add the lentils, return the mixture to a simmer, and cover the pot. Cook until the lentils are tender and the rice has absorbed all of the liquid, about 20 minutes.

4. Place the olive oil in a large skillet and warm it over medium-high heat. Add the onions and cook, stirring frequently, until they are deeply caramelized, about 20 minutes. Remove the onions from the pan with a slotted spoon and transfer them to a paper towel–lined plate. Season with salt and pepper and set the onions aside.

5. Uncover the Dutch oven, remove the bay leaves, and discard them. Stir half of the scallions and the cilantro into the rice mixture. Season with salt and pepper, transfer to a serving dish, and top with the caramelized onions and the remaining scallions. Serve with the Tahini & Yogurt Sauce and enjoy.

Fried Brussels Sprouts with Tahini & Feta
SEE PAGE 390

Glazed Okra

YIELD: 2 SERVINGS / ACTIVE TIME: 15 MINUTES / TOTAL TIME: 30 MINUTES

2 TABLESPOONS EXTRA-VIRGIN OLIVE OIL

24 OKRA PODS, TRIMMED

1 TEASPOON KOSHER SALT

1 TEASPOON BLACK PEPPER

1 TEASPOON BROWN SUGAR

1 TEASPOON WHITE VINEGAR

SMOKED POTATO PUREE (SEE PAGE 411)

1. Place the olive oil in a large cast-iron pan and warm it over high heat. Add the okra, season it with the salt and pepper, and cook until the okra is browned all over, turning it as necessary.

2. Remove the okra from the pan and set it aside. Turn off the heat but leave the pan on the stove.

3. Place the brown sugar and vinegar in the pan and stir until the mixture is syrupy. Remove the pan from heat and let the glaze cool slightly.

4. Spread the Smoked Potato Puree on a serving plate, arrange the okra in a line on top of it, drizzle the glaze over the top, and enjoy.

Horiatiki Salad

YIELD: 4 SERVINGS / ACTIVE TIME: 10 MINUTES / TOTAL TIME: 10 MINUTES

1 CUCUMBER, SLICED

1 CUP CHERRY TOMATOES, HALVED

1 CUP CRUMBLED FETA CHEESE

1 RED ONION, SLICED

½ CUP PITTED KALAMATA OLIVES

1 TEASPOON DRIED OREGANO

½ CUP EXTRA-VIRGIN OLIVE OIL

SALT AND PEPPER, TO TASTE

1. Place the cucumber, cherry tomatoes, feta, onion, olives, and dried oregano in a mixing bowl and stir gently until combined.

2. Drizzle the olive oil over the salad, season with salt and pepper, gently toss to combine, and enjoy.

Tabbouleh

YIELD: 4 CUPS / **ACTIVE TIME:** 15 MINUTES / **TOTAL TIME:** 30 MINUTES

½ CUP BULGUR

1½ CUPS BOILING WATER

½ TEASPOON KOSHER SALT, PLUS MORE TO TASTE

½ CUP FRESH LEMON JUICE

2 CUPS FRESH PARSLEY, CHOPPED

1 CUP PEELED, SEEDED, AND DICED CUCUMBER

2 TOMATOES, DICED

6 SCALLIONS, TRIMMED

1 CUP FRESH MINT LEAVES, CHOPPED

2 TABLESPOONS EXTRA-VIRGIN OLIVE OIL

BLACK PEPPER, TO TASTE

½ CUP CRUMBLED FETA CHEESE

1. Place the bulgur in a bowl and add the boiling water, salt, and half of the lemon juice. Cover and let sit for about 20 minutes, until the bulgur has absorbed all of the liquid and is tender. Drain any excess liquid if necessary. Let the bulgur cool completely.

2. When the bulgur has cooled, add the parsley, cucumber, tomatoes, scallions, mint, olive oil, pepper, and remaining lemon juice and stir until well combined.

3. Top with the feta and enjoy.

Marinated Eggplant Salad

YIELD: 4 SERVINGS / **ACTIVE TIME:** 30 MINUTES / **TOTAL TIME:** 2 HOURS AND 30 MINUTES

1 EGGPLANT, SLICED INTO ½-INCH-THICK ROUNDS

½ CUP EXTRA-VIRGIN OLIVE OIL

4 GARLIC CLOVES, MINCED

1 TABLESPOON CHOPPED FRESH DILL

1 TABLESPOON CHOPPED FRESH BASIL

1 TABLESPOON KOSHER SALT

½ CUP WHITE VINEGAR

1 CUP CHERRY TOMATOES, HALVED

2 SHALLOTS, JULIENNED

1. Warm a cast-iron skillet over high heat. Brush the eggplant with the olive oil, place it in the pan, and cook until lightly charred on each side, about 6 minutes.

2. Transfer the eggplant to a salad bowl, add the garlic, fresh herbs, salt, vinegar, and any remaining olive oil, and stir to combine.

3. Add the tomatoes and shallots, toss to combine, and refrigerate for at least 2 hours before serving.

Glazed Okra
SEE PAGE 394

Fava Beans with Pomegranates

YIELD: 4 SERVINGS / **ACTIVE TIME:** 20 MINUTES / **TOTAL TIME:** 30 MINUTES

½ RED ONION, SLICED THIN

1 TEASPOON SUMAC

1 TEASPOON RED WINE VINEGAR

½ TEASPOON KOSHER SALT, PLUS MORE TO TASTE

2 TABLESPOONS AVOCADO OIL

2 GARLIC CLOVES, CHOPPED

1½ LBS. FRESH YOUNG FAVA BEANS, PODS AND INNER SHELLS REMOVED

¼ TEASPOON BLACK PEPPER

1 TEASPOON ZA'ATAR (SEE PAGE 501)

JUICE OF ½ LEMON

½ CUP CHOPPED FRESH PARSLEY

¼ CUP CHOPPED FRESH DILL

¼ CUP FRESH MINT LEAVES

¼ CUP POMEGRANATE ARILS

1 TEASPOON POMEGRANATE MOLASSES, FOR GARNISH

2 TABLESPOONS EXTRA-VIRGIN OLIVE OIL, FOR GARNISH

2 TABLESPOONS LABNEH (SEE PAGE 67), FOR GARNISH

1. Place the onion, sumac, and red wine vinegar in a bowl, season with salt, and let the mixture sit until the onion turns bright red and becomes slightly pickled.

2. Place the avocado oil in a large saucepan and warm it over medium-low heat. Add the garlic and fava beans and cook, stirring occasionally, until the fava beans are bright green in color. Season with the salt, pepper, Za'atar, and lemon juice and stir to combine.

3. Remove the pan from heat and stir in the fresh herbs and pomegranate arils.

4. Transfer to a serving bowl, garnish with the onion, pomegranate molasses, olive oil, and Labneh, and enjoy.

Braised Leeks

YIELD: 12 SERVINGS / **ACTIVE TIME:** 20 MINUTES / **TOTAL TIME:** 1 HOUR

½ CUP EXTRA-VIRGIN OLIVE OIL

6 LARGE LEEKS, TRIMMED, RINSED WELL, AND HALVED LENGTHWISE

SALT AND PEPPER, TO TASTE

2 TABLESPOONS AVOCADO OIL

4 SHALLOTS, CHOPPED

2 GARLIC CLOVES, MINCED

1 TEASPOON DRIED THYME

1 TEASPOON LEMON ZEST

½ CUP WHITE WINE

2 CUPS VEGETABLE STOCK (SEE PAGE 484)

1. Preheat the oven to 400°F. Place the olive oil in a large skillet and warm it over medium-high heat. Season the leeks with salt and pepper, place them in the pan, cut side down, and sear until golden brown, about 5 minutes.

2. Season the leeks with salt and pepper, turn them over, and cook until browned on that side, about 2 minutes. Transfer the leeks to a baking dish.

3. Place the avocado oil in the skillet and warm it over medium-high heat. Add the shallots and cook until they start to brown, about 5 minutes.

4. Add the garlic, thyme, lemon zest, salt, and pepper to the pan and cook until just fragrant, about 1 minute.

5. Add the wine and cook until it has reduced by half, about 10 minutes. Add the stock and bring the mixture to a boil. Remove the pan from heat and pour the mixture over the leeks until they are almost, but not quite, submerged.

6. Place the dish in the oven and braise the leeks until tender, about 30 minutes.

7. Remove from the oven, transfer to a serving dish, and enjoy.

Moroccan Carrots

YIELD: 2 SERVINGS / **ACTIVE TIME:** 15 MINUTES / **TOTAL TIME:** 15 MINUTES

2 LARGE CARROTS, PEELED

1 TABLESPOON AVOCADO OIL

1 TABLESPOON RAS EL HANOUT (SEE PAGE 505)

2 TEASPOONS HONEY

2 TEASPOONS TAHINI PASTE

2 PINCHES OF SESAME SEEDS, FOR GARNISH

1. Cut the carrots into matchsticks that are approximately ½ inch wide and 3 inches long.

2. Place the avocado oil in a large skillet and warm it over high heat. Add the carrots to the pan, making sure to leave as much space between them as possible. Sprinkle the Ras el Hanout over the carrots and sear them until lightly charred all over, about 6 minutes, turning them as necessary.

3. Transfer the carrots to a paper towel–lined plate to drain.

4. Divide the carrots between the serving plates and drizzle the honey and tahini over each portion. Garnish with the sesame seeds and enjoy.

Couscous with Seven Vegetables

YIELD: 6 SERVINGS / **ACTIVE TIME:** 20 MINUTES / **TOTAL TIME:** 50 MINUTES

3 TABLESPOONS AVOCADO OIL

1 LARGE YELLOW ONION, DICED

SALT AND PEPPER, TO TASTE

2 GARLIC CLOVES, MINCED

2 TOMATOES, SEEDED AND DICED

1 TABLESPOON TOMATO PASTE

2 TEASPOONS CUMIN

1 TEASPOON PAPRIKA

1 TEASPOON GROUND GINGER

1 TEASPOON CINNAMON

¼ TEASPOON CAYENNE PEPPER

2 RED BELL PEPPERS, STEMS AND SEEDS REMOVED, CHOPPED

2 ZUCCHINIS, HALVED AND CHOPPED

3 SMALL TURNIPS, PEELED AND CHOPPED

1 BUNCH OF CARROTS, PEELED AND CHOPPED

1 BUTTERNUT SQUASH, PEELED, SEEDED, AND CUBED

4 CUPS VEGETABLE STOCK (SEE PAGE 484)

1 (14 OZ.) CAN OF CHICKPEAS, DRAINED AND RINSED

1 (10 OZ.) BOX OF COUSCOUS

2 TEASPOONS RAS EL HANOUT (SEE PAGE 505)

FRESH PARSLEY, CHOPPED, FOR GARNISH

HANDFUL OF SLIVERED ALMONDS, FOR GARNISH

1. Place the avocado oil in a Dutch oven and warm it over medium heat. Add the onion and cook, stirring occasionally, until it has softened, about 5 minutes.

2. Season the onion with salt and pepper, add the garlic and tomatoes, and cook, stirring frequently, until the tomatoes start to collapse, about 5 minutes. Stir in the tomato paste, cumin, paprika, ginger, cinnamon, and cayenne and cook, stirring frequently, until the mixture is fragrant, 2 to 3 minutes.

3. Add the peppers, zucchini, turnips, carrots, squash, and stock and bring to a boil. Reduce the heat, cover the pan, and simmer until the vegetables are tender, 10 to 15 minutes.

4. Remove the cover and add the chickpeas. Simmer until the chickpeas are warmed through and the stew has thickened, 5 to 10 minutes.

5. Meanwhile, make the couscous according to the directions on the package.

6. Stir the Ras el Hanout into the stew, taste, and adjust the seasoning as necessary.

7. To serve, spread the couscous on a platter. Spoon the vegetable stew over the couscous, garnish with the parsley and slivered almonds, and enjoy.

Moroccan Carrots
SEE PAGE 400

Beets with Walnut Dukkah

YIELD: 2 SERVINGS / **ACTIVE TIME:** 30 MINUTES / **TOTAL TIME:** 1 HOUR AND 30 MINUTES

2 LARGE BEETS

PINCH OF KOSHER SALT

2 TABLESPOONS CHOPPED WALNUTS

2 TABLESPOONS CHOPPED HAZELNUTS

2 TEASPOONS BLACK PEPPER

2 TEASPOONS POPPY SEEDS

2 TEASPOONS BLACK SESAME SEEDS

1 TABLESPOON AVOCADO OIL

¼ CUP LABNEH (SEE PAGE 67)

1 CINNAMON STICK

1. Place the beets and salt in a saucepan with at least 5 cups of water and bring to a boil. Cook the beets until a knife can easily pass through them, 30 to 40 minutes.

2. Drain the beets, run them under cold water, and peel off the skins and stems; it is easiest to do this while the beets are still hot. Cut the peeled beets into ¾-inch cubes and set them aside.

3. Place the nuts in a resealable bag and use a rolling pin to crush them. Transfer to a small bowl, add the black pepper and seeds, and stir to combine. Set the mixture aside.

4. Place the avocado oil in a large skillet and warm it over high heat. Place the beets in the pan and sear until well browned all over, about 5 minutes, turning the beets as necessary. Transfer the beets to a paper towel–lined plate to drain.

5. To serve, spread the Labneh across a shallow bowl, pile the beets on top, and sprinkle the dukkah over the dish. Grate the cinnamon stick over the beets until the dish is to your taste and enjoy.

Roasted Pepper Salad

YIELD: 6 SERVINGS / **ACTIVE TIME:** 10 MINUTES / **TOTAL TIME:** 30 MINUTES

3 RED BELL PEPPERS

2 YELLOW BELL PEPPERS

1 GREEN BELL PEPPER

½ CUP PLUS 1 TABLESPOON AVOCADO OIL

½ ONION, SLICED THIN

1 TEASPOON WHITE VINEGAR

¼ TEASPOON KOSHER SALT

⅛ TEASPOON BLACK PEPPER

½ TEASPOON CUMIN

¼ BUNCH OF FRESH CILANTRO, CHOPPED

1. Roast the peppers on a grill or over the flame of a gas burner until they are charred all over and tender. Place the peppers in a baking dish, cover it with plastic wrap, and let them steam for 10 minutes.

2. Remove the charred skins and the seed pods from the peppers and discard them. Slice the roasted peppers into strips and set them aside.

3. Place 1 tablespoon of the avocado oil in a saucepan and warm it over medium heat. Add the onion and cook, stirring occasionally, until it has softened, about 5 minutes. Remove the pan from heat and let the onion cool.

4. Place the peppers, onion, remaining avocado oil, the vinegar, salt, pepper, cumin, and cilantro in a bowl, stir until combined, and enjoy.

Roasted Root Vegetables

YIELD: 4 SERVINGS / **ACTIVE TIME:** 15 MINUTES / **TOTAL TIME:** 50 MINUTES

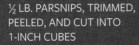

½ LB. PARSNIPS, TRIMMED, PEELED, AND CUT INTO 1-INCH CUBES

1 CELERIAC, TRIMMED, PEELED, AND CUT INTO 1-INCH CUBES

½ LB. BRUSSELS SPROUTS, TRIMMED AND HALVED

1 LB. NEW POTATOES

6 SHALLOTS, QUARTERED

4 GARLIC CLOVES, MINCED

2 TEASPOONS FRESH THYME

1 TEASPOON CHOPPED FRESH ROSEMARY

1 TABLESPOON HONEY

6 TABLESPOONS EXTRA-VIRGIN OLIVE OIL

SALT AND PEPPER, TO TASTE

2 TABLESPOONS CHOPPED FRESH PARSLEY

1 TABLESPOON CAPERS, DRAINED AND CHOPPED

ZEST AND JUICE OF 1 LEMON

1. Preheat the oven to 425°F. Place the parsnips, celeriac, Brussels sprouts, potatoes, shallots, garlic, thyme, rosemary, honey, and ¼ cup of the olive oil in a mixing bowl and toss to coat. Season the mixture with salt and pepper and spread the mixture on a baking sheet in a single layer.

2. Place the vegetables in the oven and roast until golden brown and tender, 30 to 35 minutes. Remove the vegetables from the oven and let them cool.

3. Place the parsley, capers, lemon zest, lemon juice, and remaining olive oil in a mixing bowl and whisk to combine.

4. Drizzle the sauce over the roasted vegetables, toss to coat, and enjoy.

Cucumber, Mint & Sumac Salad

YIELD: 4 SERVINGS / **ACTIVE TIME:** 15 MINUTES / **TOTAL TIME:** 15 MINUTES

12 PERSIAN CUCUMBERS, QUARTERED LENGTHWISE ON A BIAS

1½ TABLESPOONS SUMAC

¼ CUP EXTRA-VIRGIN OLIVE OIL

¼ CUP FRESH LEMON JUICE

1 TEASPOON KOSHER SALT, PLUS MORE TO TASTE

¼ CUP FRESH MINT LEAVES, FOR GARNISH

1. Place the cucumbers, 1 tablespoon of the sumac, the olive oil, lemon juice, and salt in a large bowl and toss to combine.

2. Transfer the salad to a serving bowl, taste, and adjust the seasoning as necessary. Sprinkle the remaining sumac on top, garnish with the mint, and enjoy.

Beets with Walnut Dukkah
SEE PAGE 404

Romano Beans with Mustard Vinaigrette & Walnuts

YIELD: 8 SERVINGS / **ACTIVE TIME:** 15 MINUTES / **TOTAL TIME:** 30 MINUTES

1 CUP WALNUTS

SALT AND PEPPER, TO TASTE

3 LBS. ROMANO BEANS, TRIMMED

3 TABLESPOONS RED WINE VINEGAR

2 TABLESPOONS DIJON MUSTARD

1 GARLIC CLOVE, FINELY GRATED

2 TABLESPOONS EXTRA-VIRGIN OLIVE OIL, PLUS MORE TO TASTE

ZEST OF ½ LEMON

¾ CUP CHOPPED FRESH PARSLEY

1. Preheat the oven to 350°F. Place the walnuts on a rimmed baking sheet, place them in the oven, and toast until browned and fragrant, 8 to 10 minutes, tossing halfway through.

2. Remove the walnuts from the oven and let them cool. When the walnuts have cooled slightly, chop them and set aside.

3. Bring salted water to a boil in a large saucepan and prepare an ice bath. Place the beans in the boiling water and cook until bright green and tender, 8 to 10 minutes. Using a slotted spoon, transfer them to the ice bath and let them cool. Drain, pat the beans dry, and set them aside.

4. Place the vinegar, mustard, garlic, and olive oil in a large mixing bowl and whisk until thoroughly combined. Let the dressing rest for 10 minutes.

5. Add the walnuts and beans to the dressing. Sprinkle the lemon zest and parsley over the beans, season with salt and pepper, and toss to coat. Transfer to a platter, drizzle more olive oil over the top, and enjoy.

Roasted Radicchio

YIELD: 2 SERVINGS / **ACTIVE TIME:** 10 MINUTES / **TOTAL TIME:** 30 MINUTES

1 HEAD OF RADICCHIO

¼ CUP EXTRA-VIRGIN OLIVE OIL

1 TEASPOON KOSHER SALT

¼ CUP BALSAMIC VINEGAR

1 TABLESPOON CAPERS, DRAINED AND RINSED

¼ CUP CRUMBLED FETA CHEESE

1. Preheat the oven to 450°F. Cut the head of radicchio in half and remove the stem. Separate the leaves and place them in a mixing bowl. Add the olive oil and salt and toss to coat.

2. Arrange the radicchio on a baking sheet in a single layer. Place it in the oven and roast until the radicchio is brown and slightly wilted, 10 to 15 minutes. Remove from the oven and leave the oven on.

3. Distribute the vinegar and capers over the radicchio and return it to the oven. Roast until the vinegar starts to bubble, 5 to 10 minutes.

4. Remove the radicchio from the oven and place it in a serving dish. Sprinkle the feta over the top and enjoy.

Olive Salad

YIELD: 6 SERVINGS / **ACTIVE TIME:** 15 MINUTES / **TOTAL TIME:** 15 MINUTES

2 CUPS GREEN OLIVES, PITS REMOVED

2 GARLIC CLOVES, MINCED

1 CUP POMEGRANATE ARILS

⅓ CUP POMEGRANATE JUICE

⅓ CUP CHOPPED FRESH MINT, PLUS MORE FOR GARNISH

⅓ CUP EXTRA-VIRGIN OLIVE OIL

1 TEASPOON KOSHER SALT

¼ TEASPOON BLACK PEPPER

ROASTED WALNUTS, CRUSHED, FOR GARNISH

1. Place the olives, garlic, and pomegranate arils in a bowl and stir until well combined.

2. Place the pomegranate juice, mint, and olive oil in a separate bowl and stir until combined.

3. Pour the dressing over the olive mixture and stir until evenly coated. Add the salt and pepper, garnish with the walnuts and additional mint, and enjoy.

Smoked Potato Puree

YIELD: 4 SERVINGS / **ACTIVE TIME:** 30 MINUTES / **TOTAL TIME:** 1 HOUR AND 15 MINUTES

½ CUP WOOD CHIPS

2 SWEET POTATOES, PEELED AND CHOPPED

1 YUKON GOLD POTATO, PEELED AND CHOPPED

2 TEASPOONS KOSHER SALT, PLUS MORE TO TASTE

½ CUP HEAVY CREAM

2 TABLESPOONS UNSALTED BUTTER

1. Preheat the oven to 250°F. Place the wood chips in a cast-iron skillet and place the pan over high heat. When the wood chips start to smoke, place the skillet in a deep roasting pan. Set the sweet potatoes and potato in the roasting pan (not in the skillet) and cover the roasting pan with aluminum foil. Place it in the oven and smoke for 30 minutes.

2. While the potatoes are smoking in the oven, bring water to a boil in a large saucepan.

3. Remove the potatoes from the oven, add the salt to the boiling water, and then add the potatoes. Cook until they are fork-tender, 20 to 25 minutes. Drain, place the potatoes in a mixing bowl, and add the remaining ingredients. Mash until smooth, season with salt, and serve immediately.

Taro Ulass

YIELD: 4 SERVINGS / **ACTIVE TIME:** 25 MINUTES / **TOTAL TIME:** 40 MINUTES

½ CUP VEGETABLE STOCK (SEE PAGE 484)

JUICE FROM ½ LEMON

1 LB. TARO ROOT, PEELED AND CUBED

1 LARGE BUNCH OF RED CHARD, STEMS AND LEAVES SEPARATED AND CHOPPED

½ BUNCH OF FRESH CILANTRO, CHOPPED

1 TABLESPOON EXTRA-VIRGIN OLIVE OIL

2 GARLIC CLOVES, CHOPPED

1. Place the stock, lemon juice, and taro in a saucepan, bring to a simmer over medium heat, and cook until the taro is tender, about 8 minutes. Remove the pan from heat and set it aside.

2. Place the chard leaves and cilantro in a pan containing approximately ¼ cup water. Cook over medium heat until the chard is wilted and most of the liquid has evaporated. Transfer the mixture to a food processor and blitz until pureed.

3. Place the olive oil in a large skillet and warm it over medium heat. Add the garlic and the chard stems and cook, stirring frequently, until the garlic starts to brown slightly, about 1½ minutes.

4. Stir in the taro mixture and the chard puree, cook until heated through, and enjoy.

Sumac & Apple Cauliflower

YIELD: 4 SERVINGS / **ACTIVE TIME:** 15 MINUTES / **TOTAL TIME:** 1 HOUR AND 15 MINUTES

1 APPLE, PEELED AND QUARTERED

1 ONION, QUARTERED

1 TABLESPOON SUMAC

1 TABLESPOON KOSHER SALT

1 TABLESPOON SUGAR

½ CUP WATER

1 HEAD OF CAULIFLOWER, TRIMMED

2 TABLESPOONS HONEY

2 TABLESPOONS TAHINI PASTE

1. Preheat the oven to 400°F. Place the apple, onion, sumac, salt, sugar, and water in a food processor and pulse until combined.

2. Place the cauliflower in a roasting pan and pour the apple-and-sumac mixture over it. Cover the pan with aluminum foil, place it in the oven, and roast until the cauliflower is fork-tender, about 45 minutes.

3. Raise the oven's temperature to 450°F and remove the aluminum foil. Roast the cauliflower until crispy, about 10 minutes.

4. Remove the cauliflower from the oven, drizzle the honey and tahini over the top, and serve.

Pickled Green Beans

YIELD: 4 SERVINGS / **ACTIVE TIME:** 15 MINUTES / **TOTAL TIME:** 2 DAYS

1 LB. GREEN BEANS, TRIMMED

2 TABLESPOONS CHOPPED FRESH DILL

2 GARLIC CLOVES, MINCED

1 TABLESPOON KOSHER SALT

1 TABLESPOON SUGAR

2 CUPS WHITE VINEGAR

1 TABLESPOON EXTRA-VIRGIN OLIVE OIL

1 TABLESPOON HONEY

1. Place the green beans, dill, garlic, salt, and sugar in a large mason jar. Pour the vinegar over the mixture, cover the jar, and shake to combine. Chill the green beans in the refrigerator for 48 hours.

2. Preheat the oven to 450°F. Remove the green beans from the liquid and place them on a baking sheet. Drizzle the olive oil over them and toss to coat.

3. Place the green beans in the oven and roast until browned, about 20 minutes.

4. Remove the green beans from the oven, drizzle the honey over them, and enjoy.

Roasted Brussels Sprouts with Warm Honey Glaze

YIELD: 4 SERVINGS / **ACTIVE TIME:** 30 MINUTES / **TOTAL TIME:** 1 HOUR

1½ LBS. BRUSSELS SPROUTS, TRIMMED AND HALVED

¼ CUP AVOCADO OIL

½ TEASPOON SEA SALT, PLUS MORE TO TASTE

BLACK PEPPER, TO TASTE

¼ CUP HONEY

¼ CUP SHERRY VINEGAR OR RED WINE VINEGAR

¾ TEASPOON CRUSHED RED PEPPER FLAKES

3 TABLESPOONS UNSALTED BUTTER

3 SCALLIONS, TRIMMED AND SLICED THIN ON A BIAS

1 TEASPOON LEMON ZEST

1. Position a rack in the bottom third of the oven and set a rimmed baking sheet on it. Preheat the oven to 450°F.

2. In a large bowl, combine the Brussels sprouts and oil, toss to coat, and season with salt and pepper.

3. Carefully remove the baking sheet from the oven. Using tongs, arrange the Brussels sprouts, cut side down, on the hot baking sheet. Place it back on the low rack and roast the Brussels sprouts until they are tender and deeply browned, 20 to 25 minutes.

4. While the Brussels sprouts are roasting, place the honey in a small saucepan and bring to a simmer over medium-high heat. Reduce the heat to medium-low and cook, stirring frequently, until the honey is a deep amber color but not burnt (it will be foamy), about 3 minutes. Remove from heat, carefully add the vinegar and red pepper flakes, and stir until incorporated.

5. Place the saucepan back over medium heat, stir in the butter and ½ teaspoon salt, and cook, whisking constantly, until the glaze is glossy, bubbling, and has thickened, about 4 minutes.

6. Remove the Brussels sprouts from the oven, transfer them to a large bowl, and add the glaze. Toss to coat, top with the scallions and lemon zest, and enjoy.

Sumac & Apple Cauliflower
SEE PAGE 412

Farro Salad with Olive & Whole Lemon Vinaigrette

YIELD: 8 SERVINGS / **ACTIVE TIME:** 15 MINUTES / **TOTAL TIME:** 1 HOUR

2 CUPS FARRO

SALT AND PEPPER, TO TASTE

2 CUPS GREEN OLIVES

1 LEMON

2 SHALLOTS, MINCED

½ CUP EXTRA-VIRGIN OLIVE OIL

FRESH LEMON JUICE, TO TASTE

2 CUPS CHOPPED FRESH MINT OR CILANTRO

2 CUPS CHOPPED FRESH PARSLEY

1. Place the farro in a large, wide saucepan and toast it over medium heat, stirring frequently, until it is golden brown and fragrant, about 4 minutes. Remove the pan from heat, cover the farro by 1 inch with cold water, and add a generous handful of salt.

2. Place the pan over medium-high heat and bring to a boil. Reduce the heat and simmer the farro, skimming any foam from the surface, until it is tender but still has some bite, 25 to 35 minutes. Drain and transfer the farro to a large bowl.

3. Crush the olives to break them up into large, craggy pieces. Discard the pits and place the olives in a large bowl.

4. Halve the lemon, remove the seeds, and finely dice the entire lemon, peel and all. Add the lemon and shallots to the olives, toss to combine, and season with salt and pepper. Let the dressing stand for 5 minutes to allow the flavors to meld.

5. Place the olive oil in a small saucepan and warm it over medium heat. Add the dressing and cook, swirling the pan occasionally, until the dressing is warmed through and the shallots have softened slightly, about 4 minutes.

6. Add the dressing to the farro and toss to combine. Taste and season with salt, pepper, and lemon juice. Add the fresh herbs, fold to incorporate them, and enjoy.

Za'atar Okra & Lemons

YIELD: 4 SERVINGS / **ACTIVE TIME:** 20 MINUTES / **TOTAL TIME:** 20 MINUTES

2 TABLESPOONS AVOCADO OIL

1 LB. OKRA, TRIMMED

1 LEMON, CUT INTO WEDGES

SALT, TO TASTE

ZA'ATAR (SEE PAGE 501), TO TASTE

FRESH PARSLEY, CHOPPED, FOR GARNISH

1. Place the avocado oil in a large skillet and warm it over high heat. Add the okra and lemon wedges, season with salt, and cook, stirring frequently, until the okra and lemon begin to char.

2. Remove the pan from heat and stir in the Za'atar. Place the mixture in a serving bowl, garnish with parsley, and enjoy.

Za'atar Okra & Lemons
SEE PAGE 417

DESSERTS

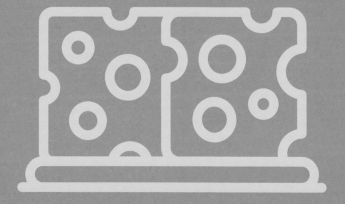

Baklava

YIELD: 30 PIECES / **ACTIVE TIME:** 30 MINUTES / **TOTAL TIME:** 1 HOUR AND 30 MINUTES

1 CUP PLUS 2 TABLESPOONS SUGAR

¾ CUP WATER

½ CUP HONEY

1 CINNAMON STICK

5 WHOLE CLOVES

¼ TEASPOON FINE SEA SALT

1½ CUPS SLIVERED ALMONDS

1½ CUPS WALNUTS

1 TEASPOON CINNAMON

¼ TEASPOON GROUND CLOVES

1 LB. PHYLLO DOUGH, THAWED

1 CUP UNSALTED BUTTER, MELTED

1. Place 1 cup of the sugar, the water, honey, cinnamon stick, whole cloves, and half of the sea salt in a saucepan and bring the mixture to a boil, stirring to dissolve the sugar. Reduce the heat and simmer until the mixture is syrupy, about 5 minutes. Remove the pan from heat and let the syrup cool. When it is cool, strain the syrup and set it aside.

2. Place the almonds in a food processor and pulse until finely chopped. Place the almonds in a bowl, add the walnuts to the food processor, and pulse and they are finely chopped. Add them to the bowl along with the cinnamon, ground cloves, and remaining sugar and salt and stir until combined. Set the mixture aside.

3. Preheat the oven to 300°F. Line a 10 x 8–inch baking pan with parchment paper. Place one sheet of phyllo in the pan and keep the remaining phyllo covered. Brush the sheet with some of the melted butter and place another sheet of phyllo on top. Repeat this four more times, so that you have a layer of 10 buttered phyllo sheets.

4. Spread 1 cup of the nut mixture over the phyllo. Top this with another layer of 10 buttered phyllo sheets, spread another cup of the nut mixture over it, and repeat.

5. Top the baklava with another layer of 10 buttered phyllo sheets. Using a serrated knife, cut the baklava into diamonds, making sure not to cut all the way through the bottom layer. Place the baklava in the oven and bake until it is golden brown, about 45 minutes, rotating the pan halfway through.

6. Remove the baklava from the oven and pour the syrup over it. Let the baklava cool completely, cut it all the way through, and enjoy.

Fig, Orange & Anise Honey Balls

YIELD: 20 BALLS / **ACTIVE TIME:** 30 MINUTES / **TOTAL TIME:** 2 HOURS

½ CUP PLUS ⅓ CUP SUGAR

1 CUP PLUS 2 TABLESPOONS WATER

2 TABLESPOONS HONEY

ZEST AND JUICE OF 1 ORANGE

SEEDS OF ½ VANILLA BEAN

2 CUPS DRIED FIGS

½ TEASPOON FENNEL SEEDS

1 CUP WALNUTS, TOASTED AND CHOPPED

1 TABLESPOON PERNOD

½ LB. FROZEN KATAIFI, THAWED

¼ CUP EXTRA-VIRGIN OLIVE OIL

1. Place ⅓ cup of the sugar, 2 tablespoons of the water, the honey, orange zest, orange juice, and vanilla seeds in a small saucepan and bring the mixture to a boil, stirring to dissolve the sugar. Reduce the heat and simmer the mixture until it is syrupy, about 5 minutes. Remove the pan from heat, let the syrup cool, and strain it. Set the syrup aside.

2. Line a baking sheet with parchment paper. Place the figs, fennel seeds, and remaining sugar and water in a saucepan and bring the mixture to a boil, stirring to dissolve the sugar. Reduce the heat and simmer the mixture until the liquid is syrupy, about 10 minutes. Remove the pan from heat and let it cool.

3. Place the cooled fig mixture in a food processor and blitz until it is a paste, scraping down the side of the work bowl frequently. Add the walnuts and Pernod and pulse until combined.

4. Form tablespoons of the mixture into balls and place them on the baking sheet. You should have about 20 balls. Place them in the refrigerator and chill for 30 minutes.

5. Preheat the oven to 350°F. Place the kataifi in a mixing bowl, slowly drizzle in the olive oil, and gently fold until the kataifi is evenly coated.

6. Grab a small amount of the kataifi and wrap it around one of the balls. Place the ball back on the baking sheet and repeat until all of the balls have been wrapped in kataifi.

7. Place the baking sheet in the oven and bake until the kataifi is golden brown, about 10 minutes, rotating the pan halfway through.

8. Remove the balls from the oven and let them cool.

9. Pour ½ tablespoon of the syrup over each ball and enjoy.

Meyer Lemon Curd

YIELD: 3 CUPS / **ACTIVE TIME:** 25 MINUTES / **TOTAL TIME:** 2 HOURS

¾ CUP FRESH MEYER LEMON JUICE

4 EGGS

¾ CUP SUGAR

⅛ TEASPOON KOSHER SALT

¼ TEASPOON PURE VANILLA EXTRACT

½ CUP UNSALTED BUTTER, SOFTENED

1. Fill a small saucepan halfway with water and bring it to a gentle simmer.

2. Place the lemon juice in a small saucepan and warm it over low heat.

3. Combine the eggs, sugar, salt, and vanilla in a metal mixing bowl. Place the bowl over the simmering water and whisk the mixture continually until it is 135°F on an instant-read thermometer.

4. When the lemon juice comes to a simmer, gradually add it to the egg mixture while whisking constantly.

5. When all of the lemon juice has been incorporated, whisk the curd until it has thickened and is 155°F. Remove the bowl from heat, add the butter, and stir until thoroughly incorporated.

6. Transfer the curd to a mason jar, place plastic wrap directly on its surface, and let it cool. Once cool, serve the curd or store it in the refrigerator, where it will keep for up to 2 weeks.

Goat Cheese & Honey Panna Cotta

YIELD: 4 SERVINGS / **ACTIVE TIME:** 30 MINUTES / **TOTAL TIME:** 5 HOURS

2 TABLESPOONS WATER

1 ENVELOPE OF UNFLAVORED GELATIN

2½ CUPS HEAVY CREAM

4 OZ. CREAMY GOAT CHEESE

½ CUP HONEY, PLUS MORE FOR GARNISH

FRESH BERRIES, FOR GARNISH

1. Place the water in a medium saucepan and warm it over medium heat. Sprinkle the gelatin over the water and stir until thoroughly combined. The mixture will very quickly become a paste—remove the pan from heat as soon as it does and set it aside.

2. Place the cream in another small saucepan and warm it over medium heat. Stir in the goat cheese and cook until it has dissolved. Add the honey and cook until it has been incorporated.

3. Place the gelatin over low heat and gradually add the cream mixture, stirring continually. When all of the cream mixture has been incorporated, raise the heat to medium and cook the mixture until it has thickened, about 10 minutes, stirring frequently.

4. Remove the pan from heat and pour the mixture into 4 oz. ramekins or mason jars. Place them in the refrigerator and chill until they have set, 4 to 5 hours.

5. To serve, garnish each portion with fresh berries and a drizzle of honey.

Yogurt Mousse with Blueberry Compote & Granola

YIELD: 4 SERVINGS / **ACTIVE TIME:** 40 MINUTES / **TOTAL TIME:** 1 HOUR

2 SHEETS OF GELATIN

2 TABLESPOONS FRESH LEMON JUICE

⅓ CUP SUGAR

SEEDS AND POD OF ½ VANILLA BEAN

1 CUP HEAVY CREAM

1 CUP FULL-FAT GREEK YOGURT

BLUEBERRY COMPOTE (SEE PAGE 491)

GRANOLA (SEE PAGE 491)

1. Place the sheets of gelatin in a bowl, cover them with cold water, and let them sit.

2. Place the lemon juice, sugar, and vanilla seeds and pod in a saucepan and bring to a simmer. Remove the pan from heat.

3. Remove the sheets of gelatin from the water and squeeze them to remove excess moisture. Add them to the warm syrup and stir until they have dissolved. Strain the gelatin into a bowl and let it cool until it is just slightly warm.

4. Place the cream in the work bowl of a stand mixer fitted with the whisk attachment and whip until it holds soft peaks. Set the whipped cream aside.

5. Add the yogurt to the gelatin and gently fold to combine. Add the whipped cream and fold to combine.

6. To serve, spoon the mousse into a serving dish and top each portion with some of the compote and Granola.

Pasteli

YIELD: 20 BARS / **ACTIVE TIME:** 20 MINUTES / **TOTAL TIME:** 1 HOUR

2 CUPS SESAME SEEDS

1 CUP HONEY

½ TEASPOON KOSHER SALT

1 TEASPOON PURE VANILLA EXTRACT

1. Preheat the oven to 350°F. Line a square 8-inch baking pan with parchment paper. Place the sesame seeds on a baking sheet, place them in the oven, and toast until golden brown, about 5 minutes. Remove from the oven and let the sesame seeds cool.

2. Place the honey in a small saucepan and warm it over medium-high heat. Boil the honey until it reaches 310°F.

3. Remove the pan from heat, stir in the salt, vanilla, and toasted sesame seeds, and pour the mixture into the baking pan. Let the mixture cool for 15 minutes.

4. Cut the bars into the desired shape; they should still be warm. Enjoy immediately or at room temperature.

Fermented Banana Fritters

YIELD: 2 SERVINGS / **ACTIVE TIME:** 25 MINUTES / **TOTAL TIME:** 4 TO 5 DAYS

2 BANANAS

1 TEASPOON ACTIVE DRY YEAST

2 CUPS WATER, PLUS MORE AS NEEDED

½ CUP ALL-PURPOSE FLOUR

1 TEASPOON BAKING POWDER

2 TABLESPOONS SUGAR

1 TABLESPOON CINNAMON

CANOLA OIL, AS NEEDED

2 TABLESPOONS PEANUT BUTTER

1. Peel the bananas, slice them into ½-inch-thick rounds, and place them in a mason jar. Add the yeast and then cover the bananas with the water. It is important that the bananas are completely covered, so add more water as necessary.

2. Cover the jar and place it in a cupboard, keeping it at roughly 70°F, for 4 to 5 days, until the bananas start to smell a little like alcohol, though not funky. Any bananas at the top that brown should be thrown away.

3. Drain the bananas, place them in a mixing bowl, and mash them. Add the flour and baking powder and stir until well combined.

4. Place the sugar and cinnamon in a bowl and stir to combine. Set the cinnamon sugar aside.

5. Add canola oil to a medium saucepan until it is about 1 inch deep and warm it to 325°F. Scoop tablespoons of the batter and fry until they are puffy and golden brown on one side, 1½ to 2 minutes. Turn the fritters over and cook until they are puffy and golden brown all over.

6. Remove the fritters from the hot oil, place them in the cinnamon sugar, and toss to coat.

7. Place the peanut butter in a microwave-safe bowl and microwave on medium in 10-second increments until it has liquefied.

8. To serve, spread the melted peanut butter on a small plate and pile the fritters on top.

Blueberry & Ginger Malabi

YIELD: 4 SERVINGS / **ACTIVE TIME:** 30 MINUTES / **TOTAL TIME:** 5 HOURS

2 CUPS LIGHT CREAM

1 TABLESPOON SUGAR

1 TEASPOON GRATED FRESH GINGER

½ CUP BLUEBERRIES

¼ CUP COLD WATER

2 TABLESPOONS CORNSTARCH

1. Place the cream, sugar, ginger, and blueberries in a small saucepan and warm the mixture over medium heat. When the mixture begins to bubble at the edge, reduce the heat to low and let it simmer for 30 minutes.

2. Puree the mixture using an immersion blender (or a food processor). Strain the mixture, place the liquid in a clean saucepan, and warm it over medium-high heat.

3. In a small bowl, combine the water and cornstarch. While stirring continually, gradually add the slurry to the cream mixture. As the mixture starts to thicken, reduce the heat to medium. Cook until the mixture acquires a pudding-like consistency, about 5 minutes.

4. Divide the mixture among 4 oz. ramekins or mason jars, place them in the refrigerator, and chill for 4 hours before serving.

Lemon Rice Pudding with Roasted Vanilla Cherries & Lemon Crème

YIELD: 4 SERVINGS / **ACTIVE TIME:** 45 MINUTES / **TOTAL TIME:** 2 HOURS

SEEDS OF 1 VANILLA BEAN

4 CUPS WHOLE MILK

½ CUP SUGAR

ZEST OF 1 LEMON

1 CUP RICE

ROASTED VANILLA CHERRIES (SEE PAGE 490)

LEMON CRÈME (SEE PAGE 488)

1. Place the vanilla bean seeds, milk, sugar, lemon zest, and rice in a saucepan and bring the mixture to a simmer over medium-low heat. Cook, stirring frequently, until the rice is cooked through and the mixture has thickened to the consistency of yogurt, 20 to 30 minutes. Remove the pan from heat and let the mixture cool.

2. To serve, divide the rice pudding between the serving bowls and top each portion with some of the roasted cherries and Lemon Crème.

Black Lime & Strawberry Crostata

YIELD: 6 SERVINGS / **ACTIVE TIME:** 30 MINUTES / **TOTAL TIME:** 2 HOURS AND 30 MINUTES

1¾ CUPS ALL-PURPOSE FLOUR, PLUS MORE AS NEEDED

1 CUP SUGAR

1 TEASPOON BAKING POWDER

10 TABLESPOONS UNSALTED BUTTER, SOFTENED AND CHOPPED, PLUS MORE AS NEEDED

2 EGGS, AT ROOM TEMPERATURE

2 BLACK LIMES

1 CUP WATER

1 CUP HULLED AND SLICED FRESH STRAWBERRIES

1. Place the flour, ½ cup of the sugar, and the baking powder in the work bowl of a mixer fitted with the paddle attachment and stir to combine.

2. Add the butter and 1 egg, as well as the yolk of the second egg. Reserve the egg white for the egg wash. Beat the mixture until it comes together as a soft dough. Cover it in plastic wrap and chill in the refrigerator for 30 minutes.

3. Open the black limes and pull out the sticky pith from inside. Place it in a small saucepan with the remaining sugar, the water, and strawberries. Bring the mixture to a boil and cook until it has reduced and is 220°F. Remove the pan from heat and let the mixture cool.

4. Preheat the oven to 350°F. Coat an 8-inch pie plate with butter.

5. Remove the dough from the refrigerator, divide it into two, and place it on a flour-dusted work surface. Roll each piece out to ⅛ inch thick and place one crust in the pie plate, trimming away any excess dough.

6. Fill the crust with the jam. Cut the remaining dough into strips. Lay the strips over the filling and trim any excess. To make a lattice crust, lift every other strip and fold back so you can place another strip across those strips that remain flat. Lay the folded strips back down over the cross-strip. Fold back the strips that you laid the cross-strip on top of and repeat until the lattice covers the surface of the crostata. Beat the remaining egg white until scrambled and brush the strips with it, taking care not to get any egg on the filling.

7. Place the crostata in the oven and bake until the crust is golden brown, about 30 minutes. Remove the crostata from the oven, place it on a wire rack, and let it cool to room temperature before enjoying.

Cardamom Biscotti

YIELD: 8 SERVINGS / **ACTIVE TIME:** 30 MINUTES / **TOTAL TIME:** 1 HOUR AND 30 MINUTES

1½ CUPS ALL-PURPOSE FLOUR

¾ TEASPOON BAKING POWDER

PINCH OF FINE SEA SALT

¼ CUP SUGAR

⅓ CUP LIGHT BROWN SUGAR

¾ TEASPOON CARDAMOM

½ TEASPOON CINNAMON

¼ TEASPOON GROUND GINGER

⅛ TEASPOON GROUND CLOVES

⅛ TEASPOON FRESHLY GRATED NUTMEG

ZEST OF 1 ORANGE

2 EGGS, BEATEN

¼ CUP EXTRA-VIRGIN OLIVE OIL

1 TEASPOON PURE VANILLA EXTRACT

1. Preheat the oven to 350°F. Line a baking sheet with parchment paper. Place the flour, baking powder, salt, sugars, and spices in a mixing bowl and whisk until combined.

2. Add the remaining ingredients and work the mixture by hand until it comes together as a smooth dough. Roll the dough into a log that is about 6 inches long and about 2 inches wide. Place the log on the baking sheet, place it in the oven, and bake until golden brown, about 20 minutes.

3. Remove the biscotti from the oven and let it cool.

4. Cut the biscotti into the desired shape and size. Place the biscotti back in the oven bake until it is crispy, about 20 minutes.

5. Remove the biscotti from the oven, transfer to a wire rack, and let them cool completely before enjoying.

Sufganiyot

3½ TABLESPOONS UNSALTED BUTTER, CHOPPED, PLUS MORE AS NEEDED

3½ CUPS ALL-PURPOSE FLOUR, PLUS MORE AS NEEDED

½ TEASPOON FINE SEA SALT

¼ CUP SUGAR

1 TABLESPOON INSTANT YEAST

1 EGG

1¼ CUPS LUKEWARM MILK (85°F)

AVOCADO OIL, AS NEEDED

½ CUP STRAWBERRY OR RASPBERRY JAM

¼ CUP CONFECTIONERS' SUGAR

1. Coat a mixing bowl with some butter and set it aside. Sift the flour into the work bowl of a stand mixer fitted with the dough hook. Add the salt, sugar, and yeast and stir to incorporate.

2. Add the egg and butter to the mixture and mix to incorporate. Gradually add the milk and work the mixture until it comes together as a soft dough, 8 to 10 minutes.

3. Form the dough into a ball and place it in the buttered mixing bowl. Cover with a linen towel and let it rise until doubled in size, about 2 hours.

4. Line two baking sheets with parchment paper. Place the dough on a flour-dusted work surface and roll it out until it is about ¾ inch thick. Cut the dough into 2-inch circles, place them on the baking sheets, and cover with a linen towel. Let them rise for another 20 minutes.

5. Add avocado oil to a Dutch oven until it is about 2 inches deep and warm it to 325°F. Add the dough in batches of 4 and fry until golden brown, about 6 minutes, turning them over halfway through.

6. Drain the sufganiyot on a paper towel–lined plate. Fill a piping bag with the jam and make a small slit on the top of each sufganiyah. Place the piping bag in the slit and fill until you see the filling coming back out. Sprinkle with confectioners' sugar and enjoy.

Paste di Mandorla Siciliane

YIELD: 20 COOKIES / **ACTIVE TIME:** 20 MINUTES / **TOTAL TIME:** 1 HOUR AND 40 MINUTES

2 EGG WHITES

7 OZ. ALMOND FLOUR

4.9 OZ. CONFECTIONERS' SUGAR

3 TABLESPOONS WATER OR LIQUEUR, PLUS MORE AS NEEDED

3 DROPS OF BITTER ALMOND EXTRACT

ALMONDS, FOR TOPPING (OPTIONAL)

CANDIED CHERRIES, HALVED, FOR TOPPING (OPTIONAL)

1. Place the egg whites in the work bowl of a stand mixer fitted with the whisk attachment and whip them until they are very firm.

2. Place the flour and sugar in a bowl and stir to combine. Add the water and almond extract and stir until the mixture comes together.

3. Add the egg whites and fold until the mixture is soft enough to be squeezed out of a piping bag. If the mixture feels too hard, incorporate a splash of water.

4. Place the dough in a piping bag and chill it in the refrigerator for 1 hour.

5. Preheat the oven to 330°F and line a baking sheet with parchment paper. Pipe small dollops of the dough onto the baking sheet.

6. Press either almonds or candied cherries into the centers of the cookies. Place them in the oven and bake until they are golden brown, about 15 minutes.

7. Remove the cookies from the oven and let them cool on the baking sheet for a few minutes before transferring them to wire racks to cool completely.

Sufganiyot
SEE PAGE 436

Pistoccheddus de Cappa

YIELD: 40 COOKIES / **ACTIVE TIME:** 1 HOUR / **TOTAL TIME:** 2 HOURS

FOR THE DOUGH

8.8 OZ. ALL-PURPOSE
FLOUR, PLUS MORE AS
NEEDED

8.8 OZ. FINELY GROUND
DURUM WHEAT FLOUR

1 TEASPOON BAKING
POWDER

1 TEASPOON BAKER'S
AMMONIA

½ CUP WHOLE MILK

4 EGG YOLKS

3½ OZ. SUGAR

1 TEASPOON PURE VANILLA
EXTRACT

ZEST OF 1 LEMON

2 OZ. LARD, SOFTENED

FOR THE GLAZE

4 EGG WHITES

2 CUPS CONFECTIONERS'
SUGAR

COLORED SUGAR
SPRINKLES, FOR TOPPING
(SILVER ARE THE MOST
TYPICAL)

1. Preheat the oven to 350°F and line two baking sheets with parchment paper. To begin preparations for the dough, sift the flours into a mixing bowl, add the baking powder, and stir to combine.

2. Place the baker's ammonia and milk in a separate bowl, stir to dissolve the baker's ammonia, and set the mixture aside.

3. Place the egg yolks and sugar in a separate mixing bowl and whisk until the mixture is pale yellow. Stir in the vanilla, lemon zest, and lard, add the flour mixture, and work the mixture until it comes together.

4. Place the mixture on a flour-dusted work surface, add the milk mixture, and work the mixture until it is a smooth dough. Tear the dough into pieces that are the size of a large walnut and roll each piece into a cylinder. Shape the cylinders into ovals, circles, hearts, or S-shaped cookies.

5. Place the cookies on the baking sheets, place them in the oven, and bake until they are a light golden brown, about 20 minutes.

6. To prepare the glaze, place the egg whites and confectioners' sugar in a heatproof bowl and whisk to combine. Bring a few inches of water to a boil in a medium saucepan and place the bowl over it. Whisk until the sugar has dissolved.

7. Remove the cookies from the oven, turn them over, and brush their bottoms with the glaze.

8. Reduce the oven's temperature to 250°F. Place the cookies back in the oven and bake for 10 minutes, making sure the glaze does not brown.

9. Remove the cookies from the oven, turn them over, and brush their tops with the glaze. Sprinkle the sugar sprinkles over the cookies, place them back in the oven, and bake for 10 minutes.

10. Remove the cookies from the oven and let them cool on the baking sheets for a few minutes before transferring them to wire racks to cool completely.

Halvah

YIELD: 12 SERVINGS / **ACTIVE TIME:** 20 MINUTES / **TOTAL TIME:** 36 HOURS

1½ CUPS TAHINI PASTE, STIRRED WELL

2 CUPS HONEY

2 CUPS SLICED ALMONDS, TOASTED

1. Coat a 9 x 5–inch loaf pan with nonstick cooking spray. Place the tahini in a small saucepan.

2. Place the honey in a saucepan fitted with a candy thermometer and warm it over medium heat until it reaches 240°F. Remove the pan from heat.

3. Warm the tahini to 120°F.

4. Add the warmed tahini to the honey and stir the mixture with a wooden spoon. It will look broken at first, but after a few minutes the mixture will come together smoothly. Add the nuts and continue to stir the mixture until it starts to stiffen, 6 to 8 minutes.

5. Pour the mixture into the loaf pan and let it cool to room temperature. Cover the pan tightly with plastic wrap and refrigerate for 36 hours. This will allow sugar crystals to form, which will give the halvah its distinctive texture.

6. Invert the halvah to remove it from the pan and use a sharp knife to cut it into the desired portions.

Buccellati

YIELD: 20 COOKIES / **ACTIVE TIME:** 40 MINUTES / **TOTAL TIME:** 3 HOURS

FOR THE DOUGH

9.7 OZ. ALL-PURPOSE FLOUR, PLUS MORE AS NEEDED

7.9 OZ. FINELY GROUND DURUM WHEAT FLOUR, PLUS MORE AS NEEDED

5 OZ. LARD, SOFTENED

5.3 OZ. SUGAR

2 TEASPOONS BAKER'S AMMONIA

1 TEASPOON PURE VANILLA EXTRACT

1 CUP LUKEWARM WHOLE MILK (90°F)

FOR THE FILLING

3 CUPS DRIED FIGS, CHOPPED

¼ CUP ALMONDS, FINELY CHOPPED

¼ CUP HONEY OR FIG JAM

1¾ OZ. DARK CHOCOLATE, GRATED

1 CUP CANDIED ORANGE PEELS

COLORED SUGAR SPRINKLES, FOR TOPPING

1. To prepare the dough, place the flours in a large mixing bowl, add the lard, and use a pastry cutter to work the mixture until it is like wet sand.

2. Add the sugar, baker's ammonia, vanilla, and milk, and work the mixture until it just comes together as a dough.

3. Transfer the dough to a flour-dusted work surface and quickly knead the dough until it is smooth and dense. Cover the dough with plastic wrap and chill it in the refrigerator for 1 hour.

4. To prepare the filling, place all of the ingredients in a mixing bowl and stir to combine.

5. Preheat the oven to 350°F and line a baking sheet with parchment paper.

6. Place the dough on a flour-dusted work surface and roll it out into a ½-inch-thick rectangle. Spread the filling over the dough and then roll the dough up tightly, starting from a long side.

7. Cut the dough into 1-inch-thick slices, place them on the baking sheet, and gently press down on them to flatten them slightly.

8. Sprinkle sugar sprinkles over the cookies, place them in the oven, and bake until they are golden brown, about 25 minutes.

9. Remove the cookies from the oven and let them cool on the baking sheet for a few minutes before transferring them to wire racks to cool completely.

Sfratti

YIELD: 6 SERVINGS / **ACTIVE TIME:** 30 MINUTES / **TOTAL TIME:** 3 HOURS

3 CUPS ALL-PURPOSE FLOUR, PLUS MORE AS NEEDED

1 CUP SUGAR

PINCH OF FINE SEA SALT

⅓ CUP UNSALTED BUTTER, CHILLED

⅔ CUP DRY WHITE WINE, CHILLED

1 CUP HONEY

2 CUPS CHOPPED WALNUTS

2 TEASPOONS ORANGE ZEST

¾ TEASPOON CINNAMON

¼ TEASPOON GROUND GINGER

DASH OF FRESHLY GRATED NUTMEG

¼ TEASPOON BLACK PEPPER

1 LARGE EGG

1 TABLESPOON WATER

1. Combine the flour, sugar, and salt in a mixing bowl. Add the butter and work the mixture with a pastry cutter until it resembles coarse crumbs. Add the wine a little at a time, mixing it in with a fork to moisten the dough. Continue adding wine until the mixture just comes together as a dough. Divide the dough in half and form each piece into a ball. Flatten the balls into disks, cover them with plastic wrap, and refrigerate for 1 hour.

2. Remove the dough from the refrigerator and let it stand at room temperature until malleable but not soft.

3. Place the honey in a saucepan and bring it to a boil. Boil for 5 minutes, lowering the heat if the honey starts to foam over the edge of the pan. Add the remaining ingredients, except for the egg and water, cook, stirring constantly, for another 3 to 5 minutes, and remove the pan from heat. If the mixture begins to turn dark, it is starting to burn—remove from the heat immediately and keep stirring.

4. Let the mixture stand, stirring occasionally, until it is cool enough to handle. Pour the mixture onto a flour-dusted surface, divide it into 6 equal portions, and shape each portion into a 14-inch-long log.

5. Preheat the oven to 350°F. Line a large baking sheet with parchment paper. On a flour-dusted work surface, roll each piece of dough into a 14 x 12–inch rectangle, then cut each rectangle lengthwise into 3 long rectangles. Place one of the rods of filling near a long side of each rectangle, then roll the dough around the filling.

6. You will have 6 long sticks of dough with filling in each. Cut these into 2-inch-long sticks. Place the cookies, seam side down, on the baking sheet, leaving 1 inch between the cookies. Place the egg and water in a cup and beat until combined. Brush the cookies with the egg wash.

7. Place the cookies in the oven and bake them until golden brown, about 20 minutes. Remove from the oven, transfer the cookies to a wire rack, and let them cool completely before serving.

Classic Malabi

YIELD: 6 SERVINGS / **ACTIVE TIME:** 30 MINUTES / **TOTAL TIME:** 4 HOURS AND 30 MINUTES

FOR THE PUDDING

4 CUPS MILK

⅔ CUP CORNSTARCH

1 TEASPOON ROSE WATER

1 CUP HEAVY CREAM

½ CUP SUGAR

½ CUP ROASTED PEANUTS OR PISTACHIOS, FOR GARNISH

SHREDDED COCONUT, FOR GARNISH

FOR THE SYRUP

½ CUP WATER

½ CUP SUGAR

1 TEASPOON ROSE WATER

3 DROPS OF RED FOOD COLORING

1. To begin preparations for the pudding, place 1 cup of the milk in a bowl, add the cornstarch and rose water, and stir until the mixture is smooth. Set aside.

2. Place the remaining milk, heavy cream, and sugar in a saucepan. Bring to a simmer, stirring constantly, reduce the heat to low, and stir in the cornstarch mixture.

3. Cook, stirring constantly, until the mixture starts to thicken, 3 to 4 minutes. Pour the pudding into ramekins or small mason jars, place plastic wrap directly on the surface to prevent a skin from forming, and let the pudding cool completely. When it has cooled, chill in the refrigerator for 4 hours.

4. To prepare the syrup, place the water, sugar, and rose water in a saucepan and bring to a boil, stirring to dissolve the sugar. Stir in the food coloring, boil for another 2 minutes, and remove the pan from heat. Let the syrup cool completely.

5. When the malabi has chilled for 4 hours, pour 1 to 2 tablespoons of the syrup over each portion, and garnish with peanuts or pistachios and shredded coconut.

Lemon Poppy Seed Cake

YIELD: 1 CAKE / **ACTIVE TIME:** 30 MINUTES / **TOTAL TIME:** 24 HOURS

⅔ CUP POPPY SEEDS, PLUS MORE FOR TOPPING

1 CUP FULL-FAT GREEK YOGURT

3 CUPS ALL-PURPOSE FLOUR, PLUS MORE AS NEEDED

1 TABLESPOON BAKING POWDER

1½ TEASPOONS FINE SEA SALT

1⅓ CUPS SUGAR

5 EGGS

1 CUP EXTRA-VIRGIN OLIVE OIL

ZEST AND JUICE OF 2 LEMONS

LEMON GLAZE (SEE PAGE 488)

1. Place the poppy seeds and yogurt in a small bowl and stir to combine. Place the mixture in the refrigerator and let it chill overnight.

2. Preheat the oven to 350°F. Coat a 6-quart Bundt pan with nonstick cooking spray and sprinkle some flour over it, knocking out any excess flour. Sift the flour, baking powder, and salt into a small bowl and set the mixture aside.

3. Place the sugar, eggs, and olive oil in the work bowl of a stand mixer fitted with the whisk attachment and whip the mixture until it is pale yellow, frothy, and comes off a rubber spatula in ribbons, about 5 minutes, scraping down the work bowl as necessary.

4. Add the poppy seed yogurt and whip until it has been incorporated. Add the dry mixture and gently fold until incorporated. Add the lemon zest and lemon juice and stir until incorporated.

5. Pour the batter into the Bundt pan, place it in the oven, and bake until a toothpick inserted into the cake's center comes out clean, about 40 minutes, rotating the pan halfway through.

6. Remove the cake from the oven and let it cool completely.

7. Invert the cake onto a platter. Pour the glaze over the cake, let it set for a few minutes, and sprinkle additional poppy seeds over the top. Let the glaze set for 15 minutes before slicing and serving.

Gluten-Free Spiced Honey Cake

YIELD: 8 SERVINGS / **ACTIVE TIME:** 20 MINUTES / **TOTAL TIME:** 1 HOUR AND 20 MINUTES

2 CUPS GLUTEN-FREE ALL-PURPOSE BAKING FLOUR

1½ TEASPOONS BAKING POWDER

½ TEASPOON BAKING SODA

½ TEASPOON SEA SALT

1½ TEASPOONS CINNAMON

½ TEASPOON GROUND GINGER

⅛ TEASPOON FRESHLY GRATED NUTMEG

⅔ CUP SUGAR

¼ CUP LIGHT BROWN SUGAR

½ CUP AVOCADO OIL

½ CUP HONEY

1 LARGE EGG

1 LARGE EGG YOLK

SEEDS FROM ½ VANILLA BEAN

½ CUP FRESH ORANGE JUICE

½ CUP BUTTERMILK

1. Preheat the oven to 350°F. Coat a round 9-inch cake pan with nonstick cooking spray and line the bottom with a circle of parchment paper.

2. Place the flour, baking powder, baking soda, salt, cinnamon, ginger, and nutmeg in a mixing bowl and stir to combine.

3. Combine the sugar, brown sugar, avocado oil, honey, egg, and egg yolk in the work bowl of a stand mixer fitted with the paddle attachment. Add the vanilla seeds and beat the mixture on medium until it is pale and thick, about 4 minutes. Reduce the speed to medium-low and gradually pour in the orange juice and buttermilk. Beat until frothy, about 2 minutes. Reduce the speed to low and gradually incorporate the dry mixture. Beat until the mixture comes together as a thin, pancake-like batter.

4. Pour the batter into the prepared pan and bake until the cake is golden brown and the center springs back when you gently press down on it (a cake tester inserted will not come out clean), 45 to 55 minutes.

5. Remove the cake from the oven, place the pan on a wire rack, and let the cake cool for 20 minutes. Run a knife around the edge of the cake to loosen it and invert it onto the rack. Let the cake cool completely before enjoying.

Sumac, Spelt & Apple Cake

YIELD: 4 SERVINGS / **ACTIVE TIME:** 20 MINUTES / **TOTAL TIME:** 1 HOUR AND 20 MINUTES

FOR THE APPLESAUCE

2 LARGE GRANNY SMITH APPLES, PEELED, CORED, AND CHOPPED

1 TABLESPOON FRESH LEMON JUICE

½ CUP WATER

FOR THE CAKE

1⅔ CUPS SPELT FLOUR

½ CUP GROUND ALMONDS

1 TABLESPOON SUMAC, PLUS MORE FOR TOPPING

1 TEASPOON BAKING POWDER

1 TEASPOON BAKING SODA

¼ CUP AVOCADO OIL

½ CUP PLUS 2 TABLESPOONS SUGAR

3 GOLDEN APPLES, PEELED, CORED, AND FINELY DICED

½ CUP CONFECTIONERS' SUGAR, PLUS MORE AS NEEDED

1 TABLESPOON FRESH LEMON JUICE, PLUS MORE AS NEEDED

1. To prepare the applesauce, place all of the ingredients in a saucepan and bring to a simmer. Cook until the apples are completely tender, 10 to 12 minutes. Remove the pan from heat and mash the apples until smooth. Set the applesauce aside.

2. Preheat the oven to 350°F. Coat a 1-pound loaf pan with nonstick cooking spray and line it with parchment paper. To begin preparations for the cake, place the flour, ground almonds, sumac, baking powder, and baking soda in a mixing bowl and stir to combine.

3. Place the avocado oil, sugar, and 1½ cups of the applesauce in a separate bowl and stir to combine. Add the wet mixture to the dry mixture and gently stir until the mixture comes together as a thick batter, making sure there are no clumps of flour. Stir in the apples.

4. Pour the batter into the loaf pan, place it in the oven, and bake until a cake tester inserted into the center of the cake comes out clean, 45 to 50 minutes.

5. Remove the cake from the oven and let it cool completely in the pan.

6. Place the confectioners' sugar and lemon juice in a mixing bowl and whisk the mixture until it is thick enough to coat the back of a wooden spoon. If it's too thin, add more sugar; if too thick, add more lemon juice.

7. Drizzle the icing over the cake, top with additional sumac, and enjoy.

Sfenj

YIELD: 15 SERVINGS / **ACTIVE TIME:** 40 MINUTES / **TOTAL TIME:** 3 HOURS

4 CUPS ALL-PURPOSE FLOUR

2 TEASPOONS INSTANT YEAST

1 TEASPOON FINE SEA SALT

1 TABLESPOON SUGAR

2 LARGE EGG YOLKS

1½ CUPS LUKEWARM WATER (90°F)

AVOCADO OIL, AS NEEDED

CONFECTIONERS' SUGAR OR HONEY, FOR TOPPING

1. Place the flour, yeast, salt, and sugar in a mixing bowl and stir to combine. Add the egg yolks and slowly drizzle in the water while mixing by hand.

2. Knead the mixture until it comes together as a sticky, smooth, and soft dough.

3. Spray the dough with nonstick cooking spray and cover the bowl with plastic wrap. Let the dough rise at room temperature for 2 hours.

4. Coat a large baking sheet with some avocado oil. Set it aside.

5. Divide the dough into 15 parts, roll each piece into a ball, and place it on the greased baking sheet. Cover the balls of dough with a slightly damp linen towel and let them rise for another 30 minutes.

6. Add avocado oil to a large, deep skillet until it is one-third to halfway full and warm it to 375°F. Using your forefinger and thumb, make a hole in the center of each dough ball and, working in batches, gently slip them into the hot oil. Fry until lightly golden brown all over, turning the sfenj as necessary.

7. Top the fried sfenj with confectioners' sugar or honey and enjoy immediately.

Biscotti all'Amarena

YIELD: 10 COOKIES / **ACTIVE TIME:** 1 HOUR / **TOTAL TIME:** 1 HOUR AND 30 MINUTES

FOR THE FROLLA

10.6 OZ. ALL-PURPOSE FLOUR, PLUS MORE AS NEEDED

4.2 OZ. SUGAR

4.2 OZ. UNSALTED BUTTER, SOFTENED AND CHOPPED INTO PIECES

1 EGG

1 EGG YOLK

1 TEASPOON BAKING POWDER

1 TEASPOON PURE VANILLA EXTRACT

FOR THE FILLING

¾ LB. LEFTOVER SPONGE CAKE, CRUMBLED

5½ TABLESPOONS UNSWEETENED COCOA POWDER

1 CUP PLUS 2 TABLESPOONS SOUR CHERRIES OR BLACK CHERRY JAM

2 TABLESPOONS ALCHERMES OR ANOTHER SWEET LIQUEUR

FOR THE GLAZE

1 CUP PLUS 2 TABLESPOONS CONFECTIONERS' SUGAR

2 TABLESPOONS EGG WHITES

BLACK CHERRY JAM, AS NEEDED

1. To begin preparations for the frolla, place all of the ingredients in a mixing bowl and quickly work the mixture with your hands until it just comes together as a dough. Place the dough on a flour-dusted surface and shape it into a compact ball. Cover the dough with plastic wrap and chill it in the refrigerator for 30 minutes.

2. To prepare the filling, place all of the ingredients in a bowl and stir until well combined.

3. Place the dough on a flour-dusted work surface and roll it into a rectangle.

4. Line a baking sheet with parchment paper. Shape the filling into a log that is the same length as the dough. Place the filling in the center of the dough and roll the long sides of the dough over the filling, making sure the sides meet at the center. Pinch the seam closed, turn the dough over, and place it on the baking sheet. Chill the dough in the refrigerator for 15 minutes.

5. To prepare the glaze, place the confectioners' sugar and egg whites in a small bowl and beat until the mixture is a thick glaze. Set the glaze aside.

6. Preheat the oven to 350°F. Take the dough out of the refrigerator and trim away the two ends that have little filling inside. Spread the glaze evenly over the dough.

7. Using a toothpick, cut two long strips in the glaze. Place cherry jam in a piping bag fitted with a fine tip and pipe the jam into the strips.

8. Cut the dough into 1½-inch-thick slices, place them in the oven, and bake until they are golden brown, about 20 minutes.

9. Remove the cookies from the oven and let them cool on the baking sheet for a few minutes before transferring them to a wire rack to cool completely.

Sfenj
SEE PAGE 450

Spicy Chocolate Halvah

YIELD: 4 SERVINGS / **ACTIVE TIME:** 30 MINUTES / **TOTAL TIME:** 1 HOUR

1 CUP TAHINI PASTE

1 CUP SUGAR

1 CUP WATER

3 OZ. DARK CHOCOLATE

1 TEASPOON CAYENNE PEPPER

1. Place the tahini in a small saucepan and warm it over medium heat.

2. Place the sugar and water in a separate small saucepan that is fitted with a candy thermometer. Bring the mixture to a boil over high heat, stirring to dissolve the sugar. Boil until the syrup is 265°F.

3. As you wait for the syrup to reach the proper temperature, add the chocolate and cayenne to the tahini and stir until the chocolate has melted.

4. Once the syrup reaches 265°F, immediately remove the pan from heat and stir the syrup into the tahini, making sure not to overwork the mixture, as this will cause the halvah to crack.

5. Pour the mixture into a container—a silicone mold, small loaf pan, or Tupperware are all acceptable. The halvah should set relatively quickly (30 minutes or less) and can be stored in the refrigerator for up to 2 weeks. Serve at room temperature.

Salted Honey & Apple Upside-Down Cake

YIELD: 6 SERVINGS / **ACTIVE TIME:** 20 MINUTES / **TOTAL TIME:** 1 HOUR AND 20 MINUTES

¾ CUP ALL-PURPOSE FLOUR

1 TEASPOON BAKING POWDER

¾ TEASPOON KOSHER SALT

½ TEASPOON CINNAMON

¼ CUP SOUR CREAM, PLUS MORE FOR SERVING

¼ CUP AVOCADO OIL

2 TEASPOONS PURE VANILLA EXTRACT

½ CUP SUGAR

2 EGGS

½ TABLESPOON UNSALTED BUTTER

¼ CUP HONEY, PLUS MORE FOR SERVING

1 BAKING APPLE, CORED AND SLICED INTO THIN ROUNDS

MALDON SEA SALT, FOR GARNISH

1. Preheat the oven to 350°F. Place the flour, baking powder, ½ teaspoon of the salt, and the cinnamon in a small bowl and whisk until combined.

2. Place the sour cream, avocado oil, and vanilla in a separate bowl and stir until combined. Place the sugar and eggs in a separate bowl and whisk until the mixture is foamy, about 2 minutes.

3. Add half of the flour mixture to the egg mixture and gently stir to incorporate it. Stir in half of the sour cream mixture, add the remaining flour mixture, and stir until incorporated. Add the remaining sour cream mixture and stir until the mixture just comes together. Set the batter aside.

4. Butter the bottom and sides of an 8-inch cast-iron skillet or springform pan and add the honey, swirling the pan to ensure the honey covers as much of the pan as possible. Sprinkle the remaining salt over the honey.

5. Arrange the apples on top the honey, overlapping them to fit the pan. Pour the cake batter over the apples and tap the pan on a counter a few times to remove any large bubbles.

6. Place the cake in the oven and bake until it is golden brown and springs back when gently touched with a finger, about 30 minutes.

7. Remove the cake from the oven and let it cool in the pan for 10 minutes. Run an offset spatula or knife around the pan and invert the cake onto a cooling rack (or unmold and then invert, if using a springform pan). Let the cake cool for another 20 minutes before transferring to a platter and sprinkling the Maldon sea salt over the top. Serve with additional sour cream and honey.

Pignoli

YIELD: 36 COOKIES / **ACTIVE TIME:** 15 MINUTES / **TOTAL TIME:** 40 MINUTES

1¾ CUPS UNSWEETENED ALMOND PASTE

1½ CUPS CONFECTIONERS' SUGAR

2 TABLESPOONS HONEY

PINCH OF CINNAMON

PINCH OF FINE SEA SALT

2 LARGE EGG WHITES, AT ROOM TEMPERATURE

ZEST OF 1 LEMON

¾ CUP PINE NUTS

1. Preheat the oven to 350°F and line two baking sheets with parchment paper. In the work bowl of a stand mixer fitted with the paddle attachment, beat the almond paste until it is thoroughly broken up. Add the confectioners' sugar and beat the mixture on low until combined.

2. Add the honey, cinnamon, salt, egg whites, and lemon zest, raise the speed to medium, and beat until the mixture is very thick, about 5 minutes.

3. Drop tablespoons of dough onto the prepared baking sheets and gently pat pine nuts into each of the cookies. Place the cookies in the oven and bake until golden brown, 12 to 14 minutes. Remove from the oven and let the cookies cool on the baking sheets.

Black & White Halvah

YIELD: 16 SERVINGS / **ACTIVE TIME:** 35 MINUTES / **TOTAL TIME:** 3 HOURS AND 40 MINUTES

¾ CUP WHITE TAHINI PASTE

1 TEASPOON KOSHER SALT

1⅓ CUPS SUGAR

¾ CUP BLACK TAHINI PASTE

1. Lightly coat an 8 x 4–inch loaf pan with nonstick spray and line it with parchment paper, leaving a 2-inch overhang on the long sides. Place a sheet of parchment paper on a work surface and lightly coat it with nonstick cooking spray. Place the white tahini and ½ teaspoon of the salt in the work bowl of a stand mixer fitted with the paddle attachment and beat on low until the mixture is smooth.

2. Place ⅓ cup of the sugar in a small saucepan. Place the remaining sugar in another small saucepan. Add ¼ cup water to each saucepan and place both saucepans over low heat. Cook, stirring to dissolve the sugar, for about 4 minutes. Keep one saucepan over low heat. Raise the heat under the other saucepan to medium-high and fit it with a thermometer. Cook the syrup, brushing down the side of the saucepan with a wet pastry brush to dissolve any crystals that form, until the syrup is 248°F, 7 to 10 minutes.

3. Remove the boiling syrup from heat. With the mixer running at medium speed, gradually stream the boiling syrup into the salted tahini, aiming for the space between the side of the bowl and the paddle. Beat just until the mixture comes together in a smooth mass, less than a minute. Take care not to overwork the mixture, or it will be crumbly.

4. Working quickly, scrape the mixture onto the prepared parchment and flatten it with a spatula until it is ¾ inch thick. Invert a medium bowl over the halvah to keep it warm. Rinse any hardened sugar off the candy thermometer and clip it to the second saucepan. Raise the heat to medium-high and cook the syrup, brushing down the side of the saucepan with a wet pastry brush, until the syrup is 248°F.

5. While the syrup is cooking, place the black tahini and remaining salt in the work bowl of the stand mixer (no need to clean it out, unless you have lots of hardened sugar stuck around the sides) and beat until smooth. With the mixer running, stream in the syrup and repeat Step 4.

6. Uncover the white halvah and scrape the black halvah on top; flatten it to about the same shape as the white halvah. Using the sides of the parchment to lift the edges of the stacked halvah, fold it in half and flatten slightly. Repeat this folding and flattening motion 4 to 5 times, rotating the halvah as you work to create a marbled effect.

7. Press the halvah into the prepared loaf pan. Fold the parchment paper over the halvah and let it cool for at least 3 hours. Using the parchment paper, lift the halvah out of the pan. Peel away the parchment paper and cut the halvah into ½-inch-thick slices. Enjoy or store in an airtight container at room temperature for up to 3 days.

Candied Hazelnuts

YIELD: ½ CUP / **ACTIVE TIME:** 30 MINUTES / **TOTAL TIME:** 1 HOUR

½ CUP HAZELNUTS

½ CUP MAPLE SYRUP

2 CUPS CANOLA OIL

1 TABLESPOON SUGAR

½ TEASPOON FINE SEA SALT

1. Line a baking sheet with parchment paper. Place the hazelnuts and maple syrup in a small saucepan and bring to a boil. Reduce the heat and simmer for 5 minutes.

2. Transfer the hazelnuts to the baking sheet. Using a fork, separate the hazelnuts so that they don't stick together when cool. Let the hazelnuts cool completely.

3. Place the canola oil in a Dutch oven and warm it to 350°F. Working in batches to avoid crowding the pot, add the hazelnuts and fry until golden brown. Transfer the fried hazelnuts to a paper towel–lined plate to drain, sprinkle the sugar and salt over them, and let them cool completely.

Susamielli

YIELD: 12 COOKIES / **ACTIVE TIME:** 40 MINUTES / **TOTAL TIME:** 1 HOUR

¾ CUP BLANCHED ALMONDS, PLUS MORE FOR TOPPING

3½ OZ. SUGAR

8.8 OZ. ALL-PURPOSE FLOUR

½ TEASPOON BAKER'S AMMONIA

2 TEASPOONS PISTO (SEE PAGE 492)

¾ CUP HONEY

1 EGG WHITE, BEATEN

1. Preheat the oven to 350°F and line a baking sheet with parchment paper. Place the almonds and sugar in a food processor and blitz until the almonds are finely ground.

2. Place the almond mixture, flour, baker's ammonia, Pisto, and honey in the work bowl of a stand mixer fitted with the paddle attachment and beat until the mixture comes together as a smooth dough.

3. Divide the dough into 2 pieces and form them into logs. Tear each log into 2 oz. pieces, roll these pieces into thin logs, and shape them into an S.

4. Place the cookies on the baking sheet, brush them with the egg white, and press almonds into the tops.

5. Place the cookies in the oven and bake until they are golden brown, about 15 minutes.

6. Remove the cookies from the oven and let them cool on the baking sheet for a few minutes before transferring them to wire racks to cool completely.

Taralli Dolci Pugliesi

YIELD: 60 COOKIES / **ACTIVE TIME:** 40 MINUTES / **TOTAL TIME:** 1 HOUR AND 15 MINUTES

17.6 OZ. ALL-PURPOSE
FLOUR, PLUS MORE AS
NEEDED

2 TEASPOONS BAKING SODA

4.6 OZ. SUGAR, PLUS MORE
FOR COATING

5.3 OZ. EXTRA-VIRGIN OLIVE
OIL

¾ CUP SWEET WHITE WINE

1. Preheat the oven to 340°F and line two baking sheets with parchment paper. Sift the flour into a mixing bowl, add the baking soda and sugar, and stir to combine. Add the olive oil and wine and work the mixture until it comes together as a shaggy dough.

2. Transfer the dough to a flour-dusted work surface and knead it until it is soft and smooth.

3. Tear the dough into walnut-sized pieces and roll them into 4-inch-long logs. Join the ends together to form rings and gently press down on the seams.

4. Fill a small bowl with sugar and dip the taralli in it until evenly coated.

5. Place the taralli on the baking sheets, place them in the oven, and bake until they are golden brown, about 25 minutes.

6. Remove the taralli from the oven and let them cool on the baking sheets for a few minutes before transferring them to wire racks to cool completely.

Debla

YIELD: 12 COOKIES / **ACTIVE TIME:** 20 MINUTES / **TOTAL TIME:** 1 HOUR

5 LARGE EGGS, BEATEN

1 TEASPOON BAKING SODA

3 CUPS ALL-PURPOSE FLOUR

AVOCADO OIL, AS NEEDED

2 CUPS SUGAR

⅛ TEASPOON FRESH LEMON JUICE

⅛ TEASPOON ORANGE BLOSSOM WATER

⅛ TEASPOON ROSE WATER

⅛ TEASPOON PURE VANILLA EXTRACT

1. Place the eggs, baking soda, and 2½ cups of the flour in a mixing bowl and work the mixture until it comes together as a dough. Separate the dough into five pieces. Roll out each piece until it is paper thin.

2. Add avocado oil to a deep skillet until it is 1 inch deep and warm it to 325°F.

3. Cut the dough into strips that are 2 inches wide and about 12 inches long. Prick the strips all over with a fork.

4. Wrap a strip around one prong of a wide fork and fry it, coiling the dough around itself as it fries until it is lightly browned all over. Transfer the fried debla to a paper towel–lined colander and let it drain. Repeat with the remaining dough.

5. Place the remaining ingredients and 1½ cups water in a saucepan, cover the pan, and simmer the mixture over low heat until it is a thick syrup, about 45 minutes. Stir the syrup and remove the pan from heat.

6. Dip the debla into the warm syrup, soaking them well. Place them in a colander and let them drain. When the syrup has cooled and hardened, arrange the debla on a serving platter and enjoy.

Mostaccioli

YIELD: 15 COOKIES / **ACTIVE TIME:** 40 MINUTES / **TOTAL TIME:** 1 HOUR

17.6 OZ. ALL-PURPOSE FLOUR, PLUS MORE AS NEEDED

5.3 OZ. ALMOND FLOUR

5.3 OZ. HONEY

5.3 OZ. SUGAR

1½ TEASPOONS BAKER'S AMMONIA

2 TEASPOONS PISTO (SEE PAGE 492)

1.2 OZ. UNSWEETENED COCOA POWDER

ZEST AND JUICE OF 1 ORANGE

3½ OZ. HOT WATER (140°F), PLUS MORE AS NEEDED

7 OZ. BITTERSWEET CHOCOLATE, CHOPPED

1. Preheat the oven to 350°F and line two baking sheets with parchment paper. Place the flours, honey, sugar, baker's ammonia, Pisto, cocoa powder, orange zest, and orange juice in the work bowl of a stand mixer fitted with the paddle attachment. With the mixer running, gradually add the hot water and work the mixture until it comes together as a soft, smooth dough. Depending on the all-purpose flour you end up using, you may not need to use all of the water; you also may need to add more water if the dough is too stiff.

2. Place the dough on a flour-dusted work surface and roll it out until it is about ½ inch thick. Cut the dough into diamonds and place them on the baking sheets.

3. Place the cookies in the oven and bake until they are golden brown, 10 to 15 minutes. Remove the cookies from the oven and let them cool.

4. While the cookies are cooling, bring a few inches of water to a simmer in a medium saucepan. Place the chocolate in a heatproof bowl, place it over the simmering water, and stir until the chocolate has melted.

5. Using kitchen tongs, dip the cookies into the melted chocolate and place them on wire racks. Let the chocolate set before serving.

Celli Pieni

YIELD: 40 COOKIES / **ACTIVE TIME:** 40 MINUTES / **TOTAL TIME:** 1 HOUR AND 30 MINUTES

¾ CUP CRUSHED BISCUITS OR OTHER DRY COOKIES

⅔ CUP FINELY CHOPPED, BLANCHED, AND TOASTED ALMONDS

1⅓ CUPS GRAPE JAM

ZEST OF 1 LEMON

2 TEASPOONS UNSWEETENED COCOA POWDER

½ TEASPOON CINNAMON

⅔ CUP DRY WHITE WINE

2 TABLESPOONS SUGAR, PLUS MORE FOR TOPPING

⅔ CUP EXTRA-VIRGIN OLIVE OIL

17.6 OZ. ALL-PURPOSE FLOUR, PLUS MORE AS NEEDED

1. Place the cookies and almonds in a bowl and stir to combine. Add the jam, lemon zest, cocoa powder, and cinnamon and stir to incorporate. Let the mixture rest for 30 minutes.

2. Place the wine and sugar in a saucepan and warm the mixture over medium heat, stirring to dissolve the sugar.

3. Place the wine syrup in a heatproof bowl, add the olive oil and flour, and work the mixture with your hands until it comes together as a smooth dough. Cover the dough and let it rest for 30 minutes.

4. Preheat the oven to 350°F and line two baking sheets with parchment paper. Place the dough on a flour-dusted work surface and roll it out into a very thin sheet. It is also possible to use a pasta maker to get the dough thin enough.

5. Distribute teaspoons of the jam mixture on the dough, leaving 1 inch between each dollop. Use a glass or ring cutter to cut out rounds of dough with the jam mixture in the center. Fold the rounds over the filling, shape them into crescents, and pinch the seams to seal the cookies. Bring the two points of the crescents together to form the shape of a fortune cookie or tortellino. Dust the cookies with sugar and place them on the baking sheets.

6. Place the cookies in the oven and bake until they are a light golden brown, about 15 minutes.

7. Remove the cookies from the oven and let them cool on the baking sheets for a few minutes before transferring them to wire racks to cool completely.

Reginelle

YIELD: 40 COOKIES / **ACTIVE TIME:** 30 MINUTES / **TOTAL TIME:** 2 HOURS

17.6 OZ. ALL-PURPOSE FLOUR, PLUS MORE AS NEEDED

5.3 OZ. SUGAR

¼ TEASPOON SAFFRON THREADS

1 TEASPOON BAKER'S AMMONIA

1½ TABLESPOONS WHOLE MILK

5 OZ. LARD OR UNSALTED BUTTER

2 EGGS

ZEST OF 1 LEMON

PINCH OF KOSHER SALT

1 CUP SESAME SEEDS

1. Place the flour, sugar, and saffron in a mixing bowl and stir to combine.

2. Place the baker's ammonia and milk in a bowl and stir until the baker's ammonia has dissolved. Add the milk mixture, lard (or butter), eggs, lemon zest, and salt to the mixing bowl and work the mixture until it just comes together.

3. Place the dough on a flour-dusted work surface and knead it until it is smooth. Form the dough into a ball, cover it with plastic wrap, and chill it in the refrigerator for 30 minutes.

4. Preheat the oven to 390°F and line two baking sheets with parchment paper.

5. Place the dough on a flour-dusted work surface, divide it into 8 pieces, and roll each piece into a 1-inch-thick cylinder. Cut the cylinders into 2-inch-long pieces.

6. Place the sesame seeds in a bowl, spray the pieces of dough with water, and roll them in the sesame seeds until they are completely coated.

7. Place the cookies on the baking sheets, place them in the oven, and bake them until they are golden brown, 10 to 15 minutes.

8. Reduce the oven's temperature to 300°F and bake the cookies for another 15 minutes.

9. Remove the cookies from the oven and let them cool on the baking sheets for a few minutes before transferring them to wire racks to cool completely.

Pepatelli Molisani

YIELD: 40 COOKIES / **ACTIVE TIME:** 30 MINUTES / **TOTAL TIME:** 1 HOUR

17.6 OZ. WHOLE WHEAT FLOUR

1 TEASPOON BAKING SODA

17.6 OZ. HONEY

3 CUPS BLANCHED AND TOASTED ALMONDS

ZEST OF 1 ORANGE

1 TABLESPOON BLACK PEPPER

1. Line a 13 x 9–inch baking dish with parchment paper. Sift the flour into a large bowl, add the baking soda, and stir to combine. Set the mixture aside.

2. Place the honey in a medium saucepan and warm it over medium heat. Stir in the almonds, orange zest, and pepper, add the flour mixture, and stir vigorously until the mixture comes together as a dough.

3. Pour the dough into the baking dish and level it until it is about 1 inch thick. Let the dough cool completely.

4. Preheat the oven to 340°F. Line two baking sheets with parchment paper. Cut the dough into 2 x ½–inch strips and place them on the baking sheets.

5. Place the cookies in the oven and bake until they are a light golden brown, about 15 minutes. Turn off the oven and leave the cookies in the cooling oven for 5 minutes.

6. Remove the cookies from the oven and let them cool on the baking sheets for a few minutes before transferring them to wire racks to cool completely.

Sfogliatelle di Frolla

YIELD: 12 SFOGLIATELLE / **ACTIVE TIME:** 1 HOUR / **TOTAL TIME:** 3 HOURS

1⅔ CUPS WHOLE MILK

PINCH OF KOSHER SALT

½ CUP UNSALTED BUTTER

1 LEMON PEEL, PITH REMOVED

¾ CUP COARSE SEMOLINA FLOUR

1 EGG

2 CUPS CONFECTIONERS' SUGAR

1 TEASPOON PURE VANILLA EXTRACT

1 TEASPOON ORANGE BLOSSOM WATER

PINCH OF CINNAMON

½ CUP CANDIED CITRUS PEELS, FINELY CHOPPED

1 CUP RICOTTA CHEESE

PASTA FROLLA NAPOLETANA (SEE PAGE 489)

ALL-PURPOSE FLOUR, AS NEEDED

1 EGG YOLK, BEATEN

1. Place the milk, salt, half of the butter, and the lemon peel in a medium saucepan and bring the mixture to a boil.

2. Remove the lemon peel and discard it. Add the semolina and stir continually until the mixture thickens.

3. Remove the pan from heat, cover it with plastic wrap, and let the mixture cool.

4. Place the remaining butter, the egg, confectioners' sugar, vanilla, orange blossom water, cinnamon, and candied citrus peels in another bowl and whisk to combine. Incorporate the ricotta a little bit at a time. When all of the ricotta has been incorporated, add the semolina mixture gradually and whisk until incorporated.

5. Cover the mixture with plastic wrap and chill it in the refrigerator for 1 hour.

6. Line two baking sheets with parchment paper. Place the frolla on a flour-dusted work surface and beat it with a rolling pin to soften it. Divide the frolla into 12 pieces and roll out each piece into a ¼-inch-thick oval.

7. Place 1 tablespoon of the ricotta cream on the bottom half of each oval, making sure to maintain a small border around the edge, and fold the other half of the dough over the filling.

8. Press down on the edges of the sfogliatelle to seal them and trim away any excess dough.

9. Place the sfogliatelle on the baking sheets and chill them in the refrigerator for 1 hour.

10. Preheat the oven to 390°F (if your oven has convection mode, set it to that).

11. Brush the sfogliatelle with the egg yolk, place them in the oven, and bake until they are golden brown, about 15 minutes.

12. Remove the sfogliatelle from the oven and let them cool slightly before serving.

Caramelized Honey Tart

YIELD: 8 SERVINGS / **ACTIVE TIME:** 35 MINUTES / **TOTAL TIME:** 1 HOUR AND 30 MINUTES

FOR THE CRUST

1½ CUPS ALL-PURPOSE FLOUR, PLUS MORE AS NEEDED

¼ CUP CONFECTIONERS' SUGAR

½ TEASPOON KOSHER SALT

½ CUP UNSALTED BUTTER, CHILLED AND CHOPPED, PLUS MORE AS NEEDED

2 LARGE EGG YOLKS

1 TABLESPOON WATER

FOR THE FILLING

¼ CUP HONEY

1 TABLESPOON WATER

¼ CUP SUGAR

4 CUPS HEAVY CREAM

4 TABLESPOONS UNSALTED BUTTER

2 TABLESPOONS LIGHT CORN SYRUP

½ TEASPOON KOSHER SALT

½ TEASPOON PURE VANILLA EXTRACT

2 CUPS UNSALTED AND ROASTED MIXED NUTS (PECANS, HAZELNUTS, PEANUTS, PISTACHIOS, AND/OR SLICED ALMONDS)

⅓ CUP UNSALTED AND ROASTED SUNFLOWER SEEDS

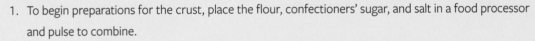

1. To begin preparations for the crust, place the flour, confectioners' sugar, and salt in a food processor and pulse to combine.

2. Add the butter and pulse until the mixture is a coarse meal with a few pea-size pieces of butter remaining.

3. Place the egg yolks and water in a small bowl and beat until combined. With the food processor running, add the egg yolks to the mixture and blitz until it comes together as a dough.

4. Coat a 9-inch springform pan with butter. Using lightly flour-dusted hands, place the dough in the pan and press it about 1 inch up the side and evenly in the bottom of the pan, making sure the side of the crust is slightly thicker than the bottom. Use a flour-dusted, straight-sided measuring cup or glass to compact and smooth the dough. Place the crust in the freezer until it is solid, 15 to 20 minutes.

5. Preheat the oven to 350°F. Prick the bottom of the crust with a fork, place it in the oven, and bake until it is golden brown, 20 to 25 minutes.

6. Remove the crust from the oven and place the pan on a wire rack. Leave the oven on.

7. To begin preparations for the filling, place the honey and water in a small saucepan and bring it to a simmer over low heat, swirling the pan frequently. Simmer until the mixture has darkened and gives off a nutty fragrance, about 2 minutes.

8. Carefully add the sugar, heavy cream, butter, corn syrup, salt, and vanilla to the pan and stir until the mixture is smooth. Raise the heat to medium and bring the mixture to a boil. Cook, swirling the pan, until the caramel has darkened slightly and is thick enough to coat a wooden spoon, 5 to 8 minutes.

9. Remove the pan from heat and stir the nuts and seeds into the caramel.

10. Scrape the filling into the crust, making sure it is evenly distributed. Place the tart in the oven and bake until the filling is a deep golden brown and bubbling, 25 to 30 minutes.

11. Remove the tart from the oven and let it cool completely before serving.

Honey Cake

YIELD: 1 CAKE / **ACTIVE TIME:** 1 HOUR / **TOTAL TIME:** 4 HOURS

2½ CUPS ALL-PURPOSE FLOUR

2 TEASPOONS BAKING POWDER

½ TEASPOON BAKING SODA

½ TEASPOON KOSHER SALT

2 TEASPOONS CINNAMON

¼ TEASPOON GROUND GINGER

¼ TEASPOON GROUND CLOVES

3 LARGE EGGS

1 CUP SUGAR

1¼ CUPS AVOCADO OIL

1 CUP PURE HONEY

¾ CUP LUKEWARM BREWED COFFEE

1½ TEASPOONS ORANGE ZEST

CHOCOLATE GLAZE (SEE PAGE 492)

MALDON SEA SALT, FOR TOPPING

1. Preheat the oven to 350°F and position a rack in middle. Generously coat a 12-cup Bundt pan with nonstick cooking spray.

2. Place the flour, baking powder, baking soda, salt, and spices in a large bowl and stir to combine.

3. Place the eggs in a separate bowl and beat until scrambled. Add the sugar, avocado oil, honey, coffee, and orange zest and whisk until thoroughly combined.

4. Make a well in the center of the dry mixture and place the wet mixture in it. Whisk until the mixture comes together as a smooth batter.

5. Pour the batter into the prepared pan and place it in the oven. Bake until the cake is springy to the touch and a cake tester inserted into the center comes out clean, 45 to 50 minutes.

6. Remove the cake from the oven, place the pan on a wire rack, and let it cool for 20 minutes. Loosen the cake with a thin rubber spatula. Invert the cake onto the wire rack and let it cool completely.

7. Transfer the cake to a serving platter and slowly pour the Chocolate Glaze over the top, letting it drip down the sides. Let the cake stand at room temperature until the glaze is set.

8. Sprinkle the Maldon over the glaze and serve.

Bocconotti Calabresi

YIELD: 15 BOCCONOTTI / **ACTIVE TIME:** 1 HOUR / **TOTAL TIME:** 2 HOURS

UNSALTED BUTTER, AS NEEDED

ALL-PURPOSE FLOUR, AS NEEDED

PASTA FROLLA (SEE PAGE 489)

1½ CUPS BLACK GRAPE MARMALADE (MOSTARDA D'UVA)

1 EGG YOLK

CONFECTIONERS' SUGAR, FOR TOPPING

1. Coat the wells of a muffin pan with butter, dust them with flour, and knock out any excess.

2. Preheat the oven to 350°F. Place the frolla on a flour-dusted work surface and beat it with a rolling pin to soften it. Roll out the frolla into a ¼-inch-thick rectangle and use a glass or ring cutter to cut out rounds that are large enough to cover the bottom and sides of the wells in the muffin pan. Place the rounds in the wells and trim away any excess dough. Roll the excess dough out into a thin sheet that will cover the muffin pan.

3. Fill each pastry with a heaping spoonful of the marmalade.

4. Cut rounds slightly larger than the wells from the sheet of dough. Place them over the bocconotti and press down on the edges to seal so that the tops hold tight in the oven.

5. Prick the tops of the bocconotti with a toothpick. Beat the egg yolk and brush the bocconotti with it.

6. Place the bocconotti in the oven. Baking times will depend on the depth of the wells in the muffin pan. For deeper wells, bake for about 30 minutes. For shallower wells, bake for about 20 minutes. Also, do not worry if the tops detach; they will be reattached later.

7. Remove the bocconotti from the oven and let them cool for 5 minutes. Cover the pan with a similarly sized tray, invert the pan, and let it rest on the counter for 1 hour.

8. Turn the pan back over, remove the bocconotti from the pan, dust them generously with confectioners' sugar, and enjoy.

Bocconotti Calabresi
SEE PAGE 471

Zeppole with Meyer Lemon Curd

YIELD: 4 SERVINGS / **ACTIVE TIME:** 30 MINUTES / **TOTAL TIME:** 2 HOURS

1½ CUPS ALL-PURPOSE FLOUR

1 TABLESPOON PLUS 1 TEASPOON BAKING POWDER

¼ TEASPOON FINE SEA SALT

2 EGGS

2 TABLESPOONS SUGAR

2 CUPS RICOTTA CHEESE

ZEST OF 1 ORANGE

1 CUP MILK

1 TEASPOON PURE VANILLA EXTRACT

CANOLA OIL, AS NEEDED

¼ CUP CONFECTIONERS' SUGAR, FOR TOPPING

MEYER LEMON CURD (SEE PAGE 425)

1. Sift the flour, baking powder, and salt into a bowl. Set the mixture aside.

2. Place the eggs and sugar in a separate bowl and whisk to combine. Add the ricotta, whisk to incorporate, and then stir in the orange zest, milk, and vanilla.

3. Gradually incorporate the dry mixture into the wet mixture until it comes together as a smooth batter. Place the batter in the refrigerator and chill for 1 hour.

4. Add canola oil to a Dutch oven until it is about 2 inches deep and warm it to 350°F. Drop tablespoons of the batter into the hot oil, taking care not to crowd the pot, and fry until the zeppole are golden brown. Transfer the fried zeppole to a paper towel–lined plate and dust them with confectioners' sugar.

5. To serve, spread some Meyer Lemon Curd on each serving plate and top with 2 or 3 zeppole.

Cassatelle di Agira

YIELD: 20 CASSATELLE / **ACTIVE TIME:** 1 HOUR AND 30 MINUTES / **TOTAL TIME:** 24 HOURS

7 OZ. ALMONDS, TOASTED

ZEST OF 1 LEMON

½ CUP UNSWEETENED COCOA POWDER

¾ CUP SUGAR

1 TEASPOON CINNAMON, PLUS MORE FOR TOPPING

1 TEASPOON PURE VANILLA EXTRACT

1½ CUPS WATER

½ (HEAPING) CUP CHICKPEA FLOUR, PLUS MORE AS NEEDED

PASTA FROLLA AL LARDO (SEE PAGE 490)

ALL-PURPOSE FLOUR, AS NEEDED

CONFECTIONERS' SUGAR, FOR TOPPING

1. Place the almonds and lemon zest in a food processor and blitz until the mixture is a slightly coarse powder.

2. Place the ground almond mixture, cocoa powder, sugar, cinnamon, vanilla, and water in a medium saucepan and stir to combine. Bring the mixture to a simmer over low heat and cook until it thickens, stirring continually.

3. Remove the pan from heat, sift the chickpea flour into the pan, and stir vigorously until the mixture is smooth.

4. Transfer the filling to an airtight container and let it sit at room temperature overnight.

5. Preheat the oven to 350°F and line two baking sheets with parchment paper. Place the frolla on a flour-dusted work surface and roll it out until it is a ⅛-inch-thick rectangle. Use a glass or ring cutter to cut 4-inch rounds out of the dough.

6. Place a teaspoon of the filling in the center of each round and fold the rounds into half-moons. Press down on the edge to seal the dumplings and trim away any excess dough using a pasta wheel. Place the cassatelle on the baking sheets.

7. Place the cassatelle in the oven and bake until they are just about to start browning, 10 to 15 minutes.

8. Remove the cassatelle from the oven and let them cool completely.

9. Place confectioners' sugar and cinnamon in a shallow bowl and stir to combine. Sprinkle the mixture over the cassatelle and enjoy.

Casadinas

YIELD: 15 CASADINAS / **ACTIVE TIME:** 1 HOUR / **TOTAL TIME:** 2 HOURS

10.6 OZ. FINELY GROUND DURUM WHEAT FLOUR, PLUS MORE AS NEEDED

2.8 OZ. LARD

5.6 OZ. LUKEWARM WATER (90°F)

PINCH OF FINE SEA SALT

2 CUPS RICOTTA CHEESE (BEST IF FROM SHEEP'S MILK)

1 CUP CONFECTIONERS' SUGAR

2 TABLESPOONS ALL-PURPOSE FLOUR

1 EGG

PINCH OF SAFFRON THREADS

ZEST OF 1 ORANGE

ZEST OF 1 LEMON

1. Place the flour, lard, water, and salt in a mixing bowl and work the mixture until it comes together as a smooth dough.

2. Cover the dough with plastic wrap and let it rest for 30 minutes.

3. Place the ricotta cheese, confectioners' sugar, all-purpose flour, egg, saffron threads, orange zest, and lemon zest in a mixing bowl. Stir until well combined.

4. Preheat the oven to 350°F and line two baking sheets with parchment paper.

5. Place the dough on a flour-dusted work surface and roll it out until it is about ⅛ inch thick. Cut the dough into 4-inch rounds and place them on the baking sheets.

6. Place a tablespoon of the ricotta mixture in the center of each round.

7. To shape the casadinas, pinch the edge of the rounds around the filling, forming a sort of small basket that encases it. Generally, the perimeter of the pastry has 7 or 8 corners.

8. Place the casadinas in the oven and bake until the filling is golden brown and puffy, about 30 minutes.

9. Remove the casadinas from the oven and let them cool slightly before enjoying.

Pastiera Napoletana

YIELD: 1 PIE / **ACTIVE TIME:** 1 HOUR / **TOTAL TIME:** 24 HOURS

8.8 OZ. COOKED WHEAT BERRIES

⅔ CUP WHOLE MILK

1½ CUPS SUGAR

1½ TABLESPOONS UNSALTED BUTTER, PLUS MORE AS NEEDED

1½ CUPS RICOTTA CHEESE, DRAINED (RICOTTA MADE FROM SHEEP'S MILK PREFERRED)

2 EGGS

2 EGG YOLKS

1½ (HEAPING) TABLESPOONS ORANGE BLOSSOM WATER

SEEDS OF 1 VANILLA BEAN

¼ CUP CANDIED CITRUS PEELS, FINELY DICED

¼ CUP CANDIED ORANGE PEELS, FINELY DICED

PASTA FROLLA (SEE PAGE 489)

ALL-PURPOSE FLOUR, AS NEEDED

CONFECTIONERS' SUGAR, FOR TOPPING

1. Place the wheat berries, milk, sugar, and butter in a saucepan and bring the mixture to a boil over low heat, stirring continually. Cook until the mixture thickens, about 15 minutes.

2. Remove the pan from heat and let the mixture cool.

3. Add the ricotta, eggs, egg yolks, orange blossom water, vanilla seeds, candied citrus peels, and candied orange peels and stir to combine.

4. Preheat the oven to 340°F. Place the frolla on a flour-dusted work surface, remove a 3½ oz. piece of dough, and set it aside. Beat the remaining dough with a rolling pin to soften it and roll it out into a ⅛-inch-thick disk.

5. Coat a 9-inch pie plate with butter, dust it with flour, and knock out any excess. Place the dough in the pie plate, prick it with a fork, and trim away any excess dough.

6. Roll out the 3½ oz. piece of dough into a ⅛-inch-thick disk and cut it into 7 strips.

7. Pour the filling into the dough and arrange the strips of dough in a lattice pattern over the filling.

8. Place the pastiera in the oven and bake until the crust is golden brown, about 1 hour.

9. Remove the pastiera from the oven and let it cool completely. Cover it with plastic wrap and chill it in the refrigerator overnight.

10. Dust the pastiera with confectioners' sugar and serve.

APPENDIX

Fish Stock

YIELD: 6 CUPS / **ACTIVE TIME:** 20 MINUTES / **TOTAL TIME:** 4 HOURS

¼ CUP EXTRA-VIRGIN OLIVE OIL

1 LEEK, TRIMMED, RINSED WELL, AND CHOPPED

1 LARGE YELLOW ONION, UNPEELED, ROOT CLEANED, CHOPPED

2 LARGE CARROTS, PEELED AND CHOPPED

1 CELERY STALK, CHOPPED

¾ LB. WHITEFISH BODIES

4 SPRIGS OF FRESH PARSLEY

3 SPRIGS OF FRESH THYME

2 BAY LEAVES

1 TEASPOON BLACK PEPPERCORNS

1 TEASPOON KOSHER SALT

8 CUPS WATER

1. Place the olive oil in a stockpot and warm it over low heat. Add the vegetables and cook until the liquid they release has evaporated.

2. Add the whitefish bodies, the aromatics, peppercorns, salt, and water to the pot, raise the heat to high, and bring to a boil. Reduce the heat so that the stock simmers and cook for 3 hours, skimming to remove any impurities that float to the surface.

3. Strain the stock through a fine sieve, let it cool slightly, and place in the refrigerator, uncovered, to chill. When the stock is completely cool, remove the fat layer from the top and cover. The stock will keep in the refrigerator for 3 to 5 days and in the freezer for up to 3 months.

Chicken Stock

YIELD: 8 CUPS / **ACTIVE TIME:** 20 MINUTES / **TOTAL TIME:** 6 HOURS

7 LBS. CHICKEN BONES, RINSED

4 CUPS CHOPPED YELLOW ONIONS

2 CUPS CHOPPED CARROTS

2 CUPS CHOPPED CELERY

3 GARLIC CLOVES, CRUSHED

3 SPRIGS OF FRESH THYME

1 TEASPOON BLACK PEPPERCORNS

1 BAY LEAF

1. Place the chicken bones in a stockpot and cover with cold water. Bring to a simmer over medium-high heat and use a ladle to skim off any impurities that rise to the surface.

2. Add the remaining ingredients, reduce the heat to low, and simmer for 5 hours, while skimming to remove any impurities that rise to the surface.

3. Strain, allow to cool slightly, and transfer the stock to the refrigerator. Leave it uncovered and let the stock cool completely. Remove the layer of fat and cover. The stock will keep in the refrigerator for 3 to 5 days and in the freezer for up to 3 months.

Lobster Stock

YIELD: 8 CUPS / **ACTIVE TIME:** 30 MINUTES / **TOTAL TIME:** 4 HOURS AND 30 MINUTES

5 LBS. LOBSTER SHELLS AND BODIES

2 TABLESPOONS EXTRA-VIRGIN OLIVE OIL

½ LB. CARROTS, PEELED AND CHOPPED

½ LB. ONIONS, CHOPPED

10 TOMATOES, CHOPPED

1 CUP V8

5 SPRIGS OF FRESH THYME

5 SPRIGS OF FRESH PARSLEY

5 SPRIGS OF FRESH TARRAGON

5 SPRIGS OF FRESH DILL

1 GARLIC CLOVE

2 CUPS WHITE WINE

1. Preheat the oven to 350°F. Arrange the lobster bodies and shells on two baking sheets, place them in the oven, and roast them for 30 to 45 minutes. Remove the roasted bodies and shells from the oven and set them aside.

2. While the lobster bodies and shells are in the oven, place the olive oil in a stockpot and warm it over medium heat. Add the carrots and onions and cook, stirring occasionally, until the onions start to brown, about 10 minutes. Remove the pan from heat.

3. Add the lobster bodies and shells and the remaining ingredients to the stockpot. Add enough water to cover the mixture, raise the heat to high, and bring to a boil. Reduce the heat and simmer the stock for at least 2 hours, occasionally skimming to remove any impurities that rise to the surface.

4. When the flavor of the stock has developed to your liking, strain it through a fine-mesh sieve or a colander lined with cheesecloth. Place the stock in the refrigerator and chill until it is completely cool.

5. Remove the fat layer from the top of the cooled stock. The stock will keep in the refrigerator for 3 to 5 days and in the freezer for up to 3 months.

Vegetable Stock

YIELD: 6 CUPS / ACTIVE TIME: 20 MINUTES / TOTAL TIME: 3 HOURS

2 TABLESPOONS EXTRA-VIRGIN OLIVE OIL

2 LARGE LEEKS, TRIMMED AND RINSED WELL

2 LARGE CARROTS, PEELED AND SLICED

2 CELERY STALKS, SLICED

2 LARGE YELLOW ONIONS, SLICED

3 GARLIC CLOVES, UNPEELED BUT SMASHED

2 SPRIGS OF FRESH PARSLEY

2 SPRIGS OF FRESH THYME

1 BAY LEAF

8 CUPS WATER

½ TEASPOON BLACK PEPPERCORNS

SALT, TO TASTE

1. Place the olive oil and vegetables in a stockpot and cook over low heat until the liquid they release has evaporated. This will allow the flavor of the vegetables to become concentrated.

2. Add the garlic, parsley, thyme, bay leaf, water, peppercorns, and salt. Raise the heat to high and bring to a boil. Reduce the heat so that the stock simmers and cook for 2 hours, while skimming to remove any impurities that float to the surface.

3. Strain through a fine sieve, let the stock cool slightly, and place in the refrigerator, uncovered, to chill. Remove the fat layer and cover the stock. The stock will keep in the refrigerator for 3 to 5 days and in the freezer for up to 3 months.

Beef Stock

YIELD: 8 CUPS / ACTIVE TIME: 20 MINUTES / TOTAL TIME: 6 HOURS

7 LBS. BEEF BONES, RINSED

4 CUPS CHOPPED YELLOW ONIONS

2 CUPS CHOPPED CARROTS

2 CUPS CHOPPED CELERY

3 GARLIC CLOVES, CRUSHED

3 SPRIGS OF FRESH THYME

1 TEASPOON BLACK PEPPERCORNS

1 BAY LEAF

1. Place the beef bones in a stockpot and cover them with cold water. Bring to a simmer over medium-high heat and use a ladle to skim off any impurities that rise to the surface.

2. Add the remaining ingredients, reduce the heat to low, and simmer for 5 hours, occasionally skimming the stock to remove any impurities that rise to the surface.

3. Strain the stock, let it cool slightly, and transfer it to the refrigerator. Leave the stock uncovered and let it cool completely. Remove the layer of fat and cover. The stock will keep in the refrigerator for 3 to 5 days and in the freezer for up to 3 months.

Confit Tuna

YIELD: 4 SERVINGS / **ACTIVE TIME:** 10 MINUTES / **TOTAL TIME:** 30 MINUTES

½ LB. YELLOWFIN TUNA STEAK

1 CUP EXTRA-VIRGIN OLIVE OIL, PLUS MORE AS NEEDED

ZEST OF 1 ORANGE

1 GARLIC CLOVE

1 BAY LEAF

5 BLACK PEPPERCORNS

SLICES OF BAGUETTE, TOASTED, FOR SERVING

1. Place the tuna and olive oil in a small saucepan. The tuna needs to be completely covered by the olive oil; if it is not, add more olive oil as needed.

2. Add the orange zest, garlic, bay leaf, and peppercorns and warm the mixture over low heat. Cook until the internal temperature of the tuna is 135°F.

3. Remove the tuna from the oil and let it cool completely. Serve with toasted slices of baguette or chill in the refrigerator.

Bouquet Garni

YIELD: 1 BOUQUET / **ACTIVE TIME:** 2 MINUTES / **TOTAL TIME:** 2 MINUTES

2 BAY LEAVES

3 SPRIGS OF FRESH THYME

3 SPRIGS OF FRESH PARSLEY

1. Cut a 2-inch section of kitchen twine. Tie one side of the twine around the herbs and knot it tightly.

2. To use, attach the other end of the twine to one of the pot's handles and slip the herbs into the broth. Remove before serving.

Dukkah

YIELD: 1½ CUPS / **ACTIVE TIME:** 1 HOUR / **TOTAL TIME:** 1 HOUR

1 HEAD OF GARLIC

1 LARGE SHALLOT

¾ CUP EXTRA-VIRGIN OLIVE OIL

1 CUP SHELLED RAW PISTACHIOS

2 TABLESPOONS CORIANDER SEEDS

2 TABLESPOONS BLACK SESAME SEEDS

2 TABLESPOONS WHITE SESAME SEEDS

1½ TABLESPOONS PINK PEPPERCORNS

1 TABLESPOON MALDON SEA SALT

2 TEASPOONS SUMAC

2 TEASPOONS ALEPPO PEPPER

1½ TABLESPOONS DRIED MINT

1½ TABLESPOONS DRIED THYME

1. Preheat the oven to 325°F.

2. Peel the garlic cloves, trim the ends of each clove, and slice them as thinly and evenly as you can. Trim the ends of the shallot, halve it lengthwise, and slice it as thin as possible.

3. Place the garlic and shallot in a cold skillet, add the olive oil, and cook over low heat until they are a deep, even golden brown, 30 to 40 minutes, stirring occasionally to make sure the heat circulates evenly. This long cook time allows them to build flavor without also becoming bitter, so don't try to speed it up with a higher flame.

4. While the garlic and shallot are cooking, place the pistachios on a baking sheet, place them in the oven, and roast until fragrant, 6 to 7 minutes. Remove the pistachios from the oven and let them cool.

5. Line a plate with paper towels. Strain the garlic and shallot over a clean bowl and spread them on the plate in an even layer. Wipe out the skillet and fill it with the reserved oil. Add the coriander seeds, black sesame seeds, and white sesame seeds. Toast, over low heat, until the seeds are crunchy and aromatic, about 8 minutes. Drain and place the seeds on the same plate as the shallot and garlic.

6. Place the shallot, garlic, and seeds in a large resealable plastic bag with the pistachios and the remaining ingredients. Pound the mixture with a rolling pin or mallet until everything is roughly crushed. Use immediately or store in an airtight container in the refrigerator.

Lemon Crème

YIELD: 4 SERVINGS / **ACTIVE TIME:** 20 MINUTES / **TOTAL TIME:** 20 MINUTES

ZEST AND JUICE OF 2
LEMONS

½ CUP SUGAR

3 EGGS

6 TABLESPOONS UNSALTED
BUTTER

PINCH OF FINE SEA SALT

1. Place the lemon zest, lemon juice, and half of the sugar in a small saucepan and bring the mixture to a boil, stirring to dissolve the sugar. Remove the pan from heat.

2. Place the remaining sugar and the eggs in a small mixing bowl and whisk until combined. While whisking vigorously, slowly pour the hot syrup into the mixture. Place the tempered mixture in the saucepan, place it over low heat, and stir until it starts to thicken, about 5 minutes.

3. Remove the pan from heat and incorporate the butter 1 tablespoon at a time. When all of the butter has been incorporated, stir in the salt and then pour the crème into a bowl. Place plastic wrap directly on the surface to prevent a skin from forming and chill the crème in the refrigerator until ready to use.

Lemon Glaze

YIELD: 4 SERVINGS / **ACTIVE TIME:** 5 MINUTES / **TOTAL TIME:** 5 MINUTES

3 TABLESPOONS FRESH
LEMON JUICE

2 TABLESPOONS FULL-FAT
GREEK YOGURT

2 CUPS CONFECTIONERS'
SUGAR

SEEDS OF ½ VANILLA BEAN

1. Place all of the ingredients in a mixing bowl and whisk to combine.

Pasta Frolla

YIELD: 1 SHORT-CRUST PASTRY / **ACTIVE TIME:** 15 MINUTES / **TOTAL TIME:** 1 HOUR AND 15 MINUTES

4.2 OZ. SUGAR

5.4 OZ. UNSALTED BUTTER, SOFTENED

1 EGG

2 EGG YOLKS

ZEST OF 1 LEMON

10.6 OZ. ALL-PURPOSE FLOUR

PINCH OF BAKING POWDER

PINCH OF FINE SEA SALT

1. Place the sugar and butter in the work bowl of a stand mixer fitted with the paddle attachment and cream until the mixture is light and fluffy.

2. Add the egg, egg yolks, and lemon zest and beat until incorporated.

3. Sift the flour, baking powder, and salt into the work bowl and beat until the dough just comes together.

4. Form the dough into a ball, cover it with plastic wrap, and chill it in the refrigerator for 1 hour before using.

Pasta Frolla Napoletana

YIELD: 1 SHORT-CRUST PASTRY / **ACTIVE TIME:** 15 MINUTES / **TOTAL TIME:** 1 HOUR AND 15 MINUTES

3½ OZ. SUGAR

1¾ OZ. LARD

1¾ OZ. UNSALTED BUTTER

1¾ OZ. WATER

1 TEASPOON PURE VANILLA EXTRACT

ZEST OF ½ LEMON

8.8 OZ. ALL-PURPOSE FLOUR

PINCH OF BAKER'S AMMONIA

PINCH OF FINE SEA SALT

1. Place the sugar, lard, and butter in the work bowl of a stand mixer fitted with the paddle attachment and cream until the mixture is light and fluffy.

2. Add the water, vanilla, and lemon zest and beat until incorporated.

3. Sift the flour, baker's ammonia, and salt into the work bowl and beat until the dough just comes together.

4. Form the dough into a ball, cover it with plastic wrap, and chill it in the refrigerator for 1 hour before using.

Pasta Frolla al Lardo

YIELD: 1 SHORT-CRUST PASTRY / **ACTIVE TIME:** 15 MINUTES / **TOTAL TIME:** 1 HOUR AND 15 MINUTES

8.8 OZ. SUGAR

8.8 OZ. LARD

3 SMALL EGGS

ZEST OF 1 LEMON

17.6 OZ. ALL-PURPOSE FLOUR

½ TEASPOON BAKING POWDER

PINCH OF FINE SEA SALT

1. Place the sugar and lard in the work bowl of a stand mixer fitted with the paddle attachment and cream until the mixture is light and fluffy.

2. Add the eggs and lemon zest and beat until incorporated.

3. Sift the flour, baking powder, and salt into the work bowl and beat until the dough just comes together.

4. Form the dough into a ball, cover it with plastic wrap, and chill it in the refrigerator for 1 hour before using.

Roasted Vanilla Cherries

YIELD: 4 SERVINGS / **ACTIVE TIME:** 25 MINUTES / **TOTAL TIME:** 24 HOURS

24 CHERRIES

PINCH OF FINE SEA SALT

¼ CUP BRANDY

SEEDS OF ½ VANILLA BEAN OR 1 TEASPOON PURE VANILLA EXTRACT

2 TABLESPOONS DEMERARA SUGAR

1. Place the cherries, salt, brandy, and vanilla in a bowl and let the mixture marinate at room temperature overnight.

2. Preheat the oven to 400°F. Strain the cherries, reserve the liquid, and place the cherries on a baking sheet. Sprinkle the sugar over the cherries, place them in the oven, and roast until the sugar starts to caramelize, 8 to 10 minutes, making sure that the sugar does not burn.

3. Remove the cherries from the oven, pour the reserved liquid over them, and place them back in the oven. Roast for another 5 minutes, remove the cherries from the oven, and let them cool. When they are cool enough to handle, remove the pits from the cherries. Chill the cherries in the refrigerator until ready to use.

Blueberry Compote

YIELD: 4 SERVINGS / **ACTIVE TIME:** 10 MINUTES / **TOTAL TIME:** 30 MINUTES

1½ CUPS FROZEN BLUEBERRIES, THAWED

2 TABLESPOONS SUGAR

JUICE OF 1 ORANGE

2 CINNAMON STICKS

1 STAR ANISE POD

1. Place all of the ingredients in a small saucepan and cook over low heat, stirring occasionally, until the mixture has thickened and most of the liquid has evaporated, 5 to 7 minutes.

2. Remove the cinnamon sticks and star anise and let the compote cool.

3. When the compote has cooled, use immediately or store in the refrigerator until needed.

Granola

YIELD: 3 CUPS / **ACTIVE TIME:** 10 MINUTES / **TOTAL TIME:** 45 MINUTES

2 CUPS ROLLED OATS

¼ CUP PURE MAPLE SYRUP

1 CUP PECAN HALVES

2 TEASPOONS KOSHER SALT

1 TEASPOON CINNAMON

⅔ CUP DRIED CRANBERRIES

1. Preheat the oven to 350°F and line a baking sheet with a Silpat mat. Place all of the ingredients in a mixing bowl and toss to combine.

2. Spread the mixture on the baking sheet in an even layer. Place it in the oven and bake until browned and fragrant, about 20 minutes. Remove from the oven and let the granola cool completely before serving.

Chocolate Glaze

YIELD: 1 CUP / **ACTIVE TIME:** 10 MINUTES / **TOTAL TIME:** 25 MINUTES

6 TABLESPOONS UNSWEETENED COCONUT MILK, STIRRED WELL

2 TEASPOONS LIGHT CORN SYRUP

4 OZ. DARK CHOCOLATE, FINELY CHOPPED

1. Place the coconut milk and corn syrup in a small saucepan and bring to a simmer over medium heat, stirring until combined.

2. Remove the pan from heat and add the chocolate. Let the mixture stand for 1 minute. Stir until the chocolate has melted and the glaze is smooth.

3. Let the glaze stand, stirring occasionally, until it has thickened slightly but is still pourable.

Pisto

YIELD: ¼ CUP / **ACTIVE TIME:** 5 MINUTES / **TOTAL TIME:** 5 MINUTES

4 TEASPOONS CINNAMON

2 TEASPOONS CORIANDER

2 TEASPOONS BLACK PEPPER

2 TEASPOONS FRESHLY GRATED NUTMEG

1 TEASPOON GROUND CLOVES

½ TEASPOON GROUND STAR ANISE

1. Place all of the ingredients in a bowl, stir to combine, and use immediately or store in an airtight container.

Pistachio Gremolata

YIELD: 2 CUPS / **ACTIVE TIME:** 5 MINUTES / **TOTAL TIME:** 5 MINUTES

1½ CUPS FRESH MINT LEAVES

½ CUP SHELLED, ROASTED, AND SALTED PISTACHIOS

2 GARLIC CLOVES

2 TEASPOONS LEMON ZEST

¼ TEASPOON KOSHER SALT

¼ TEASPOON BLACK PEPPER

2 TABLESPOONS EXTRA-VIRGIN OLIVE OIL

1. Place the mint, pistachios, garlic, lemon zest, salt, and pepper in a food processor and pulse until the mixture is combined and coarsely chopped.

2. Add the olive oil in a slow stream and pulse until the mixture is just combined, making sure not to overprocess the gremolata—you want it to have some texture. Use as desired.

Spicy Honey Mayonnaise

YIELD: ½ CUP / **ACTIVE TIME:** 5 MINUTES / **TOTAL TIME:** 15 MINUTES

½ CUP MAYONNAISE

2 TABLESPOONS HONEY

1 TABLESPOON SRIRACHA

1. Place all of the ingredients in a small bowl and stir until thoroughly combined.

2. Chill the mayonnaise in the refrigerator for 10 minutes before serving.

Tahini Mayonnaise

YIELD: 1 CUP / **ACTIVE TIME:** 10 MINUTES / **TOTAL TIME:** 10 MINUTES

2 EGG YOLKS

¼ CUP TAHINI PASTE

3 TABLESPOONS FRESH LEMON JUICE

1 TABLESPOON WATER

1 TEASPOON KOSHER SALT

½ CUP EXTRA-VIRGIN OLIVE OIL

1. Place the egg yolks, tahini, lemon juice, water, and salt in a food processor and blitz until they are combined.

2. With the food processor running, gradually add the olive oil in a slow stream. Blitz until the mayonnaise is extremely thick and velvety. Be thorough in this step; a tight emulsion is the difference between having all of those flavors hit you in equal measure or having them fall flat.

3. Use the mayonnaise immediately or store it in the refrigerator, where it will keep for a few days.

Passion Fruit Emulsion

YIELD: 1 CUP / **ACTIVE TIME:** 5 MINUTES / **TOTAL TIME:** 5 MINUTES

1 SHALLOT, CHOPPED

1 CUP PASSION FRUIT PUREE

1 CUP CANOLA OIL

1. Place the shallot and passion fruit puree in a blender and puree on medium until smooth.

2. Reduce the speed to low and slowly drizzle in the canola oil until it has emulsified. Use immediately or store in the refrigerator.

Meyer Lemon Marmalade

YIELD: 2 CUPS / **ACTIVE TIME:** 45 MINUTES / **TOTAL TIME:** 2 HOURS

5 MEYER LEMONS

2 FRESNO CHILE PEPPERS, STEMS AND SEEDS REMOVED, DICED

4 GARLIC CLOVES, MINCED

1 TABLESPOON KOSHER SALT

1 TEASPOON BLACK PEPPER

1 CUP WATER

1 CUP WHITE VINEGAR

2 CUPS SUGAR

1. Cut the lemons, rind and all, into ½-inch chunks.

2. Place all of the ingredients in a saucepan and bring the mixture to a boil over high heat. Reduce the heat to medium-high and simmer, stirring occasionally, until everything has softened, about 45 minutes.

3. raise the heat back to high and cook until the mixture reaches 220°F.

4. Remove the pan from heat and let it cool completely. Use immediately or store in the refrigerator.

Tahini & Yogurt Sauce

YIELD: 1 CUP / **ACTIVE TIME:** 5 MINUTES / **TOTAL TIME:** 5 MINUTES

¾ CUP FULL-FAT GREEK YOGURT

1 GARLIC CLOVE, MINCED

2 TABLESPOONS TAHINI PASTE

JUICE OF 1 LEMON

½ TEASPOON CUMIN

SALT AND PEPPER, TO TASTE

1 TABLESPOON BLACK SESAME SEEDS

1 TABLESPOON EXTRA-VIRGIN OLIVE OIL

1. Place the yogurt, garlic, tahini, lemon juice, and cumin in a small bowl and whisk to combine.

2. Season the sauce with salt and pepper, add the sesame seeds and olive oil, and whisk until incorporated. Use immediately or store in the refrigerator until needed.

Romesco Sauce

YIELD: 2 CUPS / **ACTIVE TIME:** 5 MINUTES / **TOTAL TIME:** 20 MINUTES

¾ CUP DAY-OLD BREAD PIECES (½-INCH CUBES), CRUST REMOVED

2 TABLESPOONS SLIVERED ALMONDS

¾ CUP ROASTED RED PEPPERS IN OLIVE OIL, DRAINED AND CHOPPED

1 PLUM TOMATO, SEEDED AND CHOPPED

1 TABLESPOON EXTRA-VIRGIN OLIVE OIL

2 TEASPOONS RED WINE VINEGAR

1 GARLIC CLOVE, MINCED

2 PINCHES OF CAYENNE PEPPER

SALT AND PEPPER, TO TASTE

1. Preheat the oven to 350°F. Place the bread and almonds on separate sections of a baking sheet, place the pan in the oven, and toast until the bread and almonds are golden brown, 5 to 7 minutes. Remove from the oven and let them cool.

2. Place the toasted bread and almonds in a food processor and pulse until they are finely ground.

3. Add the peppers and pulse until combined. Add the remaining ingredients and blitz until smooth.

4. Taste, adjust the seasoning as necessary, and use as desired.

Champagne Vinaigrette

YIELD: 2½ CUPS / **ACTIVE TIME:** 5 MINUTES / **TOTAL TIME:** 5 MINUTES

¼ CUP CHAMPAGNE VINEGAR

¼ CUP WATER

2 TABLESPOONS DIJON MUSTARD

½ TEASPOON KOSHER SALT

½ TEASPOON BLACK PEPPER

2 TABLESPOONS HONEY

1½ CUPS EXTRA-VIRGIN OLIVE OIL

1. Place all of the ingredients, except for the olive oil, in a bowl and whisk until well combined.

2. While whisking, add the oil in a slow stream until it has emulsified. Use immediately or store in the refrigerator.

Pomegranate Vinaigrette

YIELD: 4 CUPS / **ACTIVE TIME:** 30 MINUTES / **TOTAL TIME:** 30 MINUTES

2 CUPS POMEGRANATE JUICE

½ CUP RED WINE VINEGAR

2 TABLESPOONS DIJON MUSTARD

2 TABLESPOONS HONEY

1 TABLESPOON ZA'ATAR (SEE PAGE 501)

2 TEASPOONS SUMAC

2 TABLESPOONS KOSHER SALT

1 TABLESPOON BLACK PEPPER

1 TABLESPOON CHOPPED FRESH OREGANO

1 TABLESPOON CHOPPED FRESH BASIL

1 TABLESPOON CHOPPED FRESH PARSLEY

1 TABLESPOON CHOPPED FRESH MINT

3 CUPS EXTRA-VIRGIN OLIVE OIL

1. Place the pomegranate juice in a small saucepan and bring it to a boil over medium-high heat. Boil until it has reduced to ¼ cup. Remove the pan from heat and let it cool.

2. Place the pomegranate reduction and the remaining ingredients, except for the olive oil, in a blender and puree until smooth.

3. With the blender on, drizzle in the oil. Puree until it has emulsified. Use immediately or store in the refrigerator.

THE ENCYCLOPEDIA OF MEDITERRANEAN

Red Zhug

YIELD: 2½ CUPS / **ACTIVE TIME:** 10 MINUTES / **TOTAL TIME:** 10 MINUTES

4 FRESNO CHILE PEPPERS, STEMS AND SEEDS REMOVED, ROUGHLY CHOPPED

2 CUPS FRESH PARSLEY

1 ONION, QUARTERED

5 GARLIC CLOVES

JUICE OF 1 LEMON

1 TABLESPOON KOSHER SALT

1 TEASPOON CAYENNE PEPPER

1 TABLESPOON CUMIN

2 TABLESPOONS PAPRIKA

¾ CUP EXTRA-VIRGIN OLIVE OIL

1. Place the chiles, parsley, onion, garlic, and lemon juice in a food processor and pulse until combined.

2. Add the salt, cayenne, cumin, and paprika and, with the food processor on high, slowly pour in the olive oil. Blitz until the mixture is emulsified, adding water as needed to get the desired texture. Use immediately or store in the refrigerator.

Lemony Yogurt Sauce

YIELD: 2½ CUPS / **ACTIVE TIME:** 5 MINUTES / **TOTAL TIME:** 5 MINUTES

6 TABLESPOONS FRESH LEMON JUICE

1 GARLIC CLOVE, GRATED

1 TEASPOON KOSHER SALT

1 TEASPOON BLACK PEPPER

2 CUPS FULL-FAT GREEK YOGURT

1. Place all of the ingredients in a mixing bowl and stir until thoroughly combined. Use immediately or store in the refrigerator.

Green Zhug

YIELD: 2½ CUPS / **ACTIVE TIME:** 10 MINUTES / **TOTAL TIME:** 10 MINUTES

4 JALAPEÑO CHILE PEPPERS, STEMS AND SEEDS REMOVED, ROUGHLY CHOPPED

2 CUPS FRESH PARSLEY

¼ CUP FRESH CILANTRO

6 FRESH MINT LEAVES

1 ONION, QUARTERED

5 GARLIC CLOVES

JUICE OF 1 LEMON

1 TABLESPOON KOSHER SALT

½ CUP EXTRA-VIRGIN OLIVE OIL

1. Place the jalapeños, parsley, cilantro, mint, onion, garlic, and lemon juice in a food processor and pulse until combined.

2. Add the salt and, with the food processor on high, slowly pour in the olive oil. Blitz until the mixture is emulsified, adding water as needed to get the desired texture. Use immediately or store in the refrigerator.

Tahini Sauce

YIELD: ¾ CUP / **ACTIVE TIME:** 10 MINUTES / **TOTAL TIME:** 10 MINUTES

5 OZ. TAHINI PASTE

½ CUP WATER

3 GARLIC CLOVES

1 TEASPOON KOSHER SALT

JUICE OF 1 LEMON

PINCH OF CUMIN

1. Place the tahini and water in a food processor and pulse to combine. Let the mixture sit for 30 seconds.

2. Add the garlic, salt, lemon juice, and cumin. Blitz on high for 2 to 3 minutes, until the sauce is creamy and smooth. Use immediately or store in the refrigerator.

INTRODUCTION

Spanning 21 countries, three continents, and regions as disparate as North Africa, the Levant, Catalonia, Italy, and Provence, the Mediterranean is a region unlike any other—particularly when it comes to cuisine.

This book is a vibrant conversation between the many cultures and perspectives that inhabit the region. It celebrates what is unique to each, while also capturing their shared flair for using simple, straightforward methods to produce dynamic flavors. By leaning heavily upon the wonderful produce available in the region, this flair results in dishes that are as nutritious as they are delectable, a rare combination that has made "Mediterranean" a buzzword in wellness and weight-loss circles over the last decade.

Though this is not a dieting or wellness book, there is no avoiding the reality that emulating the Mediterranean approach to eating—a prevalence of vegetables, fruits, whole grains, seafood, and olive oil, only occasional encounters with poultry and beef, and a complete avoidance of seed oils and processed foods—will keep the pounds off, and help you feel better in general. At a time when a number of countries are having issues with obesity and chronic disease, Mediterranean cuisine's effortless ability to improve one's health has taken on an almost mystical air.

But the rush to brand the food of the Mediterranean as an antidote to modernity's ills paints an incomplete picture of the cuisine, excising the pasta and bread that make up a not-insignificant part of people's diets in the region. It is not that the people of the Mediterranean have unlocked the secrets of which foods to eat and which to ignore.

Instead, the mystique is tied to the fact that they continue to follow the principles that carried humanity for so long before capitalism and globalism began to reign—eat what is plentiful locally, and enjoy everything in moderation. Such an approach is not a magic bullet, but it will supply your diet with far more balance, significantly broaden your palate, and connect you with a way of life that has enriched the people of the Mediterranean for millennia.

One of the staples of the region's cuisine that many are already acquainted with is the mezze platter, a collection of delicious small bites that has ridden the contemporary love for tapas and small plates to worldwide popularity. A section with all of the elements you need to compose your own leads off the book, filled with nutritious, delectable bites and luscious dips and spreads. Once that course has been completed, a year's worth of mains follow, featuring everything from handmade pastas and light and quick weeknight dinners to sumptuous dishes that are suitable for a feast day. When the weather turns cold and something comforting is called for, the soups and stews in the next chapter are there. And to make sure your table always has the proper balance—aka plenty of vegetables—the penultimate chapter contains a staggering collection of plant-forward salads and side dishes. Finally, there's a collection of toothsome desserts that will soothe your sweet cravings when they inevitably arise.

As you'll soon see, wherever one finds themselves in their quest for better health or better food, the Mediterranean is the ultimate destination.

CONTENTS

Encyclopedia of Mediterranean

Copyright © 2024 by Cider Mill Press Book Publishers LLC. •
This is an officially licensed book by Cider Mill Press Book Publishers
LLC. • All rights reserved under the Pan-American and International Copyright
Conventions. • No part of this book may be reproduced in whole or in part, scanned,
photocopied, recorded, distributed in any printed or electronic form, or reproduced in
any manner whatsoever, or by any information storage and retrieval system now known or
hereafter invented, without express written permission of the publisher, except in the case of
brief quotations in critical articles and reviews. • The scanning, uploading, and distribution of
this book via the internet or via any other means without permission of the publisher is illegal and
punishable by law. Please support authors' rights, and do not participate in or encourage piracy of
copyrighted materials. • 13-Digit ISBN: 978-1-40034-463-5 • 10-Digit ISBN: 1-40034-463-8 • This
book may be ordered by mail from the publisher. Please include $5.99 for postage and handling.
Please support your local bookseller first! • Books published by Cider Mill Press Book Publishers are
available at special discounts for bulk purchases in the United States by corporations, institutions,
and other organizations. For more information, please contact the publisher. • Cider Mill Press
Book Publishers • "Where good books are ready for press" • 501 Nelson Place • Nashville,
Tennessee 37214 • cidermillpress.com • Typography: Hansief, Freight Sans, Freight Serif
• Image Credits: Pages 4–5, 6, 9, 12, 35, 44–45, 48–49, 52–53, 68–69, 110–111, 113, 126–
127, 135, 145, 150–151, 166–167, 175, 187, 189, 197, 204–205, 209, 213, 217, 223,
245, 254–255, 258–259, 299, 302–303, 323, 342–343, 372–373, 438–439,
441, 452–453, 461, 467, 472–473, 479, and 511 used under official
license from Shutterstock. All other photos courtesy of Cider
Mill Press. • Printed in Malaysia • 24 25 26 27 28
COS 5 4 3 2 1 • First Edition

THE ENCYCLOPEDIA OF

MEDITERRANEAN

OVER 350 RECIPES FROM THE CENTER OF THE CULINARY WORLD

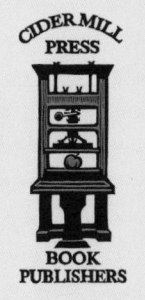

CIDER MILL PRESS

BOOK PUBLISHERS

THE ENCYCLOPEDIA OF

MEDITERRANEAN

Za'atar

YIELD: 1½ CUPS / **ACTIVE TIME:** 5 MINUTES / **TOTAL TIME:** 5 MINUTES

1 TABLESPOON CUMIN

1 TABLESPOON SUMAC

1 TABLESPOON DRIED THYME

2 TEASPOONS HEMP SEEDS

2 TEASPOONS CRUSHED TOASTED SUNFLOWER SEEDS

2 TABLESPOONS SESAME SEEDS

2 TABLESPOONS KOSHER SALT

1 TABLESPOON BLACK PEPPER

2 TABLESPOONS CHOPPED FRESH OREGANO

2 TABLESPOONS CHOPPED FRESH BASIL

2 TABLESPOONS CHOPPED FRESH PARSLEY

1 TABLESPOON GARLIC POWDER

1 TABLESPOON ONION POWDER

1. Place all of the ingredients in a large bowl and stir until thoroughly combined. Use immediately or store in an airtight container.

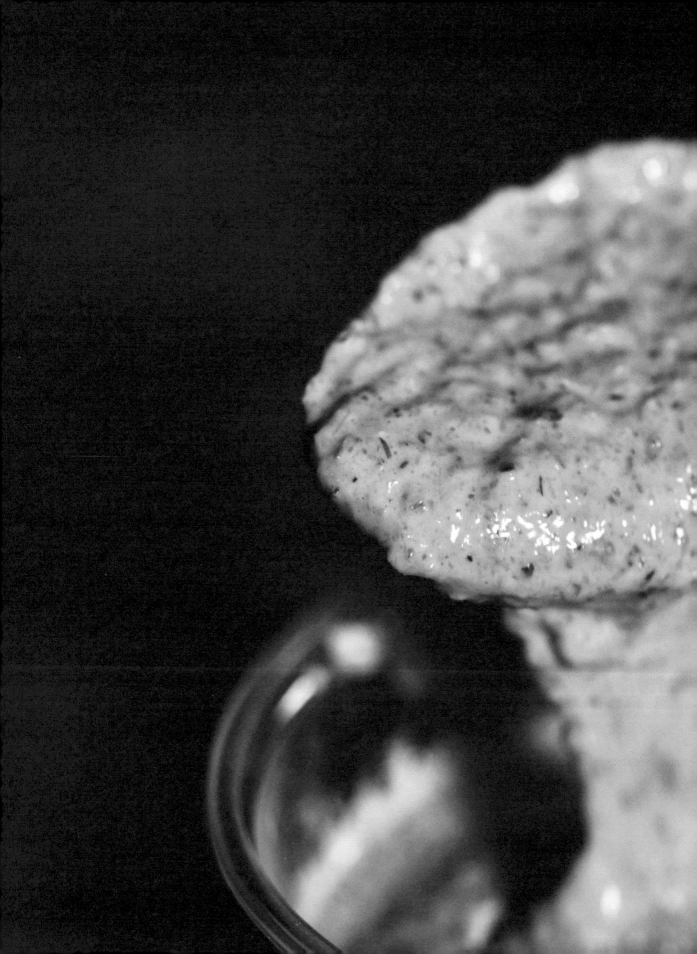

Green Zhug
SEE PAGE 500

Tomato Sauce

YIELD: 4 CUPS / **ACTIVE TIME:** 15 MINUTES / **TOTAL TIME:** 45 MINUTES

2 TABLESPOONS AVOCADO
OIL

1 LARGE GARLIC CLOVE,
CHOPPED

1 TEASPOON GRATED FRESH
GINGER

1 CINNAMON STICK

1 (28 OZ.) CAN OF
CHOPPED SAN MARZANO
TOMATOES, WITH THEIR
LIQUID

½ TEASPOON CUMIN

¼ TEASPOON CORIANDER

⅛ TEASPOON CAYENNE
PEPPER

1. Place the avocado oil in a large saucepan and warm it over medium heat. Add the garlic and ginger and cook, stirring frequently, until fragrant, about 1 minute.

2. Add the cinnamon stick and cook for 30 seconds. Add the remaining ingredients and bring the sauce to a boil.

3. Reduce the heat and simmer the sauce until the flavor has developed to your liking, about 30 minutes.

4. Remove the cinnamon stick from the sauce and use as desired.

Chermoula Sauce

YIELD: 5 CUPS / **ACTIVE TIME:** 5 MINUTES / **TOTAL TIME:** 10 MINUTES

1 TABLESPOON SAFFRON
THREADS

4 CUPS MAYONNAISE

1 TABLESPOON RAS EL
HANOUT (SEE OPPOSITE
PAGE)

1 TABLESPOON BERBERE
SEASONING

2 TABLESPOONS ZA'ATAR
(SEE PAGE 501)

1 TABLESPOON SUMAC

2 CUPS CHOPPED FRESH
HERBS (TARRAGON,
PARSLEY, CHIVES, AND
CILANTRO)

1 TABLESPOON DRIED
OREGANO

1 TABLESPOON KOSHER
SALT

1 TABLESPOON BLACK
PEPPER

1. Place the saffron in ¼ cup water and let it bloom. Remove the saffron from the water and reserve the liquid for another preparation (it's really good in a tomato sauce, for example)—using it in the sauce will make it too loose.

2. Place the saffron and the remaining ingredients in a large bowl and stir until thoroughly combined. Use immediately or transfer to an airtight container and store in the refrigerator.

Salsa Verde

YIELD: 1 CUP / **ACTIVE TIME:** 5 MINUTES / **TOTAL TIME:** 5 MINUTES

1 CUP FRESH PARSLEY

1 GARLIC CLOVE

1 TABLESPOON FRESH
LEMON JUICE

1 TABLESPOON CHOPPED
FRESH ROSEMARY

1 TEASPOON KOSHER SALT

1 STRIP OF LEMON ZEST

1 TABLESPOON CAPERS,
DRAINED

½ TEASPOON RED PEPPER
FLAKES BLACK PEPPER, TO
TASTE

¼ CUP EXTRA-VIRGIN OLIVE
OIL

1. Place all of the ingredients, except for the olive oil, in a food processor and blitz until it is nearly smooth, scraping down the work bowl as needed.

2. With the food processor running, slowly drizzle in the olive oil and blitz until it has emulsified.

3. If not using immediately, refrigerate and let the sauce come to room temperature before serving.

Ras el Hanout

YIELD: ½ CUP / **ACTIVE TIME:** 5 MINUTES / **TOTAL TIME:** 5 MINUTES

1 TEASPOON TURMERIC

1 TEASPOON GROUND
GINGER

1 TEASPOON CUMIN

¾ TEASPOON CINNAMON

1 TEASPOON BLACK PEPPER

½ TEASPOON CORIANDER

½ TEASPOON CAYENNE
PEPPER

½ TEASPOON ALLSPICE

½ TEASPOON FRESHLY
GRATED NUTMEG

¼ TEASPOON GROUND
CLOVES

1 TEASPOON FINE SEA SALT

1. Place all of the ingredients in a bowl, stir to combine, and use immediately or store in an airtight container.

Chermoula Sauce
SEE PAGE 504

Fig Vinaigrette

YIELD: 1½ CUPS / **ACTIVE TIME:** 5 MINUTES / **TOTAL TIME:** 5 MINUTES

3 TABLESPOONS BALSAMIC VINEGAR

1 TABLESPOON WATER

1 FIG JAM

1 TABLESPOON DIJON MUSTARD

1 SHALLOT, MINCED

½ CUP EXTRA-VIRGIN OLIVE OIL

½ CUP DICED FIGS

2 TABLESPOONS CHOPPED FRESH CHIVES

SALT AND PEPPER, TO TASTE

1. Place the vinegar, water, jam, mustard, and shallot in a mixing bowl and whisk to combine.

2. While whisking continually, add the olive oil in a slow, steady stream until it has emulsified.

3. Add the figs and chives, whisk to incorporate, and season the vinaigrette with salt and pepper. Use immediately or store in the refrigerator until needed.

Balsamic Glaze

YIELD: ½ CUP / **ACTIVE TIME:** 10 MINUTES / **TOTAL TIME:** 25 MINUTES

1 CUP BALSAMIC VINEGAR

¼ CUP BROWN SUGAR

1. Place the vinegar and sugar in a small saucepan and bring the mixture to a boil.

2. Reduce the heat to medium-low and simmer for 8 to 10 minutes, stirring frequently, until the mixture has thickened.

3. Remove the pan from heat and let the glaze cool for 15 minutes before using.

Toum

YIELD: 1½ CUPS / **ACTIVE TIME:** 10 MINUTES / **TOTAL TIME:** 40 MINUTES

1 CUP AVOCADO OIL

⅓ CUP GARLIC CLOVES

2 TABLESPOONS FRESH LEMON JUICE

2 TABLESPOONS ICE WATER

SALT, TO TASTE

1. Place the avocado oil in the freezer for 30 minutes. This will help the sauce emulsify.

2. Place the garlic, lemon juice, ¼ cup of the chilled avocado oil, and 1 tablespoon of the ice water in a food processor and pulse until the mixture is smooth. With the food processor running, slowly drizzle in another ½ cup of the avocado oil.

3. Scrape down the work bowl and slowly drizzle in the remaining avocado oil with the food processor running, until the mixture has emulsified and comes together as a thick sauce—it should cling to a spoon.

4. Add the remaining ice water, season the toum with salt, and pulse to incorporate. This whole process will take 8 to 10 minutes, so remain patient. Use immediately or store in the refrigerator.

Skordalia

YIELD: 4 CUPS / **ACTIVE TIME:** 25 MINUTES / **TOTAL TIME:** 35 MINUTES

2 CUPS PEELED AND CHOPPED YELLOW POTATOES (½-INCH CUBES)

4 GARLIC CLOVES, GRATED OR MASHED

2 TABLESPOONS RED WINE VINEGAR

1 CUP DAY-OLD BREAD PIECES

½ CUP WARM WATER (105°F)

2 TABLESPOONS EXTRA-VIRGIN OLIVE OIL

3 TABLESPOONS FULL-FAT GREEK YOGURT

SALT AND PEPPER, TO TASTE

1. Bring water to a boil in a medium saucepan. Add the potatoes, reduce the heat, and simmer the potatoes until they are fork-tender, 15 to 20 minutes. Drain the potatoes and let them cool until they have stopped steaming.

2. Place the garlic, vinegar, bread, and water in a mixing bowl, stir to combine, and let the mixture sit for 5 minutes.

3. Using a fork, mash the bread mixture until it is smooth. Use a potato ricer or a fork to mash the potatoes, add them to the bowl, and stir until the mixture is smooth.

4. Stir in the olive oil and yogurt, season the sauce with salt and pepper, and use as desired.

Three-Pepper Harissa Sauce

YIELD: 1 CUP / **ACTIVE TIME:** 10 MINUTES / **TOTAL TIME:** 1 HOUR

3 OZ. GUAJILLO CHILE PEPPERS, STEMS AND SEEDS REMOVED, TORN

1 OZ. DRIED CHIPOTLE CHILE PEPPERS, STEMS AND SEEDS REMOVED, TORN

1 TABLESPOON NIGELLA SEEDS

1 TEASPOON CORIANDER SEEDS

2 GARLIC CLOVES

1 TABLESPOON CUMIN

1 TEASPOON KOSHER SALT

½ TEASPOON ALEPPO PEPPER

½ CUP EXTRA-VIRGIN OLIVE OIL

2 TABLESPOONS WHITE WINE VINEGAR

1. Place the guajillo and chipotle chiles in a large heatproof bowl and cover them with boiling water. Let the chiles soak until they have softened, 40 to 45 minutes.

2. Drain the chiles and set them aside.

3. Grind the nigella seeds and coriander seeds into a powder using a spice mill or a mortar and pestle. Transfer the powder to a food processor and add the garlic, cumin, salt, and Aleppo pepper. Pulse until the garlic is very finely chopped.

4. Add the chiles and pulse until they are chopped.

5. Add the olive oil and vinegar and pulse until the sauce is a chunky paste.

Pesto

YIELD: 2 CUPS / **ACTIVE TIME:** 10 MINUTES / **TOTAL TIME:** 10 MINUTES

2 CUPS PACKED FRESH BASIL LEAVES

1 CUP PACKED BABY SPINACH

2 CUPS GRATED PARMESAN CHEESE

¼ CUP PINE NUTS

1 GARLIC CLOVE

2 TEASPOONS FRESH LEMON JUICE

SALT AND PEPPER, TO TASTE

½ CUP EXTRA-VIRGIN OLIVE OIL

1. Place all of the ingredients, except for the olive oil, in a food processor and pulse until pureed.

2. Transfer the puree to a mixing bowl. While whisking, add the olive oil in a slow stream until it is emulsified. Use immediately or store in the refrigerator.

Pistachio & Raisin Sauce

YIELD: 1 CUP / **ACTIVE TIME:** 5 MINUTES / **TOTAL TIME:** 5 MINUTES

2 SHALLOTS, CHOPPED

⅓ CUP CHOPPED FRESH PARSLEY

½ CUP ORANGE JUICE

⅓ CUP RAISINS

¼ CUP SHELLED PISTACHIOS, TOASTED

½ TEASPOON CINNAMON

1 TABLESPOON WHITE WINE VINEGAR

2 TABLESPOONS EXTRA-VIRGIN OLIVE OIL

SALT AND PEPPER, TO TASTE

1. Place the shallots, parsley, orange juice, raisins, pistachios, cinnamon, and vinegar in a food processor and blitz until the mixture is a thick paste.

2. With the food processor running, add the olive oil in a slow stream and blitz until it has emulsified. Season the sauce with salt and pepper and use immediately or store in the refrigerator.

Eggplant & Pine Nut Ragout

YIELD: 2 CUPS / **ACTIVE TIME:** 20 MINUTES / **TOTAL TIME:** 40 MINUTES

1 TABLESPOON EXTRA-VIRGIN OLIVE OIL

1 EGGPLANT, TRIMMED AND CHOPPED (¾-INCH CUBES)

½ TEASPOON RAS EL HANOUT (SEE PAGE 505)

1 TABLESPOON RAISINS

2 TABLESPOONS PINE NUTS, TOASTED

1 TEASPOON LEMON ZEST

SALT AND PEPPER, TO TASTE

1. Place the olive oil in a large saucepan and warm it over medium heat. Add the eggplant, cover the pan, and cook the eggplant, stirring occasionally, for 5 minutes. Remove the cover and cook, stirring occasionally, until the eggplant is browned, about 10 minutes.

2. Stir in the remaining ingredients and cook, stirring occasionally, until the eggplant has collapsed and the flavor has developed to your liking, 10 to 15 minutes. Use immediately or store in the refrigerator.

Hot Sauce, Yemeni Style

YIELD: 8 CUPS / **ACTIVE TIME:** 45 MINUTES / **TOTAL TIME:** 2 HOURS

8 CUPS WHITE VINEGAR

4 FRESNO CHILE PEPPERS, STEMS REMOVED

1 BUNCH OF FRESH CILANTRO, CHOPPED

½ WHITE ONION, CHOPPED

4 GARLIC CLOVES

1 TEASPOON CUMIN

2 TEASPOONS KOSHER SALT

2 TABLESPOONS RENDERED CHICKEN FAT

1. Place the vinegar, chiles, cilantro, onion, garlic, cumin, and salt in a saucepan and bring the mixture to a boil over high heat. Reduce the heat to medium and simmer the mixture, stirring occasionally, for 45 minutes to 1 hour.

2. Remove the pan from heat and let the mixture cool.

3. Place the mixture in a food processor or blender and pulse until the solids are finely chopped and it is well combined.

4. Strain the liquid into a bowl or mason jar and discard the solids.

5. Place the chicken fat in a small saucepan and warm it over low heat.

6. Add the chicken fat to the sauce and stir until it has a velvety texture. Use immediately or store in the refrigerator.

Spiced Yogurt

YIELD: 1¼ CUPS / **ACTIVE TIME:** 5 MINUTES / **TOTAL TIME:** 5 MINUTES

1 CUP FULL-FAT GREEK YOGURT

¼ CUP GREEN ZHUG (SEE PAGE 500)

1 TEASPOON FRESH LEMON JUICE

2 GARLIC CLOVES, MINCED

SALT AND PEPPER, TO TASTE

1. Place all of the ingredients in a mixing bowl and whisk until combined. Use immediately or store in the refrigerator.

Smoked Egg Aioli

YIELD: 1 CUP / **ACTIVE TIME:** 20 MINUTES / **TOTAL TIME:** 45 MINUTES

2 EGG YOLKS

½ CUP WOOD CHIPS

1 TABLESPOON WHITE VINEGAR

1 TEASPOON KOSHER SALT

1 CUP AVOCADO OIL

1. Place the yolks in a metal bowl and set the bowl in a roasting pan.

2. Place the wood chips in a cast-iron skillet and warm them over high heat. Remove the pan from heat, light the wood chips on fire, and place the skillet in the roasting pan beside the bowl. Cover the roasting pan with aluminum foil and allow the smoke to flavor the yolks for 20 minutes.

3. Place the yolks and vinegar in a bowl, gently break the yolks, and let the mixture sit for 5 minutes.

4. Add the salt to the egg yolk mixture. Slowly drizzle the avocado oil into the mixture while beating it with an electric mixer or immersion blender until it is thick and creamy. Use immediately or store in the refrigerator.

Roasted Garlic Aioli

YIELD: ½ CUP / **ACTIVE TIME:** 10 MINUTES / **TOTAL TIME:** 40 MINUTES

1 HEAD OF GARLIC

½ CUP EXTRA-VIRGIN OLIVE OIL, PLUS MORE AS NEEDED

SALT AND PEPPER, TO TASTE

1 EGG YOLK

1 TEASPOON FRESH LEMON JUICE

1. Preheat the oven to 350°F. Cut off the top ½ inch of the head of garlic. Place the remainder in a piece of aluminum foil, drizzle olive oil over it, and season it with salt.

2. Place the garlic in the oven and roast until the garlic cloves have softened and are caramelized, about 30 minutes. Remove from the oven, remove the cloves from the head of garlic, and squeeze the garlic out of their skins into a mixing bowl.

3. Add the egg yolk and lemon juice and whisk to combine. While whisking continually, add the olive oil in a slow stream. When all the oil has been emulsified, season the aioli with salt and pepper and serve.

Pizza Sauce

YIELD: 2 CUPS / **ACTIVE TIME:** 5 MINUTES / **TOTAL TIME:** 5 MINUTES

1 LB. PEELED WHOLE SAN MARZANO TOMATOES, WITH THEIR LIQUID, CRUSHED BY HAND

1½ TABLESPOONS EXTRA-VIRGIN OLIVE OIL

SALT, TO TASTE

DRIED OREGANO, TO TASTE

1. Place the tomatoes and their juices in a bowl, add the olive oil, and stir until it has been thoroughly incorporated.

2. Season the sauce with salt and oregano and stir to incorporate. If using within 2 hours, leave the sauce at room temperature. If storing in the refrigerator, where the sauce will keep for up to 3 days, return to room temperature before using.

Charred Scallion Sauce

YIELD: 1 CUP / **ACTIVE TIME:** 10 MINUTES / **TOTAL TIME:** 10 MINUTES

3 SCALLIONS, TRIMMED

2 GARLIC CLOVES, MINCED

2 BIRD'S EYE CHILE PEPPERS, STEMS AND SEEDS REMOVED, MINCED

¼ CUP CHOPPED FRESH CILANTRO

1 TABLESPOON GRATED FRESH GINGER

1 TABLESPOON SESAME OIL

½ CUP SOY SAUCE

1 TABLESPOON SAMBAL OELEK

2 TABLESPOONS FRESH LIME JUICE

1 TEASPOON SUGAR

1 TABLESPOON SESAME SEEDS

SALT AND PEPPER, TO TASTE

1. On a grill or over an open flame on a gas stove, char the scallions all over. Remove the charred scallions from heat and let them cool.

2. Slice the charred scallions, place them in a mixing bowl, and add the remaining ingredients. Stir to combine, taste the sauce, and adjust the seasoning as necessary. Use immediately or store in the refrigerator until needed.

Agristada Sauce

YIELD: 2 CUPS / **ACTIVE TIME:** 10 MINUTES / **TOTAL TIME:** 20 MINUTES

4 EGGS

2 CUPS WARM WATER

2 TABLESPOONS ALL-PURPOSE FLOUR

¼ CUP AVOCADO OIL

¼ CUP FRESH LEMON JUICE

½ TEASPOON KOSHER SALT

1. Place the eggs in a medium saucepan and whisk until scrambled. Set the eggs aside.

2. Place the warm water and flour in a mixing bowl and vigorously whisk the mixture until there are no visible lumps in it. Strain the mixture into the saucepan.

3. Add the avocado oil, lemon juice, and salt and warm the mixture over medium-low heat, stirring constantly with a wooden spoon. Cook until the sauce has thickened, 10 to 12 minutes.

4. When the sauce is just about to boil, remove the pan from heat, stir for another minute, and then strain the sauce into a bowl.

5. Taste, adjust the seasoning as necessary, and place plastic wrap directly on the surface of the sauce to prevent a skin from forming. Let the sauce cool to room temperature before serving or storing in the refrigerator.

Gremolata

YIELD: ½ CUP / **ACTIVE TIME:** 5 MINUTES / **TOTAL TIME:** 5 MINUTES

8 GARLIC CLOVES, MINCED

ZEST OF 8 LEMONS

¼ CUP CHOPPED FRESH PARSLEY

1. Place all of the ingredients in a bowl, stir to combine, and use immediately or store in the refrigerator.

Dijon Dressing

YIELD: 1 CUP / **ACTIVE TIME:** 5 MINUTES / **TOTAL TIME:** 5 MINUTES

JUICE OF 2 LEMONS

1 TABLESPOON MINCED SHALLOT

1 TABLESPOON CHOPPED FRESH BASIL

2 TEASPOONS FRESH THYME

2 TEASPOONS CHOPPED FRESH OREGANO

2 TEASPOONS DIJON MUSTARD

2 ANCHOVIES IN OLIVE OIL, DRAINED AND FINELY CHOPPED

2 TEASPOONS CAPERS, DRAINED AND CHOPPED

SALT AND PEPPER, TO TASTE

¾ CUP EXTRA-VIRGIN OLIVE OIL

1. Place all of the ingredients, except for the olive oil, in a food processor and blitz to combine.

2. With the food processor running, add the olive oil in a slow stream until it has emulsified. Use immediately or store in the refrigerator.

Pickled Applesauce

YIELD: 6 CUPS / **ACTIVE TIME:** 20 MINUTES / **TOTAL TIME:** 1 HOUR

3 LBS. GRANNY SMITH APPLES, PEELED AND SLICED

1 TEASPOON CINNAMON

PINCH OF GROUND CLOVES

½ CUP SUGAR

1½ CUPS WHITE VINEGAR

1. Place the ingredients in a large saucepan and bring to a boil over high heat.

2. Reduce the heat to medium-high and simmer until the liquid has reduced by one-third. Remove the pan from heat and let it cool to room temperature.

3. Place the mixture in a food processor and blitz on high until smooth, about 2 minutes. Serve immediately or store in the refrigerator.

Creamy Balsamic & Mushroom Sauce

YIELD: 2 CUPS / **ACTIVE TIME:** 30 MINUTES / **TOTAL TIME:** 30 MINUTES

4 TABLESPOONS UNSALTED BUTTER

2 CUPS SLICED MUSHROOMS

2 ONIONS, DICED

2 TEASPOONS TOMATO PASTE

1 CUP VEGETABLE STOCK (SEE PAGE 484)

1 CUP HEAVY CREAM

SALT AND PEPPER, TO TASTE

2 TEASPOONS BALSAMIC VINEGAR

2 TEASPOONS DRIED THYME

¼ CUP CHOPPED FRESH PARSLEY

2 TABLESPOONS CORNSTARCH

1. Place 2 tablespoons of the butter in a large skillet and melt it over medium heat. Add the mushrooms and cook, stirring one or two times, until browned all over, about 10 minutes. Remove the mushrooms from the pan and set them aside.

2. Place the remaining butter in the pan, add the onions, and cook, stirring occasionally, until they have softened, about 5 minutes. Add the tomato paste and cook, stirring continually, for 2 minutes.

3. Deglaze the pan with the stock and heavy cream, scraping up any browned bits from the bottom of the pan. Cook until the liquid has been reduced by half.

4. Add the mushrooms back to the pan and season the sauce with salt and pepper. Stir in the vinegar, thyme, and parsley and let the mixture simmer.

5. Place the cornstarch in a small bowl and add a splash of water. Whisk to combine and then whisk the slurry into the sauce. Continue whisking until the sauce has thickened, about 2 minutes, and use as desired.

Paprika Oil

YIELD: 2 CUPS / **ACTIVE TIME:** 5 MINUTES / **TOTAL TIME:** 5 MINUTES

½ CUP SWEET PAPRIKA

2 CUPS AVOCADO OIL

1. Place the paprika and avocado oil in a mason jar and shake until thoroughly combined.

2. Store the oil in a dark, dry place and always shake before using.

Saffron & Tomato Coulis

YIELD: 4 CUPS / **ACTIVE TIME:** 5 MINUTES / **TOTAL TIME:** 25 MINUTES

1 TABLESPOON SAFFRON

2 TABLESPOONS EXTRA-VIRGIN OLIVE OIL

¼ CUP MINCED ONION

¼ CUP SLICED GARLIC

3 BAY LEAVES

3 TABLESPOONS KOSHER SALT

2 TABLESPOONS BLACK PEPPER

½ CUP WHITE WINE

1 (14 OZ.) CAN OF DICED SAN MARZANO TOMATOES, DRAINED

1. Place the saffron in a bowl and add 1 cup of water. Let the saffron steep for 10 minutes.

2. Place the olive oil in a saucepan and warm it over medium heat. Add the onion, garlic, bay leaves, salt, and pepper and cook, stirring frequently, until the onion is translucent, 3 to 4 minutes.

3. Deglaze the pan with the wine and bring the mixture to a simmer.

4. Add the saffron and soaking liquid, along with the tomatoes, and cook for 5 minutes.

5. Taste, adjust the seasoning as necessary, and use as desired.

METRIC CONVERSION CHART

Weights

1 oz. = 28 grams

2 oz. = 57 grams

4 oz. (¼ lb.) = 113 grams

8 oz. (½ lb.) = 227 grams

16 oz. (1 lb.) = 454 grams

Volume Measures

⅛ teaspoon = 0.6 ml

¼ teaspoon = 1.23 ml

½ teaspoon = 2.5 ml

1 teaspoon = 5 ml

1 tablespoon (3 teaspoons) = ½ fluid oz. = 15 ml

2 tablespoons = 1 fluid oz. = 29.5 ml

¼ cup (4 tablespoons) = 2 fluid oz. = 59 ml

⅓ cup (5⅓ tablespoons) = 2.7 fluid oz. = 80 ml

½ cup (8 tablespoons) = 4 fluid oz. = 120 ml

⅔ cup (10⅔ tablespoons) = 5.4 fluid oz. = 160 ml

¾ cup (12 tablespoons) = 6 fluid oz. = 180 ml

1 cup (16 tablespoons) = 8 fluid oz. = 240 ml

Temperature Equivalents

°F	°C	Gas Mark
225	110	¼
250	130	½
275	140	1
300	150	2
325	170	3
350	180	4
375	190	5
400	200	6
425	220	7
450	230	8
475	240	9
500	250	10

Length Measures

1/16 inch = 1.6 mm

⅛ inch = 3 mm

¼ inch = 6.35 mm

½ inch = 1.25 cm

¾ inch = 2 cm

1 inch = 2.5 cm

THE ENCYCLOPEDIA OF MEDITERRANEAN

THE ENCYCLOPEDIA OF MEDITERRANEAN

ABOUT CIDER MILL PRESS BOOK PUBLISHERS

Good ideas ripen with time. From seed to harvest, Cider Mill Press brings fine reading, information, and entertainment together between the covers of its creatively crafted books. Our Cider Mill bears fruit twice a year, publishing a new crop of titles each spring and fall.

"Where Good Books Are Ready for Press"

501 Nelson Place
Nashville, TN 37214

cidermillpress.com